SOUTH CAROLINA MARRIAGES
VOLUME IV 1787-1875
IMPLIED IN THE MISCELLANEOUS
RECORDS OF SOUTH CAROLINA

Barbara R. Langdon

LANGDON & LANGDON
GENEALOGICAL RESEARCH
132 LANGDON ROAD
AIKEN, SC 29801-9536

Other books in this series:

Abbeville County Marriages 1780-1879
Implied in Abbeville County, S.C.
Equity Records
ISBN 0-938741-10-1          250 pages

Barnwell County Marriages 1764-1859
Implied in Barnwell County, S.C. Deeds
ISBN 0-938741-04-7          118 pages

Barnwell County Marriages 1775-1879
Implied in Barnwell County, S.C.
Probate and Equity Records
ISBN 0-938741-01-2          188 pages

Chester County Marriages 1778-1879
Implied in Chester County, S.C.
Probate and Equity Records
ISBN 0-938741-02-0          221 pages

Spartanburg County Marriages 1785-1911
Implied in Spartanburg County, S.C.
Probate Records
ISBN 0-938741-07-1          317 pages

South Carolina Marriages Volume I
1749-1867 Implied in
South Carolina Equity Reports
ISBN 0-938741-06-3          204 pages

South Carolina Marriages Volume II
1735-1885 Implied in
South Carolina Law Reports
ISBN 0-938741-08-X          172 pages

South Carolina Marriages Volume III
1671-1791 Implied in the
Provincial and Miscellaneous Records
of South Carolina
ISBN 0-938741-09-8          224 pages

Copyright 1994 Barbara R. Langdon
ISBN 0-938741-11-X

INTRODUCTION

Marriages were not recorded in South Carolina until the twentieth century. This book is part of a series designed as an aid to discover South Carolina marriages. This collection of 2,271 marriage references and relationships is the result of the searching of the Miscellaneous Records of South Carolina Volumes A through Z and AA through CC. The year 1787 was the date of the earliest record found and 1875 was the latest found in the volumes searched. These records may be found at the South Carolina Department of Archives and History in Columbia. The Archives will answer requests for specific information by mail.

The original bound volumes of the Miscellaneous Records of South Carolina contain various types of recorded documents. Among the records from which they are comprised are primarily mortgages, bills of sale and marriage settlements. Many of these documents are available only in this recorded form as many of the originals have not survived.

Please note that this book contains evidence of and in many cases only clues to marriages. It is not a collection of marriage records. Proof or verification is left to the user of this book.

Husband-wife relationships appear in some of these recorded documents. Marriage settlements or references to marriage settlements may contain the woman's maiden name or the name of a previous husband as well as specific dates. Occasionally there are other vital statistics.

This book is divided into two alphabetically ordered sections Men and Women. In each section the man's or woman's name is followed by the spouse, the volume and page numbers of the record volume in which the reference is found and the year one or both were living. Usually the year is that of the document in which the couple is mentioned, not necessarily the date of marriage. The couple may have lived many years prior to the date of the document.

Each entry in this book contains only the information discernable from that document alone and possibly an additional document in which instance reference to this other source is given. The other reference or references may be needed to correlate and support the evidence in the first citation.

Why are some first names of men and women left blank? The document may merely show that John Smith married a daughter of James Jones. The entry in this book will leave the first name of the woman blank. Likewise, a woman may appear with her married name among her brothers, revealing the last name of her spouse, but not his first name. Thus the man's first name is left blank.

The name of a woman's father or former husband may have been found. Also given are brothers of some of the women with the idea of leading the researcher to the woman's surname. A Subindex to these persons mentioned in notations below some of the references is provided at the end of the book.

Geographical clues concerning the county or parish of residence for the couple may appear with the reference.

When looking through this book for clues to a marriage, it is important to check all possible variations in the spelling of names. Every attempt has been made to spell the names as they appear in the records. A couple may be referred to in more than one document with sometimes drastically different spellings and different dates. In all cases all should be searched. The user of this book will have to make his own judgement as to which of the spelling variants is correct.

It is hoped that this book will assist the descendants of these South Carolina families in their research.

Barbara R. Langdon

KEY TO SOURCES

| ABBREVIATION | VOLUME OF RECORDS |
|---|---|
| A | Miscellaneous Records Volume A 1776-1801 |
| B | Miscellaneous Records Volume B 1801-1812 |
| C | Miscellaneous Records Volume C 1812-1819 |
| D | Miscellaneous Records Volume D 1818-1822 |
| E | Miscellaneous Records Volume E 1822-1827 |
| F | Miscellaneous Records Volume F 1827-1829 |
| G | Miscellaneous Records Volume G 1829-1831 |
| H | Miscellaneous Records Volume H 1831-1834 |
| I | Miscellaneous Records Volume I 1834-1837 |
| THERE IS NO VOLUME J | |
| K | Miscellaneous Records Volume K 1837-1840 |
| L | Miscellaneous Records Volume L 1839-1842 |
| M | Miscellaneous Records Volume M 1842-1843 |
| N | Miscellaneous Records Volume N 1843-1844 |
| O | Miscellaneous Records Volume O 1844-1845 |
| P | Miscellaneous Records Volume P 1845-1846 |
| Q | Miscellaneous Records Volume Q 1788-1839 |
| R | Miscellaneous Records Volume R 1846-1847 |
| S | Miscellaneous Records Volume S 1847-1849 |
| T | Miscellaneous Records Volume T 1849-1850 |
| U | Miscellaneous Records Volume U 1850-1851 |
| V | Miscellaneous Records Volume V 1851-1852 |
| W | Miscellaneous Records Volume W 1852-1853 |
| X | Miscellaneous Records Volume X 1853-1855 |

KEY TO SOURCES

| ABBREVIATION | VOLUME OF RECORDS |
|---|---|
| Y | Miscellaneous Records Volume Y |
| Z | Miscellaneous Records Volume Z 1856-1857 |
| AA | Miscellaneous Records Volume AA 1857-1860 |
| BB | Miscellaneous Records Volume BB 1860-1864 |
| CC | Miscellaneous Records Volume CC 1864-1875 |

DOUBLE LETTER ALPHABET STOPS

KEY TO TERMS AND ABBREVIATIONS:

common-law marriage = couple was not married by law
LIVED = usually date of document in which couple appears
VOLUME = bound original manuscript book

Implied South Carolina Marriages Volume IV 1787-1875

MAN                     WOMAN                   VOL    PAGES       LIVED

(A)

Abney, Matthew W.       Caroline S. Blocker     2B     161-164     1860
    (in Edgefield District) (daughter of James Blocker)
Adams, _____           Margaret Johnston       W      557-559     1853
    (Johnson) (daughter of Samuel Johnston of
    Winnsborough, Fairfield District, who died 13 May 1853)
Adams, H. P.            Mary E. Mace            2B     607-608     1863
    (marriage agreement 11 March 1863) (in Marion District)
Adams, Harry W.         Rebecca S. Johnston     O      418-420     1845
    (of Richland District) (daughter of Samuel Johnston of
    Winnsborough, Fairfield District)
Adams, Harry W.         Rebecca S. Johnston     P      339-340     1846
    (daughter of Samuel Johnston of
    Winnsborough, Fairfield District)
Adams, Henry            Mary G. Evans           G      216-217     1830
    (marriage settlement 12 October 1830)
Adams, J. R.            Nancy Dewalt            2A     327-332     1858
    (daughter of Daniel Dewalt Senr. of
    Newberry District, who died 6 November 1853) [See also
    pages 364-368, 495-499, 541-544, 631-634, 673-677]
Adams, James F.         Tabitha Tillman         X      208-211     1853
    (marriage settlement 3 May 1853) (he was married before)
    (widow) (both of Edgefield District)
Adams, James P.         Margaret C. Johnston    U      7-9         1850
    (of Richland District) (daughter of Samuel Johnston of
    Winnsborough, Fairfield District)
Adams, John P.          Amy G. Adams            2C     206-208     1866
    (marriage settlement 17 November 1866)
Adams, Jonathan         Polly Bright            G      370-371     1831
Adams, Joseph           Frances Adams           X      208-211     1853
    (daughter of James F. Adams of Edgefield
    District)
Adams, R. Wright        Clara Peterson          2B     762-764     1863
    (in Edgefield District) (daughter of Basil Peterson)
Adams, Thomas J.        Mary Jemima Chatham     Z      444-445     1856
    (of Edgefield District) (daughter of Thomas Chatham of
    Abbeville District)
Addison, _____         Elizabeth Bledsoe       2A     571         1857
    (daughter of Lewis Bledsoe of Edgefield
    District)
Addison, John           Sarah Cartledge         E      433-434     1825
    (marriage contract 26 June 1825) (both of Edgefield
    District)

Implied South Carolina Marriages Volume IV 1787-1875

| MAN | WOMAN | VOL | PAGES | LIVED |
|---|---|---|---|---|
| Addison, John A. | Susan M. Mosley | Y | 253-255 | 1855 |

(marriage settlement 2 June 1855) (daughter of John Mosley) (both of Edgefield District)

Agnew, Samuel T.　　　Julia F. Stephens　　2A　580-581　　1856
　(marriage settlement 7 April 1856) (in Newberry District)

Alexander, \_\_\_\_\_　　Frances C. Harris　　G　36-37　　1829
　(daughter of John Harris of Abbeville District)

Alexander, \_\_\_\_\_　　\_\_\_\_\_ Swaford　　X　585-586　　1854
　(daughter of John Swaford of Pickens District)

Alexander, \_\_\_\_\_　　\_\_\_\_\_ Swoford　　Y　280-281　　1855
　(daughter of John Swoford of Pickens District)

Alexander, James H.　Eliza S. Reid　　Z　3-4　　1856
　(of Union District) (daughter of William Reid Senr.)

Alexander, James H.　Eliza Smith Ried　U　385-386　　1851
　(Reid) (daughter of William Ried Sr. of Spartanburgh District) [Must also see pages 447-448; Volume V, pages 198-199]

Alexander, Sample　　Lucie H. Clawson　　2A　758-760　　1860
　(marriage settlement 16 January 1860) (in York District)

Allen, \_\_\_\_\_　　Marion Gourdine Gaillard　　2A　608-612　　1859

Allen, Elijah G.　　Mary Louisa Kirkland　P　85-86　　1845
　(daughter of George Kirkland of Barnwell District)

Allen, John R.　　Mary Lucia Allen　　G　33-35　　1823
　(marriage settlement \_\_ June 1823) (widow of George Allen of Richmond County, Georgia) (John R. Allen of Richmond County, Georgia)

Allen, Joseph　　Sarah E. Allen　　N　191　　1826
　(reference to marriage settlement recorded 12 April 1826)

Allen, Joseph Duncan　Ann Louisa Myers　K　258　　1838
　(daughter of Col. David Myers) (of Richland District)

Allen, Joseph Junr.　Sarah E. Allen　　E　439-441　　1826
　(marriage settlement 19 January 1826) (widow of Josiah G. Allen) (both of Barnwell District)

Allen, Josiah G.　　Sarah E. Bryan　　E　439-441　　1826
　(daughter of Joseph Bryan)

Allen, Paul H.　　Zilphia Z. Allen　　2B　831-834　　1864
　(marriage contract 7 July 1864) (both of Barnwell District)

Implied South Carolina Marriages Volume IV 1787-1875

| MAN | WOMAN | VOL | PAGES | LIVED |
|---|---|---|---|---|
| Allen, William D. | Susan W. Hughes | 2B | 571-572 | 1862 |

(married 27 April 1862) (he of Houston County, Georgia) (she of Barnwell District, S.C.)

| Allen, Young | Susannah Richardson | E | 497-498 | 1826 |
|---|---|---|---|---|

(in Edgefield District)

| Allen, Young | Susannah Richardson | F | 347 | 1828 |
|---|---|---|---|---|

(she of Edgefield District)

| Allgary, William S. | Sarah F. Anderson | 2A | 581-584 | 1859 |
|---|---|---|---|---|

(marriage settlement 1 March 1859) (widow of Richard L. Anderson) (both of Abbeville District)

| Allsbrook, _____ | Mary Walker (widow) | P | 150-152 | 1845 |
|---|---|---|---|---|
| Alton, Elihu | Mary F. Vance | U | 111-112 | 1850 |

(of Pontotoc County, Mississippi) (in Laurens District, S.C.)

| Ancrum, William A. | Charlotte E. Douglas | T | 429-430 | 1850 |
|---|---|---|---|---|

(daughter of James K. Douglas of Kershaw District)

| Anderson, _____ | Mary Butler | Z | 298 | 1856 |
|---|---|---|---|---|

(of Edgefield District) (daughter of Seth Butler of Edgefield District)

| Anderson, _____ | Eliza R. Levy | K | 522 | 1839 |
|---|---|---|---|---|
| Anderson, _____ | Mary Nesbett | I | 398-399 | 1836 |
| Anderson, _____ | Harriet A. Stark (widow) | O | 22-24 | 1844 |
| Anderson, David Q. | Pernecy C. Griffith | 2B | 565-566 | 1856 |

(married about 1856) (separation agreement 12 January 1863) (daughter of Stephen Griffith) (in Laurens District)

| Anderson, Doctor William Wallace | Elizabeth Waties | H | 470-471 | 1833 |
|---|---|---|---|---|

(marriage settlement 29 October 1833) (daughter of Hon. Thomas Waties) (both of Stateburg, Claremont)

| Anderson, Dr David L. | Mary Elizabeth Nickels | R | 404-405 | 1846 |
|---|---|---|---|---|

(of Laurens District) (daughter of John Nickels of Laurens District)

| Anderson, Edward K. | Elizabeth K. Kincaid | T | 234-237 | 1849 |
|---|---|---|---|---|

(in Fairfield District)

| Anderson, James L. | Nancy C. Dunn | L | 426-428 | 1841 |
|---|---|---|---|---|

(marriage settlement 7 September 1841) (widow) (both of Abbeville District)

| Anderson, John Henry | Caroline Ashley | Z | 619-621 | 1856 |
|---|---|---|---|---|

(marriage settlement 31 December 1856) (widow of Barnett Ashley)

| Anderson, _____ | Frances C. Mars Lovezinski | 2B | 782-783 | 1864 |
|---|---|---|---|---|

(of Newberry District) (daughter of John A. Mars of Abbeville District)

Implied South Carolina Marriages Volume IV 1787-1875

| MAN | WOMAN | VOL | PAGES | LIVED |
|---|---|---|---|---|
| Anderson, Lovinski | Frances Cornelia Mars | Z | 793-794 | 1857 |

(of Newberry District) (daughter of John A. Mars of Abbeville District)

| Anderson, Robert | Mary Pickens | W | 100-102 | 1852 |
|---|---|---|---|---|

(in Abbeville District) (daughter of Ezekiel Pickens)

| Anderson, Robert | Mary Barksdale Pickens | H | 153-155 | 1832 |
|---|---|---|---|---|

(marriage settlement 10 July 1832) (daughter of Ezekiel Pickens)

| Anderson, Robert | Catharine L. Sullivan | U | 272-274 | 1851 |
|---|---|---|---|---|

(of Edgefield District)

| Anderson, Robert J. | Susan Rebecca McKnight | Z | 686-688 | 1857 |
|---|---|---|---|---|

(marriage settlement 5 February 1857) (he of Sumter District) (she of Williamsburg District)

| Anderson, Thomas R. | Mary Ann Miller | P | 316-317 | 1846 |
|---|---|---|---|---|

(daughter of James Miller of Edgefield District) [See also Volume U, pages 60-61]

| Anderson, William | Sarah B. Douglass | F | 451-452 | 1829 |
|---|---|---|---|---|

(daughter of James K. Douglass of Camden, Kershaw District)

| Anderson, William J. | Margaret Frierson | Z | 404-406 | 1856 |
|---|---|---|---|---|

(of Sumter District) (widow)

| Andrews, David J. | Janette L. Hewitt | Z | 131-133 | 1856 |
|---|---|---|---|---|

(marriage settlement 28 February 1856) (widow of Frances M. Hewitt of Darlington District) (of Darlington District)

| Andrews, Michael | Susannah Rogers | D | 344-345 | 1820 |
|---|---|---|---|---|
| Ansly, William S. (Ansley) | Jane Hearst | O | 66-68 | 1844 |

(daughter of John Hearst of Abbeville District)

| Anthony, ____ | Avarilla Griffin | 2A | 728-729 | 1859 |
|---|---|---|---|---|

(in Pickens District)

| Anthony, Edward L. | Margaret ____ Roy | K | 117-118 | 1838 |
|---|---|---|---|---|

(marriage settlement 29 January 1838) (both of Edgefield District)

| Arant, Christian | Margaret Smith | F | 330 | 1828 |
|---|---|---|---|---|

(marriage settlement 26 August 1828) (widow of Robert Smith of Orangeburgh District) (of Orangeburgh District) [Must also see pages 405-407, 412-413]

| Arant, Christian | Margaret Smith | H | 344-346 | 1829 |
|---|---|---|---|---|

(in Orangeburgh District) (daughter of Robert Smith)

| Archer, John | Sarah A. Calhoun | L | 329-331 | 1841 |
|---|---|---|---|---|

(marriage settlement 15 April 1841) (both of Abbeville District)

4

Implied South Carolina Marriages Volume IV 1787-1875

| MAN | WOMAN | VOL | PAGES | LIVED |
|---|---|---|---|---|
| Ard, Thomas M. | Frances A. Brough | 2A | 81-82 | 1857 |

(both of Abbeville District)

| Ardis, Abram | Sarah R. M. Bender | B | 594-595 | 1809 |

(marriage agreement 24 April 1809) (he was married before) (widow of George Bender) (of Edgefield District)

| Ardis, David | Eliza. C. Gray | W | 465-466 | 1851 |
| Ardis, David | Eliza Corby Gray | F | 43-45 | 1827 |

(marriage settlement 1 February 1827) (daughter of John J. Gray of Beach Island, Edgefield District) (in Edgefield District)

| Arick, Lee D. | Sarah Arledge | K | 169-170 | 1838 |

(marriage settlement 28 June 1838) (widow) (both of Fairfield District)

| Armstrong, _____ | Jane Lesly | W | 21-24 | 1852 |

("Jane Lesly, afterwards Jane Armstrong")

| Arnold, _____ | Elizabeth Yancey | S | 293-294 | 1848 |

Groves (daughter of Joseph Groves of Abbeville District)

| Arp, Caleb A. | Francis McKie | M | 255-256 | 1842 |

(daughter of Daniel McKie of Edgefield District)

| Arthur, _____ | Mary A. Kinsler | 2B | 52-61 | 1859 |
| Arthur, Benjamin F. | Ann E. Dogan | X | 163-166 | 1854 |

(daughter of Joseph H. Dogan of Union District)

| Arthur, Henry | Harriet Seibles | 2C | 358-360 | 1867 |

(of Lexington District)

| Arthur, J. R. | Mary Y. Simmons | S | 40-41 | 1848 |

(in Abbeville District)

| Arthur, Joseph R. | Mary Y. _____ | G | 389-390 | 1827 |

(reference to marriage settlement - no date given)

| Askew, John M. | Susan R. Little | 2A | 429-430 | 1858 |

(marriage contract 24 September 1858) (in Union District)

| Atkinson, A. W. | Lucretia Patterson | 2B | 457-458 | 1861 |

(in Barnwell District) (daughter of Angus Patterson)

| Atkinson, Ephraim | Adeline Oneal | W | 621-622 | 1853 |

H. (of Chester District) (daughter of Richard Oneal of Columbia, Richland District)

| Aull, Harmon | Eve Werts (Wertz) | H | 140-143 | 1832 |

(marriage settlement 8 May 1832) (widow of John Werts) (in Newberry District)

| Austin, Elijah | Julia Salton | 2B | 156-157 | 1860 |

(daughter of Michael Salton of Lexington District)

| Austin, William | Margaret Gramling | I | 451-452 | 1836 |

(marriage settlement 7 May 1836)

Implied South Carolina Marriages Volume IV 1787-1875

| MAN | WOMAN | VOL | PAGES | LIVED |
|---|---|---|---|---|

(B)

Bacon, _____  Juliana James          H    325-328   1833
                 (daughter of Walter James)
Bacon, Henry W.  Julia Ann (Julian)     G    59-61     1829
                 James
     (marriage settlement 8 October 1829) (daughter of Walter
     James) (Bacon of Georgia) (she of Sumter District, S.C.)
Bacon, Thomas G. Angelina Gallman       L    36-37     1839
                 (daughter of Harman Gallman)
Bacon, William H. Julian James          M    334-336   1839
     (in Sumter District)
Bacot, Cyrus     Anna H. Brown          F    152-153   1827
     (marriage settlement 20 September 1827) (widow of Wm.
     Brown) (Bacot of Darlington District) (she of
     Marlborough District)
Bacot, Peter S. A. Sarah J. Fountain    2A   796-799   1860
     (marriage settlement 23 February 1860) (daughter of
     George H. Fountain) (both of Darlington District)
Bacot, R.        Mary Ann Fountain      2A   560-564   1859
     Brockington Jr. (marriage settlement 24 February 1859)
     (daughter of George H. Fountain) (both of Darlington
     District)
Bacot, Washington Martha Amanda         2A   432-435   1858
     Murphy       Fountain
     (marriage settlement 7 October 1858) (daughter of George
     Fountain) (both of Darlington District)
Bailey, _____ Malinda Foster         P    28-29     1845
                 [daughter of Jariahr (Josiah?) Foster of
                 Union District]
Bailey, _____ Elizabeth Norman       U    132-134   1850
Bailey, _____ Elizabeth Sims         Z    396-398   1856
Bailey, Jehu Sr. Margaret Crenshaw      2C   214-216   1856
     (reference to marriage contract 7 October 1856)
Bailey, Jesse    Sarah Hollis           W    606-607   1853
     (marriage settlement 28 April 1853) (in Union District)
Bailey, Jesse    Francis McDaniel       2A   144-146   1857
     (marriage contract 13 November 1857) (both of Edgefield
     District)
Bailey, W. J.    Martha A. Moye         M    178-180   1842
Bailey, William J. Martha A. Moye       I    612-614   1837
     (marriage settlement 22 May 1837) (in Darlington
     District)

Implied South Carolina Marriages Volume IV 1787-1875

| MAN | WOMAN | VOL | PAGES | LIVED |
|---|---|---|---|---|
| Bailey, William T. | Elizabeth McCaw | Z | 467-469 | 1856 |

(marriage settlement 27 November 1856) (widow) (he of Oglethorpe County, Georgia) (she of Abbeville District, S.C.)

| Bailey, William T. | Elizabeth McCaw | 2A | 186-187 | 1856 |
|---|---|---|---|---|

(reference to marriage settlement 7 November 1856)

| Baker, _____ | Eliza Jane P. Moses | W | 479-480 | 1853 |
|---|---|---|---|---|

(daughter of Franklin J. Moses of Sumter District)

| Baker, Alpheus | Eliza H. Courtney | D | 208-210 | 1820 |
|---|---|---|---|---|

(marriage contract 9 April 1820) (he of Abbeville District, S.C.) (she of Wilkes County, Georgia)

| Baker, Charles R. | Jacqueline Chandler | 2C | 113-115 | 1866 |
|---|---|---|---|---|

F. (marriage settlement 19 January 1866) (widow of Genl. Samuel R. Chandler) (Baker of Clarendon District) (she of Sumter District)

| Baldaree, Starling | Ruth Waters | D | 133-136 | 1819 |
|---|---|---|---|---|

(Sterling) (Baldree) (marriage settlement 6 February 1819) (widow of Philemon Waters Senr.) (of Newberry District)

| Ball, John the Younger | Elizabeth Bryan | C | 321-323 | 1810 |
|---|---|---|---|---|

(daughter of John Bryan)

| Ballard, Franklin M. | Ellen Spann | H | 518-520 | 1833 |
|---|---|---|---|---|

(of Sumter District)

| Ballard, Lewis W. | Emma Gerald | R | 383-385 | 1844 |
|---|---|---|---|---|

(in Sumter District) [See also pages 386-388, 408-409]

| Ballard, William | Evelina A. Richardson | I | 428-429 | 1836 |
|---|---|---|---|---|

(marriage settlement 30 April 1836) (both of Sumter District)

| Barkley, Hugh | Jane Barber | H | 351-354 | 1833 |
|---|---|---|---|---|
| Barksdale, J. H. | Juanda A. Allen | S | 177-178 | 1848 |

(daughter of Bannister Allen of Abbeville District)

| Barnes, _____ | Mary Cunningham | 2B | 213-217 | 1860 |
|---|---|---|---|---|

(widow)

| Barnes, Ephraim | Adela Garvin | X | 472-474 | 1853 |
|---|---|---|---|---|

(daughter of David Garvin of Hall County, Georgia)

| Barnes, James T. | Emila Josephine Moseley | 2A | 682-683 | 1859 |
|---|---|---|---|---|

(daughter of John M. Moseley of Abbeville District)

| Barnes, John N. | Mary Louisa Dart | Y | 32-33 | 1855 |
|---|---|---|---|---|

(in Pickens District)

| Barnes, W. J. | M. M. Witherspoon | U | 115-117 | 1850 |
|---|---|---|---|---|

(in Darlington District) (daughter of John S. Witherspoon)

Implied South Carolina Marriages Volume IV 1787-1875

| MAN | WOMAN | VOL | PAGES | LIVED |
|---|---|---|---|---|

Barnes, William E.   Betsy M. Meyer          2A    282-284    1857
   (marriage settlement 16 April 1857) (daughter of David
   Meyer) (Barnes of Augusta, Georgia) (she of Barnwell
   District, S.C.)
Barnes, Zephaniah    A. A. R. Dart           Y     32-33      1855
   W.
Barnwell, Robert W.  Mary Carter             2A    359-360    1858
   Jr.               Singleton
   (marriage settlement 23 June 1858) (daughter of John C.
   Singleton and granddaughter of Richard Singleton) (both
   of Richland District)
Barrett, Colbert     Mary Lenhardt           Z     461-462    1856
   (of Greenville District) (daughter of Lawrence Lenhardt
   of Greenville District)
Barrett, Judah       Judith Bookter          B     446-449    1806
   (marriage settlement 19 November 1806) (widow of Jacob
   Bookter and a prior marriage with _____ Frost) (of
   Columbia, Richland District)
Bartlett, Julius L.  Agnes P. White          2C    392-396    1867
   (of Sumter)       (daughter of Leonard White)
Barton, _____       Catharine Hightower     2A    90-91      1851
Barton, _____       Louisa Hightower        2A    90-91      1851
Barton, Dr. Edward   Agnes Wallace           S     375-376    1848
   H.                (daughter of Andrew Wallace of Richland
   District, S.C.) (of New Orleans, Louisiana)
Barton, Dr. Edward   Agnes Wallace           T     326-328    1849
   H.                (daughter of Andrew Wallace of Richland
   District, S.C.) (of New Orleans, Louisiana)
Barwick, _____      Martha Thompson         Z     187-188    1856
                     (daughter of John Thompson)
Baskin, John C.      Margaret Gaskins        W     493-496    1853
   (of Kershaw District) (daughter of Daniel Gaskins Sr. of
   Kershaw District)
Bass, Isaac M.       Hannah Louisa Smith     F     405-407    1825
                     (daughter of Robert Smith of Orangeburgh
                     District)
Bass, Isaac M.       Hannah Louisa Smith     H     344-346    1829
   (in Orangeburgh District) (daughter of Robert Smith)
Bates, Joseph        Martha Matilda Scott    Z     470-471    1857
                     (daughter of John Scott of Richland
                     District)
Baugh, Robert        Georgiana Bates         T     544-547    1850
                     (daughter of John Bates of Lexington
                     District)
Baxter, Francis M.   Mary E. Ervins          R     90-91      1809
   (reference to marriage contract 24 November 1809)

Implied South Carolina Marriages Volume IV 1787-1875

| MAN | WOMAN | VOL | PAGES | LIVED |
|---|---|---|---|---|

Bealer, George B.   Elizabeth E. Bacot   W   200-203   1852
   (marriage settlement 14 December 1852) (daughter of
   Samuel Bacot) (he now of Chesterfield District) (she of
   Darlington District)
Beard, James M.   Rebecca Turnipseed   U   148-150   1850
   (daughter of Felix Turnipseed of Richland
   District)
Beck, Elijah J.   Margaret Boyett   U   160-161   1850
   (marriage settlement 9 September 1850) (in Barnwell
   District)
Beckham, _____   Rebecca Jones   H   208-209   1831
   (widow)
Beckham, Dr.   Mary Hannah Bates   2A   312   1857
   Francis M.   (daughter of John Bates of Richland
   District)
Beckham, William   Eleanor Duren   G   406   1831
   (daughter of Thomas Duren)
Beckham, William   Amelia Ragsdale   2A   388-389   1858
   (daughter of Burr Ragsdale of Chester
   District)
Beckham, William H.   Elizabeth Massey   2B   213-217   1860
   (marriage agreement 22 November 1860) (daughter of James
   R. Massey of Lancaster District) (Beckham of Chester
   District)
Beckham, William M.   Martha R. Bates   U   98-100   1850
Bedenbaugh, John A.   Lucy C. Wright   P   83-84   1845
   (of Newberry District) (daughter of Zacheus Wright of
   Newberry District)
Bedon, Richard S.   Julia Dain   Y   515-516   1855
   (of Colleton District) (daughter of Hyder A. Dain)
Beecham, _____   Lucy Wilson   K   29   1837
   (widow) (she of Newberry District)
Belcher, William W.   Mary M. Martin   2A   774-775   1860
   (of Abbeville District)
Belk, Thomas M.   Elizabeth R. Hood   2A   619-621   1859
   (marriage settlement 9 May 1859) (widow) (both of
   Lancaster District)
Bell, James   Rachael Jennings   E   499-500   1826
   (marriage settlement 27 July 1826) (in Orangeburgh
   District) [See also pages 544-545]
Bell, James   Mary Eleanor   2A   550-552   1859
   McPherson (daughter of James McPherson)
Bell, O. R.   Ann Albert   V   570-571   1852
Bell, William M.   Elizabeth A. Cleckly   Z   594-596   1857
   (marriage settlement 13 January 1857) (widow of D. F.
   Cleckly) (in Abbeville District)

Implied South Carolina Marriages Volume IV 1787-1875

| MAN | WOMAN | VOL | PAGES | LIVED |
|---|---|---|---|---|
| Bellinger, Carnot | Sarah B. Hails | H | 28-29 | 1832 |

(marriage settlement 1 February 1832) (daughter of Capt. Robert Hails)

| | | | | |
|---|---|---|---|---|
| Bellinger, E. Jr. | C. W. Allen | Y | 401-404 | 1855 |

(of Barnwell District) (daughter of John C. Allen)

| | | | | |
|---|---|---|---|---|
| Belser, Laurence H. | Mary Anastasia Staggers | Z | 97-101 | 1856 |

(daughter of William Staggers of Williamsburg District)

| | | | | |
|---|---|---|---|---|
| Belton, John | Hannah Frean | 2A | 639-640 | 1859 |
| Bennett, _____ | Sophronia Sims | Z | 396-398 | 1856 |
| Benson, John B. | Elizabeth A. Norton | 2C | 208-209 | 1866 |

(of Hart County, Georgia) (daughter of Jeptha Norton of Pickens District, S.C.)

| | | | | |
|---|---|---|---|---|
| Bethune, _____ | Elizabeth N. Horton | 2B | 309-312 | 1861 |
| Betsel, _____ | Sarah Tucker | R | 438-440 | 1824 |
| Bevill, William A. H. | Sarah Bently | O | 357-358 | 1822 |

(married 2 September 1822) (daughter of Joel Bently) (both of Union District)

| | | | | |
|---|---|---|---|---|
| Billingsley, John B. | Catharine Bedgegood | Z | 170-182 | 1851 |

(widow of Malachi N. Bedgegood of Marlborough District)

| | | | | |
|---|---|---|---|---|
| Billingsley, John B. | Catherine Bedgegood | F | 73-78 | 1827 |

(marriage settlement 7 July 1827) (widow of Malachi N. Bedgegood) (in Marlborough District)

| | | | | |
|---|---|---|---|---|
| Birchette, Richard | Elizabeth T. Mitchell | G | 327-328 | 1831 |

(marriage settlement 1 January 1831) (in Union District)

| | | | | |
|---|---|---|---|---|
| Bird, _____ | Behithland Brooks | T | 315-324 | 1848 |

(daughter of Col. Zachariah S. Brooks of Edgefield District, who died April 1848)

| | | | | |
|---|---|---|---|---|
| Bird, _____ | Lucinda Brooks | T | 315-324 | 1848 |

(daughter of Col. Zachariah S. Brooks of Edgefield District, who died April 1848)

| | | | | |
|---|---|---|---|---|
| Bird, Daniel | Beheathland Simkins | F | 104-106 | 1827 |

(marriage agreement 17 August 1827) (widow of Jesse Simkins of Edgefield District) (of Edgefield District)

| | | | | |
|---|---|---|---|---|
| Black, Ewel | Nancy Dunlap | I | 31 | 1834 |

(daughter of William Dunlap)

| | | | | |
|---|---|---|---|---|
| Black, James A. | Elizabeth S. Logan | M | 70-71 | 1841 |

(of York District)

| | | | | |
|---|---|---|---|---|
| Black, James E. | Christiana Rountree | Y | 598-599 | 1855 |

(daughter of Dudley Rountree of Edgefield District)

| | | | | |
|---|---|---|---|---|
| Black, James E. | Christiann Rountree | P | 294-296 | 1845 |

(daughter of Dudley Rountree of Edgefield District)

| | | | | |
|---|---|---|---|---|
| Black, John L. | Mary P. Black | 2A | 35-38 | 1857 |

Implied South Carolina Marriages Volume IV 1787-1875

| MAN | WOMAN | VOL | PAGES | LIVED |
|---|---|---|---|---|
| Black, Joseph A. | Martha K. Peay (daughter of Austin F. Peay of Fairfield District) | L | 199-200 | 1841 |
| Black, Joseph A. | Martha K. Peay (daughter of Austin F. Peay of Fairfield District) | 2A | 35-38 | 1857 |
| Black, Robert | Maria Welbourn (marriage agreement 21 February 1837) (both of Union District) | I | 555 | 1837 |
| Black, Sam R. | Martha Ann Kirkland (in Fairfield District) | Z | 123-124 | 1856 |
| Black, Samuel R. | Martha A. Kirkland (marriage settlement 13 June 1846) (daughter of John D. Kirkland) | R | 16-19 | 1846 |
| Black, Thomas | Nancy Gladney (of Fairfield District) | Y | 561-562 | 1855 |
| Black, William C. | Martha Ann Griffin (in Abbeville District) (daughter of Ira Griffin) | I | 35-36 | 1834 |
| Black, William E. | Antoinette E. Brown (marriage settlement __ February 1855) (widow) | Y | 195-197 | 1855 |
| Blackburn, ____ | Maria Clark (widow) | 2B | 671-673 | 1863 |
| Blackwell, ____ | Sarah Ann Harrell (daughter of James Harrell) | W | 189-191 | 1852 |
| Blain, James W. | Sarah Razor (of Abbeville District) (widow) | Z | 493-495 | 1857 |
| Blair, John P. | Martha C. Ray | G | 414-415 | 1831 |
| Bland, Elza the Elder | Sofey Johnson (in Edgefield District) | N | 285-287 | 1844 |
| Blanding, ____ | Leonora M. McFaddin (daughter of James D. McFaddin of Sumter District) | 2B | 823-824 | 1864 |
| Blanding, James D. | Leonora A. McFaddin (daughter of James D. McFaddin of Sumter District) | Y | 606-607 | 1855 |
| Blizzard, Jacob | Sarah Wilson (in Fairfield District) (widow of James Wilson Senr.) [See also pages 309-314] | L | 314-316 | 1840 |
| Blocker, Barkley M. | Nancy Brooks (daughter of Col. Zachariah Smith Brooks of Edgefield District, who died April 1848) [Must also see pages 315-324] [See also Volume T, pages 10-11] | H | 212-213 | 1832 |
| Blue, Archibald | Margaret C. Chapman (of Cheraw, Chesterfield District) (daughter of Allen Chapman Sr. of Chesterfield District) | Z | 82-86 | 1855 |
| Boatner, Lewis | Sarah Suber (widow) | I | 25-26 | 1834 |
| Boatwright, ____ | Sophia Watson | 2A | 198 | 1858 |

Implied South Carolina Marriages Volume IV 1787-1875

| MAN | WOMAN | VOL | PAGES | LIVED |
|---|---|---|---|---|
| Boatwright, Burrell | Sophia Watson | S | 279-280 | 1848 |

(in Edgefield District)

Boatwright, Burrell  Sophia Watson    2A   564-565   1859
   T. (in Edgefield District) [Must also see page 742]
Boatwright, John H.  Mary E. Tradewell   Z   196-200   1855
   (in Richland District)
Bobo, William M.    Martha L. Carey    N   196-197   1841
   (married 21 July 1841) (daughter of W. H. Carey) (he of
   Union District) (she of Edgefield District)
Boland, John M.    Mary M. Reddle    2A   799-800   1860
   (of Newberry District)
Bomar, Edward      Mary Tredaway     I    39-40    1834
   (marriage settlement 17 April 1834) (he was married
   before) (of Spartanburgh District)
Bomar, J. Edward   Elizabeth Eugenia  2A   736-737   1859
                   Earle (daughter of James W. Earle)
   (in Anderson District)
Bonham, Simion S.  Elizabeth Amanda   F    379-380   1829
                   Wardlaw (daughter of James Wardlaw of
   Abbevile District) (of Abbeville District)
Boozer, _____     Elizabeth C. Atkin  I    564     1837
                   (Akin) (daughter of David Atkin of
                   Newberry District)
Boozer, _____     Elizabeth A.       2A   188-189   1858
                   McKellar (daughter of John W. McKellar)
Boozer, David      Amelia Burton      S    413-414   1848
   (of Newberry District) (widow of Peter Burton of
   Columbia, Richland District)
Boozer, George     Lavinia C. Ruff    2C   16-18    1864
   Burder (marriage settlement 26 October 1864) (widow)
   (both of Newberry District)
Bossard, John P.   Charlotte White    H    307-308   1832
                   (daughter of Joseph B. White of Sumter
                   District)
Bouchillon, _____  Martha Gardner    G    345-346   1831
Bouchillon, _____  Martha F. Gardner  K    66      1837
                   (daughter of Jeremiah Gardner of
                   Abbeville District)
Boulware, Allbin   Regina Smith       2B   201-202   1860
                   (she of Fairfield District)
Boulware, Allen    Reginia Smith      O    400-401   1845
   (marriage contract 16 January 1845) (in Fairfield
   District)
Bowden, James F.   Jane A. McNeel     W    138-139   1852
   (to be married 5 October 1852) (marriage settlement 5
   October 1852) (he of Talladega County, formerly Shelby
   County, Alabama) (she of Chester District, S.C.)

Implied South Carolina Marriages Volume IV 1787-1875

| MAN | WOMAN | VOL | PAGES | LIVED |
|---|---|---|---|---|

Bowen, Richard C.　　Rebecca Hodges　　W　258-259　1852
　(of Mississippi) (daughter of Gabriel Hodges of
　Abbeville District, S.C.)
Bowen, William　　Sarah Bradley　　Y　256-258　1855
　(marriage settlement 5 July 1855) (widow of Isaac
　Bradley) (Bowen of Pickens District) (she of Greenville
　District)
Bowers, James L.　　Sarah Ann Graham　　M　426-427　1842
　(daughter of James Graham of Newberry
　District)
Bowers, James M.　　Elizabeth Sapp Bush　O　427-428　1845
　(daughter of George Bush of Barnwell
　District)
Bowers, John B.　　Harriet E. Wilson　　S　221-222　1848
　(of Barnwell District)
Bowie, John　　Jane Eliza Hamilton　I　371　1836
　(daughter of Alexander C. Hamilton) (of
　Aiken, Barnwell District) [See also Volume K, pages 166-168]
Bowman, Archibald　　Margaret Pickens　　B　497　1807
　(did not marry; had child only) (he to Stokes County,
　North Carolina) (she in Pendleton District, S.C.)
Bowman, John M.　　Violet Smithson　　Z　659-660　1851
　(marriage settlement 11 July 1851) (in Pickens District)
Boyce, _____　　Mary E. Pearson　　W　74-81　1845
　(daughter of George B. Pearson Sr. of
　Fairfield District)
Boyce, John　　Martha Elizabeth　　O　195-197　1844
　　　　Rosanna Boyce
　(marriage contract 10 July 1844) (both of Union
　District)
Boyd, William B.　　Lucinda Payne　　2A　348-349　1858
　(marriage settlement 17 April 1858) (widow of John W.
　Payne) (both of Laurens District)
Boykin, Burwell　　Mary Whitaker　　A　243-246　1793
　(marriage settlement 21 October 1793) (both of Kershaw
　County)
Boykin, Jonathan　　Maria Bracy　　G　92-93　1830
　(marriage settlement 24 January 1830)
Boyle, Cunningham　　Martha J. Fullwood　2A　472-473　1858
　(marriage settlement __ December 1858) (widow of Robert
　Fullwood) (Boyle of Richland District) (she of Sumter
　District)
Boylston, Samuel　　Margaret C. DuBose　2B　663-665　1863
　Cordes (marriage settlement 15 September 1863) (daughter
　of Samuel DuBose of Fairfield District) (Boylston of
　Charleston) (to Florida?)

Implied South Carolina Marriages Volume IV 1787-1875

| MAN | WOMAN | VOL | PAGES | LIVED |
|---|---|---|---|---|
| Bozeman, _____ | Susan Quarles | G | 345-346 | 1831 |
| Bracey, James | Charlotte Alston Waties | F | 366-367 | 1818 |

(marriage settlement 2 February 1818)

Bracey, William R.　　Anna Eleanor Yates　　L　　439-441　　1841
(marriage settlement 6 November 1841) (both of Sumter District)

Bracy, Solly　　Maria (Mariah)　　D　　187-188　　1820
　　　　　　Darrington [her last name illegible]
(daughter of Robert Darrington) (in Kershaw District)

Bradford, John S.　　Vermeille _____　　Z　　746-748　　1857
(reference to marriage settlement - no date given)

Bradford, John S.　　Vermeille Rees　　K　　300-302　　1839
(marriage settlement 8 January 1839) (widow of F. W. Rees) (of Sumter District) [See also Volume L, pages 360-363, 406-408]

Bradford, John S.　　Vermeille Rees　　X　　376-381　　1839
(marriage settlement 8 January 1839) (widow of F. W. Rees) (both of Sumter District)

Bradley, _____　　Mahazra (Mahaza) R.　　U　　208-210　　1850
　　　　　　Boykin (she of Sumter District)

Bradley, Isaac　　Sarah Shockley　　Y　　256-258　　1855

Bradley, James　　Anna Adeline Lacoste　　R　　450-451　　1847
(daughter of Stephen Lacoste of Sumter District)

Bradley, John Anderson　　Eliza Catherine Johnson　　2B　　152-154　　1860
(marriage settlement 12 July 1860) (he of Chester District) (she in Anderson District)

Bradley, Richard H.　　Emily Snelling　　R　　310-313　　1847
(marriage settlement 17 February 1847) (daughter of Henry Snelling) (both of Barnwell District)

Bradly, Archibald　　Jane Patterson　　W　　184-188　　1852
(in Abbeville District)

Bradwell, Ravenel　　Anna E. Brumby　　W　　536-539　　1853
S. (marriage settlement 5 April 1853) (both of Sumter District)

Bradwell, Ravenel　　Anna E. Brumby　　2A　　587-589　　1853
S. (reference to marriage settlement 5 April 1853) (in Sumter District)

Brady, B. H.　　M. E. Roach　　2B　　239-240　　1861
(daughter of Dr. Thomas J. Roach of Richland District)

Brady, Thomas C.　　Jane Ann Barnett　　Z　　646-648　　1857
(both of Spartanburg District) (daughter of Jorial Barnett)

Implied South Carolina Marriages Volume IV 1787-1875

| MAN | WOMAN | VOL | PAGES | LIVED |
|---|---|---|---|---|
| Brailsford, Robert | Elizabeth ____ | L | 208-209 | 1803 |

(reference to marriage settlement 14 April 1803)

| Brailsford, Robert | Elizabeth James | A | 228-238 | 1803 |

(marriage settlement 14 April 1803) (daughter of John James) (Brailsford of Charleston) (she of St. Mark's Parish, Clarendon County)

| Brailsford, Theodore W. | Margaret Ann Mary Lesesne | P | 192-194 | 1845 |

(marriage settlement 29 November 1845) (daughter of Charles Lesesne of Sumter District) (both of Sumter District)

| Braithwaite, Edward F. | Caroline Parr | I | 413 | 1836 |
| Branch, A. F. | Violet Baxter | S | 139-141 | 1847 |

(marriage settlement 4 October 1847) (both of York District)

| Brand, William | Martha Jane Kennedy | H | 100-101 | 1832 |

(marriage settlement 24 January 1832) (widow of John M. Kennedy) (in Sumter District)

| Brandenburg, Morgan | Caroline Stack | W | 167-168 | 1852 |

(marriage settlement 14 September 1852) (of St. Matthew's Parish, Orangeburg District)

| Branham, Richard | Sophenisba E. M. Wingate | F | 424-425 | 1829 |

[See also pages 430-431, 439]

| Bratton, Dr. John | Betsey Porcher DuBose | 2B | 186-187 | 1860 |

(daughter of Theodore S. DuBose of Fairfield District) (of Fairfield District)

| Breaker, Charles M. | Caroline A. Stubbs | O | 68-69 | 1844 |

(marriage settlement 22 April 1844) (in Marlboro District)

| Breeden, ____ | Elizabeth B. Ayer | Y | 524-526 | 1855 |
| Breeden, James B. | Elizabeth B. Ayer | Y | 371-372 | 1854 |

(both of Marlborough District)

| Brenan, Thomas | Nancy A. Phillips | G | 333 | 1831 |

(daughter of Zachariah Phillips)

| Brevard, Theodorus W. | ____ Hopkins | G | 338-339 | 1828 |

(daughter of James Hopkins of Richland District)

| Bristow, Thomas C. | Emily Hamer | 2C | 182-183 | 1866 |

(marriage settlement 31 July 1866) (widow of Thomas C. Hamer) (in Marlboro District)

| Britt, Daniel A. | Martha Ann Shields | Z | 496-497 | 1856 |

(daughter of James Shields)

| Britton, Daniel L. | Sarah Steed | H | 99-100 | 1832 |

(widow of Griffin Steed)

Implied South Carolina Marriages Volume IV 1787-1875

| MAN | WOMAN | VOL | PAGES | LIVED |
|---|---|---|---|---|
| Britton, Henry | Mary Ann Grier | N | 73-75 | 1843 |

(reference to marriage settlement - no date given) (his first marriage)
Brockman, _____    Kezia J. Bryson    2C    175-177    1866
Brodie, Alexander    Charlotte Sharp    E    32-34    1822
(marriage settlement 21 March 1822) (he of Columbia) (she of Lexington District)
Brogdon, Isaac B.    Martha Ann Ellen    2B    247-248    1860
   Tindal Butler (daughter of Peter M. Butler of Clarendon District)
Bronson, Horace W.    Tabitha Sanders    H    31-33    1832
   (daughter of Robert Sanders of Sumter District)
Brooks, _____    Taphenis B. Lipscomb    F    263    1828
   (in Abbeville District)
Brooks, Col.    Frances Johnson    E    174-175    1824
Zachariah S.    (widow of Taley Johnson)
(marriage settlement 3 February 1824) (both of Edgefield District)
Brooks, James C.    Anna B. Nicholson    2B    550-552    1862
(marriage settlement 20 November 1862) (in Edgefield District)
Broom, Lucus A.    Charlotte Arledge    L    463    1841
   (Arlege) (daughter of Isaac Arledge Senr. of Fairfield District) (of Fairfield District)
Broughton, Thomas    Martha E. Stark    O    22-24    1844
N. (marriage settlement 27 February 1844) (in Sumter District)
Broughton, Thomas    Martha E. Stark    T    531    1844
N. (reference to marriage settlement 27 February 1844)
Brown, _____    Elizabeth Kelly    E    390-391    1825
   (daughter of John Kelly)
Brown, _____    Antoinette Pressley    Y    188-191    1855
   (daughter of Samuel P. Pressley who died in Georgia)
Brown, _____    Elizabeth E. Watts    V    377-378    1852
   (daughter of Richard Watts of Laurens District)
Brown, Angus P.    Martha Teresa Bowers    R    513-516    1847
(marriage contract 24 September 1847) (he of Barnwell District) (she of Edgefield District)
Brown, Cornelius    Elizabeth Greenland    3A    290    1791
Brown, Geo.    Ellen Robertson    P    178-180    1845
(of Mississippi) (daughter of William Robertson of Fairfield District, S.C.)

Implied South Carolina Marriages Volume IV 1787-1875

| MAN | WOMAN | VOL | PAGES | LIVED |
|---|---|---|---|---|
| Brown, Henry | Mary Elizabeth Reed | G | 86 | 1830 |

(daughter of John Reed of Camden, who died 22 April 1821)

Brown, Horatio N.   Laura Ann Fraser   Z   794-799   1857
(marriage settlement 25 April 1857) (daughter of Ladson L. Fraser and granddaughter of John Baxter Fraser) (both of Sumter District)

Brown, James   Rosannah Caldwell   G   202-204   1828
(marriage settlement 23 July 1828) (in Newberry District)

Brown, Jesse   Nancy Brown   P   243-244   1845
(marriage contract 30 November 1845) (he of Spartanburgh District) (she of Laurens District)

Brown, John W.   Phebe Parker   G   69-70   1830
(daughter of Elisha Parker of Chesterfield District)

Brown, Joseph   Rebecca W. Allen   I   200-201   1835
(of Sumter District) (daughter of Francis Allen of Camden)

Brown, Manning   Elizabeth Ann Deveaux   2A   360-362   1848
(reference to marriage settlement 28 November 1848)

Brown, Manning   Lizzie A. Deveaux   W   33-36   1852
(marriage settlement 3 June 1852) (daughter of Stephen G. Deveaux of Charleston District) (Brown of Richland District)

Brown, Pressly   Eliza V. Berry   2A   513-514   1859
(of Columbia, Richland District)

Brown, Robert C.   Elizabeth E. Watts   Y   214-215   1855
(in Abbeville District)

Brown, Samuel   Rebecca Scott Gaillard   2A   608-612   1859
(marriage settlement 26 April 1859) (in Anderson District)

Brown, Thomas R.   Elizabeth Stroman   E   368-369   1811
(marriage settlement 4 June 1811)

Brown, Thomas T.   Caroline C. Blasingame   Y   232-234   1855
(in Anderson District)

Brown, Thomson B.   Ellen L. Lamb   2C   420-423   1868
(reference to antenuptial settlement 15 January 1868)

Brown, Vincent   Eliza Wilmore   H   351-354   1833
(marriage settlement 11 April 1833) (widow) (he of Chester District) (she of Fairfield District)

Brown, William   Emily H. Ioor   M   410-412   1842
(marriage settlement 22 December 1842) (he of Richmond County, Georgia) (she of Edgefield District, S.C.)

Implied South Carolina Marriages Volume IV 1787-1875

| MAN | WOMAN | VOL | PAGES | LIVED |
|---|---|---|---|---|
| Brown, William C. | Caroline E. Peckham | Y | 411-412 | 1856 |

(of Columbia, Richland District) (daughter of James Peckham of Columbia, Richland District)

| | | | | |
|---|---|---|---|---|
| Browne, Horatio N. | Laura Ann Fraser | 2A | 311 | 1858 |

(daughter of Ladson L. Fraser of Sumter District)

| | | | | |
|---|---|---|---|---|
| Browning, William B. | Mary Ann Ellison | W | 54-56 | 1851 |

(in Laurens District)

| | | | | |
|---|---|---|---|---|
| Brownlee, Wm. A. | _____ Scott | 2A | 745-746 | 1846 |
| Brumby, Thomas M. | Elizabeth Rose | F | 59-61 | 1827 |

(marriage settlement 20 April 1827) (widow) (both of Sumter District)

| | | | | |
|---|---|---|---|---|
| Brumley, Robert H. | Elizabeth Murphy | E | 81-82 | 1822 |

(reference to marriage contract 25 November 1822) (of Sumter District)

| | | | | |
|---|---|---|---|---|
| Brunson, D. O. | M. E. Johnson | Z | 695-696 | 1857 |

(marriage settlement 27 January 1857) (in Clarendon District)

| | | | | |
|---|---|---|---|---|
| Brunson, Daniel | Sarah Wilder | N | 104-105 | 1843 |

(of Sumter District)

| | | | | |
|---|---|---|---|---|
| Brunson, John T. | Elizabeth Alice Vaughan | 2A | 33-35 | 1857 |

(marriage settlement 20 June 1857) (granddaughter of William Vaughan) (in Sumter District)

| | | | | |
|---|---|---|---|---|
| Brunson, Manning D. | Epsey Richardson | U | 105-107 | 1850 |

(in Sumter District)

| | | | | |
|---|---|---|---|---|
| Brunson, Peter A. | Joana Catherine McLeod | P | 15-21 | 1845 |

(marriage settlement 8 May 1845) (widow of James Henry McLeod) (in Sumter District)

| | | | | |
|---|---|---|---|---|
| Brunson, Robert D. | Margaret C. Hollingsworth | 2C | 170-174 | 1866 |

(marriage settlement 9 May 1866) (granddaughter of John Hollingsworth) (Brunson of Edgefield District) (she of Abbeville District) [See also page 263]

| | | | | |
|---|---|---|---|---|
| Brunson, William C. | Mary Stephenson | M | 263-265 | 1842 |

(marriage settlement 30 June 1842) (both of Darlington District)

| | | | | |
|---|---|---|---|---|
| Buchanan, Andrew H. | Sarah Howell Bossard | P | 326-328 | 1846 |

(in Sumter District)

| | | | | |
|---|---|---|---|---|
| Buchanan, John M. | Eugenia M. Felder | 2B | 469-471 | 1862 |

(daughter of John H. Felder of Orangeburg District)

| | | | | |
|---|---|---|---|---|
| Buchanan, Malcom | Christian McArn | O | 442-444 | 1833 |

(married 1833) (of Cheraw, Chesterfield District)

| | | | | |
|---|---|---|---|---|
| Buchannon, _____ | Jane Ross (widow) | U | 186-190 | 1845 |

(in Spartanburgh District)

Implied South Carolina Marriages Volume IV 1787-1875

| MAN | WOMAN | VOL | PAGES | LIVED |
|---|---|---|---|---|
| Buford, John | Mary Box | C | 147-150 | 1814 |

(marriage settlement 1 December 1814) (widow of Thomas Box) (both of Beaufort District, S.C.) (Buford late of Screven County, Georgia)

| Bull, William R. | Julia A. Carson | L | 109-110 | 1840 |
|---|---|---|---|---|

(in Orangeburgh District)

| Bumpass, Augustin | Margaret Dobbs | A | 303 | 1796 |
|---|---|---|---|---|

(did not marry; had child only)

| Bunch, John | Mary Thomas | B | 51 | 1801 |
|---|---|---|---|---|

(of Richland District)

| Burchall, William | Elizabeth ___ | E | 259-260 | 1824 |
|---|---|---|---|---|

F. (separation agreement 9 June 1824) (in Columbia)

| Burgess, Warren H. | Agnes Herriot | I | 85-88 | 1834 |
|---|---|---|---|---|

(marriage contract 6 November 1834)

| Burke, ___ | Rachael Smith | G | 109-110 | 1830 |
|---|---|---|---|---|

(widow) (she in Richland District)

| Burnett, S. J. | Lucinda Thornton | 2B | 647-648 | 1863 |
|---|---|---|---|---|

(marriage contract 1 June 1863) (widow) (he of Edgefield District) (she of Abbeville District)

| Burns, W. H. | Jane T. Allen | X | 506 | 1854 |
|---|---|---|---|---|

(of Greenville District) (daughter of Thomas Allen)

| Burt, A. | Martha C. Calhoun | G | 357 | 1831 |
|---|---|---|---|---|

(daughter of William Calhoun of Abbeville District)

| Burt, Oswell | Nancy Raiford | H | 256-257 | 1832 |
|---|---|---|---|---|

(Oswald) E.

| Burt, Robert | Martha Cantelou | F | 378-379 | 1828 |
|---|---|---|---|---|

(marriage agreement 30 December 1828) (widow of Lemuel Cantelou) (of Edgefield District)

| Burton, George W. | Rebecca Zimmerman | Z | 295-297 | 1856 |
|---|---|---|---|---|

(marriage settlement 10 June 1856) (both of Edgefield District)

| Busby, Nathan | Elizabeth T. Martin | P | 310-311 | 1846 |
|---|---|---|---|---|

(in Fairfield District)

| Bush, ___ | Caroline A. Foreman | V | 392-395 | 1852 |
|---|---|---|---|---|
| Bussey, Jeremiah | Harriet Hightower | D | 415 | 1811 |

(marriage settlement 12 October 1811) (of Edgefield District)

| Bussey, Joseph | Nancy C. Morgan | 2B | 619-620 | 1863 |
|---|---|---|---|---|

(marriage contract 21 May 1863) (both of Edgefield District)

| Butler, ___ | Elizabeth L. Benson | 2C | 429-430 | 1868 |
|---|---|---|---|---|
| Butler, Dr. Pierce | Arsinoe M. Jeter | 2B | 210-213 | 1860 |

P. (marriage settlement 17 October 1860) (in Union District)

Implied South Carolina Marriages Volume IV 1787-1875

| MAN | WOMAN | VOL | PAGES | LIVED |
|---|---|---|---|---|
| Butler, Edward C. | Honor Quick | H | 200-202 | 1832 |

(marriage settlement 25 August 1832) (both of Marlborough District)

| Butler, George | Fanny Townes | 2B | 537-538 | 1862 |
|---|---|---|---|---|

(in Greenville District) (daughter of S. A. Townes)

| Butler, William F. | Sarah Bowman | 2A | 249-250 | 1857 |
|---|---|---|---|---|

(daughter of John A. Bowman)

| Bynum, _____ | Cyntha L. Moore | R | 117-118 | 1846 |
|---|---|---|---|---|

(in York District) (daughter of James Moore)

| Byrd, Miller | Elizabeth Leister | R | 93-96 | 1846 |
|---|---|---|---|---|

(widow of Craven Leister) (she of Darlington District)

(C)

| Calbreth, _____ | Behethlen Yarbrough | Z | 12-14 | 1856 |
|---|---|---|---|---|
| Caldwell, _____ | Eliza W. Moseley | 2B | 596 | 1862 |

(daughter of Henry Moseley of Coosa County, Alabama)

| Caldwell, Col. Wm. | Biddy Ellington | G | 367-369 | 1831 |
|---|---|---|---|---|

H. (marriage contract 10 February 1831) (he was married before) (widow) (both of Abbeville District)

| Caldwell, George W. | Caroline Elizabeth Charles | 2B | 539-540 | 1862 |
|---|---|---|---|---|

(he of Hempstead County, Arkansas) (in Greenville District, S.C.)

| Caldwell, James | Jane Davenport | K | 118-119 | 1838 |
|---|---|---|---|---|
| Caldwell, James | Sallie A. McFaddin | 2B | 529-530 | 1862 |

(daughter of James D. McFaddin of Sumter District)

| Caldwell, James | Elizabeth Reid | U | 176-178 | 1850 |
|---|---|---|---|---|
| Caldwell, John G. | Josephine P. Fair | Y | 36-39 | 1854 |

(separation agreement 28 December 1854) (daughter of James Fair) (in Abbeville District)

| Caldwell, John M. | Nancy P. Goode | 2A | 152-153 | 1857 |
|---|---|---|---|---|

(marriage settlement 4 November 1857) (widow of George M. Goode) (in York District)

| Calhoun, Charles M. | Emily C. Nelson | 2B | 112-117 | 1858 |
|---|---|---|---|---|

(married 19 October 1858)

| Calhoun, John | Elizabeth McLarin (McLaurin) | 2A | 422-423 | 1858 |
|---|---|---|---|---|

(marriage settlement 19 July 1858) (both of Marlboro District)

Implied South Carolina Marriages Volume IV 1787-1875

| MAN | WOMAN | VOL | PAGES | LIVED |
|---|---|---|---|---|
| Calhoun, W. L. | Margaret W. Cloud | Z | 105-106 | 1853 |

(daughter of William Cloud of Chester District)

Calmes, Washington W.    Virginia P. Pratt    U    449-451    1849
(marriage agreement 31 January 1849) (daughter of Thomas Pratt) (of Laurens District)

Cammer, James    Tabitha Adkinson    I    474-476    1836
(marriage agreement 31 October 1836) (of Newberry District)

Campbell, Archibald C.    Elizabeth Pringle Adams    2A    670-673    1859
(marriage settlement 12 July 1859) (he of Anderson District) (she of Pickens District)

Campbell, Archibald Chaplis    Emily C. Hannon    K    96-98    1836
(marriage settlement 8 September 1836) (in Anderson District)

Campbell, Francis L.    Ellen M. King    2B    533-537    1862
(marriage settlement 5 November 1862) (daughter of Mitchell King of Charleston, S.C.) (Campbell of Henderson County, North Carolina)

Campbell, William H.    Caroline Matilda Lewis    U    224-226    1850
(marriage settlement 12 December 1850) (both of Greenville District)

Cannon, _____    Mary S. Dubose    W    529-531    1851
Cannon, David    Mary Magdalena Folk    H    440-442    1833
(in Newberry District)

Cannon, Gabriel    Mary A. Caldwell    2A    131    1857
(marriage settlement 21 October 1857) (in Spartanburg District)

Cannon, John E.    Mary A. W. Cook    F    419    1829
(marriage settlement 2 April 1829) (both of Darlington District)

Cannon, Richard S.    Phebe Griffin    S    245-247    1848
Cannon, Wm M.    Margaret Jane Ervin    M    68-70    1842
Cantelou, Lewis C.    Mary Ann Rainsford    H    329-331    1833
(marriage settlement 28 February 1833) (both of Edgefield District)

Cantey, Edward B.    Mary Whitaker Boykin    2C    85-87    1866
(daughter of A. Hamilton Boykin of Kershaw District)

Cantey, Joseph Junr    Susannah Herrington    B    368-369    1805
(marriage settlement 10 May 1805) (of Sumter District)

Cantey, Major Edward B.    Mary Boykin    2B    706-707    1863
(daughter of Alexander Hamilton Boykin of Kershaw District)

Implied South Carolina Marriages Volume IV 1787-1875

| MAN | WOMAN | VOL | PAGES | LIVED |
|---|---|---|---|---|

Cantey, Zachariah    Sarah A. Adamson    T    139-148    1848
    (in Kershaw District) [See also Volume W, pages 247-250,
    619-620]
Capehart, _____    _____ Gibson    2B    73    1860
    (in Pickens District) (daughter of Absolom Gibson)
Capers, Ellison    Charlotte R. Palmer    2A    568-570    1859
    (marriage settlement 24 February 1859) (he now of
    Winnsboro) (she of St. John's Berkley Parish)
Cappleman, _____    Mariah Wilson    M    71-72    1842
    (daughter of James Wilson of Newberry
    District)
Capplepower, _____    Barbara Ostman    B    659-670    1810
Caraway, George H.    Margaret J. Lucas    2B    392-394    1861
    (marriage settlement 30 November 1861) (daughter of
    Benjamin Lucas) (both of Darlington District)
Carrigan, _____    Mary W. Spann    2B    51    1860
    (in Sumter District) (widow)
Carroll, John L.    Sarah E. Culler    2B    88-89    1860
    (marriage settlement 14 February 1860) (widow of Jacob
    Culler of Orangeburg District)
Carter, Robert    Jane Sophia Myers    2A    176-177    1858
Carter, Samuel D.    Margaret Anderson    G    89-90    1830
    (marriage settlement 5 January 1830) (daughter of John
    Anderson Junr. and granddaughter of John Anderson Senr.)
    (both of Sumter District)
Cartin, John W.    Rachel Robinson    F    314-315    1828
    (marriage settlement 20 February 1828) (both of
    Orangeburgh District)
Cartledge, _____    Margaret Cunningham    F    357-358    1825
    (in Edgefield District)
Cary, Lemuel    Ann Hiron    C    433-435    1807
    (marriage agreement 30 July 1807) (widow of John Hiron)
    (both of Columbia)
Cash, Ellerbe    Allan Eunice Ellerbe    V    57-62    1848
    Boggan Crawford (married 28 November 1848) (daughter of
    William C. Ellerbe) (Cash of Chester District) (she of
    Kershaw District)
Cassels, Hugh G.    Frances M. Vaughan    V    323-325    1851
Cassels, Hugh G.    Francis M. Vaughan    O    179    1844
    [See also pages 101-103, 176-178]
Cater, Edwin    Margaret R. Barr    2A    539-540    1859
    (marriage settlement 15 February 1859) (daughter of
    William H. Barr)
Cater, Thomas A.    Sarah C. Giles    2B    104-106    1860
    (marriage settlement 3 May 1860) (in Abbeville District)
Cates, Robert    A. E. Zimmerman    R    13-16    1846
    (daughter of John C. Zimmerman)

Implied South Carolina Marriages Volume IV 1787-1875

| MAN | WOMAN | VOL | PAGES | LIVED |
|---|---|---|---|---|

Cates. See Kates
Cathcart, Robert    Jane Elder    N    133-135    1843
  (marriage settlement 19 May 1843) (both of Winnsborough,
  Fairfield District)
Cathey, John    Mary Cathey    R    354-356    1847
  (marriage settlement 8 February 1847) (in York District)
Cauthen, Thomas    Rebecca Flemming    U    172-176    1850
  Senr. (marriage settlement 26 September 1850) (in
  Lancaster District)
Cauthen, William B.    Nancy Sims    Z    396-398    1856
  (in Lancaster District) (widow of Forney Sims)
Cavens, _____    Amelia Ann Otterson    Y    224-225    1855
Center, Thomas R.    Sarah E. Waring    2A    231-233    1858
  (marriage settlement 12 January 1858) (widow) [See also
  pages 627-629]
Chalmers, Thomas B.    Henrietta Wilson    O    138-140    1844
  (granddaughter of James Wilson Senior)
Chalmers, Thomas B.    Sarah Wilson    T    449-452    1844
  (granddaughter of James Wilson)
Chambers, B. W.    Mary D. Ferguson    X    580-581    1854
  (marriage settlement 16 November 1854) (he of
  Charleston) (she of Darlington District)
Chambers, Sylvanus    Caroline Johnston    U    237-238    1850
  (daughter of Samuel Johnston of Fairfield
  District)
Chambers, William    Mary Ann Arthur    S    222-225    1848
  E. (marriage settlement 30 May 1848) (both of Columbia,
  Richland District)
Chambliss, John    Mary C. Mauldin    2B    397-398    1861
  Alexander (marriage contract 22 October 1861) (daughter
  of Samuel Mauldin) (Chambliss of Sumter) (she of
  Greenville) [See also pages 568-569]
Chandler, Ezekiel    Sarah J. Lemon    X    495    1854
  (in Sumter District)
Chandler, Samuel    Nancy F. Gordon    E    304-305    1825
  (daughter of Charles F. Gordon) (in Sumter District)
Chapman, Allen    Eliza Ann Hubbard    Y    209-212    1855
  (marriage settlement 25 April 1855) (daughter of William
  Hubbard) (both of Chesterfield District)
Chappell, Paul G.    Silina G. Deveaux    W    486-487    1853
  (of Richland District)
Chiles, Thomas    Mary Eddins    E    437-438    1826
  (marriage settlement 6 March 1826) (widow) (both of
  Edgefield District)
China, Alfred    Mary Roach    L    325-326    1833
  (in Sumter District)

23

Implied South Carolina Marriages Volume IV 1787-1875

| MAN | WOMAN | VOL | PAGES | LIVED |
|---|---|---|---|---|

Chunn, James F.    Maria P. Cross         2B    337-338    1861
  (marriage settlement 25 April 1861) (in Richland
  District)
Clark, _____       Catherine W. H.        V     385-389    1852
                    Turpin
Clark, Aaron A.    Elizabeth S. _____    V     474-475    1852
  (reference to marriage settlement - no date given) (of
  Edgefield District)
Clark, Aaron A.    Elizabeth S. Glover    T     37-38      1848
  (marriage contract 16 December 1848) (widow) (both of
  Edgefield District)
Clark, Aaron A.    Elizabeth S. Glover    Z     808-811    1857
  (reference to marriage settlement - no date given)
  (widow) (in Edgefield District)
Clark, Aaron A.    Elizabeth S. Glover    2A    85-86      1857
  (reference to marriage settlement - no date given) (in
  Edgefield District)
Clark, Dr. Michael  Anna Frances          Y     437-439    1855
  R.            Ledingham (daughter of John Ledingham of
  Richland District, S.C.) (of Richland District, S.C.)
  (to Franklin County, Mississippi)
Clark, Henry Senr   Charity Smith         A     255-259    1794
  (marriage settlement 6 December 1794) (widow of Edward
  Smith) (both of Claremont County)
Clark, J. L.       Martha Scott           T     395-398    1849
Clark, Lieut.      Ada W. Bacot           2B    728-732    1863
  Thomas A. G. (marriage settlement 10 November 1863)
  (widow) (she of Darlington District)
Clark, Wilburn D.  Mary Caroline McCoy    S     458-459    1848
  (marriage contract 30 November 1848) (daughter of Joseph
  McCoy) (of Sumter District)
Clark, Willburn    Lavinia McCoy          M     205-206    1842
  (marriage settlement 9 April 1842) (both of Sumter
  District)
Clarke, Caleb      Elizabeth McKelvey     M     368-369    1842
  (marriage settlement 18 September 1842) (widow) (in
  Fairfield District)
Clarke, David M.   Susan Ann Bauskett     Z     791-792    1857
                   (daughter of John Bauskett of Columbia,
                   Richland District)
Clarke, Lemuel     Caroline Beaumont      2A    300-301    1858
  Clarence         Clarkson (daughter of Thomas B. Clarkson
                   Senior of Richland District)
Clarke, William    Anna C. Clarke         V     266-270    1851
  (marriage settlement 1 December 1851) (daughter of Caleb
  Clarke) (in Fairfield District)

Implied South Carolina Marriages Volume IV 1787-1875

| MAN | WOMAN | VOL | PAGES | LIVED |
|---|---|---|---|---|
| Clarkson, Thomas Boston | Sarah Caroline Heriot | 2C | 78-83 | 1830 |

(reference to marriage settlement 25 February 1830)

| Clay, William H. | Mourning Gay | E | 196 | 1824 |
|---|---|---|---|---|

(of Caswell County, North Carolina)

| Cleckley, James D. | Harriet L. Jennings | 2B | 381-383 | 1861 |
|---|---|---|---|---|

(marriage settlement 3 July 1861) (both of Orangeburg District)

| Clendening, James | J. S. Rawls | 2C | 223-224 | 1866 |
|---|---|---|---|---|

(antenuptial settlement 18 September 1866) (widow) (in Richland District)

| Clifford, Benjamin | Catharine L. Bailey | H | 4-5 | 1831 |
|---|---|---|---|---|

(of Edgefield District)

| Cline, _____ | Jane Ann Black | G | 181-185 | 1830 |
|---|---|---|---|---|

(daughter of John Black of Columbia, Richland District)

| Cloud, _____ | Elizabeth Noble | 2A | 375-378 | 1845 |
|---|---|---|---|---|

(daughter of William Noble)

| Clowney, Joseph | Henrietta W. Aiken | Z | 660-661 | 1857 |
|---|---|---|---|---|

(daughter of James Aiken of Fairfield District)

| Coate, Marmaduke | Nancy Rotten | H | 65-66 | 1831 |
|---|---|---|---|---|

(marriage settlement 29 December 1831) (of Edgefield District)

Cobb. See Kobb

| Cochran, Hansford A. | Caroline A. Bush | V | 392-395 | 1852 |
|---|---|---|---|---|

(marriage settlement 4 February 1852) (widow) (both of Barnwell District)

| Cochran, Nesbit | Jane Henderson | W | 21-24 | 1852 |
|---|---|---|---|---|
| Cocke, George Pleasant | Mary M. Moore | H | 503-505 | 1834 |

(marriage agreement 16 January 1834) (widow of Col. Richard Moore)

| Coggeshall, Peter C. | _____ Wilds | 2B | 480-490 | 1861 |
|---|---|---|---|---|
| Coggeshall, Peter C. | Mary Ann Wilds | E | 41-43 | 1822 |

(marriage settlement 13 June 1822) (in Darlington District)

| Coggeshall, Peter C. | Nancy L. Wilds | X | 385-391 | 1854 |
|---|---|---|---|---|

(marriage settlement 12 April 1854) (daughter of Peter A. Wilds of Darlington District) (both of Darlington District)

| Cole, John | Anne Jones | F | 434-435 | 1818 |
|---|---|---|---|---|

(both of Newberry District) (widow of Elijah Jones)

| Cole, John B. | Bethaniah Burton | G | 348 | 1831 |
|---|---|---|---|---|

(daughter of Aaron Burton of Newberry District)

Implied South Carolina Marriages Volume IV 1787-1875

| MAN | WOMAN | VOL | PAGES | LIVED |
|---|---|---|---|---|
| Cole, Mason G. | Harriet Duke | C | 442-445 | 1817 |

(marriage settlement 6 October 1817)

| | | | | |
|---|---|---|---|---|
| Coleman, James B. | Elizabeth M. Blewer | K | 221-224 | 1838 |

(marriage settlement 9 August 1838) (widow of John G. Blewer of Lexington District) (Coleman was married before) (of Edgefield District)

| | | | | |
|---|---|---|---|---|
| Coleman, John A. | Eustatia Floyd | X | 110-112 | 1853 |
| Coleman, Wiley | Mary Seymore (Seamore) | E | 182 | 1824 |

(marriage settlement 1 January 1824) (in Fairfield District)

| | | | | |
|---|---|---|---|---|
| Collins, Jesse | Barbara E. Henry | V | 304-314 | 1852 |

(daughter of James Henry of Richland District)

| | | | | |
|---|---|---|---|---|
| Collum, Vincent E. | Sarah R. Jeter (widow) | L | 99-100 | 1840 |
| Colvin, Daniel | Sarah Egan | D | 383-384 | 1822 |

("Sarah Colvin otherwise called Sarah Egan") (separation agreement 17 January 1822)

| | | | | |
|---|---|---|---|---|
| Colzy, _____ | Elizabeth C. Allen | F | 369 | 1828 |

(daughter of Francis Allen of Camden)

| | | | | |
|---|---|---|---|---|
| Conally, William L. | Elizabeth Pressey | F | 274-275 | 1828 |

(marriage settlement 9 February 1828) (widow of Samuel Pressey) (of Barnwell District)

| | | | | |
|---|---|---|---|---|
| Conger, Wilson | Mary E. Hamer | G | 39-42 | 1829 |

(of Warren County, Mississippi)

| | | | | |
|---|---|---|---|---|
| Converse, _____ | Mary S. Kellog | S | 205-208 | 1845 |

(daughter of Daniel Kellogg) (of Claremont County, Sumter District)

| | | | | |
|---|---|---|---|---|
| Converse, Augustus L. | Mary Ann Kellogg (daughter of Daniel Kellogg) | O | 445-448 | 1845 |
| Converse, Augustus L. | Videau Marion Singleton (daughter of Richard Singleton) | 2A | 665-668 | 1859 |

(in Sumter District)

| | | | | |
|---|---|---|---|---|
| Converse, Reverend Augustus L. | Videau Marion Deveaux | T | 156-160 | 1849 |

(marriage settlement 27 March 1849) (in Sumter District) [See also page 252; Volume U, pages 178-180]

| | | | | |
|---|---|---|---|---|
| Conway, Augustus | Susan V. Mellett | M | 240-242 | 1842 |

(marriage settlement 20 July 1842) (both of Sumter District)

| | | | | |
|---|---|---|---|---|
| Conwell, Baily | Catharine Schumpert | P | 135 | 1845 |

(daughter of Fred. Schumpert of Newberry District)

| | | | | |
|---|---|---|---|---|
| Conyers, James | Martha Montgomery | B | 341-342 | 1804 |

(marriage settlement 24 August 1804) (widow of William Montgomery) (both of Sumter District)

Implied South Carolina Marriages Volume IV 1787-1875

| MAN | WOMAN | VOL | PAGES | LIVED |
|---|---|---|---|---|
| Cook, ____ | Susan Miles | 2B | 506-507 | 1862 |
| Cook, Daniel Jr. | Fanny Cockran | 2A | 325-327 | 1858 |

(of Barnwell District)
Cook, Dr Horatio R. Helena H. M. Miller  S  469-472  1849
 (of Edgefield District) (daughter of John Miller)
Cook, Jacob  Margaret Aul  E  27-30  1822
 (marriage settlement 22 August 1822) (of Newberry District)
Cook, John  Susannah Jones  I  615  1837
 (marriage agreement 1 August 1837) (he was married before) (in Laurens District)
Cook, John W.  Caroline Elizabeth  U  426-427  1851
 Lewis (daughter of Joseph Lewis of Chester District) (Cook of Fairfield District)
Cook, Joseph  Martha Hutchinson  Y  436-437  1855
 (granddaughter of James Boatwright)
Cooke, Revd. John  Mary Lequeux  R  442-446  1847
P. (marriage settlement 29 May 1847) (he of Columbia, Richland District) (she of Winnsborough, Fairfield District)
Cooner, Frederick  Harriett ____  M  359-362  1842
W. (separation agreement 21 November 1842)
Cooner, Frederick  Harriett ____  O  55-56  1842
W. (separation agreement 21 November 1842)
Cooper, ____  Susahan Norman  U  132-134  1850
Cooper, Agrippa  Anna Pulliam  D  174-178  1819
 (of Abbeville District)
Cooper, Jesse  Nancy D. Wescott  M  13-14  1842
 (daughter of Thomas Wescott)
Corley, Bailey, Jr. Sarah E. Presley  2B  472-473  1862
 (of Edgefield District) (daughter of Edward Presley of Edgefield District)
Costner, Adam  Sarah Mullen  E  168-169  1824
 (Mellen) ("Sarah Mullen sometimes called Sarah Ware") (marriage settlement 25 March 1824) (of Lincoln County, North Carolina)
Coulter, Jedediah  Rachel Moore  F  403-404  1828
 (marriage settlement 28 November 1828) (in York District)
Counts, ____  Rebecca Ruff  U  69-71  1850
 (daughter of John Henry Ruff)
Counts, Andrew J. Anna C. Bright  2B  208-210  1860
 (marriage settlement 13 November 1860) (in Lexington District)
Cowen, ____  Margaretta Harris  G  36-37  1829
 (daughter of John Harris of Abbeville District)

Implied South Carolina Marriages Volume IV 1787-1875

| MAN | WOMAN | VOL | PAGES | LIVED |
|---|---|---|---|---|

Cox, John          Frances Langley      Q    60        1803
 (he was born 28 February 1777 in Portsmouth, Hampshire,
 England) (she was born 27 June 1778 in Dewsberry,
 Yorkshire, England) (arrived Charleston, S.C., 16
 February 1800) (to Columbia, S.C.)
Cox, Sherwood L.    Sarah A. Robeson    Y   206-209   1855
 (marriage settlement 19 April 1855) (widow of Peter L.
 Robeson) (Cox of Anson County, North Carolina) (she of
 Chesterfield District, S.C.)
Cox, William      Sarah Caps        R    420       1847
 (marriage contract 16 February 1847) (in Greenville
 District)
Coxe, Edward      Charlotte Victoria  C   456-457   1818
                      James (daughter of Matthew James of
 Sumter District, S.C.) (Coxe of Wilkes County, Georgia)
Craft. See Kraft
Craig, James C.    Laura S. Pervis     S    76-78    1848
                      (daughter of John Pervis of Chesterfield
                      District)
Crane, _____       Frances Adaline     2A   3-4      1857
                      Wilson (daughter of Absalom Wilson of
                      Sumter District)
Crane, Charles     Mary Margaret       R   450-451   1847
                      Lacoste (daughter of Stephen Lacoste of
                      Sumter District)
Crane, Noah       Sarah E. Wright     K   442-444   1839
 (marriage settlement 11 July 1839) (both of Sumter
 District)
Crawford, James F.  Amasillas Hawthorn  P    87-91    1845
Crawford, Newton E. Eleanor S. Ash      W   124-125   1852
 (Cranford)       (daughter of Samuel Ash)
Crawford, Robert   Huldah Logan        G    28       1829
                      (daughter of Andrew Logan of Abbeville
 District) (of Abbeville District)
Crawley, John F.   Eliza C. Owens      X    59-62    1846
 (reference to marriage settlement 22 December 1846)
 (widow) (in Barnwell District)
Creber, William B.  Jane Henry         V   304-314   1852
                      (daughter of James Henry of Richland
                      District)
Creighton, William  Elizabeth Reynolds  I    422      1832
                      (Renolds, Runnels)
 (marriage contract 13 February 1832)
Crimm, Thomas     Jane Nettles        G   363-364   1809
 (married 23 June 1809) (daughter of Zachariah Nettles)

Implied South Carolina Marriages Volume IV 1787-1875

| MAN | WOMAN | VOL | PAGES | LIVED |
|---|---|---|---|---|
| Crocker, Elhanon | Elizabeth Young | C | 229-230 | 1815 |

(marriage settlement 11 November 1815) (in Laurens District)

| Croghan, Hubert | Mary O'Brien | U | 30-35 | 1850 |
|---|---|---|---|---|

(marriage settlement 23 February 1850) (widow of William O'Brien) (both of Sumter District)

| Cromer, Jacob | Tenah Suber | G | 445-446 | 1831 |
|---|---|---|---|---|

(marriage settlement 11 July 1831) (widow) (both of Newberry District)

| Crooks, William T. | Mary Ruff | U | 122-123 | 1849 |
|---|---|---|---|---|

(of Union District)

| Crosland, ___ | Nancy Britton Shields | Z | 496-497 | 1856 |
|---|---|---|---|---|
| Cross, ___ | Cornelia L. Bird | T | 315-324 | 1848 |

(in Edgefield District)

| Cross, Charles B. | Cornelia L. ___ | P | 80-81 | 1845 |
|---|---|---|---|---|

(granddaughter of Z. S. Brooks of Edgefield District)

| Cross, Leonard J. | Isabella G. Jones | H | 143-144 | 1832 |
|---|---|---|---|---|

(marriage settlement 16 June 1832) (daughter of Samuel P. Jones)

| Crosson, J. T. P. | Rosannah Catherine Cook | 2B | 298-300 | 1861 |
|---|---|---|---|---|

(daughter of John Cook of Newberry District)

| Crumpton, Thomas | Elizabeth E. Rabb | O | 319-320 | 1845 |
|---|---|---|---|---|

(in Fairfield District) (daughter of John Rabb of Fairfield District)

| Culler, John H. G. | Ann Senn | G | 61-63 | 1829 |
|---|---|---|---|---|

(marriage settlement 19 December 1829) (widow) (of Lexington District) [See also pages 212-214]

| Culpepper, Joseph | Ann Geiger | D | 57-58 | 1818 |
|---|---|---|---|---|

(of Abbeville District)

| Cumming, James | Rosena Melton | Y | 154-155 | 1843 |
|---|---|---|---|---|

(married 1 July 1843) (daughter of Elisha Melton) (of Edgefield District)

| Cummings, Joseph T. | Sarah R. Watts | U | 331 | 1851 |
|---|---|---|---|---|

(daughter of Hampton Watts of Sumter District)

| Cummings, Joseph T. | Sarah R. Watts | Z | 485-487 | 1856 |
|---|---|---|---|---|

(daughter of Hampton Watts of Sumter District)

| Cunningham, ___ | Mary Massey | 2B | 213-217 | 1860 |
|---|---|---|---|---|
| Cunningham, Joel J. | Ellen Verdier ___ | 2A | 463-465 | 1858 |

(separation agreement 19 August 1858) (in Abbeville District)

Implied South Carolina Marriages Volume IV 1787-1875

| MAN | WOMAN | VOL | PAGES | LIVED |
|---|---|---|---|---|

Cunningham, Joseph   Esther (Hester) A.   L   385-386   1841
　　　　　　　　　　 Niles
　　(marriage contract 20 July 1841) (he of Liberty Hill)
　　(she of Camden)
Cureton, _____　　　Julia Gilmore　　　 2B　 561　　 1862
　　(in Chester District)
Cureton, Cunningham Nancy Cunningham　　Z　 499-501　 1856
　　B. (marriage settlement 16 December 1856) (daughter of
　　John S. Cunningham) (both of Kershaw District)
Cureton, John　　　Mary E. Gallagher　 T　 430-433　 1849
　　(marriage settlement 30 October 1849) (daughter of Mack
　　Lamar of Edgefield District) (of Edgefield District)
Current, Alpheus W. Margaret H. Poole　 2B　 205-207　 1860
　　(of Spartanburg District) (daughter of John Poole)
Curry, David　　　　Sarah Elizabeth Mayo V　 75-79　 1851
　　(marriage settlement 27 October 1851) (he of Oktibbeha
　　County, Mississippi) (she of Fairfield District, S.C.)
Curtis, Revd. L. W. Nancy Caldwell　　　U　 283-285　 1850
　　(reference to antenuptial agreement 29 July 1850) (in
　　Union District)
Curton, James　　　 Sarah Schumpert　　P　 138-139　 1845
　　(of Coweta County, Georgia) (daughter of Frederick
　　Schumpert of Newberry District, S.C.)
Cuttino, David W.　 Mary Ann Wells　　 2A　 782-783　 1860
　　(of Clarendon District) (daughter of Henry H. Wells of
　　Sumter District)

(D)

Daniel, John S.　　 Eliza A. Mixson　　W　 613-617　 1853
　　(marriage settlement 28 June 1853) (daughter of William
　　J. Mixson) (Daniel late of Barnwell District, now of
　　Edgefield District)
Darby, Dr. Artemas　Margaret C. Thomson I　 45-49　　 1834
　　T. (marriage settlement 19 April 1834) (daughter of John
　　L. Thomson and granddaughter of William R. Thomson) (of
　　Richland District) [Must also see pages 449-450, 452]
Darby, James　　　　Elizabeth Simpson　2A　 579-580　 1858
　　(marriage settlement 11 November 1858) (both of Chester
　　District)
Darby, Osgood A.　　Rachel C. Withers　2A　 466-468　 1858
　　(marriage settlement 22 November 1858) (widow of
　　Benjamin F. Withers) (in York District)
Dargan, Charles A.　Serena L. Bacot　　2A　 721-722　 1859
　　(marriage settlement 24 August 1859)

Implied South Carolina Marriages Volume IV 1787-1875

| MAN | WOMAN | VOL | PAGES | LIVED |
|---|---|---|---|---|

Dargan, George W.    Ida L. Hunter    2B    250-253    1861
    (marriage settlement 2 January 1861) (in Darlington
    District)
Dargan, John M.    Emily E. Vaughan    O    176-179    1844
    (in Sumter District) [See also pages 101-103]
Dargan, Kemp S.    Margaret C. Mushatt    Z    700-702    1857
Dargan, Theodore A. Maria Louisa Bacot    O    236-238    1844
    (marriage settlement 5 November 1844) (both of
    Darlington District)
Dargan, Timothy    Clara Louise Dargan    2C    211-214    1866
    George (marriage settlement 15 November 1866)
Dargan, William    Hannah E. Coggeshall    X    178-181    1853
    Jas. (marriage settlement 22 December 1853) (daughter of
    Peter C. Coggeshall) (in Darlington District)
Darlington, John    Martha Hankinson    F    23-24    1826
    (in Barnwell District)
Darracott, Thomas    Martha H. Palmer    2B    207-208    1860
    B.    (daughter of Champion D. Palmer of
    Abbeville District, S.C.) (she of Brooks County,
    Georgia)
Davega, Abraham H.    Eliza J. McLure    2A    465-466    1858
    (in Chester District) (daughter of Hugh McLure)
Davidson, Nathaniel Martha H. Ruff    U    123-124    1845
    W. (in Newberry District)
Davis, _____    Martha Ann Sowden    V    305-306    1852
    [See also pages 310-311]
Davis, _____    Martha Watson    I    210    1835
    (widow of Mathew Watson)
Davis, Advil    Susan (Susannah)    W    252-254    1852
    Brunson
    (marriage settlement __ December 1852) (in Sumter
    District)
Davis, Charles H.    Mary J. McAdams    I    481    1836
    (widow of Hiram A. McAdams)
    (Davis of Newberry District) (she of Camden, Kershaw
    District)
Davis, Charles W.    Mary C. Skinner    Y    406-407    1855
    (marriage settlement 14 August 1855) (daughter of Harvey
    Skinner) (both of Sumter District)
Davis, George    Sarah Boyd    E    484-486    1826
    (marriage settlement 25 April 1826) (both of York
    District)
Davis, James    Zilpah Mercer    2A    147-148    1844
    (in Darlington District) (daughter of Thomas Mercer of
    Darlington District)
Davis, John    Margaret Griffin    E    45-46    1821
    (in Fairfield District)

Implied South Carolina Marriages Volume IV 1787-1875

| MAN | WOMAN | VOL | PAGES | LIVED |
|---|---|---|---|---|
| Davis, John M. | Jane F. Kirven | K | 498-501 | 1839 |

(marriage settlement 9 September 1839)

| Davis, Lemuel B. | Lenora McClary | I | 302 | 1835 |
|---|---|---|---|---|

(marriage settlement 15 April 1835) (widow) (both of Sumter District)

| Davis, Lemuel B. | Rebecca McLane | G | 90-91 | 1830 |
|---|---|---|---|---|

(in Sumter District) (widow)

| Davis, Reverend | Martha Watson | G | 73 | 1830 |
|---|---|---|---|---|

Chesley (marriage settlement 14 January 1830) (in Abbeville District)

| Davis, Richard | Martha Ann Sowden | W | 214-216 | 1853 |
|---|---|---|---|---|
| Davis, Warren E. | Mary Whitmire | 2A | 229-230 | 1858 |

(marriage settlement 2 February 1858) (widow) (in Union District)

| Davis, Wiley J. | Sarah H. Jones | 2A | 252-255 | 1858 |
|---|---|---|---|---|

(Wylie) (marriage settlement 12 January 1858) (widow of Ralph Jones of Fairfield District) [Must also see pages 504-508]

| Davis, William | Elizabeth Yarbrough | M | 92-96 | 1842 |
|---|---|---|---|---|

(marriage settlement 17 January 1842) (he of Monroe County, Georgia) (she of Abbeville District, S.C.)

| Davis, William K. | Sarah A. Zimmerman | R | 374-375 | 1847 |
|---|---|---|---|---|

(in Darlington District)

| Davis, William | Martha Cantey | A | 202-211 | 1792 |
|---|---|---|---|---|

Ransom (marriage settlement 19/20 June 1792) (he of Stateburgh, Camden District) (she of Camden District)

| Davis, Zimmerman | Cornelia J. McIver | 2A | 179-182 | 1857 |
|---|---|---|---|---|

(marriage settlement 9 November 1857) (in Darlington District)

| Dean, Moses | Narcass Lewis | 2B | 824-827 | 1843 |
|---|---|---|---|---|

(in Anderson District)

| Debruhl, ___ | Susan Cammer | H | 169 | 1832 |
|---|---|---|---|---|

(daughter of James Cammer of Richland District)

| de Caradeuc, | Eliza Ann ___ | X | 560-561 | 1854 |
|---|---|---|---|---|

Achille (postnuptial settlement 10 October 1854) (in Aiken, Barnwell District)

| Deen, William Sr | Sarah Adams | F | 359-360 | 1828 |
|---|---|---|---|---|

(marriage settlement 12 September 1828) (widow)

| DeGraffenreid, Doct | Rebecca Hill | G | 357-358 | 1831 |
|---|---|---|---|---|

Trezevant

| Dejarnett, James | Eliza Ann Pegues | K | 236-238 | 1838 |
|---|---|---|---|---|

Jerry

| Delane, Freeman | Ann Hirons | B | 214-217 | 1803 |
|---|---|---|---|---|

(marriage settlement 22 March 1803) (widow of John Hirons) (both of Columbia, Richland District) [See also Volume C, pages 102, 433-435]

Implied South Carolina Marriages Volume IV 1787-1875

| MAN | WOMAN | VOL | PAGES | LIVED |
|---|---|---|---|---|
| DeLoach, William T. | Ellen Garrot | P | 122-123 | 1845 |

(marriage settlement 7 December 1845) (in Sumter District)

| Delorme, Charles | Elizabeth Britton | N | 73-75 | 1843 |
|---|---|---|---|---|

(in Sumter District)

| DeLorme, Charles H. | Anna Jane Dove | Z | 307-313 | 1856 |
|---|---|---|---|---|

(marriage settlement 25 June 1856) (daughter of Daniel Dove of Darlington District) (both of Darlington District)

| DeLorme, John F. | Adaline O. Nettles | X | 603-605 | 1855 |
|---|---|---|---|---|

(of Darlington District)

| Delorme, William M. | Mary Ann White | G | 48-49 | 1829 |
|---|---|---|---|---|

(daughter of Joseph B. White of Sumter District) (of Sumter District)

| Dendy, Marcus | Susan P. Grant | Z | 477 | 1856 |
|---|---|---|---|---|

(marriage settlement 23 December 1856) (he was married before) (both of Laurens District)

| Dendy, Thomas M. | Harriet Elizabeth Ann Still | N | 89-90 | 1843 |
|---|---|---|---|---|

(marriage settlement 9 March 1843) (both of Edgefield District)

| Denson, James | Mary Elvira Brumby | E | 447-448 | 1826 |
|---|---|---|---|---|

(marriage settlement 28 February 1826) (both of Sumter District)

| Dent, James | Christina W. Hornsby | Y | 71-73 | 1855 |
|---|---|---|---|---|

(in Richland District) (daughter of Daniel Hornsby)

| Dent, Jesse E. | Elizabeth W. Terrill | M | 364 | 1842 |
|---|---|---|---|---|

(common-law marriage?) (of Columbia, Richland District)

| Dent, Peter | Christina Hornsby | Y | 125-126 | 1855 |
|---|---|---|---|---|

(in Richland District)

| Dent, William | Catherine Zeigler | D | 168-169 | 1820 |
|---|---|---|---|---|

(daughter of Nicholas Zeigler) [See also pages 169-172]

| Deveaux, ____ | Videau Marion Singleton | T | 252 | 1849 |
|---|---|---|---|---|

(daughter of Richard Singleton) (in Sumter District) [Must also see pages 156-160]

| DeVeaux, Robert Marion | ____ Singleton | 2B | 496-502 | 1855 |
|---|---|---|---|---|

(daughter of Richard Singleton and granddaughter of John Singleton)

| Devore, Dr. James A. | Rachel B. Prescott | 2B | 193-197 | 1860 |
|---|---|---|---|---|

(daughter of Daniel Prescott of Edgefield District)

| Dexter, Andrew A. | Harrietta Sarah Williams | M | 300 | 1840 |
|---|---|---|---|---|

(of Alabama) (daughter of Wm. W. Williams)

33

Implied South Carolina Marriages Volume IV 1787-1875

| MAN | WOMAN | VOL | PAGES | LIVED |
|---|---|---|---|---|
| Dick, Leonard W. | Leonora Ida Colclough | 2B | 263-265 | 1860 |

(marriage settlement 20 December 1860) (daughter of John A. Colclough) (both of Sumter District)

| | | | | |
|---|---|---|---|---|
| Dick, Robert J. | Catherine M. McDowell | 2B | 93-95 | 1860 |

(marriage settlement 30 March 1860) (in Sumter District)

| | | | | |
|---|---|---|---|---|
| Dickert, Claiborne | Elizabeth Kibler | T | 31-33 | 1848 |
| Dickert, George H. | Christiana Barbara Kibler | T | 31-33 | 1848 |
| Dickert, Henry | Edna (Edney) Stephens | I | 469-470 | 1836 |

(marriage agreement 2 August 1836) (widow of John Stephens of Newberry District) (in Newberry District)

| | | | | |
|---|---|---|---|---|
| Dicketts, William | Ann (Nancy) \_\_\_\_ | E | 216-217 | 1824 |

(marriage settlement 20 September 1824) (both of Columbia, Richland District)

| | | | | |
|---|---|---|---|---|
| Dickson, Hugh | Nancy G. Benson | 2B | 335-337 | 1861 |

(in Pickens District) (widow of William P. Benson)

| | | | | |
|---|---|---|---|---|
| Dickson, Thomas | Mary Eliza Howell | 2A | 270-271 | 1857 |

(marriage contract 8 December 1857) (daughter of Joseph Howell) (both of York District)

| | | | | |
|---|---|---|---|---|
| Dickson, Thomas | \_\_\_\_ Scott | 2A | 745-746 | 1846 |
| Dillard, \_\_\_\_ | Martha W. Norman | U | 132-134 | 1850 |
| Dillard, C. H. | D. E. L. Tarrant | V | 385-389 | 1852 |

(marriage contract 3 January 1852) (widow) (both of Union District)

| | | | | |
|---|---|---|---|---|
| Dingle, R. Rutledge | Sallie H. McKnight | W | 219-221 | 1852 |

(marriage settlement 4 November 1852) (both of Sumter District)

| | | | | |
|---|---|---|---|---|
| Dinkins, Langdon H. | Frances James | M | 334-336 | 1839 |

(in Sumter District)

| | | | | |
|---|---|---|---|---|
| Dinkins, Langdon H. | Francis L. James | K | 303-305 | 1838 |

(marriage settlement 22 December 1838) (daughter of Walter James) (in Sumter District)

| | | | | |
|---|---|---|---|---|
| Dinkins, Micajah | Elizabeth Stone | D | 207-208 | 1820 |

(daughter of Enoch Stone of Lexington District)

| | | | | |
|---|---|---|---|---|
| Dinkins, Tyre J. | Esther A. \_\_\_\_ | N | 130 | 1843 |

(reference to marriage settlement - no date given)

| | | | | |
|---|---|---|---|---|
| Dinkins, Tyre J. | Esther A. \_\_\_\_ | Z | 51-56 | 1856 |

(reference to marriage settlement - no date given)

| | | | | |
|---|---|---|---|---|
| Dinkins, Tyre J. | Amanthes James | M | 334-336 | 1839 |

(in Sumter District)

Implied South Carolina Marriages Volume IV 1787-1875

| MAN | WOMAN | VOL | PAGES | LIVED |
|---|---|---|---|---|

Dinkins, Tyre J.　Esther Amanthus　H　325-328　1833
　　　　　　　　　James
　(marriage settlement 8 March 1833) (daughter of Walter
　James) (both of Sumter District)
Dixon, _____　　　Mary Perry　　　　N　310　　　1844
　(widow) (she of Lancaster District)
Dixon, J. L.　　　Sarah Elizabeth　　U　221　　　1850
　　　　　　　　　Butler (daughter of Peter M. Butler of
　　　　　　　　　Sumter District)
Doby, J. W.　　　 Martha Gerald　　　R　383-385　1844
　(in Sumter District) [See also pages 386-388, 408-409]
Donald, David L.　Elzira Barmore　　 X　677-679　1854
　(in Abbeville District)
Donald, John　　　Mary Ann Razor　　 Z　493-495　1857
Donaldson, John R. Margaret A. Haskew N　314-317　1844
　(marriage settlement 22 February 1844) (daughter of
　Zacheus Haskew of Marlboro District) (of Marlboro
　District)
Donaldson, William Tabitha Wilkinson E　22-24　  1822
　(marriage contract 27 June 1822) (both of York District)
Donnelly, Revd　　Mariah Williams　 W　68-73　  1852
　James　　　　　　_____ [no last name]
　(separation agreement 17 May 1852) (of Abbeville
　District)
Donnelly, Samuel　Mary R. Ewart　　 K　155-157　1838
　(marriage settlement 11 June 1838)
Donnelly, Samuel　Mary R. Ewart　　2B　217-219　1860
　(reference to marriage settlement - no date given)
Doolittle. See Doulittle
Dorithy, William O. Sarah Bradham　  U　329-331　1851
　W. (marriage settlement 9 January 1851) (in Sumter
　District)
Douglas, Jilson B. M. Carolina　　　2A　516-518　1859
　　　　　　　　　Coggeshall
　(marriage settlement 19 January 1859) (both of
　Darlington District)
Douglass, _____　 Matilda C. Lomax　L　57-58　　1836
　(daughter of G. Lomax of Abbeville
　District)
Doulittle, Seaburn Mary McKie　　　 M　255-256　1842
　(daughter of Daniel McKie of Edgefield
　District)
Doyle, John　　　 Mary McElroy　　　E　281-282　1824
　(marriage settlement 26 December 1824)
Doyley, Charles W. Sarah E. Baker　 G　107-109　1817
　(Doyly) (reference to marriage settlement 14 April 1817)
　(in Greenville District)

35

Implied South Carolina Marriages Volume IV 1787-1875

| MAN | WOMAN | VOL | PAGES | LIVED |
|---|---|---|---|---|
| Dozier, _____ | Caroline Yarbrough | Z | 12-14 | 1856 |
| Dozier, Arthur | Mense L. _____ | Z | 320-321 | 1856 |

(granddaughter of Bennet Perry of Edgefield District)

| Dozier, Smith W. | Elizabeth Bright | G | 370-371 | 1831 |
| Dozier, Thomas | Sarah B. Gause | T | 351-355 | 1849 |

Jefferson (marriage settlement 5 November 1849) (both of Marion District)

| Drafts, Jesse | _____ Lorick | T | 387-389 | 1849 |

(widow of John Lorick)

| Drake, James F. | Ann Eliza Tomlinson | 2A | 426-429 | 1858 |

(marriage settlement 11 September 1858) (daughter of Henry M. Tomlinson)

| Drake, James F. | Ann Eliza Tomlinson | 2B | 493-496 | 1858 |

(reference to antenuptial settlement 11 September 1858) (daughter of Henry M. Tomlinson) (in Chesterfield District)

| Dreher, Godfrey | Margaret Leapheart | S | 450-452 | 1848 |

(marriage settlement 20 November 1848) (widow of William Leapheart) (in Lexington District)

| Drehr, John | Catharina Leever | A | 308-311 | 1797 |

(marriage settlement 21 July 1797) (widow of Jacob Leever) (both of Orangeburgh District)

| Drenan, Wm. T. | _____ Scott | 2A | 745-746 | 1846 |
| Drennon, William T. | Mary D. Scott | 2A | 566 | 1859 |
| DuBose, David | Margaret Ann Johnson | G | 329-332 | 1831 |

St. Piere (marriage contract 3 January 1831) (both of Sumter District)

| Dubose, Isaac | Catharine Dubose | A | 311-315 | 1797 |

(marriage settlement 6 July 1797) (both of Camden, Kershaw County)

| DuBose, Peter | Amanda Crosswell | Y | 553-555 | 1855 |

(marriage settlement 18 December 1855) (both of Darlington District)

| Duckworth, Jacob J. | Mary A. Smith | 2A | 195-197 | 1858 |

(marriage settlement 13 January 1858) (widow) (she of Anderson District)

| Due, John S. | Emma Wiggins | R | 212-213 | 1846 |

(of Fairfield District)

| Duke, _____ | Ann Montgomery | N | 102 | 1836 |

(daughter of David Montgomery of Kershaw District)

| Dulin, Rice | Martha B. Mickle | I | 569 | 1837 |

(of Columbia) (daughter of Joseph Mickle of Kershaw District)

Implied South Carolina Marriages Volume IV 1787-1875

| MAN | WOMAN | VOL | PAGES | LIVED |
|---|---|---|---|---|
| Dunbar, William | Sarah Myddleton (Middleton) | A | 259-262 | 1794 |

(marriage settlement 7 July 1794) (he of Winton County) (she of Orangeburgh District)

| Duncan, _____ | Medora Rice | 2B | 777-778 | 1864 |

(daughter of B. H. Rice of Union District)

| Duncan, Darling P. | Rosa Aldrich | 2B | 761-762 | 1864 |

(in Barnwell District) (daughter of Alfred P. Aldrich)

| Dunn, _____ | Nancy C. Calvert | L | 426-428 | 1841 |

(daughter of Jesse Calvert)

| Dunovant, R. G. M. | Ellen S. Brooks | T | 468-469 | 1849 |

(daughter of Whitfield Brooks of Edgefield District)

| Dunovant, Williams | Mary M. Mobley | Y | 294-296 | 1855 |

(marriage settlement 30 May 1855) (daughter of John M. Mobley) (in Chester District)

| Dunsford, William W. | Frances Stack Lorick | Z | 369-372 | 1856 |

(of Richland District) (daughter of John Lorick of Richland District and stepdaughter of Jesse Drafts)

| DuPre, James | Drucilla Mace | Y | 128-129 | 1855 |

(Dupree) (marriage settlement 6 March 1855) (in Marion District)

| DuPre, James | Drucilla Mace | Z | 478-480 | 1855 |

(reference to marriage settlement 6 March 1855) (in Marion District)

| Dupree, Franklin | Mary P. Huckabee | Z | 518-519 | 1857 |

(daughter of G. W. Huckabee)

| Durant, Joseph S. | Margaret E. Muldrow | 2B | 732-735 | 1864 |

(marriage settlement 13 January 1864) (daughter of Robert B. Muldrow of Sumter District) (Durant of Clarendon District) (she of Sumter District)

| Durant, Sidney P. | Elizabeth M. Cureton | 2A | 502-504 | 1859 |

(of Sumter District) (daughter of Jere Cureton Jr. and granddaughter of Jere Cureton Sr.)

| Durbec, Eugene Sr. | Clara Aveilhe | M | 281-283 | 1842 |

(of Aiken, Barnwell District)

| Durham, John | Mary Wagner Mobley | 2B | 756-757 | 1863 |

Woodward (of Fairfield District) (daughter of Dr. Isaiah Mobley)

| Duvall, Gideon | Caroline Ellerbe | L | 441-444 | 1841 |

(marriage settlement 20 November 1841) (widow of Thomas G. Ellerbe)

| Duvall, Gideon W. | Sarah Powe | O | 156-158 | 1844 |

(marriage settlement 29 May 1844) (daughter of Thomas Powe) (both of Chesterfield District)

Implied South Carolina Marriages Volume IV 1787-1875

| MAN | WOMAN | VOL | PAGES | LIVED |
|---|---|---|---|---|
| Dwight, Dr. Samuel J. | Sarah Ann Scott (daughter of John Scott of Richland District) | W | 140-141 | 1852 |
| Dwight, William Moultrie | Elizabeth P. Gaillard | 2B | 254-255 | 1861 |

(marriage settlement 30 January 1861) (he of Abbeville District) (she of Fairfield District)

| Dwyer, Samuel | Elizabeth Dubose | D | 198-201 | 1820 |
|---|---|---|---|---|

(marriage settlement 3 June 1820) (both of Sumter District)

| Dyke, Samuel A. | Mary Ann Elizabeth Cheatham | 2B | 530-531 | 1862 |
|---|---|---|---|---|

(daughter of Guthredge Cheatham of Edgefield District) (of Abbeville District)

| Dyson, _____ | Nancy E. West | K | 318-320 | 1830 |
|---|---|---|---|---|

(in Sumter District)

| Dyson, Archibald S. | Hannah S. Bacot | 2A | 415-417 | 1858 |
|---|---|---|---|---|

(marriage settlement 15 July 1858) (both of Darlington District)

(E)

| Eadie, James | Katharine Paterson | D | 109-114 | 1818 |
|---|---|---|---|---|

(daughter of James Paterson) (of Clackmanan, Scotland)

| Earle, Dr M. B. | Harriet H. Maxwell | V | 23-24 | 1851 |
|---|---|---|---|---|

(of Greenville) (daughter of John Maxwell of Anderson District)

| Earle, George W. | Ann Eliza McCall | 2B | 167-168 | 1860 |
|---|---|---|---|---|

(daughter of James S. McCall Senr. of Darlington District)

| Easterling, Joel | Frances (Fannie) Thomas | 2A | 527-528 | 1859 |
|---|---|---|---|---|

(marriage settlement 19 February 1859) (widower) (widow) (both of Marlborough District) [See also page 748]

| Eccles, Reverend Samuel | Ann Pettigrew | B | 498-505 | 1808 |
|---|---|---|---|---|

(marriage settlement 21 April 1808) (widow of Alexander Pettigrew) (of Darlington District)

| Eddy, William H. | Susan E. Hunter | 2A | 531 | 1859 |
|---|---|---|---|---|

(daughter of Joseph Y. Hunter of Newberry District)

| Edmonds, Jefferson L. | Dorothy Ann Wadlington | I | 107-108 | 1834 |
|---|---|---|---|---|
| Edmonson, John | Susannah Turner | F | 175 | 1826 |

(marriage contract 29 January 1826) (both of Newberry District)

Implied South Carolina Marriages Volume IV 1787-1875

| MAN | WOMAN | VOL | PAGES | LIVED |
|---|---|---|---|---|
| Edmunds, ___ | Polly Bussey | Y | 73-75 | 1855 |

(daughter of Demcy Bussey Sr.)
Edmunds, ___         Agnes Zinn         C    201-207   1815
   (daughter of Jacob Zinn Senior of Be<u>a</u>ch
   Island, Edgefield District)
Edwards, Augustus    Elizabeth S. Hart  2A   708-709   1859
   F. (in Darlington District)
Edwards, J. Gadsden  Eliza Gabriella    2B   317-319   1861
                     Gibbes
   (marriage settlement 29 April 1861) (both of Columbia)
Edwards, Philip      Anna Margaret      2B   716-717   1840
   Gadsden           Guignard
   (reference to postnuptial settlement 4 May 1840) (he died
   1847) (of Charleston)
Eigleberger,         Effie Hughey       U    5-7       1850
   William           (daughter of Daniel Hughey of Fairfield
   District)
Eigleburger, John    Sarah Priester     D    365-367   1821
   (marriage agreement 13 September 1821) (both of Newberry
   District)
Elders, ___          Mary Wescott       M    13-14     1842
   (widow) (she of Richland District)
Elders, John         Sarah Rowe         C    306-307   1816
   (of Richland District) ("formerly Sarah Autry")
Elders, William      Mary Boucher       C    222-223   1816
   (marriage agreement 13 January 1816) (widow)
Ellerbe, Joseph      Elizabeth Ellerbe  H    81-83     1832
   (of Chesterfield District) (daughter of William Ellerbe)
Ellerbe, Thomas G.   Caroline Powe      L    441-444   1841
   (daughter of Thomas Powe of Chesterfield
   District)
Ellerbe, William C.  Mary E. Sanders    2C   412-413   1868
   S.                (daughter of William Sanders of Sumter
   District)
Ellerbie, ___        Mary C. Powe       I    439       1836
   (in Chesterfield District) (daughter of Erasmus Powe)
Ellison, ___         Margaret Adger     X    144-145   1850
Elmore, Franklin H.  Harriet Chesnut    H    26-27     1831
                     Taylor (daughter of John Taylor of
                     Columbia, Richland District)
Elmore, John         Eliza Taylor       Y    608-609   1855
   (marriage settlement 3 December 1855) (widow) (both of
   Newberry District) [See also pages 613-615]
English, John        Maria Means        2A   546-547   1858
Epting, Draton       Kezia Salton       2B   156-157   1860
                     (daughter of Michael Salton of Lexington
                     District)

39

Implied South Carolina Marriages Volume IV 1787-1875

| MAN | WOMAN | VOL | PAGES | LIVED |
|---|---|---|---|---|
| Ervin, _____ | _____ Brown | R | 398-400 | 1847 |

(daughter of James Brown of Darlington District)

Ervin, Samuel J.   Sarah A. Coggeshall   X   7-11   1853
(marriage settlement 8 August 1853) (daughter of Peter C. Coggeshall) (both of Darlington District)

Erwin, James D.   Annabella Martha   Z   452-454   1856
Tucker (daughter of Daniel R. Tucker of Baldwin County, Georgia) (Erwin of Barnwell District, S.C.)

Erwin, Ulysses M.   Mary Ann Elizabeth   Z   450-452   1856
Tucker (daughter of Daniel R. Tucker of Baldwin County, Georgia) (Erwin of Barnwell District, S.C.)

Erwin, Wm G.   Eliza A. Steel   W   62-64   1852
(marriage settlement 15 June 1852) (widow of J. J. Steel) (in York District)

Eubanks, Joseph   Margaret E. Wood   2C   438-440   1868
(daughter of Wiley Wood of Union District)

Evans, Capt. John   Frances Anna Augusta   F   411   1828
Jane Knight
(marriage settlement 24 June 1828) (both of Hamburg, Edgefield District)

Evans, David R.   Martha K. Aiken   2A   746-747   1859
(daughter of James Aiken of Fairfield District, S.C.) (Evans late of Fairfield District, S.C., now of Louisiana)

Evans, Edward   Sally Chesnut Taylor   S   377-384   1848
Edwards (marriage settlement 15 November 1848) (daughter of John Chesnut Taylor) (in Richland District)

Evans, John E. B.   Sarah Eliza Clark   Z   406-407   1856
(of Richland District) (daughter of J. W. Clark of Columbia, Richland District)

Evans, Joseph   Elizabeth Havis   E   139-145   1823
(in Fairfield District) (daughter of Jesse Havis Senior)

Evans, Moses   Catharine Gowen   D   191-194   1820
(marriage settlement 24 April 1820) (widow of John Gowen of York District) (of York District)

Evans, Robert E.   Rebecca F. Robeson   2C   285-287   1867
(daughter of Thomas W. Robeson of Chesterfield District)

Evans, Samuel W.   Alescina Wallace   S   34-35   1848
(of Chesterfield District) (daughter of Andrew Wallace of Richland District)

Eveleigh, Cleland   Ann Simmons   A   335-338   1787

Implied South Carolina Marriages Volume IV 1787-1875

| MAN | WOMAN | VOL | PAGES | LIVED |
|---|---|---|---|---|

Exum, Joseph J.    Sarah A. Atkinson    I    26-27    1834
 (marriage agreement 19 February 1834) (he of Kershaw
 District) (she of Sumter District)

(F)

Fair, Samuel    Mary D. DeBruhl    W    412-415    1853
 (of Richland District) (daughter of Jesse DeBruhl of
 Richland District)
Fairbarn, E. G.    Mary Boozer    2A    50-51    1857
 (of Laurens District) (daughter of George Boozer of
 Newberry District)
Fairey, Philip W.    Elizabeth R. Griffis    2C    351-353    1867
 (marriage settlement 14 May 1867) (he of Orangeburg
 District) (she of Colleton District)
Fant, John A.    Sarah Thomas    2A    206-208    1857
 (marriage contract 24 October 1857) (widow) (of Union
 District)
Farnandis, James    Sarah Johnston    H    103    1832
 (Johnson) (daughter of John Johnston of
 Fairfield District)
Farnandis, Lemuel    Sarah Shelton    F    229-230    1827
Farr, J. H. R.    Margaret W. Smith    P    302-304    1846
 (to be married 5 February 1846) (marriage settlement 5
 February 1846) (both of Union District)
Farr, Robert G. H.    Margarett L. Beatty    H    213-215    1828
 (of Union District) (daughter of Jonathan Beatty)
Farrow, _____    Susannah Baskerville    F    367    1828
 (widow)
Fayssoux, Templar S.    Melinda A. McFadden    Y    34    1855
 (daughter of Isaac McFadden of Chester
 District)
Feaster, Nathan Andrew McClanahan)    Annette C. McClanahan (daughter    2B    144-145    1860
 (of Greenville District) of Samuel G.
Felder, Edwin D.    Caroline Macon    X    548    1854
 Brunson (daughter of William L. Brunson)
 (in Sumter District)
Felder, Erwin D.    Caroline Macon    2B    225-228    1860
 Brunson (daughter of William L. Brunson
 of Sumter District)
Felkel, Derrill M.    Rachael A. _____    Y    219-220    1852
 (separation agreement 29 October 1852) (in Orangeburg
 District)
Fenly, _____    Elizabeth Kinsler    2B    52-61    1859

41

Implied South Carolina Marriages Volume IV 1787-1875

| MAN | WOMAN | VOL | PAGES | LIVED |
|---|---|---|---|---|
| Ferguson, Elisha A. | Mary Catherine Richardson (daughter of Noah T. Richardson of Anderson District) (Ferguson of Pickens District) | 2B | 246-247 | 1859 |
| Ferrel, ____ | Mariah Robinson | L | 352-354 | 1841 |
| Fladger, C. J. | S. A. Bethea (marriage settlement 16 August 1859) (widow of W. S. Bethea) (both of Marion District) | 2A | 694-695 | 1859 |
| Fleming, Andrew B. | Ann Murph (marriage contract 16 August 1854) (in Spartanburg District) | 2B | 135-136 | 1854 |
| Flinn, Christopher | Elizabeth Byrd (marriage settlement 13 October 1846) (widow of Miller Byrd) (both of Darlington District) | R | 94-96 | 1846 |
| Flinn, Henry K. W. | Ann D. Ervin (marriage settlement 26 July 1851) (in Darlington District) | V | 16-18 | 1851 |
| Flowers, John | Hannah Ann Huson | H | 461 | 1833 |
| Flud, John M. | Eliza C. K. ____ (reference to marriage settlement - no date given) | 2B | 654 | 1863 |
| Flyn, Patrick | Hetty McKenney | U | 417-418 | 1851 |
| Folger, ____ | Cassandra Lucy Dean (daughter of John Dean of Spartanburgh District) | S | 226-227 | 1848 |
| Folk, David | Pirmelia Angeline Kibler | T | 31-33 | 1848 |
| Folk, John A. | Christena Cannon (marriage contract 27 June 1840) (he was married before) (widow) (both of Newberry District) | L | 103-104 | 1840 |
| Fooshe, Charles | Gracy Wood (marriage settlement 13 June 1820) (in Abbeville District) | D | 201-202 | 1820 |
| Ford, ____ | Mary Robeson (daughter of Peter L. Robeson of Chesterfield District) | F | 393 | 1828 |
| Ford, Malachi | Margaret Ann Sanders | B | 173-175 | 1792 |
| Ford, Thomas | Mary Walter (marriage settlement 16 December 1805) (widow of Richard Charles Walter who died 17__) (Ford of Black River) (she of Stateburg) | B | 391-398 | 1805 |
| Foster, George | Cynthia Bailey (in Union District) | L | 351 | 1841 |
| Foulkes, Nathaniel W. | Eliza Ann Rice (marriage settlement 2 August 1836) (widow of David B. Rice) (both of York District) | I | 466-468 | 1836 |
| Fowke, R. C. | H. S. Allen (daughter of John C. Allen) | Z | 527-528 | 1857 |

Implied South Carolina Marriages Volume IV 1787-1875

MAN                WOMAN              VOL   PAGES        LIVED

Fowler, John F.    Sarah P. Henderson   2A   552-554      1859
   (marriage settlement 31 January 1859) (widow of Hugh L.
   Henderson) (in Laurens District)
Frank, John        Catharine _____      Z    489-491      1857
   (separation agreement 22 January 1857) (of Richland
   District)
Fraser, _____      Jane A. Lesly        Z    422-423      1856
   (she in Abbeville District)
Fraser, John W.    Ann Clayton          X    15-18        1853
   (Frasier) (marriage settlement 9 July 1853) (widow of
   Edmond Clayton) (in Barnwell District)
Fraser, Ladson L.  Hannah A. _____      W    239-243      1824
   (reference to marriage settlement 8 December 1824)
Fraser, Ladson L.  Hannah A. _____      Z    794-799      1824
   (reference to marriage settlement 8 December 1824)
Fraser, Ladson L.  Mary Adelaide D.     2B   583-584      1862
   Jr.             _____ [no last name]
   (in Sumter District) (granddaughter of Joseph B. White
   Sr.)
Fraser, Lansden    Hannah Atkinson      E    277-279      1824
   (marriage settlement 8 December 1824) (both of Sumter
   District)
Fraser, Revr. M. D. Hessy Crawford      N    271-272      1843
Fraser, Thomas B.  Sarah M. _____       Z    188-189      1856
   (reference to marriage settlement - no date given)
Fraser, Thomas B.  Sarah Margaret       V    422-426      1852
                   McIver
   (marriage settlement 24 March 1852) (he of Sumterville)
   (she of Yorkville)
Fraser, William W. Martha A. McCutchen  2B   566-568      1862
   (in Sumter District)
Frean, Thomas      Hannah Elmore        D    152-154      1819
                   (daughter of Mathias Elmore) (Frean of
   Charleston, formerly of Newberry District) [See also
   Volume V, page 163; Volume 2A, pages 639-640]
Freeman, _____     Eliza A. A.          2B   332-335      1861
                   Hollingsworth
Frierson, _____    Margaret Muldrow     Z    404-406      1856
                   (daughter of Matthew E. Muldrow of Salem
                   County, Sumter District)
Frierson, John N.  Catharine K.         S    205-208      1845
                   Converse (granddaughter of Daniel
   Kellogg) (Frierson of Claremont County, Sumter District)
Frierson, John N.  Catherine K.         O    423-424      1845
                   Converse (daughter of Augustus L.
   Converse of Sumter District) (Frierson of Claremont
   County, Sumter District) [Must also see pages 445-448]

43

Implied South Carolina Marriages Volume IV 1787-1875

| MAN | WOMAN | VOL | PAGES | LIVED |
|---|---|---|---|---|

Fritzmann, Sebastian    Sarah Wood    M    253    1842
(marriage settlement 30 June 1842) (in Newberry District)
Fuller, James L.    Catharine ____    G    279-280    1830
(separation agreement 4 September 1830)
Fullwood, Robert    Martha J. Perrit    2A    472-473    1858
Fullwood, Robert H.    Eliza Orr    S    438-441    1848
(marriage settlement 13 September 1848) (widow of Joab Orr) (Fullwood of York District, S.C.) (she of Mecklenburg County, North Carolina)
Fulmer, William P.    Amanda L. Fulmer    2B    814-815    1864
(marriage settlement 19 May 1864) (widow of John H. Fulmer) (both of Newberry District)
Futrell, ____    Agnes Miles    2B    506-507    1862

(G)

Gaillard, Franklin    Catharine Cordes Porcher    W    500-506    1853
(marriage settlement 28 March 1853) (he of Winnsborough, Fairfield District) (she of Charleston)
Gaillard, Lewis C.    Eliza Jane Harkness    S    414-415    1848
(in Anderson District) (daughter of John Harkness)
Gailliard, C. L.    Alethea L. Creswell    R    433-435    1847
(marriage settlement 1 March 1847) (widow) (in Anderson District)
Galbreath, ____    Ann Davidson    E    171-172    1824
(daughter of Robert Davidson of York District)
Galespy, Solomon    Barbara Vaughn    V    11-13    1851
(Galespe) (separation agreement 13 May 1851) (daughter of John Vaughn) (in Laurens District)
Gallagher, ____    Mary E. Lamar    T    430-433    1849
(daughter of Mack Lamar of Edgefield District)
Galluchat, Joseph    Rebecca M. Gill    R    131-132    1846
(to be married 22 October 1846) (marriage settlement 19 October 1846) (daughter of Lewis Gill) (in Lancaster District)
Gantt, ____    Emma Francis Groves    S    293-294    1848
(daughter of Joseph Groves of Abbeville District)
Gantt, Thomas W.    Francis Emala Groves    V    522-524    1852
(in Abbeville District)

Implied South Carolina Marriages Volume IV 1787-1875

| MAN | WOMAN | VOL | PAGES | LIVED |
|---|---|---|---|---|

Gardener, Wm J.    Martha J. McMullin    Y    124-125    1855
  (separation agreement 19 February 1855) (daughter of
  Cullin McMullin) (in Spartanburg District)
Gardner, _____    Mary Zinn    C    201-207    1815
  (daughter of Jacob Zinn Senior of Beach
  Island, Edgefield District)
Gardner, James T.    Rebecca Nail    Z    275-278    1856
  (separation agreement 10 June 1856) (daughter of Casper
  Nail) (in Edgefield District)
Gardner, Jeremiah    Elizabeth Williams    K    66    1837
  (of Abbeville District)
Gardner, John Henry Mary Caroline Geiger    2A    635-637    1859
  (marriage settlement 22 June 1859) (daughter of Godfrey
  H. Geiger and granddaughter of Michael Lorick)
Gardner, William Q.  Anna J. _____    2A    572-573    1859
  (separation agreement 11 April 1859) (of Edgefield
  District, S.C., late of Louisiana)
Garlington, Edwin    Elener (Eleanor)    C    231-233    1815
                     Griffin
  (marriage settlement 23 November 1815) (in Laurens
  District)
Garlington, H. W.    Mary Teague    T    398-400    1849
Garner, _____    Mary Miles    2B    506-507    1862
Garner, Charles W.    Winny Parrott    N    348-349    1844
  (daughter of Benjamin Parrott of
  Darlington District)
Garner, Gilbert    Caroline    2B    274-275    1861
                   Killingsworth
  (marriage settlement 30 January 1861) (widow) (both of
  Richland District)
Garrett, Jesse    Mary Shermon    2B    525-527    1862
  (of Anderson District)
Garrett, John W.    Caroline Middleton    M    15    1841
  (of Edgefield District) (daughter of John Middleton of
  Edgefield District)
Garvin, Daniel    Dorothy Ables    T    255-256    1849
  (of Orangeburgh District) (daughter of John J. Ables of
  Lexington District)
Garvin, David    Nancy Kirksey    X    472-474    1853
  (of Hall County, Georgia) (daughter of William Kirksey
  Senr. of Pickens District, S.C.)
Garvin, W. W.    Sarah C. Ratchford    2A    234-237    1858
  (both of Barnwell District) [See also pages 240-241]
Gaskins, John    Matilda Addison    T    232-233    1849
  (marriage settlement 14 June 1849) (in Edgefield
  District)

Implied South Carolina Marriages Volume IV 1787-1875

| MAN | WOMAN | VOL | PAGES | LIVED |
|---|---|---|---|---|
| Gaulden, Wade H. | Ann M. Cheves (Chivers) | C | 392-394 | 1816 |

(marriage settlement 25 November 1816) (both of Sumter District)

Gayer, William J.    Cora E. Carter    2A    709-711    1859
(of Charleston) (daughter of Larkin G. Carter of Abbeville District)
Gee, Charles    Mary Elizabeth    G    175-176    1829
    Vernon    [See also pages 39-42]
Gee, Wilson P.    Drusilla M. E.    R    220-222    1847
Gilliam (daughter of Reuben Gilliam of Union District)
Gent, Daniel    Nancy Anderson    F    265-266    1828
(marriage settlement 15 April 1828) (widow of James Anderson) (in Edgefield District)
George, Darling    Mary Elizabeth Scott    X    602-603    1854
(or David) J.    (daughter of John Scott of Richland District) [See also pages 640-641]
Gerald, Benjamin    Alice James    B    194-196    1802
(marriage settlement 26 June 1802) (both of Claremont County, Sumter District)
Gerald, Thomas D.    Catharine ____    Y    459-461    1855
(reference to marriage settlement - no date given) (both of Sumter District)
Gerald, Thomas D.    Catharine Osborn    L    464-465    1841
(marriage settlement 8 November 1841) (in Sumter District)
Getsam, Samuel    Mary Sullivan    K    508-510    1836
Gibbes, Robert W.    Mary How    Y    8-10    1855
Junior (marriage settlement 6 February 1855)
Gibbons, Thomas    Rebecca Beckham    H    208-209    1832
(in Lancaster District) (widow)
Gibert, Dr. J. A.    Martha C. Tennent    2A    213-214    1857
(of Abbeville District) (daughter of William Tennent of Abbeville District)
<u>Gibson,</u> ____    <u>Haret</u> Yarbrough    Z    12    1856
(Gelder) [his last name illegible] [her first name illegible]
Gibson, A. W.    Isabella Cason    R    213-214    1847
(of Fairfield District)
Gibson, Allen    Mary Ann Williams    G    177-181    1830
(marriage settlement 17 April 1830) (daughter of Eli Williams) (Gibson of Columbia, Richland District) (she of Richland District)
Gibson, Jacob    Rebecca ____    M    416-418    1843
(separation agreement 31 January 1843) (of Fairfield District)

46

Implied South Carolina Marriages Volume IV 1787-1875

| MAN | WOMAN | VOL | PAGES | LIVED |
|---|---|---|---|---|

Gibson, John    Ann M. Harper    V    608-609    1852
  Augustus (marriage settlement 24 June 1852) (widow)
  (both of Richland District)
Giles, Abraham    Annes Phillips    B    295-300    1804
  (marriage settlement 16 February 1804) (both of Marion
  District)
Giles, William    Mary Young    H    207-208    1827
  (marriage settlement 27 April 1827) (in Abbeville
  District)
Gill, Henry S.    Elizabeth A. Duke    O    387-389    1845
  (marriage settlement 10 March 1845) (of Richland
  District)
Gillam, Genl. James    Louisa L. Carruth    U    242-245    1850
  (marriage settlement 17 October 1850) (he of Abbeville
  District) (she of Anderson District)
Gillam, James    Louisa L. _____    V    558-560    1850
  (reference to marriage settlement 17 October 1850) (of
  Abbeville District)
Gillespie. See Galespy
Gilman, George    Ann Kershaw    B    736-738    1812
  (marriage settlement 7 April 1812) (widow of George
  Kershaw of Camden) (Gilman late of Camden, now of Black
  River)
Gilmer, James J.    Alathea Bowie    L    126-127    1840
  (in Abbeville District)
Gilstrap, Hardy    Lavinia Hawthorn    2C    56-59    1865
  (postnuptial settlement/separation agreement 9 October
  1865) (he was married before) (widow of Jasper N.
  Hawthorn) (in Pickens District)
Givens, Solomon W.    Susan E. McFadden    2A    537    1858
  (in Chester District)
Gladney, Richard J.    Sarah M. Harden    W    550-552    1853
  (marriage settlement 4 May 1853) (daughter of Silas
  Harden) (both of Fairfield District)
Gladney, Richard J.    Sarah M. Harden    2B    187-190    1853
  (reference to marriage settlement 4 May 1853) (in
  Fairfield District)
Glasgow, Spencer L.    Martha A. Cannon    2A    120-121    1857
  (daughter of George S. Cannon of Newberry
  District)
Glass, James B.    Julia S. Kennerly    2B    62-63    1852
  (both of Richland District) (daughter of Eli Kennerly)
Glaze, William    Harriet Ann Morgan    I    511-512    1836
  (marriage settlement 19 October 1836) (she of Columbia)
Glazener, G.    Francis Elizabeth    2B    468-469    1859
  Luwiler    Gossett
  (in Greenville District) (daughter of John T. Gossett)

47

Implied South Carolina Marriages Volume IV 1787-1875

| MAN | WOMAN | VOL | PAGES | LIVED |
|---|---|---|---|---|
| Glenn, Nathan | Permelia Coleman | M | 392-393 | 1843 |

(of Union District)

| Glenn, William C. | Elizabeth Wright | G | 258 | 1830 |
|---|---|---|---|---|

(in Union District) (daughter of Thomas Wright)

| Glover, Artemas E. | Washington Ann Pemble | X | 118-120 | 1853 |
|---|---|---|---|---|

(marriage settlement 12 November 1853) (of Orangeburg District)

| Glover, Joseph Edward | Mary E. Bellinger | 2B | 651-654 | 1863 |
|---|---|---|---|---|

(marriage settlement 7 July 1863) (daughter of Edmund C. Bellinger) (Glover of Colleton District) (she of Charleston) (in Barnwell District) [See also pages 720-721, 724, 772-773]

| Glover, Wiley | Matilda Gaskins | 2A | 622-625 | 1859 |
|---|---|---|---|---|

(marriage settlement 16 June 1859) (both of Edgefield District)

| Godbee, _____ | Loveridge Lewis Villepontoux | A | 198-199 | 1791 |
|---|---|---|---|---|
| Godefroy, Armand | Julie (Julia) Marion | H | 131 | 1831 |

(marriage agreement 12 December 1831) (both of Columbia) [See also pages 80-81]

| Godman, _____ | Emiline Ward | 2A | 47-49 | 1857 |
|---|---|---|---|---|
| Godman, Harry R. | Emeline Ward | X | 457-458 | 1854 |

(daughter of Richard Ward of Edgefield District)

| Godman, Stewart A. | Margaret E. Watts | S | 331-333 | 1848 |
|---|---|---|---|---|

(marriage settlement 24 August 1848) (in Laurens District)

| Goff, James | Sarah _____ | Z | 718-720 | 1857 |
|---|---|---|---|---|

(reference to marriage settlement 22 July 1856 - unrecorded) (of Edgefield District)

| Golding, John | Hetty Waldrop | F | 364-365 | 1828 |
|---|---|---|---|---|

(marriage settlement 23 September 1828) (in Newberry District)

| Goldthwaite, Robert Henry | Eleanor Walker | E | 155-156 | 1823 |
|---|---|---|---|---|

(married 10 August 1823) (marriage settlement 25 September 1823) (both of Lexington District) [See also pages 193-194]

| Good, James W. | Narry Cole | 2A | 369-371 | 1858 |
|---|---|---|---|---|

(of York District) (daughter of William Cole of Union District)

| Good, John | Susannah Connell | C | 281-283 | 1816 |
|---|---|---|---|---|

(marriage settlement 6 March 1816) (in Darlington District)

| Good, John B. | Amanda Cole | 2A | 369-371 | 1858 |
|---|---|---|---|---|

(daughter of William Cole of Union District)

Implied South Carolina Marriages Volume IV 1787-1875

| MAN | WOMAN | VOL | PAGES | LIVED |
|---|---|---|---|---|
| Good, Samuel F. | Mary A. Gomillion | U | 49-50 | 1850 |

(of Edgefield District)

| Goodin, _____ | Ann Hightower | 2A | 90-91 | 1851 |
|---|---|---|---|---|
| Goodin, Reuben | Jane Russell | U | 18-19 | 1850 |

(marriage settlement 23 February 1850) (she of Abbeville District)

| Goodwin, John H. | Sarah Ann Lynch | 2C | 342-344 | 1867 |
|---|---|---|---|---|

(Goodwyn) (marriage settlement 17 June 1867)

| Goodwyn, _____ | Celestine Raoul | R | 159-164 | 1847 |
|---|---|---|---|---|

(daughter of Dr. John Louis Raoul de Champmanoir) [See also pages 216-219, 258-260]

| Goodwyn, Dr. Thomas J. | Eliza Elliott Darby | 2A | 743-744 | 1859 |
|---|---|---|---|---|
| Goodwyn, Jesse H. | Sarah T. Wienchy | G | 322-323 | 1831 |
| Goodwyn, John T. | Sally C. Brown | R | 22-23 | 1846 |
| Gordon, _____ | Margaret Chandler | E | 190-191 | 1824 |

(widow of George Chandler, her first husband)

| Gordon, Eli | Nancy K. Farr | K | 398-399 | 1839 |
|---|---|---|---|---|

(of Newberry District) (daughter of John P. Farr of Union District)

Goree, Robert Kelly. See Robert Kelly

| Goudelock, John B. | Sarah M. Doggett | H | 87-88 | 1832 |
|---|---|---|---|---|

(marriage settlement 4 February 1832) (he of Union District, S.C.) (she of Rutherford County, North Carolina)

| Gracey, M. W. | Mary B. Wadlington | K | 535-542 | 1835 |
|---|---|---|---|---|
| Gradick, David | Mary Ann F. Leitner | 2B | 661-662 | 1863 |

(daughter of Daniel W. Leitner)

| Graham, _____ | Eliza C. Smith | S | 157 | 1848 |
|---|---|---|---|---|

(in Barnwell District)

| Graham, John | Martha Havis | E | 139-145 | 1823 |
|---|---|---|---|---|

(in Fairfield District) (daughter of Jesse Havis Senior)

| Graham, Joseph E. | Elizabeth H. Clark | 2B | 124-125 | 1860 |
|---|---|---|---|---|

(marriage settlement 1 April 1860) (both of Clarendon District)

| Grant, _____ | Nancy Yarbrough | Z | 12-14 | 1856 |
|---|---|---|---|---|
| Graves, George | Caroline S. Tatom | N | 297-301 | 1844 |

(marriage settlement 30 January 1844) (widow of Orville Tatom) (Graves of Jefferson County, Florida) (she of Abbeville District, S.C.)

| Gray, William | Harriet Green | D | 364-365 | 1821 |
|---|---|---|---|---|

(marriage agreement 9 June 1821) (in Richland District)

| Green, _____ | Laura A. H. Turpin | V | 385-389 | 1852 |
|---|---|---|---|---|
| Green, Charles Henry | Elizabeth Jane Green | 2A | 511-512 | 1858 |

(marriage settlement 29 December 1858) (he of Georgia) (she in Sumter District, S.C.)

Implied South Carolina Marriages Volume IV 1787-1875

| MAN | WOMAN | VOL | PAGES | LIVED |
|---|---|---|---|---|
| Green, Dr. Allen J. | Sally Scott | T | 395-398 | 1849 |

(marriage settlement 15 October 1849)

| Green, Halcot P. | Virginia Taylor | R | 189-191 | 1847 |

(daughter of Benjamin F. Taylor)

| Green, Joseph | Franc_i_s Benson | N | 71 | 1843 |

(marriage contract 3 January 1843) (both of Greenville District)

| Green, Samuel | Selina Waring | E | 317-318 | 1825 |

(marriage contract 4 August 1825) (both of Columbia, Richland District)

| Green, Thomas | Ermin Lester | 2A | 178-179 | 1857 |

(daughter of Archibald Lester)

| Green, William H. | Elizabeth Bogan Jr. | I | 400 | 1835 |

(marriage settlement 31 December 1835) (daughter of William Bogan) (in Union District)

| Greenfield, Alexander | Mary Hays Hibben | 2A | 281-282 | 1858 |

(marriage settlement __ January 1858) (of Greenville District)

| Greenfield, Robert | Mary C. Shaver | Y | 513-515 | 1855 |

(marriage settlement 27 October 1855) (both of Greenville District)

| Greer, David | Susannah Ward | F | 80 | 1827 |

(marriage agreement 7 June 1827) (in Laurens District)

| Gregory, Adolphus | Martha Ann Gibbs | W | 451-452 | 1853 |

(of Union District) (daughter of Churchill Gibbs of Union District)

| Gregory, Benjamin | Mary S. Vanlew | K | 79-80 | 1838 |

(marriage settlement 3 January 1838) (of Union District)

| Gregory, Doctr. James | Sarah Elvira Gregory | V | 246-247 | 1852 |

(daughter of Benjamin J. Gregory of Union District)

| Gregory, Gerard Singleton | Nancy ____ | X | 368-370 | 1854 |

(his second marriage) (in Union District)

| Gregory, John J. | E. Mary J. Smith | X | 46-47 | 1853 |

(of Union District) (daughter of John Smith of Chester District)

| Gregory, John L. | Sarah Elizabeth Cook | Z | 409-411 | 1856 |

(of Lancaster District) (daughter of Nathaniel Cook of Lancaster District)

| Gregory, Ossian (Osmund) | Ann Elizabeth Breithaupt | I | 610-612 | 1837 |

(daughter of Christian Breithaupt of Edgefield District, S.C., who died 4 December 1835) (Gregory of Macon and Savannah, Georgia)

| Griffeth, Henry (Griffith) | Matilda Morgan | 2B | 373-374 | 1861 |

(marriage contract 8 August 1861) (widow of Mark Morgan) (both of Newberry District)

Implied South Carolina Marriages Volume IV 1787-1875

| MAN | WOMAN | VOL | PAGES | LIVED |
|---|---|---|---|---|
| Griffin, Absalom | Elizabeth _____ | F | 163-164 | 1827 |

(separation agreement 29 November 1827) (of Columbia, Richland District)

| Griffin, Dr. William K. | Octavia R. Moon | 2A | 449-451 | 1858 |

(daughter of Peter Moon of Newberry District)

| Griffin, Horatio | Sarah Adeline Bates | 2A | 278-279 | 1858 |

(of Buncombe County, North Carolina) (daughter of John Bates Sr.)

| Griffin, Joseph | Catharine Threewits | K | 246-248 | 1838 |

(marriage settlement 17 September 1838) (widow) (both of Edgefield District)

| Griffin, Thomas | Ann Rowe | O | 431-432 | 1845 |

(marriage settlement 7 April 1845) (widow) (both of Fairfield District)

Griffith. See Griffeth

| Grigsby, _____ | Elizabeth Payne | H | 85 | 1831 |

(widow) (she of Newberry District) [See also page 155]

| Grimes, Graville | Martha C. Lowe | L | 271 | 1841 |

(in Richland District)

| Grimes, Henry D. | Mary M. Holman | 2A | 12-13 | 1855 |

(in Barnwell District)

| Guignard, James S. | A. M. Edwards | 2A | 171 | 1857 |

(in Richland District) (widow)

| Guignard, James S. | Anna Margaret Edwards | 2B | 716-717 | 1860 |

(widow of Philip Gadsden Edwards of Charleston) (Guignard of Columbia)

| Guignard, James Sanders | Elizabeth Sanders Ford | D | 69-70 (of Columbia) | 1818 |
| Guignard, John Gabriel | Elizabeth Sanders | B | 173-175 | 1792 |
| Gulledge, David | E. Lauretta McBride | R | 316-317 | 1847 |

(daughter of William McBride of Chesterfield District)

| Gulledge, Joel Sr. | Jerusha Sellers | Y | 615-617 | 1855 |

(marriage settlement 29 December 1855) (both of Chesterfield District)

| Gulledge, Obediah | Lavica (Levica) Boatwright | L | 128-131 | 1840 |

(marriage settlement 25 June 1840) (widow of Drury Boatwright) (both of Chesterfield District)

| Gwin, Thomas Decature | Laura M. McClanahan | 2B | 146-147 | 1860 |

(daughter of Samuel G. McClanahan) (of Greenville District)

Implied South Carolina Marriages Volume IV 1787-1875

MAN                     WOMAN                   VOL     PAGES       LIVED

(H)

Hackett, Joseph.    See Joseph Wardlaw
Hadden, Robert          Elizabeth Caldwell      U       119-122     1850
    (of Spartanburgh District)
Hagood, _____           Martha M. Hickson       T       357-359     1849
    (daughter of Levi Hickson of Barnwell
    District)
Hagood, Johnson         Eloise Brevard          X       596-597     1854
    Butler
    (marriage settlement 20 November 1854) (of Barnwell)
Haile, Edward           Mary Whitaker           V       585-588     1852
    Chesnut (daughter of John Chesnut)
    (of Kershaw District)
Haile, Thomas E.        Esther Lerena           V       582-585     1852
    Chesnut (daughter of John Chesnut)
    (of Kershaw District)
Hall, _____             Talitha Hammond         C       51-52       1813
Hall, _____             Mary Elizabeth Long     2B      267-268     1861
    (daughter of Jacob S. Long of Newberry
    District)
Hall, Laban             Elcy A. Parker          N       301-302     1844
    (marriage settlement 21 February 1844) (he of
    Chesterfield District) (she in Kershaw District)
Hall, Mansel            Jane E. McDaniel        R       482-484     1847
    (marriage contract 14 April 1847) (in Chester District)
Hall, Washington C.     Jane Miller             U       436-437     1851
    (marriage settlement 5 April 1851) (widow) (both of
    Edgefield District)
Hall, Washington C.     Martha Shibley          S       13-15       1847
    (marriage contract 28 September 1847) (widow of Jacob
    Shibley) (both of Edgefield District)
Hall, William P.        Jane Cameron            P       48-49       1845
    (of Pickens County, Alabama) (daughter of Joseph
    Cameron of Fairfield District, S.C.)
Halleman, Edmund        Sarah Ann Latimer       V       38-41       1851
    Peyton (marriage settlement 13 April 1851) (both of
    Abbeville District)
Hallonquist,            Adelaide Sams           2C      42-44       1865
    Laurent D. (marriage settlement 20 March 1865) (he of
    Montgomery County, Alabama) (she of Newberry District,
    S.C.)
Hallonquist,            Sophia Chollet          W       420-422     1853
    Lawrence D. (of Barnwell District) [See also page 206;
    Volume X, pages 338-340; Volume 2A, pages 479-485]

52

Implied South Carolina Marriages Volume IV 1787-1875

| MAN | WOMAN | VOL | PAGES | LIVED |
|---|---|---|---|---|
| Haltiwanger, ___ | ___ Kelly | E | 521 | 1826 |

(daughter of Frederick Kelly of Lexington District)

| Hamburg, Charles | Lena Goodman | 2C | 304-307 | 1867 |

(reference to marriage settlement 26 March 1867) (he of Columbia, Richland District) (she of Charleston)

| Hamilton, ___ | Angelina Jeter | 2C | 715-716 | 1875 |

(daughter of Thomas C. Jeter)

| Hamilton, Robert | Sarah Darby | S | 351-352 | 1848 |

(daughter of James Darby of Chester District)

| Hammond, Abner | Catharine M. Barsh | I | 131-135 | 1834 |

Lewis (marriage settlement 19 November 1834) [See also Volume K, pages 87-90]

| Hammond, Col. Saml. | Eliza Amelia OKeiff | G | 442-443 | 1831 |

(reference to marriage contract - no date given)

| Hammond, LeRoy | Katey ___ | B | 183-186 | 1802 |

(Cherokee Indian)
(did not marry; had child only) (of Edgefield District) [See also pages 398-402, 457-459, 683-684; Volume C, pages 51-52]

| Hammond, Philip J. | Delilah Thorn | M | 342-343 | 1842 |

(daughter of Charles Thorn)

| Hammond, Samuel | Eliza Amelia O'Keefe | B | 176-180 | 1802 |

(marriage settlement 25 May 1802) (he of Georgia)

| Hammond, William | Margaret P. McComb | 2A | 514-516 | 1858 |

Jackson (in Abbeville District)

| Hampton, Wade Jr. | Mary Singleton McDuffie | 2A | 217-218 | 1858 |

(marriage settlement 28 January 1858)

| Haney, James T. | Jane M. Havird | O | 213-215 | 1844 |

(marriage settlement 26 July 1844) (both of Edgefield District)

| Hankinson, Stephen | Mary C. Speights | E | 186-187 | 1824 |

(marriage settlement 10 April 1824) (he of Barnwell District) (she of Edgefield District)

| Hardy, ___ | Mary Cartledge | H | 449-450 | 1825 |

(daughter of Edmund Cartledge of Edgefield District)

| Hardy, ___ | Caroline Turpin | V | 385-389 | 1852 |
| Hare, Gunrod | Margaret Zeigler | D | 237-239 | 1821 |

(in Orangeburgh District) (daughter of Jacob Zeigler)

| Harkness, Robert C. | Jane Y. ___ | Z | 152-157 | 1856 |

(separation agreement 29 April 1856) (of Abbeville District) [See also pages 300-303]

Implied South Carolina Marriages Volume IV 1787-1875

| MAN | WOMAN | VOL | PAGES | LIVED |
|---|---|---|---|---|
| Harlan, William | Eliza Palmer | 2A | 14-15 | 1857 |

(of Union District) (daughter of Ellis Palmer of Union District)

| Harllee, ____ | Amelia M. Howard | Y | 510-512 | 1855 |
|---|---|---|---|---|

(widow of Charles B. Howard)

| Harmon, ____ | Susanna Snelgrove | B | 622-623 | 1810 |
|---|---|---|---|---|

(she of Newberry District)

| Harrall, J. P. | Laura A. Drake | V | 146-149 | 1851 |
|---|---|---|---|---|

(daughter of Lemuel S. Drake of Chesterfield District)

| Harrington, John W. | Mary Anna Nettles | 2B | 684-687 | 1863 |
|---|---|---|---|---|

(marriage settlement 19 September 1863) (daughter of Joseph B. Nettles) (both of Darlington District)

| Harrington, William H. | Eliza A. Hollingsworth | 2A | 521-526 | 1858 |
|---|---|---|---|---|

(marriage settlement 1 December 1858) (widow) (in Edgefield District)

| Harris, ____ | Eliza Jane Norman | U | 132-134 | 1850 |
|---|---|---|---|---|
| Harris, Abraham | Frederica Koppel | 2B | 385-386 | 1862 |

(married 13 August 1862) (daughter of Jacob Koppel) (Harris of Newberry) (she of Unionville)

| Harris, Dr. Nathaniel | Sarah (Sally) P. Cater | Z | 233-237 | 1854 |
|---|---|---|---|---|

(married 14 December 1854) (marriage contract 13 December 1854) (he of Abbeville District) (she of Anderson District)

| Harris, William | Mary Jane Ashmore | X | 605-607 | 1855 |
|---|---|---|---|---|

(daughter of William H. Ashmore of Greenville District)

| Harris, William | Sarah Jane Baker | 2B | 118-119 | 1860 |
|---|---|---|---|---|

(in Abbeville District)

| Harris, William C. | Comma M. Pressley | Y | 188-191 | 1855 |
|---|---|---|---|---|

(daughter of Samuel P. Pressley who died in Georgia)

| Harrison, ____ | Rebecca Johnston | X | 22-27 | 1853 |
|---|---|---|---|---|

(daughter of John K. Johnston of Edgefield District)

| Harrison, Benjamin Junior | Ann ____ | E | 100-102 | 1823 |
|---|---|---|---|---|

(separation agreement 27 April 1823) (of Columbia)

| Harrison, Eli | Elizabeth Douglass | Y | 485-486 | 1855 |
|---|---|---|---|---|

(of Fairfield District) (daughter of Dr. John Douglass of Chester District)

| Harrison, Nathaniel S. | Martha Sanders | 2A | 303-304 | 1857 |
|---|---|---|---|---|

Implied South Carolina Marriages Volume IV 1787-1875

| MAN | WOMAN | VOL | PAGES | LIVED |
|---|---|---|---|---|
| Harrison, Richard | Margaret Isabella Bradley | R | 391-393 | 1847 |

(marriage settlement 18 February 1847) (daughter of John Bradley of Sumter District, S.C.) (Harrison of Florida)

| Harrison, Steward (Stewart) | Frances (Fanny) Richardson | U | 394-396 | 1851 |
|---|---|---|---|---|

(marriage settlement __ March 1851) (in Edgefield District)

| Harrison, William C. | Elizabeth E. Crumpton | F | 396-397 | 1828 |
|---|---|---|---|---|

(marriage settlement 18 December 1828) (daughter of David Crumpton of Twiggs County, Georgia)

| Hart, Silvester E. | Louisa Witherspoon | U | 115-117 | 1850 |
|---|---|---|---|---|

(in Darlington District) (daughter of John S. Witherspoon)

| Harvey, ___ | Catherine Delaughter | U | 274-276 | 1850 |
|---|---|---|---|---|
| Harward, Charles P. | Rebecca Counts | U | 69-71 | 1850 |

(marriage settlement 29 April 1850) (widow) (in Lexington District)

| Hatch, Lewis M. | Emily E. Bell | 2C | 417-419 | 1837 |
|---|---|---|---|---|

(reference to marriage settlement 24 November 1837) (of Charleston) [See also pages 426-428]

| Hatcher, Benjamin W. | Elizabeth A. Long | 2A | 591-592 | 1859 |
|---|---|---|---|---|

(of Edgefield District)

| Hatton, William M. | Lucy Ann ___ | 2A | 752-753 | 1860 |
|---|---|---|---|---|

(stepdaughter of Daniel Hughey)

| Havird, Winfield | Mary Ann Watkins | Y | 141-142 | 1855 |
|---|---|---|---|---|

(of Edgefield District) (daughter of Zedekiah Watkins of Edgefield District)

| Havis, John | Patience Cassety | K | 142-143 | 1838 |
|---|---|---|---|---|

(marriage agreement 13 May 1838) (he of Leon County, Florida) (she of Fairfield District, S.C.)

| Hawley, ___ | Rebecca J. Marks | U | 4 | 1851 |
|---|---|---|---|---|

[See also Volume V, pages 41-42]

| Hawthorn, Joseph J. | Anna (Anny) Cowan | P | 87-91 | 1845 |
|---|---|---|---|---|

(in Abbeville District) (daughter of Col. Isaac Cowan)

| Haynesworth, John F. | Harriet A. Muldrow | S | 457 | 1848 |
|---|---|---|---|---|

(of Sumter District) (daughter of Matthew E. Muldrow of Salem County, Sumter District) [See also page 416]

| Haynie, Patrick C. | Louisa Pratt | T | 57-61 | 1848 |
|---|---|---|---|---|

(marriage settlement 18 December 1848) (widow of William Pratt) (Haynie of Anderson District) (she of Abbeville District)

| Haynsworth, Henry | Sarah White | T | 525-528 | 1850 |
|---|---|---|---|---|

(marriage settlement 13 February 1850) (daughter of William White) (both of Sumter District)

Implied South Carolina Marriages Volume IV 1787-1875

| MAN | WOMAN | VOL | PAGES | LIVED |
|---|---|---|---|---|

Haynsworth, Henry    Sarah White          Y    386-388    1855
    (reference to marriage settlement 13 February 1850)
Haynsworth, James    McConico G. Spann    S    72-74      1848
    L. (marriage settlement 6 January 1848) (both of Sumter
    District)
Haynsworth, John F.  Harriet A. Muldrow   I    388-389    1836
    (of Sumter District) (daughter of Matthew D. Muldrow of
    Salem County, Sumter District)
Haynsworth, Joseph   Jane C. Muldrow      W    243-246    1852
    C. (marriage settlement 17 December 1852) (both of
    Sumter District)
Haynsworth, Thomas   Elizabeth H. McCall  N    214-216    1843
    B. (marriage settlement 5 September 1843) (in Darlington
    District)
Haynsworth, William  Mary L. Charles      2A   410-412    1858
    F. B. (marriage settlement 13 July 1858) (daughter of
    Edgar W. Charles of Darlington District and
    granddaughter of Hugh Lide) (Haynsworth of Sumter
    District) [Must also see pages 529-530] [See also pages
    686-687]
Haynsworth, William  Susan Haynsworth     X    112-118    1853
    F. B.            Earle
    (marriage settlement 1 December 1853) (daughter of Elias
    Drayton Earle who died in Greenville District)
    (Haynsworth of Sumter District) (she late of Greenville
    District, now of Sumter District)
Hays, _____         Patsey Hinton        E    290-291    1824
                     (daughter of William Hinton)
Hays, _____         _____ Plowden       2B   682-684    1863
                     (daughter of Miles H. Plowden of
                     Clarendon District)
Hays, B. F.          Martha Ann Dew       2A   780-781    1860
    (marriage settlement 24 January 1860) (daughter of
    Wilson Dew) (in Marion District)
Heard, John          Jane (Jean) Barnard  B    589-593    1809
    (married 16 July 1809) (marriage contract 15 July 1809)
    (he of Pine Grove, Barnwell District) (she of Horse
    Creek, Edgefield District)
Heard, Thomas J.     Elizabeth Y. Arnold  2C   6-7        1864
    (marriage settlement 28 July 1864) (he of Elbert County,
    Georgia) (she of Abbeville District, S.C.)
Heath, John P.       Eliza L. Stewart     2B   109-110    1860
    (marriage settlement 1 March 1860) (in Lancaster
    District)

Implied South Carolina Marriages Volume IV 1787-1875

| MAN | WOMAN | VOL | PAGES | LIVED |
|---|---|---|---|---|

Hecklin, Dr. James C.    Sarah Rebecca Douglass    Y   484-485   1855
(of York District) (daughter of Dr. John Douglass of Chester District)
Hefferon, Michael    Agnes Green    X   279-280   1854
(marriage settlement 7 February 1854) (widow of Henry C. Green)
Heller, John    Mary Parrott    H   145-146   1832
(marriage settlement 14 June 1832)
Hendrix, Joshua    Sarah Mills    G   304-305   1831
(in Newberry District) (daughter of Thomas Mills)
Henning, Isaac L.    Mary Arnold    S   391-393   1844
(married 30 November 1844) (in Greenvile District)
Herbemont, Nicholas    Caroline Smyth    H   482-485   1808
(marriage agreement 21 July 1808) (both of Columbia, Richland District)
Herbert, W. W.    Emeline S. Pearson    W   74-81   1852
(daughter of George B. Pearson Sr. of Fairfield District)
Herndon, Patrick F.    _____ Glenn    H   107-108   1832
Herron, James    Ann (Anny) Long    K   514-516   1839
(marriage settlement 5 November 1839) (both of Anderson District)
Herron, Thomas (Heron)    Sarah McDowell (McDowall)    E   37-38   1822
(marriage contract 24 July 1822) (both of Abbeville District) (widow of William McDowell)
Heyward, Edward Barnwell    Katherine (Catharine) Maria Clinch    2B   588-590   1863
(marriage settlement 17 February 1863)
Heyward, Nathaniel    Elizabeth B. Smith    2B   656-658   1838
Junr. (reference to marriage settlement 30 March 1838)
Heyward, Thomas Savage    Kitty L. Boykin    2B   329-331   1861
(marriage settlement 9 April 1861)
Hickey, Andrew    Mary Cherry    C   397-398   1816
(marriage settlement 26 December 1816) (both of Orangeburgh District)
Hickey, William    Elizabeth OCain    H   273-274   1832
(marriage settlement 5 December 1832) (daughter of Daniel OCain of Orangeburgh District) (both of Orangeburgh District)
Hicks, _____    Ann V. Vernon    G   39-42   1829
Hicks, George Washington    Sarah A. Hickson    2C   98-108   1866
(marriage settlement 13 January 1866) (widow of John Hickson) (both of Barnwell District)

Implied South Carolina Marriages Volume IV 1787-1875

| MAN | WOMAN | VOL | PAGES | LIVED |
|---|---|---|---|---|
| Hickson, _____ | Elizabeth McKenzie (daughter of William McKenzie of Sumter District) | X | 509-521 | 1853 |

Hickson. See Hixon

| MAN | WOMAN | VOL | PAGES | LIVED |
|---|---|---|---|---|
| Hightower, Joseph | Ann M. Cary | M | 26-27 | 1841 |

(marriage settlement 16 August 1841) (widow of William H. Cary) (both of Edgefield District)

| MAN | WOMAN | VOL | PAGES | LIVED |
|---|---|---|---|---|
| Hill, Dr. William M. | Mary H. Crawford | 2B | 272-273 | 1861 |

(of Edgefield District) (daughter of Andrew Crawford of Columbia, Richland District)

| MAN | WOMAN | VOL | PAGES | LIVED |
|---|---|---|---|---|
| Hill, J. T. | _____ Mobley | 2A | 668-669 | 1859 |

(of Union District) (daughter of Edward P. Mobley of Fairfield District)

| MAN | WOMAN | VOL | PAGES | LIVED |
|---|---|---|---|---|
| Hill, J. Mitchell | Elizabeth A. C. Smith | 2B | 99-101 | 1858 |

(marriage settlement __ November 1858) (in Abbeville District)

| MAN | WOMAN | VOL | PAGES | LIVED |
|---|---|---|---|---|
| Hill, James L. S. | Mary A. R. Sarter (daughter of John P. Sarter of Union District) | R | 309-310 | 1847 |
| Hill, John | Christiana Dantzler | E | 452-453 | 1826 |

(marriage settlement 4 February 1826) (in Orangeburgh District)

| MAN | WOMAN | VOL | PAGES | LIVED |
|---|---|---|---|---|
| Hill, John T. | Elizabeth Mobley (daughter of Edward P. Mobley) | M | 338-339 | 1842 |
| Hillegas, George A. | Mary Williamson | F | 171-174 | 1827 |

(marriage settlement 25 October 1827) (widow)

| MAN | WOMAN | VOL | PAGES | LIVED |
|---|---|---|---|---|
| Hinckley, Samuel L. | Henrietta Elizabeth Rose | K | 110-114 | 1838 |

(marriage settlement 15 March 1838) (daughter of Daniel Rose) (Hinckley of Northampton, Massachusetts) (she of Sumter District, S.C.)

| MAN | WOMAN | VOL | PAGES | LIVED |
|---|---|---|---|---|
| Hind, _____ | Mary Caroline Allen Shields (or Caroline Mary Allen Shields) | Z | 496-497 | 1856 |
| Hinksman, Richard | Jean Jaffray | C | 326-338 | 1798 |

(daughter of Henry Jaffray of County of Stirling, Scotland) [See also pages 340-344]

| MAN | WOMAN | VOL | PAGES | LIVED |
|---|---|---|---|---|
| Hipp, John | Susannah Margaret Summer (daughter of George A. Summer Senr. of Lexington District) [See also pages 116-117] | D | 118 | 1819 |
| Hitt, Thomas E. | Lucy T. Hightower | S | 373-374 | 1848 |

(of Edgefield District)

| MAN | WOMAN | VOL | PAGES | LIVED |
|---|---|---|---|---|
| Hixon, _____ | _____ Lindsey (daughter of Benjamin Lindsey of Edgefield District) | W | 49-52 | 1852 |

Implied South Carolina Marriages Volume IV 1787-1875

| MAN | WOMAN | VOL | PAGES | LIVED |
|---|---|---|---|---|
| Hoagland, Charles | Mary Bryce Kirk | T | 126-129 | 1849 |

(of Columbia, Richland District) (daughter of Alexander Kirk of Columbia, Richland District)

| Hobbs, Burrell E. | Laura Ann Hollingsworth | I | 289-290 | 1835 |

(marriage settlement 18 July 1835) (of Edgefield District)

| Hobbs, Dr. Lewellen | Mary Ann C. Hope | Y | 584-585 | 1856 |

P. (of Lexington District) (daughter of John C. Hope of Lexington District)

| Hodge, Benjamin J. | Susan F. Sherriff | W | 259-265 | 1852 |

(marriage settlement 28 December 1852) (daughter of James W. Sherriff) (both of Sumter District)

| Hodge, Elihu | Rebecca Brunson | I | 601-602 | 1837 |

(marriage agreement 13 July 1837) (daughter of Daniel Brunson) (both of Sumter District)

| Hodge, John J. | Alice C. Harvin | 2B | 307-308 | 1861 |

(marriage settlement 27 February 1861) (in Clarendon District)

| Hodge, Samuel D. | Julia O. Clark | 2B | 229-230 | 1860 |

(marriage settlement 21 October 1860) (in Clarendon District)

| Hodges, Absalom T. | Julia S. Ioor | I | 560-561 | 1837 |

(marriage agreement 9 March 1837) (he of Abbeville District) (she in Edgefield)

| Hodges, Dr. Charles W. | Harriet S. Kelly | R | 353-354 | 1847 |

(daughter of William Kelly of Union District)

| Hogan, _____ | Martha C. Cloud | 2B | 278-280 | 1860 |

(daughter of Austin N. Cloud)

| Hogan, _____ | Margaret Jane Crankfield | R | 478-479 | 1846 |

(daughter of Littleton Crankfield of Fairfield District)

| Hogan, James | Winifred Tims | U | 396-397 | 1851 |

(marriage contract 4 March 1851) (in Chester District)

| Holcombe, Darius | Charlotte Hightower | 2A | 90-91 | 1851 |

(marriage agreement 1 February 1851) (both of Greenville District)

| Holder, Berryman S. | Sarah Tollison | F | 16-17 | 1826 |

(marriage agreement 4 December 1826) (he of Spartanburgh District, S.C.) (she of Franklin County, West Tennessee)

| Holladay, John O. | Elizabeth Brunson | F | 383-384 | 1828 |

(marriage settlement 27 November 1828) (daughter of Daniel Brunson) (in Sumter District)

| Holland, _____ | Penelope Kirksey | M | 167-168 | 1842 |

(daughter of William Kirksey of Pickens District)

Implied South Carolina Marriages Volume IV 1787-1875

| MAN | WOMAN | VOL | PAGES | LIVED |
|---|---|---|---|---|
| Holland, ____ | ____ Rutland | 2A | 772-773 | 1860 |

(daughter of Abraham Rutland of Edgefield District)

Holland, William T.    Jannet Elizabeth    Z    779    1857
   Maddon (daughter of Samuel L. Maddon) (in Laurens District)
Holleyman, Harmon    Harriet Ann Clarke    K    296-298    1838
   (marriage settlement 28 November 1838) (daughter of George Clarke) (Holleyman of Kershaw District) (she of Newberry District)
Hollingsworth, ____    Eliza A. Griffin    2A    521-526    1858
Hollingsworth, M. E.    Margaret M. Gomillion    U    48-49    1850
   (of Edgefield District)
Hollis, Thomas    Anna Pearson    S    352-355    1848
   (he was married before) (widow) (in Union District)
Hollis, William    Margaret Ford    2C    430-433    1867
   (of Chester District) (daughter of William Ford)
Holloway, Lewis    Sarah Ann Spivey    2B    301-303    1861
   (marriage settlement 1 January 1861) (he of Edgefield District, S.C.) (she of Richmond County, Georgia)
Holly, Milledge T.    Martha E. Evans    2B    383-384    1861
   (of Barnwell District) (daughter of Gideon Evans of Barnwell District)
Holman, ____    Martha Bane    2B    770-771    1863
Holmes, Anderson    Mary A. Arthur    Z    776-778    1857
   (marriage settlement 5 March 1857) (widow) (he of Alabama) (she of Columbia, S.C.)
Holmes, Dr. William F.    Anna (Annie) L. Tucker    2C    194-196    1863
   (married 29 June 1863) (widow of George A. Tucker) (both of Union District)
Holmes, George Frederick    Lavalette Floyd    O    353-355    1845
   (marriage settlement 3 February 1845) (he of S.C.) (she of Tazewell County, Virginia)
Holmes, Zelatus    Catherine N. Nickels    O    329-330    1844
   (in Spartanburg District) (daughter of John Nickels of Laurens District)
Holstein, Wade (Holston)    Laura Elizabeth ____    2B    339-342    1861
   (separation agreement 30 January 1861) (of Edgefield District)
Holsten, Lorunzey    Susannah Burton    H    30-31    1832
   (daughter of Aaron Burton of Newberry District)
Holt, John    Floride Speed    G    94    1830
   (marriage settlement 3 February 1830) (in Abbeville District)

Implied South Carolina Marriages Volume IV 1787-1875

| MAN | WOMAN | VOL | PAGES | LIVED |
|---|---|---|---|---|
| Homes, ____ | Mary A. Arthur (widow) | 2B | 52-61 | 1860 |
| Homot, Simon (divorced) | Cecile Vandeperr | Q | 63 | 1805 |

(she was born about 1757 in Bruxelles, French Flanders) (to Georgia, then S.C.)

| Hooker, Zaddock | Mary Ann Moorman | G | 358-362 | 1830 |
|---|---|---|---|---|

(marriage settlement 30 December 1830) (both of Union District)

| Hopkins, James | Keziah Goodwyn | B | 638-650 | 1804 |
|---|---|---|---|---|

(Goodwin) (widow of Jesse Goodwyn who died September 1792)

| Hopkins, John | Susan E. Kelly | M | 98-99 | 1842 |
|---|---|---|---|---|

(daughter of William Kelly of Union District)

| Hopper, Alexander | Jane Gordon | D | 3-5 | 1813 |
|---|---|---|---|---|

(marriage settlement 29 December 1813) (both of Newberry District)

| Hord, Dr. Grenville | Evalina V. Mays | W | 377-378 | 1853 |
|---|---|---|---|---|

(marriage settlement 7 February 1853) (widow of Sampson B. Mays) (both of Edgefield District)

| Hord, Dr. Grenville | Susan E. Mays | 2B | 635-636 | 1863 |
|---|---|---|---|---|

(daughter of Stephen W. Mays of Edgefield District)

| Horger, David M. | Mary E. ____ | 2C | 177-179 | 1866 |
|---|---|---|---|---|

(in Orangeburg District) (granddaughter of Thomas Pricher)

| Horn, Daniel A. | Isabella J. H. McLeod | Y | 104-110 | 1855 |
|---|---|---|---|---|

(marriage settlement 13 February 1855) (he of Cheraw, Chesterfield District) (she of Marlborough District)

| Horry, Peter | Mary Margaret Guignard | C | 287-289 | 1793 |
|---|---|---|---|---|

(marriage bond 9 February 1793) (of Richland District)

| Hortman, Adam | Caroline Singley | M | 415-416 | 1842 |
|---|---|---|---|---|

(daughter of Martin Singley of Newberry District)

| House, Daniel | Sarah Neil | F | 439 | 1829 |
|---|---|---|---|---|
| Houston, Alexander | Jane Postell | E | 505 | 1826 |

(marriage settlement 13 July 1826) (widow of Colonel James Postell) (of Abbeville District) [Must also see Volume F, pages 48-50]

| Houston, Alexander | Elizabeth Smith Tennent | Y | 221-222 | 1855 |
|---|---|---|---|---|

(daughter of William Tennent of Abbeville District) (of Abbeville District)

| Houston, Alex R. | Elizabeth S. Tennent | 2A | 214-215 | 1857 |
|---|---|---|---|---|

(daughter of William Tennent of Abbeville District)

Implied South Carolina Marriages Volume IV 1787-1875

| MAN | WOMAN | VOL | PAGES | LIVED |
|---|---|---|---|---|
| Howell, Jesse | Paulina Ann ____ | Y | 427-428 | 1855 |

(natural daughter of John E. Bobo of Newberry District) (of Jefferson County, Tennessee)

| Howell, Samuel | Mary Faster (Foster) | P | 242-243 | 1845 |

(in Union District) (daughter of Robert Faster)

| Howie, John M. | Mary Parr Russell | Y | 446-449 | 1855 |

(marriage settlement 7 November 1855) (daughter of Robert Russell)

| Hoy, Major William | Frances C. Dean | U | 355-356 | 1851 |

(daughter of Alfred Dean of Spartanburgh District)

| Hoyle, David E. | Martha Ann Ellen | 2B | 247-248 | 1860 |

Tindal Brogdon (widow of Isaac B. Brogdon)

| Huckbee, James | Anna M. Moseley | 2A | 681-682 | 1859 |

(daughter of John M. Moseley of Abbeville District)

| Hudgins, W. L. | Eliza C. Klugh | 2B | 290-291 | 1860 |

(in Abbeville District)

| Huff, John | Temperance ____ | F | 68-69 | 1825 |

(separation agreement 12 July 1825) (in Edgefield District)

| Huff, Lewis | Eliza Caroline ____ | 2A | 490-492 | 1858 |

(separation agreement 15 December 1858) (of Greenville District)

| Hufman, ____ | Jane ____ | X | 322-324 | 1854 |

(granddaughter of James Elkins of Fairfield District)

| Huger, Thomas Pinckney | Anna Maria Cheves | M | 296-299 | 1842 |

(daughter of Langdon Cheves of Anderson District) (of Abbeville District)

| Hughes, ____ | Martha Bones | N | 15 | 1842 |
| Hughes, Beverly Cooper | Agnes Elizabeth Tobin | 2A | 279-281 | 1858 |
| Hughes, Doctor John | Elizabeth (Eliza) Gahagan | C | 44-47 | 1810 |

(separation agreement 29 August 1810) (widow of John Gahagan) (of Columbia, Richland District)

| Hughes, George T. | Emilia E. Green | 2B | 559-561 | 1862 |

(marriage settlement 15 December 1862) (widow) (she of Greenville District)

| Hughes, Isaac | Polly Smith | C | 129-130 | 1814 |

(daughter of George Smith of Richland District) (of Richland District)

Implied South Carolina Marriages Volume IV 1787-1875

| MAN | WOMAN | VOL | PAGES | LIVED |
|---|---|---|---|---|
| Hughs, OBrien S. (of Texas) | Liberty Dewalt (daughter of Daniel Dewalt Senr. of Newberry District, who died 6 November 1853) [See also pages 364-368, 495-499, 541-544, 631-634, 673-677] | 2A | 327-332 | 1857 |
| Humphreyville, ____ | Elizabeth Colter (she of Mobile, Alabama) | Z | 780 | 1857 |
| Humphries, Albert A. (of Abbeville District) | Jane E. Brough (daughter of Thomas Brough of Abbeville District) | W | 632-633 | 1853 |
| Humphries, Charles | Elisabeth Holland (marriage settlement 17 February 1829) (in Union District) | F | 421-422 | 1829 |
| Humphries, Samuel (Humfris) | Sarah ____ (separation agreement 5 October 1826) (of Lancaster District) | E | 538-540 | 1826 |
| Hunt, ____ | Sarah G. Foster | O | 315-316 | 1843 |
| Hunt, ____ | Eliza E. Goodlett (daughter of Spartan Goodlett) | M | 323 | 1842 |
| Hunt, William | Asceneth Daniel | P | 164-171 | 1845 |
| Hunt, William | Aseemath Daniel (daughter of Richard Daniel Senr.) | H | 480-481 | 1833 |
| Hunter, Alexander | Jane ____ (granddaughter of Benjamin Terry of Abbeville District) (of Abbeville District) | G | 227-228 | 1830 |
| Hunter, Andrew Senr. | Mary Andrews (married 10 February 1819) (of Darlington District) | D | 119-122 | 1819 |
| Hunter, Charles D. | Mary Honoria Moore (in Sumter District) (daughter of Captain Matthew S. Moore Senr.) | M | 36-37 | 1842 |
| Hunter, Robert R. | Mary Elizabeth Spires (marriage settlement 17 December 1839) (daughter of Henry Spires) (both of Edgefield District) | L | 45-47 | 1839 |
| Huntley, Thomas | Harriet A. Edgeworth (he now of Anson County, North Carolina) (daughter of Richard L. Edgeworth Senr. of Chesterfield District, S.C.) | 2A | 598-599 | 1859 |
| Hurst, Charles M. | Amanda Ebney (married 1851) (postnuptial settlement 9 December 1856) (in Sumter District) [her last name illegible] | Z | 487-489 | 1851 |
| Husbands, Hamilton | Rebecca R. A. Clark (marriage settlement 10 June 1848) (daughter of William Clark) (in Sumter District) | S | 286-288 | 1848 |
| Husbands, James | Venetta Henstiss (marriage settlement 9 January 1851) (in Marlborough District) | U | 318-319 | 1851 |

Implied South Carolina Marriages Volume IV 1787-1875

| MAN | WOMAN | VOL | PAGES | LIVED |
|---|---|---|---|---|
| Huskerson, _____ | Malinda Green (widow) | 2C | 440-444 | 1868 |
| Huson, _____ | Eliza Eppes (daughter of William Eppes of Newberry District) | G | 290 | 1831 |
| Hutchinson, _____ | _____ Boatwright (daughter of James Boatwright) | Y | 436-437 | 1855 |
| Hutchison, Irvin | Nancy Narcissa McDowall (of Abbeville District) | Z | 511-512 | 1856 |
| Hutchison, James B. | Mary A. B. Crooks (daughter of Thomas C. Crooks of Newberry District) | Z | 508 | 1857 |
| Hutson, Thomas | Elspeth Rutherford (in Shielshaugh, County of Selkirk, Scotland) | E | 73-77 | 1820 |

(I)

| | | | | |
|---|---|---|---|---|
| Inglis, _____ | Charlotte Laura Prince (daughter of Laurence Prince) (in Chesterfield District) | K | 224-226 | 1838 |
| Inglis, Robert | Jean Rutherford (in Philipaugh, County of Selkirk and Mountevine, County of Roxburgh, Scotland) | E | 73-77 | 1820 |
| Ingraham, Gustavus | Laura M. Marsh (daughter of John Marsh of Edgefield District) | T | 373-375 | 1849 |
| Ioor, Benjamin G. | Sarah C. Walter (marriage agreement 20 April 1811) (he of Claremont County) (she of Clarendon County) | B | 702-705 | 1811 |
| Ioor, John | Emily Richardson (marriage settlement 21 March 1804) (he of Sumter District) (she of Georgetown) | B | 289-295 | 1804 |
| Ioor, John | Emily Richardson (of Wilkinson County, Mississippi) [See also pages 340-342] | G | 348-349 | 1829 |
| Ioor, Wallace B. | Martha E. Lewis (marriage settlement 30 December 1851) (both of Greenville District) | V | 143-146 | 1851 |
| Irby, James H. | Orrah E. Lyles (daughter of Reuben S. Lyles of Newberry District) | 2A | 190 | 1858 |
| Ivey, Thomas C. | Mildred Anderson (marriage contract 5 June 1856) (in Lancaster District) | Z | 283 | 1856 |

Implied South Carolina Marriages Volume IV 1787-1875

MAN                WOMAN              VOL    PAGES        LIVED

(J)

Jacks, Isaac Calmes Mary A. E. Dillard   2B    758-760      1863
                    (widow)
Jackson, James      Drusillar Heath       B    561-563      1808
(of Dinwiddie County, Virginia)
Jackson, William    Charlotte Eagerton    H    313-315      1833
(marriage settlement 16 January 1833) (of Marion
District)
Jacobs, Frederick   Loudia L. Lyons      2C    242-243      1867
C.                  (daughter of Jacob C. Lyons of Columbia,
                    Richland District)
Jaffray, Henry      Margaret Shiells      C    326-338      1798
                    (daughter of James Shiells) (of County of
Stirling, Scotland) [See also pages 340-344]
James, _____       Elizabeth Haseldon   2B    658-659      1863
James, Albert       Gracia (Gracie) Ann   V    214-215      1852
                    Bates (daughter of John Bates of Richland
                    District)
James, Holloway     Roxana Howard         D    107          1819
(marriage contract 15 March 1819)
James, Thomas L.    Elizabeth H. Timmons  P    399-400      1846
(in Marion District)
Jayroe, John R.     _____ Bradford      2A    586-587      1859
                    (daughter of William W. Bradford)
Jayroe, John R.     Lucy F. E. Ware      2C    115-117      1865
(postnuptial settlement 22 December 1865) (in Sumter
District)
Jeans, Berry W.     Mary Graham           N    200-202      1843
(Jeanes) (of Union District) (daughter of John Graham of
Newberry District)
Jeffers, _____     Lurana (Uraniah)      A    301-302      1801
                    Young
(from North Carolina to Camden District, S.C.)
Jeffrey. See Jaffray
Jenkins, Amos L.    Ann Kennerly          K    149-150      1838
                    (she of Lexington District)
Jenkins, James      Caroline E. (or M.)   Y    238-241      1855
(Jinkins)           Carter
(marriage settlement 30 May 1855) (in Darlington
District)
Jenkins, Richard G. Elizabeth Donaldson   O    316-317      1845
(marriage settlement 4 February 1845) (in Kershaw
District)

65

Implied South Carolina Marriages Volume IV 1787-1875

| MAN | WOMAN | VOL | PAGES | LIVED |
|---|---|---|---|---|
| Jenkins, W. W. | Sarah Elizabeth China | W | 169-172 | 1852 |

(marriage settlement 29 October 1852) (in Sumter District)

Jenkins, William L.   Jane Harvey Gaillard   K   360-364   1839
(marriage settlement 27 April 1839) (daughter of David Gaillard) (in Anderson District)

Jennings, \_\_\_\_\_   Elizabeth Cartlegde   H   448-449   1825
(daughter of Edmund Cartledge of Edgefield District)

Jennings, John   Jane Cannon   H   211   1832
(marriage agreement 5 August 1832) (widow of Wm Cannon of Orangeburgh District) (of Orangeburgh District)

Jennings, \_\_\_\_\_   Rebecca Gerald   R   383-385   1844
Lawrington R. (in Sumter District) [See also pages 386-388, 408-409]

Jennings, William   Ann M. Bryan   X   145-147   1854
B. (of Sumter District, S.C.) (daughter of Allen Bryan of Russell County, Alabama)

Jerry, Robert N.   Harriet E. \_\_\_\_\_   E   128   1822
(separation agreement 30 July 1823) (in Columbia, Richland District)

Jervey, Lewis   Caroline Howard Glover   2B   775-777   1864
(marriage settlement 9 March 1864) (in Greenville District)

Jervis, \_\_\_\_\_   Ann Barnard (Bernard)   B   566-569   1808
(daughter of Robert Barnard of Horse Creek, Edgefield District)

Johnsey, Thomas J.   Sarah A. Ford   2B   265-267   1860
(marriage agreement 19 December 1860) (both of Chester District)

Johnson, \_\_\_\_\_   Caroline Hickson   W   109-111   1852
(daughter of Levi Hickson of Barnwell District)

Johnson, \_\_\_\_\_   Sarah B. Wade   S   343-344   1840
(in Barnwell District)

Johnson, Daniel   Leonora Richbourg   W   440-441   1853
(marriage settlement 28 February 1853) (daughter of Eli Richbourg) (in Sumter District)

Johnson, Dr. William S.   Narcissa H. Hair (Hare)   V   69-71   1851
(marriage contract 8 November 1851) (widow) (both of Barnwell District)

Johnson, George   Betsey Lightfoot   C   111-117   1811
(of Abbeville District) (daughter of Francis Lightfoot

Implied South Carolina Marriages Volume IV 1787-1875

| MAN | WOMAN | VOL | PAGES | LIVED |
|---|---|---|---|---|
| Johnson, James A. | Mary F. Watts (daughter of Hampton Watts of Sumter District) | Z | 485-487 | 1856 |
| Johnson, Jared S. | Mary L. Cannon (daughter of George S. Cannon of Newberry District) | 2A | 119-120 | 1857 |
| Johnson, John (of Abbeville District) | Sukey Lightfoot | C | 111-117 | 1811 |
| Johnson, Laurence S. (of Edgefield District) | Amanda C. Brunson (daughter of Daniel D. Brunson of Edgefield District) | Z | 690-691 | 1857 |
| Johnson, Richard M. | Elizabeth C. Garrett (marriage settlement 6 January 1840) (daughter of Henry W. Garrett and granddaughter of John C. Garrett) (of Edgefield District) | L | 14-16 | 1840 |
| Johnson, Thomas (or Willis) J. | Sarah J. Dicker (marriage settlement 4 November 1858) (both of Williamsburgh District) | 2A | 458-460 | 1858 |
| Johnson, Toliver | Jane J. Hawthorn | P | 87-91 | 1845 |
| Johnson, Washington | Elizabeth Jennings (daughter of Joseph Jennings of Edgefield) | I | 566-567 | 1837 |
| Johnson, Willis. See Thomas Johnson | | | | |
| Johnston, \_\_\_\_\_ | \_\_\_\_\_ Royston (daughter of Thomas Royston) | A | 321-322 | 1797 |
| Johnston, John K. | Susan Willis (marriage settlement 11 July 1853) (he was married before) (widow of Robert Willis) (Johnston of Edgefield District) (she of Barnwell District) | X | 22-27 | 1853 |
| Johnston, John K. | Susan Willis (Johnson) (reference to marriage settlement 11 July 1853) (widow of Robert M. Willis) (of Barnwell District) | Z | 738-741 | 1853 |
| Johnston, Robert A. | Harriet M. F. McMorries (marriage contract 22 October 1856) (in Newberry District) | Z | 357-358 | 1856 |
| Johnston, Rufus M. | Cecelia Latta (married 29 May 1856) (daughter of Robert Latta who died 25 August 1852) | 2A | 643-656 | 1856 |
| Joiner, John | Julia Ann Hix (marriage settlement 18 September 1833) (of Union District) | H | 475-477 | 1833 |
| Joiner. See Joyner | | | | |
| Jones, \_\_\_\_\_ | Mary Boyle (widow of Cunningham Boyle) | 2A | 285-294 | 1857 |
| Jones, \_\_\_\_\_ | Charlotte Massey | 2B | 213-217 | 1860 |
| Jones, \_\_\_\_\_ | Sarah Massey | 2B | 213-217 | 1860 |

Implied South Carolina Marriages Volume IV 1787-1875

| MAN | WOMAN | VOL | PAGES | LIVED |
|---|---|---|---|---|
| Jones, ____ | Hannah O'Hanlon | F | 153-154 | 1827 |

[See also page 287]

| Jones, ____ | Eliza W. Thompson | V | 344-345 | 1850 |
|---|---|---|---|---|

(daughter of Waddy Thompson)

| Jones, ____ | Jane Williams | V | 564-567 | 1842 |
|---|---|---|---|---|

(daughter of Samuel Williams of Greenville District)

Jones, Dr. William    Elizabeth J. Parkins    W    1-4    1852
Riley (marriage settlement 19 May 1852) (daughter of Allen R. Parkins)

Jones, George    Nancy Nobles    M    316-317    1842
(marriage settlement 10 September 1842) (daughter of William Nobles) (Jones of Kentucky) (she of Edgefield District, S.C.)

Jones, James    Elizabeth Brown    E    390-391    1825
(marriage settlement 23 November 1825) (widow) (in Colleton District)

Jones, James A.    Mary Ann Leaman    W    60-62    1852
(Leeman) (daughter of Hugh Leaman of Laurens District)

Jones, James D.    Sarah C. Pegues    K    236-238    1838
Jones, James J.    Sarah Buzzard    Z    637-638    1857
(marriage contract 14 February 1857) (daughter of Jacob Buzzard) (both of Newberry District)

Jones, James L.    Caroline Rich    H    360-362    1833
(in Sumter District)

Jones, John D.    Leonora W. Wilder    P    188-189    1846
(daughter of Thomas J. Wilder Senior of Sumter District)

Jones, Joseph A. C.    Elizabeth C. Jones    2B    809-810    1864
(daughter of Lewis Jones of Edgefield District)

Jones, Osmond S.    Catharine Shedd    Z    185-186    1856
(daughter of William Shedd of Fairfield District)

Jones, Robert L.    Susan A. Watts    X    375-376    1854
(daughter of Hampton Watts of Sumter District)

Jones, Robert L.    Susan A. Watts    Z    485-487    1856
(daughter of Hampton Watts of Sumter District)

Jones, Thomas    Jannet (Jennet)    M    76    1842
Richey
(marriage contract 29 January 1842) (both of Newberry District)

Implied South Carolina Marriages Volume IV 1787-1875

| MAN | WOMAN | VOL | PAGES | LIVED |
|---|---|---|---|---|
| Jones, Thomas C. | Susan L. Hodges (daughter of Robert H. W. Hodges of Abbeville District) | 2B | 439-440 | 1861 |
| Jones, Timothy L. | Victoria A. Vaughan (widow of John H. Vaughan) | P | 196-198 | 1843 |
| Jones, William | Wilmoth M. Diseker (daughter of Jacob Diseker of Richland District) | E | 472-473 | 1825 |
| Jones, William T. | Louisa ____ (separation agreement 15 May 1843) | N | 67-70 | 1843 |
| Jordan, Daniel | Nancy Adeline Richey Jones (marriage settlement 3 May 1849) (he of Rockingham County, North Carolina) (she of Abbeville District, S.C.) | T | 224-228 | 1849 |
| Jordan, Josiah | Jane Jackson (marriage contract 3 January 1854) (both of Chester District) | X | 269-272 | 1854 |
| Joyner, ____ | Sophia Carter (daughter of Benjamin Carter) (she in Richland District) [See also pages 10-11] | E | 9 | 1820 |
| Joyner. See Joiner | | | | |
| Julin, G. W. | Sarah Looper (of Pickens District) (daughter of Jeremiah Looper Sr. of Pickens District) | 2B | 178-179 | 1860 |
| Jumelle, Peter L. | Ann Margaret Eckhard (daughter of Jacob Eckhard Senr.) [See also pages 21-24] | M | 1-4 | 1841 |

(K)

| Kaigler, ____ | Catharine Kinsler | 2B | 52-61 | 1859 |
|---|---|---|---|---|
| Kaigler, Andrew | Katy Capplepower [See also pages 654-656] | B | 659-670 | 1810 |
| Kates, Allen | Polly Scruggs (of Newberry District) (widow) | O | 32-33 | 1844 |
| Kay, James | Mary Barmore (marriage settlement 4 February 1851) (in Abbeville District) | U | 410-411 | 1851 |
| Keels, Jno. A. | Martha P. Maxwell (of Williamsburg District) (daughter of John Maxwell of Pickens District) | Z | 373-374 | 1856 |
| Keese, William S. | Adaline Cleveland (marriage settlement 11 April 1859) (widow of Benjamin Milton Cleveland) (both of Pickens District) | 2A | 602-605 | 1859 |

Implied South Carolina Marriages Volume IV 1787-1875

| MAN | WOMAN | VOL | PAGES | LIVED |
|---|---|---|---|---|
| Keith, Tarlton F. | Margaret Jane Sherly | M | 414-415 | 1842 |

(in Edgefield District)

| Keitt, William | Ann Miller | F | 224-225 | 1828 |
|---|---|---|---|---|

(marriage agreement 10 March 1828) (widower) (widow) (he of St. Matthew's Parish, Orangeburgh District) (she of Orange Parish, Orangeburgh District)

| Keller, _____ | Cynthia Lomax | L | 57-58 | 1836 |
|---|---|---|---|---|

(daughter of G. Lomax of Abbeville District)

| Kelley, Daniel Plympton | Sarah Elizabeth Falls | 2B | 626-629 | 1863 |
|---|---|---|---|---|

(marriage settlement 14 May 1863) (widow of Alexander Falls) (in Richland District)

| Kellin, Robert D. | Sarah B. Ford | N | 167-169 | 1843 |
|---|---|---|---|---|

(marriage settlement 8 August 1843) (he of Darlington District) (she in Chesterfield District)

| Kelly, James | Henrietta A. Nettles | 2A | 684 | 1859 |
|---|---|---|---|---|

(of Clarendon District) (daughter of Amos A. Nettles of Sumter District)

| Kelly, Robert | Ann Goree | L | 23-24 | 1839 |
|---|---|---|---|---|

("otherwise Robert Kelly Goree") (marriage contract 23 October 1839) (of Newberry District)

| Kemp, Archibald | Elizabeth Cloud | P | 123-125 | 1845 |
|---|---|---|---|---|

(marriage settlement 7 September 1845) (of Edgefield District)

| Kemp, Archibald | Elizabeth Cloud | 2A | 377-378 | 1845 |
|---|---|---|---|---|

(reference to marriage settlement 27 September 1845) (widow) (in Edgefield District)

| Kemp, Wiley | Mary Lewis | F | 401-402 | 1828 |
|---|---|---|---|---|

(marriage settlement 17 November 1828) (of Edgefield District)

| Kendrick, Ephraim | Martha Sanders | H | 31-33 | 1832 |
|---|---|---|---|---|

(daughter of Robert Sanders of Sumter District)

| Kendrick, Joseph | Catherine E. Faries | 2A | 148-152 | 1857 |
|---|---|---|---|---|

(marriage settlement 5 November 1857) (he of York District, S.C.) (she of Mecklenburg County, North Carolina)

| Kendrick, Thomas | Sarah A. Sanders | H | 31-33 | 1832 |
|---|---|---|---|---|

(daughter of Robert Sanders of Sumter District)

| Kennedy, John A. | Charlotte Rochell | E | 161-162 | 1824 |
|---|---|---|---|---|

(marriage settlement 5 February 1824) (he of Camden, Kershaw District) (she of Fairfield District)

Implied South Carolina Marriages Volume IV 1787-1875

| MAN | WOMAN | VOL | PAGES | LIVED |
|---|---|---|---|---|
| Kennedy, John C. | Epsey Jane Satterwhite | 2A | 335 | 1858 |

(marriage settlement 23 February 1858) (both of Edgefield District)

| Kennedy, John M. | Martha Jane Smith | H | 100-101 | 1832 |
|---|---|---|---|---|

(daughter of William Smith)

| Kennedy, Joseph | Eliza Watson | P | 108-110 | 1845 |
|---|---|---|---|---|

(of Fairfield District) (daughter of Hardiway Watson)

| Kennedy, Joseph | Eliza Ann Watson | S | 461-462 | 1845 |
| Kennedy, Joseph | Eliza Ann Watson | T | 384-385 | 1845 |

(in Fairfield District) [Must also see pages 555-557]

| Kennedy, Lionel C. | Helen Fayssoux Stevens | N | 110-111 | 1843 |
|---|---|---|---|---|

(in Spartanburgh District)

| Kennedy, Richard E. | Sarah De Graffenreid | Z | 381-385 | 1856 |
|---|---|---|---|---|

(daughter of Allen De Graffenreid)

| Kennedy, Robert W. | Nancy A. Kennedy | 2A | 189 | 1857 |
|---|---|---|---|---|

(daughter of William Kennedy of Fairfield District)

| Kennedy, William | Mary W. Haile | I | 433-434 | 1836 |
|---|---|---|---|---|

(of Camden, Kershaw District) (daughter of Benjamin Haile of Camden, Kershaw District)

| Kennedy, William A. | Jane L. Wright | V | 577-580 | 1852 |
|---|---|---|---|---|

(of Chester District) (daughter of James Wright)

| Kenner, _____ | Sarah Coger Caldwell | X | 122-123 | 1849 |
| Kennerly, _____ | Leah Whetstone | C | 373 | 1817 |
| Kennerly, A. W. | Louisa Holstein | 2A | 305-306 | 1858 |

(daughter of Wade Holstein of Edgefield District)

| Kennerly, Dr. J. C. W. | Myra Watson | 2B | 169-170 | 1860 |
|---|---|---|---|---|

(of Edgefield District) (daughter of Elijah Watson of Edgefield District)

| Kennerly, Dr. John C. W. | Myra Watson | 2C | 48-50 | 1865 |
|---|---|---|---|---|

(daughter of Elijah Watson Sr. of Edgefield District)

| Kennerly, James C. | Catharine B. Smith | F | 83-84 | 1827 |
|---|---|---|---|---|

(marriage settlement 15 May 1827) (daughter of Thomas Smith) (Kennerly of Lexington District) (she of Charleston District)

| Kennerly, Samuel J. | Henrietta C. Wolfe | O | 328-329 | 1845 |
| Kennerly, Samuel J. | Henrietta C. Wolfe | S | 328-329 | 1848 |

(in Lexington District) (daughter of Joseph A. Wolfe)

| Kenneth, James C. | Sallie C. Neuffer | 2C | 45-48 | 1865 |
|---|---|---|---|---|

(marriage settlement 8 September 1865) (daughter of Charles Neuffer) (in Richland District)

| Kennington, Samuel D. | Miriam Gregory | 2A | 703 | 1859 |
|---|---|---|---|---|

(marriage agreement 5 November 1859) (widow) (both of Lancaster District)

Implied South Carolina Marriages Volume IV 1787-1875

| MAN | WOMAN | VOL | PAGES | LIVED |
|---|---|---|---|---|
| Keown, Robert | Mary Jane Shellito | W | 16-19 | 1852 |

(daughter of John Shellito)

Keown, Thomas    Nancy _____    Q    1825
(married August 1825) (she was born about 1801 near
Castle Blany, County Monahan, Ireland) (he died 19 June
1844) (arrived Charleston, S.C. from Belfast, February
1827) (to Abbeville District, S.C.)

Kerblay, Joseph    Jeanne Marie Odette    Q    63    1805
   Marie Legrunio de Lein
(he was born about 1755 in Sarzeau, France) (she was
born about 1763 in Toulouse, France) (to Georgia, then
S.C.)

Kerr, Henry S.    Leontina Moore    Z    712-714    1857
(of Abbeville District)

Kershaw, _____    Harriet DuBose    T    422-423    1850
(daughter of Isaac DuBose) (in
Williamsburg and Georgetown Districts)

Key, John C. G.    Ann J. Ardis    M    283-285    1842
(marriage settlement 31 August 1842) (both of Edgefield
District)

Keys, James    Louisa D. Lewis    2B    824-827    1843
   Crawford                    (in Anderson District)

Kibler, John Jr.    Anna Mary    T    31-33    1848
                   Eigleberger
(he died about 1835) (she of Newberry District)

Kibler, Michael Jr    Elizabeth Koon    H    163-164    1828
(of Newberry District) [See also pages 298-304]

Killen, James F.    Caroline M. Haseldon    2B    658-659    1863
(of Darlington District)

Killingsworth,    Eliza Ware    Z    128-130    1856
   James (of Abbeville District) (daughter of William Ware
of Abbeville District)

Kinard, _____    Catharine Elizabeth    H    222-225    1832
                 Rinehart
[Must also see Volume G, pages 451-455]

Kincaid, Alexander    Jane Meriner (Mamar)    H    512-514    1834
(marriage settlement 15 January 1834) (in Fairfield
District)

Kincaid, William    Caroline B. Pratt    U    451-453    1849
(marriage agreement 31 January 1849) (daughter of Thomas
Pratt) (of Fairfield District)

King, Henry C.    Mary Jane Pope    2B    801-804    1864
(marriage settlement 14 April 1864) (both of Edgefield)

King, James    Mary E. Crawley    2B    811-812    1864
(in Darlington District) (daughter of John Crawley)

Implied South Carolina Marriages Volume IV 1787-1875

| MAN | WOMAN | VOL | PAGES | LIVED |
|---|---|---|---|---|
| King, Leonidas | Caroline E. Williams | H | 422-423 | 1833 |

(marriage settlement 8 July 1833) (in Darlington District)

| | | | | |
|---|---|---|---|---|
| King, William | Emely (Emala) Nicholas | I | 406 | 1836 |

(marriage settlement 21 January 1836) (of Edgefield District)

| | | | | |
|---|---|---|---|---|
| Kingman, Samuel | Margaret Ellen Hammond | G | 441-443 | 1831 |

(of Edgefield District)

| | | | | |
|---|---|---|---|---|
| Kingsmore, Clamage H. | M. Elliott Schumpert | 2A | 423-424 | 1858 |

(of Newberry District) (daughter of Jacob K. Schumpert of Newberry District)

| | | | | |
|---|---|---|---|---|
| Kinny, Benjamin G. | Vary L. Long | 2A | 591-592 | 1859 |

(of Louisiana)

| | | | | |
|---|---|---|---|---|
| Kinsler, ____ | Amelia B. Kennerly | 2B | 707-708 | 1863 |
| Kirk, ____ | Rebecca Sims | Z | 396-398 | 1856 |
| Kirkland, ____ | Rebecca Heath | P | 141-145 | 1845 |
| Kirkland, Samuel | Barbary Cook | S | 170-171 | 1846 |

(marriage settlement 25 March 1846) (both of Kershaw District)

| | | | | |
|---|---|---|---|---|
| Kirkland, William C. | Virginia Galluchat | M | 462 | 1843 |

(in Sumter District)

| | | | | |
|---|---|---|---|---|
| Kirven, ____ | Elizabeth Tart | X | 646-649 | 1854 |
| Kirven, Joshua E. | Hannah White | L | 156-159 | 1840 |

(marriage settlement 7 September 1840) (daughter of William White of Montgomery County, Alabama) (in Darlington District, S.C.)

| | | | | |
|---|---|---|---|---|
| Knight, James P. | Antoinette Jeter | 2A | 284-285 | 1858 |

(daughter of James R. Jeter of Union District)

| | | | | |
|---|---|---|---|---|
| Knight, Robt. | Mary Fuller | Z | 356 | 1856 |

(married 10 June 1856) (daughter of Messer Fuller)

| | | | | |
|---|---|---|---|---|
| Knighton, Moses | Sarah Cason | G | 205 | 1830 |

(of Fairfield District) (daughter of Cannon Cason of Fairfield District)

| | | | | |
|---|---|---|---|---|
| Knox, John Johnson | Sarah Ann Witherspoon | H | 467-470 | 1833 |

(marriage settlement 23 October 1833) (in Sumter District)

| | | | | |
|---|---|---|---|---|
| Knox, William | Rachel Russell | 2B | 234-235 | 1860 |

(in Abbeville District)

| | | | | |
|---|---|---|---|---|
| Kobb, Adam Logram | Ellen Susan Johnson | S | 290-291 | 1848 |

(marriage settlement __ July 1848) (both of Sumter District)

| | | | | |
|---|---|---|---|---|
| Koon, John H. | Caroline Salton | 2B | 156-157 | 1860 |

(daughter of Michael Salton of Lexington District)

Implied South Carolina Marriages Volume IV 1787-1875

| MAN | WOMAN | VOL | PAGES | LIVED |
|---|---|---|---|---|
| Kraft, Sebastian | Mary A. Lee | 2A | 208-209 | 1857 |

(marriage contract 22 December 1857) (widow of Horace Lee) (both of Union District)

(L)

| | | | | |
|---|---|---|---|---|
| Lacoste, Samuel N. | Laura E. Wells | 2A | 750-752 | 1859 |

(marriage settlement 1 November 1859) (granddaughter of Thomas Wells) (both of Sumter District)

| | | | | |
|---|---|---|---|---|
| Lambright, James | Martha S. Collins | C | 139-141 | 1814 |

(marriage settlement 23 June 1814) (of Barnwell District)

| | | | | |
|---|---|---|---|---|
| Lance, Francis | Mary _____ | 2A | 483-485 | 1858 |

(reference to marriage settlement - no date given) (of Charleston)

| | | | | |
|---|---|---|---|---|
| Landrum, Abner | Meheathlan Presley | F | 338 | 1828 |

(of Edgefield District) (daughter of John Presley)

| | | | | |
|---|---|---|---|---|
| Landrum, Amos | Elizabeth Hatcher | K | 305-306 | 1838 |

(marriage agreement 21 August 1838) (daughter of John Hatcher Senr.) (both of Edgefield District)

| | | | | |
|---|---|---|---|---|
| Lane, James H. | Maria T. Gause | T | 82-84 | 1849 |

(marriage settlement 27 January 1849) (in Marlborough District)

| | | | | |
|---|---|---|---|---|
| Lane, Micajah A. | Agnes Cox | 2B | 236-238 | 1860 |

(marriage settlement 15 December 1860) (he of Lincoln County, Georgia) (she of Abbeville District, S.C.)

| | | | | |
|---|---|---|---|---|
| Langford, William | Polly Peterson | F | 478 | 1829 |

(separation agreement 15 July 1829) (widow of David Peterson) (in Newberry District)

| | | | | |
|---|---|---|---|---|
| Langley, Christopher H. | Sarah R. Harley | P | 102-105 | 1838 |

(both of Barnwell District)

| | | | | |
|---|---|---|---|---|
| Langston, David M. | Laura E. Cannon | 2A | 696 | 1859 |

H. (of Laurens District) (daughter of David M. Cannon of Newberry District)

| | | | | |
|---|---|---|---|---|
| Lanneau, John F. (Lennau) | Julia H. Gray | W | 465-466 | 1851 |
| Lanneau, John Francis | Julia Helena Gray | M | 130-131 | 1842 |

(marriage settlement 17 March 1842) (daughter of John J. Gray) (in Edgefield District)

| | | | | |
|---|---|---|---|---|
| Lark, John | Elizabeth Darlington | B | 487-488 | 1808 |

(daughter of John Darlington of Barnwell District)

| | | | | |
|---|---|---|---|---|
| Laughon, Samuel | Mary Ann Crankfield | S | 130-132 | 1846 |

(daughter of Littleton Crankfield of Fairfield District)

74

Implied South Carolina Marriages Volume IV 1787-1875

| MAN | WOMAN | VOL | PAGES | LIVED |
|---|---|---|---|---|
| Laurence, James | Mary J. Paris | V | 504-505 | 1852 |

(in Sumter District)

| Law, _____ | Mary W. Hart | 2A | 708-709 | 1859 |
|---|---|---|---|---|
| Law, _____ | Elizabeth E. Wells | U | 107-109 | 1850 |

(daughter of Irby S. Wells and granddaughter of Thomas Wells)

| Law, Charles C. | Desda S. _____ | 2A | 618-619 | 1857 |
|---|---|---|---|---|

(reference to marriage settlement 15 January 1857)

| Law, Charles C. | Desdamona S. A. Gibson | Z | 621-625 | 1857 |
|---|---|---|---|---|

(marriage settlement 15 January 1857) (daughter of John C. Gibson) (Law of Darlington District) (she of Marion District)

| Lawhon, John W. | Sarah E. Beard | V | 30-31 | 1851 |
|---|---|---|---|---|

(in Fairfield District) (daughter of James Beard)

| Lawrence, Benjamin | Hannah Miller | Q | 62 | 1801 |
|---|---|---|---|---|

(he was born November 1757 in County of Gloucester, England) (she was born about 1748 in County of Gloucester, England) (arrived Charleston, S.C., 4 September 1801) (to Columbia, S.C.)

| Leavensworth, Melines Conkling | Ann Lamar (La Mar) | B | 222-228 | 1803 |
|---|---|---|---|---|

(marriage settlement 4 June 1803) (widow of Thomas Lamar of Horse Creek, Edgefield District) (both of Edgefield District)

| Lebby, Robert the Younger | Mary Eliza Bee | 2C | 363-368 | 1867 |
|---|---|---|---|---|

(daughter of Robert R. Bee)

| Lee, Alexander Y. | Frances E. McDonald | 2C | 4-6 | 1864 |
|---|---|---|---|---|

(of Kershaw District) (daughter of William McDonald)

| Lee, Joseph E. | Mary Elizabeth Jones | Z | 462-463 | 1856 |
|---|---|---|---|---|

(of Lexington District) (daughter of Abraham Jones of Edgefield District)

| Lee, William | Margaret Gordon | E | 190-191 | 1824 |
|---|---|---|---|---|

(marriage agreement 18 March 1824) (widower) (widow) (both of Sumter District)

| Lee, William J. | Elizabeth Watts | U | 331 | 1851 |
|---|---|---|---|---|

(daughter of Hampton Watts of Sumter District)

| Lee, William J. | Elizabeth Watts | Z | 485-487 | 1856 |
|---|---|---|---|---|

(of Sumter District) (daughter of Hampton Watts of Sumter District)

| Legg, George W. H. | Clementina Sarah Kennedy | M | 383-386 | 1842 |
|---|---|---|---|---|

(of Spartanburgh District) (daughter of Lionel H. Kennedy of Spartanburgh District)

| Leigh, David G. | Rachel Miller | L | 123-124 | 1840 |
|---|---|---|---|---|

(marriage agreement 25 June 1840) (in Kershaw District)

Implied South Carolina Marriages Volume IV 1787-1875

| MAN | WOMAN | VOL | PAGES | LIVED |
|---|---|---|---|---|

Lenoir, Isaac        Elizabeth Singleton   S    422-423    1848
   (marriage contract 1 November 1848) (both of Sumter
   District)
Lenoir, T. W.        Leonora H. Dinkins    Z    806-808    1857
   (marriage settlement 16 April 1857) (daughter of L. T.
   Dinkins)
Lesesne, Charles W.  Susanna M. _____      2A   125-126    1857
   (separation agreement 15 September 1857) (in Clarendon
   District)
Lester, William F.   Sarah Hoke Crook      2C   247-250    1866
   (marriage settlement 21 December 1866) (daughter of Dr.
   A. B. Crook and granddaughter of John Hoke) (both of
   Greenville District)
Levin, Jacob         Julia (Judith)        U    117-119    1850
                     Mordecai
   (marriage settlement 14 August 1850) (he was married
   before) (in Richland District)
Levin, Lipman T.     Charlotte Augusta     V    550-553    1844
                     Woolf
   (marriage settlement 10 January 1844) (postnuptial
   settlement 23 March 1852) (of Columbia, Richland
   District)
Levin, Lipman T.     Charlotte Augusta     X    340-343    1854
                     Woolf
   (reference to marriage settlement 10 January 1854) (of
   Columbia, Richland District)
Levingston, John     Margaret Henry        V    304-314    1852
                     (daughter of James Henry of Richland
                     District)
Lewis, _____         Eliza Maxwell         S    448-449    1848
                     (daughter of John Maxwell of Anderson
                     District)
Lewis, _____         Elizabeth S. Pearse   2B   755-756    1863
                     (daughter of Samuel Pearse of Columbia)
Lewis, Alfred        Clarissa Brewer       S    47-48      1847
   (of Anderson District) (daughter of John Brewer)
Lewis, Andrew W.     Elizabeth S. Pearce   2C   3-4        1864
   (of Richmond County, Georgia) (daughter of Samuel Pearce
   of Richland District, S.C.)
Lewis, John B.       Caroline S. Thomson   S    281-282    1848
   (of Orangeburgh District) (daughter of William R.
   Thomson)
Lewis, John B.       Caroline Sophia       K    269        1839
                     Thomson          (in Orangeburgh District)
Lewis, William       Sarah P. Mellett      U    203-206    1850
   (marriage settlement 3 September 1850) (both of Sumter
   District) [See also pages 207-208]

Implied South Carolina Marriages Volume IV 1787-1875

MAN                WOMAN              VOL   PAGES      LIVED

Lewis, William     Elizabeth T. Wilson  W   455-458    1853
    (marriage settlement 21 February 1853) (widow) (he of
    Sumterville) (she of Georgetown)
Ley, Doctr William   Mary Heron (Herron)  H   219      1832
    (marriage contract 6 September 1832) (both of Columbia)
Lide, _____        _____ Miller         Y   155-156    1847
    ("Mrs. Miller now Lide") (reference to marriage
    settlement - no date given) (widow) (she to Alabama)
Lide, Layton       Julia E. Wilds       2B  480-490    1861
    (Leighton) W. (marriage settlement 25 April 1861)
    (daughter of Peter A. Wilds) (in Darlington District)
Liddell, Moses     Bethia Frances       G   349-351    1830
                   Richardson
    (of Wilkinson County, Mississippi)
Ligon, William G.  Louisa Seibles       2C  358-360    1867
    (of Lexington District)
Lindsay, _____     Mary E. Gill         W   598        1853
    (daughter of Robert Gill of Laurens
    District)
Lindsey, Dennis    Mary S. Cunningham   2A  227-229    1858
    (marriage settlement 2 January 1858) (widow of O. H. P.
    Cunningham) (Lindsey of Hamburg, Edgefield District)
Lindsey, Elbert    Bethniah Cole        V   260-262    1851
    (both of Laurens District)
Lindsey, Mahalaleel Jane Missori        O   385-387    1845
                   Cunningham           (in Newberry District)
Lipscomb, Smith    Elizabeth Jones      H   474-475    1833
    (marriage settlement 18 September 1833) (he was married
    before) (of Spartanburgh District)
Lipscomb, Wyatt    Hannah Green (widow) F   18         1821
    (he of Spartanburgh District) (she of York District)
Lishness, Anthony  Elizabeth (Eliza)    E   212-213    1824
                   Garvin
    (marriage settlement 28 June 1824) (widow of James
    Garvin of Barnwell District)
Lister, Revd. James  Janet Jaffray      C   326-338    1798
                   (daughter of Henry Jaffray of County of
    Stirling, Scotland) [See also pages 340-344]
Little, William    Rutha Holder         R   57-58      1846
    (marriage settlement 7 September 1846) (daughter of
    Daniel Holder) (of Union District)
Littlefield, Philip  Patsey Nance       E   422-423    1825
                   (daughter of Zachariah Nance of Union
                   District)
Livingston, James  Clara Kilpatrick     2A  340-345    1858
    W. (marriage settlement 29 April 1858) (he of Abbeville,
    Abbeville District) (she of Pendleton District)

Implied South Carolina Marriages Volume IV 1787-1875

| MAN | WOMAN | VOL | PAGES | LIVED |
|---|---|---|---|---|
| Livingston, Jno: C. | Martha P. Brown | G | 354-356 | 1830 |

(daughter of Peter Brown of Abbeville District)
Livingston. See Levingston

| Lloyd, William | Elizabeth Josephine ___ [no last name] | O | 430-431 | 1845 |

(reference to marriage settlement - no date given)

| Lockhart, Samuel | Sarah Killingsworth | K | 273 | 1838 |

(of Abbeville District) (daughter of Mark Killingsworth of Abbeville District)

| Lockhart, Thomas B. | Emily H. Kemble | N | 15-17 | 1843 |

(marriage settlement 30 March 1843) (he of Laurens District) (she of Columbia, Richland District)

| Lockhart, Thomas B. | Mary Pollard | L | 222-223 | 1841 |

(in Laurens District?) (daughter of James Pollard of Abbeville District)

| Logan, ___ | Susan W. A. Richardson | U | 126-128 | 1850 |
| Lomax, William James | Catharine McFie | 2B | 603-604 | 1861 |

(of Abbeville District)

| Long, ___ | Mary A. Ayer | Y | 524-526 | 1855 |
| Long, Dr. Moses M. | Clara Ann Jones | Y | 469-470 | 1855 |

(of Edgefield District) (daughter of Abraham Jones of Edgefield District)

| Long, Jacob | Magdalina Schumpert | P | 136 | 1845 |

(daughter of Frederick Schumpert of Newberry District)

| Long, Jacob Junr. | Cusdrado Holston | N | 186-187 | 1843 |

(of Edgefield District)

| Long, Nicholas | Frances Puckett | G | 404-405 | 1831 |

(marriage settlement 21 April 1831) (both of Abbeville District)

| Long, Thomas D. | Susan Perry | 2A | 475-477 | 1858 |

(of Greenville District) (to Pickens District)

| Longshow, Levi | Anna Waldrop | F | 364-365 | 1828 |

(in Newberry District)

| Longshow, Young | Matilda Waldrop | F | 364-365 | 1828 |

(in Newberry District)

| Lorick, ___ | Susan Caroline Williams (widow of Thomas B. Williams) | 2A | 767-769 | 1860 |
| Loring, ___ | Rebecca Pitts | G | 90-91 | 1830 |

(daughter of Jeremiah Pitts of Sumter District)

| Loring, Capt. Lucius P. | Mary Marsena Brunson | 2C | 498-501 | 1868 |

(daughter of William L. Brunson of Sumter District) (in Sumter District)

Implied South Carolina Marriages Volume IV 1787-1875

| MAN | WOMAN | VOL | PAGES | LIVED |
|---|---|---|---|---|
| Loring, Lucius P. | Mary Marsena Brunson (in Sumter District) (daughter of William L. Brunson of Sumter District) | 2C | 157-166 | 1846 |
| Lorton, _____ | E. Amanda Kilpatrick (widow) | 2A | 340-345 | 1858 |
| Lott, Emsley | Morina Rutland (daughter of Abraham Rutland of Edgefield District) | 2A | 772-773 | 1860 |
| Lott, Samuel | Mahala Bartley (daughter of Thomas Bartley of Edgefield District) | Y | 519-521 | 1855 |
| Loury, William R. | Mary C. Bratten (of York District) (daughter of Dr. John S. Bratten of York District) | U | 1-4 | 1850 |
| Love, Samuel L. | Elizabeth Ann Gordon (reference to marriage agreement - no date given) (daughter of Mansfield Gordon) (in York District) | 2A | 592-594 | 1858 |
| Love, Samuel Lucian | Elizabeth Ann Gordon (marriage settlement 17 April 1855) (both of York District) | Z | 431-432 | 1855 |
| Loveless, Luellen O. | Martha G. Mosley | Y | 253-255 | 1855 |
| Lovell, James | Ann Heatly (of Orangeburgh District) [See also pages 395-397] | E | 397-400 | 1825 |
| Lucas, Benjamin S. | Ellen S. King (daughter of William King of Darlington District) | 2C | 495-497 | 1867 |
| Lumsden, Joshua Leon | Margaret D. O'Hanlon (marriage settlement 9 February 1859) (he now of Columbia) (she of Columbia) | 2A | 508-510 | 1859 |
| Lyles, Benjamin | Catherine Rook (daughter of William Rook of Laurens District) | V | 554-557 | 1824 |
| Lyles, James V. | Mary Ann Mickle (marriage settlement 9 September 1840) (daughter of Joseph Mickle) (Lyles of Columbia) (she in Kershaw District) | L | 159-161 | 1840 |
| Lynch, Dr. John | Eliza Macnamara (of Columbia) | 2B | 291-294 | 1860 |
| Lynch, Hugh P. | Cornelia Agnes Reilly (daughter of Bernard Reilly of Columbia, Richland District) | 2A | 62 | 1857 |
| Lynch, Hugh P. | Cornelia Agnes Reilly (Rielly) (daughter of Bernard Reilly of Richland District) [See also pages 375-376] | 2B | 61-62 | 1857 |

Implied South Carolina Marriages Volume IV 1787-1875

| MAN | WOMAN | VOL | PAGES | LIVED |
|---|---|---|---|---|

(Mc)

McAllister, John    Polly Lightfoot    C    111-117    1811
   (of Abbeville District) (daughter of Francis Lightfoot)
McBride, William    Ann Haseltine    2B    690-695    1863
   Trowell (daughter of James Trowell)
   (in Beaufort District)
McBryde, John    Elizabeth Mayson    F    340-342    1828
   (marriage settlement 23 July 1828) (widow of Archy
   Mayson of Edgefield District) (McBryde of Hamburgh,
   Edgefield District)
McCaa, Dr Thomas W.    Mary C. Matheson    V    516-518    1852
   (daughter of Christopher Matheson of
   Camden, Kershaw District)
McCaine, _____    Mary B. Wade    S    343-344    1840
   (in Barnwell District)
McCall, Moses S.    Catharine F. _____    X    126-128    1847
   Jr. (reference to marriage settlement 26 March 1847) (of
   Darlington District, S.C., intending to go to Texas)
McCance, _____    Elisar Watson    I    210    1835
McCann, James    Anna Davenport    K    118-119    1838
   (marriage settlement 6 March 1838) (widow of William
   Davenport) (she of Newberry District)
McCants, Robert P.    Cecelia V. Rielly    2B    374-375    1861
   (of Ocala, Florida) (daughter of Bernard Rielly of
   Richland District, S.C.)
McCarrley, George    Rachel Plowden    M    270-272    1842
   J. (of Sumter District) (widow)
McCarter, _____    Mary Otterson    Y    224-225    1855
McCarter, _____    Martha Ann Waddill    S    62-64    1847
McCarthy, Thomas    Elizabeth Elrod    R    77-79    1846
   (marriage settlement 31 August 1846) (daughter of
   Jeremiah Elrod) (in Anderson District)
McCaslan, William    Sarah E. Scott    2A    453-454    1858
McCaslan, Wm    _____ Scott    2A    745-746    1846
McCauley, James    Mary W. Keitt    2B    477-478    1861
   (marriage settlement 14 August 1861) (in Orangeburg
   District)
McCaulley, George    Rachael Plowden    T    67-69    1849
   J. (in Sumter District)
McClenaghan, _____    Mary A. Pawley    Y    182-185    1855
   (widow)
McClendon, Jesse    Aley Melton    Y    154-155    1843
   (widow of Elisha Melton)

Implied South Carolina Marriages Volume IV 1787-1875

| MAN | WOMAN | VOL | PAGES | LIVED |
|---|---|---|---|---|

McColl, Moses S.    Catharine F. McRae    R    422-424    1847
 (marriage settlement 26 May 1847 recorded in Darlington
 and Marlborough Districts)
McColl, Moses S.    Catharine F. McRae    X    32    1847
 (reference to marriage settlement 26 May 1847) (in
 Darlington and Marlborough Districts)
McColl. See McCall
McCollough, Robert    Elizabeth Wallace    F    255-256    1827
 (marriage settlement 23 January 1827) (in Union
 District)
McCollough, Robert    Elizabeth Wallace    P    369-371    1827
 (reference to marriage settlement 23 January 1827) (in
 Edgefield District)
McComb, John    Sarah Gentry    T    383-384    1849
 (of Richland District)
McConnell, John    Mary Brisbane ____    2A    39-42    1857
 Thomas (postnuptial settlement 20 June 1857) (in
 Barnwell District)
McCord, ____    Mary E. Speer    T    114-115    1849
 (daughter of William Speer of Abbeville
 District)
McCord, D. J.    Louisa S. ____    X    11-12    1853
 (reference to marriage settlement - no date given) [See
 also pages 28-30]
McCord, David J.    Louisa S. Cheves    L    88-93    1840
 (marriage settlement 20 May 1840) (he of Columbia) (she
 of St. Matthew's Parish) [See also page 414]
McCord, Joseph    Martha Turquand    A    167    1791
 (daughter of Paul Turquand of Orangeburgh
 District)
McCord, Russell    Hannah Turquand    A    166-167    1791
 (of Camden District) (daughter of Paul Turquand of
 Orangeburgh District)
McCormic_, Simeon    Rebecca Bethea    2B    159-161    1860
 P. (marriage settlement 21 August 1860) (widow of
 Francis Bethea) (both of Marion District)
McCown, Joseph J.    Martha Emma Nettles    2B    358-361    1861
 (marriage settlement __ June 1861) (both of Darlington
 District)
McCrackin, James G.    Susan E. Wilson    K    356-357    1839
 (marriage settlement 8 April 1839) (both of Newberry
 District)
McCrady, ____    Jane Johnson    G    329-332    1831
McCreight, Clough    Martha A. Peake    2A    307-308    1858
 (marriage contract 2 January 1858) (of Union District)
McCrorey, James    Sarah Thorn    M    342-343    1842
 (daughter of Charles Thorn)

Implied South Carolina Marriages Volume IV 1787-1875

| MAN | WOMAN | VOL | PAGES | LIVED |
|---|---|---|---|---|
| McCrory, James | Lucretia Mobley | 2A | 763-764 | 1860 |

(of Fairfield District) (daughter of John Mobley Senr. of Fairfield District)

| McCullough, James | Jane Martin | U | 439-440 | 1851 |

(separation agreement 10 March 1851) (both of Greenville District) (he late of Ireland)

McCullough. See McCollough

| McCully, James B. | Sarah McCreary | M | 132-134 | 1842 |

(marriage contract 5 February 1842) (widow of John McCreary) (both of Chester District)

| McCully, John | Eliza. A. Neil | Z | 415 | 1852 |

(marriage settlement 9 October 1852) (both of Fairfield District)

| McCully, Thomas | Sarah A. Walker | 2B | 562 | 1861 |

(daughter of Adam T. Walker of Chester District)

| McCurry, J. W. | Sarah E. McDonald | 2C | 169-170 | 1866 |

(of Kershaw District) (daughter of Charles A. McDonald of Kershaw District)

| McCutchen, Thomas M. | Hannah J. H. Boone | 2A | 783-784 | 1860 |

(marriage settlement 1 February 1860) (he of Williamsburg District) (she of Sumter District)

| McDaniel, James | Jacqueline H. Murdock | F | 51 | 1827 |

(marriage agreement 23 May 1827)

| McDaniel, Jefferson | Nancy Dixon | X | 121-122 | 1853 |

(daughter of Benjamin Dixon of Barnwell District)

| McDonald, Griffin | Sophia M. LaRoche | 2B | 636-642 | 1863 |

(marriage settlement 17 April 1863) (reference to marriage settlement in Macon, Georgia) (widow of J. J. LaRoche) (of Aiken, Barnwell District, S.C.)

| McDonald, Hugh | Leonora G. Colclough | H | 429-434 | 1833 |

(marriage agreement 10 July 1833) (widow of William A. Colclough) (McDonald of Charleston District) (she of Sumter District)

| McDow, _____ | Isabella F. Cunningham | Z | 499-501 | 1856 |
| McDowall, _____ | Nancy Narcissa Marshall | Z | 511-512 | 1856 |

(daughter of George Marshall of Abbeville District)

| McDowell, Davidson | Catharine D. Witherspoon | U | 302-304 | 1827 |

(reference to marriage settlement 17 December 1827)

| McDowell, Thomas | Martha E. Sutton | M | 18-19 | 1841 |

(marriage settlement 3 November 1841) (widow) (both of Fairfield District)

Implied South Carolina Marriages Volume IV 1787-1875

| MAN | WOMAN | VOL | PAGES | LIVED |
|---|---|---|---|---|

McElmurray, Robert H. Ann C. Newman E 169-171 1824
(marriage settlement 14 February 1824) (both of Barnwell District)
McElveen, Andrew J. Frances H. Mellett Y 412-416 1855
(marriage settlement 29 September 1855) (widow of Dr. James L. Mellett) (in Sumter District)
McElvine, _____ Rebecca Smith H 100-101 1832
(daughter of William Smith)
McElwee, John R. Jr Isabella McMakin R 496-498 1847
(of York District) (daughter of Thomas McMakin)
McFadden, William Sarah Yongue 2B 649-651 1863
P. (marriage settlement 9 July 1863) (widow)
McFaddin, Sidney Sarah J. Wilson U 471-473 1851
(marriage settlement 13 May 1851) (both of Sumter District)
McFarland, Sarah E. Jennings O 313-315 1845
Alexander J. (daughter of Larkin Jennings) (both of Sumter District)
McFarland. See Macfarlan
McGee, Hall T. Mary W. Warren G 486-487 1829
(daughter of Peter Warren of Camden, Kershaw District) (of Camden, Kershaw District)
McGehee, Dr. James Sarah C. Harper W 213-214 1853
A. (of Paulding County, Georgia) [See also pages 311-312]
McGehee, James A. Sarah H. Harper Y 218 1855
(of Paulding County, Georgia)
McGraw, Marshall Elizabeth M. D. Cook Y 43-44 1855
(marriage settlement 20 February 1855) (he of Fairfield District) (she of Kershaw District)
McGregor, _____ Mary Ann Taylor R 86-87 1846
(daughter of William Taylor of Kershaw District)
McGuinnis, William Ellen Kervick 2B 790-793 1864
(marriage settlement 4 February 1864) (he of Columbia) (she formerly of Charleston, now of Columbia)
McGuire, John Selenah Kimbrel 2A 500-502 1858
(Kembrell)
(marriage contract 5 February 1858) (widow of G. W. Kimbrel)
McHarg, William Ann Harker I 103 1817
(married 1817) (he died December 1824) (she was born about 1790 in Cumberland, England) (she arrived at Savannah, Georgia from Liverpool, November 1815) (of Edgefield District, S.C) (to Augusta, Georgia, June 1820)

Implied South Carolina Marriages Volume IV 1787-1875

| MAN | WOMAN | VOL | PAGES | LIVED |
|---|---|---|---|---|
| McIntosh, Benjamin | Ellen Watson | S | 138-139 | 1847 |

(daughter of Francis C. Watson of Chesterfield District)

| McIntosh, George Q. (or D.) | Jane Almira (Elmira) Wilson | H | 514 | 1833 |

(daughter of Hugh Wilson of Sumter District) [See also Volume I, pages 29-30]

| McIver, _____ | Henrietta K. Robbins | 2B | 459-466 | 1862 |

Jr.
(reference to marriage settlement - no date given)

| McIver, Francis M. | Henrietta K. Robbins | 2A | 399-407 | 1858 |

the Younger
(marriage settlement 5 August 1858) (daughter of William H. Robbins) (both of Chesterfield District)

| McIver, John H. | Margaret A. Ellerbe | 2B | 367-371 | 1861 |

(marriage settlement 22 July 1861) (of Cheraw, Chesterfield District)

| McIver, John J. | Julia R. Gregg | Z | 244-248 | 1856 |

(marriage settlement 4 June 1856) (both of Darlington District)

| McIver, Peter K. | Hannah M. Nettles | R | 521-524 | 1847 |

(marriage settlement 29 September 1847) (widow of James Nettles) (in Darlington District)

| McJunkin, Major William | Caroline Kelly | U | 440-441 | 1850 |

(daughter of William Kelly of Union District)

| McKagen, Isaac A. | Frances E. Webb | 2B | 521-523 | 1862 |

(marriage settlement 9 September 1862) (daughter of William Webb) (in Sumter District)

| McKay, Randle | Catharine Taylor Macfarlan | W | 259-265 | 1852 |

(marriage settlement 28 December 1852) (daughter of John Macfarlan) (McKay of Anson County, North Carolina) (she of Chesterfield District, S.C.)

| McKellar, Dugald | Jane Purvis | H | 170-171 | 1832 |

(marriage settlement 17 August 1832) (both of Abbeville District)

| McKellar, John W. | Sarah L. Gaskins | W | 469-472 | 1853 |

(daughter of John Gaskins of Edgefield District)

| McKenna, William | Ann C. _____ | I | 326 | 1835 |

(marriage contract 22 October 1835) (in Lancaster District)

| McKnight, Robert A. | Amanda Palmer | 2A | 15-17 | 1857 |

(of Union District) (daughter of Ellis Palmer of Union District)

| McKnight, William H. | Mary Jane Horton | 2B | 309-312 | 1861 |

(in Clarendon District) (daughter of Joseph Horton)

Implied South Carolina Marriages Volume IV 1787-1875

| MAN | WOMAN | VOL | PAGES | LIVED |
|---|---|---|---|---|
| McLane, _____ | Rebecca Loring (widow) | G | 90-91 | 1830 |

McLauren, Dan<u>el</u> B.   Agness D. Chandler    2A    512-513    1836
  (reference to marriage settlement 6 January 1836) (in
  Sumter District)
McLaurin, Daniel B. Agnes D. Chandler    I    372-373    1836
  (marriage settlement 6 January 1836) (daughter of Samuel
  Chandler) (both of Sumter District)
McLaurin, James R.   Effee (Effy) Ann    N    283-285    1844
                     McLucas
  (marriage contract 22 January 1844) (he of Richmond
  County, North Carolina) (she of Marlborough District,
  S.C.)
McLean, John D.      Margaret King       X    27-28      1853
  (of Darlington District) (daughter of Gillam King of
  Chesterfield District)
McLeod, Dr John D.   Elizabeth Lang      T    30         1849
                     Bradley (daughter of John Bradley of
                     Sumter District)
McLin, David O.      Elizabeth T.        M    166        1842
                     Caldwell (daughter of James Caldwell of
                     Abbeville District)
McMahon, Eli         Amanda E. Smith     R    467        1847
  (daughter of William Smith of Union
  District)
McMaster, Dr. J. R.  Harriet R. Mobley   Y    563-564    1856
  (of Fairfield District) (daughter of Edward P. Mobley of
  Fairfield District)
McMeekin, Dr. Jacob  Henrietta Jones     V    562-563    1852
  G. (of Fairfield District) (daughter of Abraham Jones of
  Edgefield District)
McMillan, Thomas     Louisa R. Ray       G    414-415    1831
McMillan, Wm. J.     Mary Ann Lee        I    397-398    1835
  (of Lexington District, S.C.) (to Columbus, Georgia?)
McMorries, John B.   Rosannah S. Law     X    484-486    1854
  F. (marriage settlement 6 April 1854) (widow) (he of
  Newberry District) (she of Abbeville District)
McMorries, Jonathan  Elizabeth A. Neel   X    522-524    1854
  (in Newberry District)
McNair, Murphy C.    Elizabeth Stubbs    S    201-204    1848
  (marriage settlement 21 March 1848) (both of Marlborough
  District)
McNair.  See Macnair
McNeal, Augustus     Mary Carr           F    261        1828
  (marriage settlement 3 May 1828) (both of Columbia,
  Richland District)

Implied South Carolina Marriages Volume IV 1787-1875

| MAN | WOMAN | VOL | PAGES | LIVED |
|---|---|---|---|---|
| McNeely, William | Margaret Evins | 2C | 180-182 | 1866 |

(marriage settlement 4 June 1866) (widow of M. P. Evins of Laurens District) (McNeely of Greenville)

| McNeill, Alexander | Almira Haseltine Watson | 2B | 532-533 | 1862 |

(marriage settlement 2 October 1862) (in Abbeville District)

| McQueen, _____ | Marjory Macfarlan | W | 259-265 | 1852 |
| McQueen, Thomas P. | Milby Ann Norton | Z | 401-402 | 1856 |

(of Sumter District)

| McRae, John | Isabel Scota McRae (McRa) | Y | 280-281 | 1855 |

(marriage settlement 17 July 1855) (daughter of Duncan McRae) (she of Camden)

| McWhite, Alexander | Elizabeth Greaves | N | 219-221 | 1843 |

(marriage settlement 20 November 1843) (both of Marion District)


(M)

| Macfarlan, John | Janet Taylor | W | 259-265 | 1852 |
| Macfie, _____ | Catharine McGregor | W | 519-522 | 1853 |
| Mackey, John | Margaret D. McWillie | E | 69 | 1820 |

(daughter of Adam McWillie of Beaver Dam, Kershaw District) (Mackey of Fairfield District)

| Macnair, John | Elizabeth Miller | A | 224-240 | 1793 |

(widow of Andrew Miller)

| Macon, Hartwell | Eliza D. Russell | F | 252-253 | 1828 |

(marriage settlement __ February 1828)

| Madden, _____ | Frances Arnold | 2B | 366-367 | 1861 |

(in Laurens District)

| Malcom, Capt. James R. | Mary Ann Friedeberg | 2C | 193-194 | 1866 |

(marriage settlement 11 October 1866) (widow) (he in Richland District) (she of Columbia)

| Malone, Simpson | Mary A. E. Jacks | 2B | 758-760 | 1863 |

(marriage settlement 10 December 1863) (widow of Isaac Calmes Jacks) (Malone of Union District) (she of Laurens District)

| Man, Robert | Eliza Jane Whitaker | S | 338-342 | 1848 |

(daughter of William Whitaker)

| Mangum, John W. | Mary Ellen McKenney | U | 417-418 | 1851 |
| Mantz, Christopher W. | Mary P. Jeter | G | 237-238 | 1827 |

(daughter of William Jeter) (in Edgefield District)

Implied South Carolina Marriages Volume IV 1787-1875

| MAN | WOMAN | VOL | PAGES | LIVED |
|---|---|---|---|---|
| Marchant, Silas | Mary M. Lagrone | H | 354-355 | 1832 |

(marriage settlement 25 October 1832) (widow of John
Lagrone) (of Newberry District)

| Mardney, ___ | Anne Beard | D | 9-11 | 1818 |

(daughter of Joshua Beard) (she of
Richland District)

| Marsh, John | Sarah Ann Nail | E | 545-547 | 1826 |

(marriage settlement 10 October 1826) (widow of John
Nail) (both of Edgefield District)

| Marsh, John | Sarah Ann Nail | T | 373-375 | 1826 |

(reference to marriage settlement 10 October 1826)
(widow of John Nail) (both of Edgefield District)

| Marsh, Thomas | Catherine A. Murray | H | 120-121 | 1832 |

(marriage settlement 1 March 1832) (in Edgefield
District)

| Marshall, ___ | Jane Smith | 2C | 23-25 | 1864 |

(daughter of William Smith of Abbeville
District)

| Marshall, J. Foster | Elizabeth A. DeBruhl | W | 412-415 | 1853 |

(of Abbeville District) (daughter of Jesse DeBruhl of
Richland District)

| Marshall, Thomas | Sarah H. Ayer | Y | 524-526 | 1855 |

(marriage settlement 19 November 1855) (daughter of
Hutwell Ayer) (in Marlborough District)

| Marten, David B. | Ann Anderson | K | 146-147 | 1838 |

(marriage settlement 13 April 1838) (both of Chester
District)

| Martin, ___ | Nancy Cartledge | H | 450-451 | 1825 |

(daughter of Edmund Cartledge of
Edgefield District)

| Martin, Aurelius | Francis Jennings | I | 566-567 | 1837 |

(daughter of Joseph Jennings of
Edgefield)

| Martin, Philip B. | Elmina E. Hagood | 2C | 259-262 | 1866 |

(daughter of Benjamin Hagood of Pickens
District) [See also pages 252-256]

| Martin, William | Susan Hawthorn | P | 87-91 | 1845 |
| Martindale, George L. | Martha Minerva Hutchinson | Z | 183-184 | 1856 |

(daughter of A. S. Hutchinson
of Laurens District)

| Mason, ___ | Sheba Barker | G | 214-215 | 1830 |
| Mason, George T. | Martha A. Nixon | U | 40-42 | 1850 |

(marriage settlement 2 May 1850) (daughter of Washington
F. Nixon) (Mason of North Carolina) (she of Richland
District, S.C.) [Must also see pages 4-5]

| Mason, Thomas | Mary Thorn | M | 342-343 | 1842 |

(daughter of Charles Thorn)

Implied South Carolina Marriages Volume IV 1787-1875

| MAN | WOMAN | VOL | PAGES | LIVED |
|---|---|---|---|---|

Mason. See Mayson
Matheson,         Catharine Haile     I     433         1836
  Christopher     (daughter of Benjamin Haile of Camden,
  Kershaw District) (of Camden, Kershaw District)
Mathias, William     Maria (Mariah) Bracy   D   187-188    1820
  (reference to marriage articles 7 March 1820) (widow of
  Solly Bracy) (Mathias of Camden)
Mathis, George W.    Amanda Mosley      Y   253-255    1855
Mathis, Israel G.    Jane Ingram Lenoir   E   166-167    1810
  (daughter of John Lenoir Senior)
  (of Lancaster District)
Mathis, Samuel       Margaret Cathcart   A   224-240    1793
                      Miller
  (marriage settlement 22 January 1793) (daughter of
  Andrew Miller) (Mathis of Camden) (she of Claremont
  County)
Matthews, Robert W.  Rosinna Eubanks    Z   614-618    1857
  (of Barnwell District) (daughter of James J. Eubanks of
  Barnwell District)
Maybin, Henry        Nancy Knighton     L    94-95     1839
  (of Fairfield District) (daughter of Moses Knighton of
  Fairfield District)
Mayes, Junius A.     Mary Francis Muldrow  P   98-100     1845
  (of Sumter District) (daughter of Matthew E. Muldrow of
  Salem County, Sumter District)
Mayes, Matthew P.    Martha M. McBride   V    85-88     1851
  (marriage settlement 12 September 1851) (widow of Samuel
  McBride) (both of Sumter District)
Mayrant, John Jr.    Maria P. Rees      C   117-123    1814
  (marriage settlement 11 May 1814) (daughter of William
  Rees) (both of Sumter District)
Mayrant, Robert      Frances Ann Margaret  G   364-365    1831
  Pringle          Horry Guignard
  (marriage settlement 12 May 1831) (daughter of James S.
  Guignard of Columbia) (Mayrant of Sumter District) [See
  also Volume H, pages 193-194]
Mayrant, William     Ann Richardson     G   340-342    1831
  Senr            (she in Sumter District)
Mays, John A.        Carolina A. Gray   2A   103-105    1856
  (marriage settlement 13 February 1856) (widow of M. M.
  Gray) (granddaughter of Archibald Lester) (both of
  Edgefield District)
Mays, John P.        Maria Harmon       E   196-197    1824
  (marriage settlement 26 May 1824) (both of Edgefield
  District)

Implied South Carolina Marriages Volume IV 1787-1875

| MAN | WOMAN | VOL | PAGES | LIVED |
|---|---|---|---|---|
| Mays, Larkin | Elizabeth Beacham | X | 665-667 | 1855 |

(of Anderson District) (daughter of Daniel S. Beacham of Abbeville District)

| Mayson, Henry L. | Sarah Nail | M | 378-380 | 1843 |

(daughter of Casper Nail of Edgefield District)

| Mayson, Henry Laurens (of Aiken) | Sarah Ardis | L | 368-370 | 1841 |

(widow of Abram Ardis of Beach Island, Edgefield District)

| Mayson, John C. | Nancy Bostick | E | 306 | 1817 |

(of Abbeville District)

Mayson. See Mason

| Mazyck, William | Nannie W. Taylor | 2A | 201-203 | 1858 |

St. J. (of Charleston) (daughter of Benjamin F. Taylor)

| Medlock, _____ | Milley Kinard | K | 165 | 1838 |

(widow) (she of Edgefield District)

| Meetze, Henry | Caroline Dreher | X | 310-312 | 1854 |

(of Lexington District) (daughter of Godfrey Dreher of Lexington District)

| Mellett, Robert Sidney | Sarah Ann Wheler | T | 206-209 | 1849 |

(marriage settlement 15 May 1849) (in Sumter District)

| Mellichamp, Edward K. | Mary Theodosia Vaughan | P | 196-202 | 1845 |

(marriage settlement 4 December 1845) (daughter of John H. Vaughan) (Mellichamp of Charleston) (she of Sumter District)

| Melton, Jonathan | Martha Henry | V | 304-314 | 1852 |

(daughter of James Henry of Richland District)

| Melton, Robert | Louisa Waters | U | 103-105 | 1850 |

(marriage settlement 17 July 1850) (both of Chester District)

| Meriwether, Snowden G. | Martha R. Meachem | Y | 143-144 | 1855 |

(of Edgefield District)

| Meroney, James (Maroney) | Frances America Perritt | W | 625-629 | 1853 |

(widow of Perry Bryant Perritt) (in Edgefield District)

| Mickle, John Belton | Sarah Milling | R | 141-143 | 1846 |

(marriage settlement 21 October 1846) (both of Kershaw District)

| Mickle, John Belton | Sarah Milling | Y | 41-42 | 1855 |

(of Kershaw District) (daughter of John Milling of Kershaw District)

| Mickle, Joseph | Martha Belton | B | 180-183 | 1802 |

(marriage settlement 16 August 1802) (daughter of John Belton) (of Camden)

Implied South Carolina Marriages Volume IV 1787-1875

| MAN | WOMAN | VOL | PAGES | LIVED |
|---|---|---|---|---|
| Mickle, Joseph T. | Matilda W. Milling | 2C | 30-32 | 1864 |

(marriage settlement __ November 1864) (he late of Mobile, Alabama) (she of Kershaw District, S.C.)

| Middleton, John H. | Ann Fuller | D | 412-414 | 1822 |

(marriage settlement 21 March 1822) (both of Edgefield District) [See also Volume E, pages 70-71]

| Middleton, William E. | Emily Prescott | Y | 139-140 | 1855 |

(daughter of Daniel Prescott of Edgefield District)

| Middleton, William E. | Emily Prescott | 2B | 193-197 | 1860 |

(daughter of Daniel Prescott of Edgefield District)

| Mikell, _____ | Rebecca R. Moses | 2A | 84-85 | 1857 |

(daughter of Franklin J. Moses of Sumter District)

| Mikell, Thomas P. | Rebecca R. Moses | Z | 723-724 | 1857 |

(daughter of Franklin J. Moses of Sumter District)

| Mikell, Thomas P. | Rebecca R. Moses | 2B | 66 | 1860 |

(daughter of Franklin J. Moses of Sumter District)

| Miles, Francis A. | Eliza M. Hagood | 2C | 252-256 | 1866 |

(daughter of Benjamin Hagood of Pickens District) [Must also see pages 259-262]

| Miles, L. | Nancy Teague | T | 398-400 | 1849 |

(marriage settlement 4 October 1849) (he was married before) (widow) (in Laurens District)

| Milledge, _____ | Ann Lamar | N | 293-295 | 1843 |
| Miller, _____ | Temperance Crankfield (daughter of Littleton Crankfield of Fairfield District) | S | 130-131 | 1846 |
| Miller, _____ | E. H. Haynsworth | T | 304-306 | 1849 |

(in Marion District) (daughter of Dr. James Haynsworth)

| Miller, Alexander H. | Elizabeth A. Hawthorn | P | 87-91 | 1845 |
| Miller, Andrew | Elizabeth Blount | A | 224-240 | 1793 |

(daughter of Charles Blount)

| Miller, C. W. | Elizabeth H. Haynsworth (daughter of Doctor James Haynsworth) (in Marion District) | 2A | 621-622 | 1859 |
| Miller, Charles W. | Elizabeth Haywood | V | 237-238 | 1837 |

(of Sumter District) (daughter of James Haywood of Sumter District)

| Miller, John | Lydia Ann Pedrean | F | 399-400 | 1829 |

(in Anderson District)

Implied South Carolina Marriages Volume IV 1787-1875

| MAN | WOMAN | VOL | PAGES | LIVED |
|---|---|---|---|---|
| Miller, John I. (or J.) | Harriet I. (or J.) B. Fraser | W | 239-243 | 1852 |

(marriage settlement 7 December 1852) (daughter of
Ladson L. Fraser and granddaughter of John B. Fraser)
(both of Sumter District)

| Miller, Nicholas | Mary Yarbrough | M | 92-96 | 1842 |
|---|---|---|---|---|
| Miller, William | C. Louisa Gray | W | 465-467 | 1851 |
| Milling, Dr. James S. | Mary Whitaker Milling (daughter of John Milling of | 2A | 454-455 | 1858 |

Kershaw District) (of Fairfield District)

| Milling, John McK. | Harriet Lowndes Aiken (daughter of James Aiken of | 2B | 474-475 | 1862 |
|---|---|---|---|---|

Fairfield District) (of Fairfield District)

| Mills, Edwin R. | Mary Jane Moore | Z | 596-598 | 1857 |
|---|---|---|---|---|

(marriage contract 5 February 1857) (he of Chester
District) (she of York District)

| Milner, Arnold | Isabella Saxon | P | 110-111 | 1848 |
|---|---|---|---|---|

(marriage contract 17 November 1848) (widow) (he of Cass
County, Georgia) (she of Laurens District, S.C.)

| Mims, Julius A. | Mary L. Byrd | 2B | 180-181 | 1860 |
|---|---|---|---|---|

(postnuptial settlement 2 October 1860) (daughter of
Reddin Byrd) (of Sumter District)

| Mitchell, Benjamin | Mary W. Michau | I | 374-375 | 1835 |
|---|---|---|---|---|

(marriage settlement 13 December 1835) (widow of
Manasseth Michau) (in Sumter District) [See also page
404]

| Mitchell, Benjamin | Alice D. Vaughan | O | 101-103 | 1844 |
|---|---|---|---|---|

(in Sumter District) [See also pages 176-178]

| Mitchell, Samuel C. | Leonora C. Vaughan | L | 38-40 | 1840 |
|---|---|---|---|---|

(marriage settlement 11 January 1840) (daughter of
William Vaughan) (both of Sumter District)

| Mobley, Andrew J. | Eugenia A. Bynum | 2B | 679-680 | 1863 |
|---|---|---|---|---|

(of Fairfield District) (daughter of Nathaniel Bynum of
Richland District)

| Mobley, Dr. John C. | Catharine E. Caldwell (daughter of James E. Caldwell | 2B | 280-281 | 1860 |
|---|---|---|---|---|

of Fairfield District) (of Fairfield District)

| Mobley, Edward P. | Harriet W. Hill | G | 357-358 | 1831 |
|---|---|---|---|---|
| Mobley, Edward P. | Marion R. Mobley (daughter of John Mobley Sr. of Fairfield District) | 2A | 134-135 | 1857 |
| Moffett, George | Celina Louisa Kibler (daughter of John Adam Kibler of Newberry District) | X | 102-103 | 1853 |
| Moffett, James | Mariah B. Winfield | E | 449-452 | 1826 |

(marriage settlement __ __ 1826) (he of Cheraw) (she of
Marlborough District)

91

Implied South Carolina Marriages Volume IV 1787-1875

| MAN | WOMAN | VOL | PAGES | LIVED |
|---|---|---|---|---|
| Mondy, John W. | Susannah Thomas | K | 253 | 1838 |

(Monday) (marriage settlement 15 September 1838) (widow of Charles Thomas) (both of Edgefield District)

| Moneyhan, Thomas | Aroline Murphy | 2B | 140-142 | 1860 |
|---|---|---|---|---|

(marriage settlement 21 July 1860) (in Marion District)

| Montgomery, _____ | Mary Perry | C | 45 | 1817 |
|---|---|---|---|---|

(daughter of Lamuel Perry)

| Montgomery, Edward P. | Leonora Addie | 2C | 209-211 | 1866 |
|---|---|---|---|---|

(or Addie L.) Dargan (marriage settlement 15 November 1866) (in Darlington District)

| Montgomery, Green B. | Dorcas Ingram | Y | 422-423 | 1855 |
|---|---|---|---|---|

(marriage settlement 9 October 1855) (widow) (both of Chester District)

| Montgomery, Green B. Senior | Elizabeth Sibley | V | 236-237 | 1852 |
|---|---|---|---|---|

(marriage agreement 24 January 1852) (widow) (in Chester District)

| Montgomery, James A. | Virginia E. Lesly | Z | 423-424 | 1856 |
|---|---|---|---|---|

(in Abbeville District) (daughter of William Lesly)

| Montgomery, Thomas | Hannah Davis | Y | 577-579 | 1855 |
|---|---|---|---|---|

(marriage settlement 19 December 1855) (both of Newberry District)

| Moore, _____ | Esther Westfield Benson | W | 460-462 | 1853 |
|---|---|---|---|---|

(daughter of E. B. Benson of Anderson District)

| Moore, Dr. A. P. | Elizabeth M. Taylor | K | 546-552 | 1840 |
|---|---|---|---|---|

(daughter of Henry P. Taylor and granddaughter of Col. Thomas Taylor)

| Moore, Eli P. | Elizabeth Ann Neely | 2A | 438-441 | 1858 |
|---|---|---|---|---|

(marriage agreement 30 September 1858)

| Moore, Gabriel | Martha Smith | 2A | 637-638 | 1859 |
|---|---|---|---|---|

(daughter of Enoch H. Smith of Spartanburg District)

| Moore, James S. | Margaret M. Rees | W | 600-606 | 1853 |
|---|---|---|---|---|

(marriage settlement 7 June 1853) (granddaughter of William J. Rees) (both of Sumter District) [pages 601-603 missing]

| Moore, John Burchell | Annie Peyre DeVeaux | 2B | 496-502 | 1855 |
|---|---|---|---|---|

(married 3 July 1855) (reference to marriage settlement 3 July 1855) (daughter of Robert Marion DeVeaux and granddaughter of S. G. DeVeaux) (in Sumter District)

| Moore, John J. | _____ Richardson | 2B | 496-502 | 1855 |
|---|---|---|---|---|

(daughter of Governor James B. Richardson)

| Moore, Joseph | Lucy T. Butler | H | 485-487 | 1834 |
|---|---|---|---|---|

(marriage settlement 16 January 1834) (widow) (in Edgefield District)

Implied South Carolina Marriages Volume IV 1787-1875

| MAN | WOMAN | VOL | PAGES | LIVED |
|---|---|---|---|---|

Moore, Michael    Rebecca Lunsford    B    239-243    1803
  (marriage settlement 8 May 1803) (widow of Swanson
  Lunsford) (both of Columbia, Richland District) [See
  also pages 315-316]
Moorman, Robert    Mary L. Kenner    M    285-286    1842
  (daughter of Samuel E. Kenner of Newberry
  District)
Mordecai, M. C.    Isabella R. Lyons    H    521-522    1834
  (of Charleston) (daughter of Isaac Lyons of Columbia,
  Richland District)
Morgan, Abiah    Elizabeth Tomkins    I    485-486    1836
  (Biah) (marriage agreement 1 July 1836) (widow of
  Stephen Tomkins) (both of Edgefield District)
Morgan, Francis    Phoebe Bates    X    449-450    1854
  (daughter of William Bates)
Morgan, Joseph H.    Narcissa C. Jones    2A    716-719    1859
  (marriage settlement 3 November 1859) (both of
  Orangeburg District)
Morgan, William    Elizabeth Lott    D    167-168    1819
  (marriage agreement 10 June 1819) (both of Chester
  District)
Morris, Joseph    Catherine Harvey    U    274-276    1850
  (marriage settlement 26 December 1850) (widow) (in
  Edgefield District)
Morris, Jourdan    Milly Knighton    L    93-94    1840
  (of Fairfield District) (daughter of Moses Knighton of
  Fairfield District)
Morris, Samuel    Malinda Huskerson    2C    440-444    1868
  (married about 1868) (separation agreement 4 March 1868)
  (he was married before) (widow) (in Anderson District)
Morse, George    Mary Ann Nettles    X    303-306    1854
  (marriage settlement 18 January 1854) (in Darlington
  District)
Mosely, William    Polly Maddox    L    181-185    1840
Moses, Dr. Franklin C.    Alice Cohen    2C    33-35    1864
  J. (marriage settlement 1 December 1864) (daughter of
  John J. Cohen of Columbia, Richland District)
Moss, \_\_\_\_\_ (Moses)    Agness J. Tucker    W    415-417    1853
  (daughter of Bartley Tucker of Abbeville
  District)
Moss, Roland    Lacy Ann Richardson    2A    549-550    1859
  (of Fairfield District) (daughter of Thomas Richardson
  of Fairfield District)
Mostello, \_\_\_\_\_    Frances Charles    2B    538-539    1862
  (in Greenville District, S.C.) (she of Hall County,
  Georgia)

Implied South Carolina Marriages Volume IV 1787-1875

| MAN | WOMAN | VOL | PAGES | LIVED |
|---|---|---|---|---|

Motley, Ransom L.    Rebecca Morse         2A    778-779    1858
   (marriage agreement __ September 1858) (in Richland
   District)
Mouzon, Peter        Elizabeth White       G     419-420    1830
   (of Sumter District) [See also pages 417-419]
Moye, Augustus       Louisa Amanda         P     260-264    1845
   Washington        Muldrow
   (marriage settlement 18 December 1845) (in Darlington
   District)
Moye, George H.      Anna Maria Moye       M     178-180    1842
                     (daughter of George W. Moye) (George H.
   Moye of Darlington District) (she of Chesterfield
   District)
Moye, Thomas N.      Mary Catherine        T     221-223    1849
                     Wheeler
   (marriage settlement 22 May 1849) (in Sumter District)
Mudd, William        Sarah Covington       R     314-315    1847
   (marriage contract 5 January 1847) (both of Marlborough
   District)
Murdock, _____       Matilda Davenport     K     118-119    1838
Murdock, Dr. John    Emma Wallace          T     130-131    1849
   S.                (daughter of Andrew Wallace of Richland
   District, S.C.) (to Jacksonville, Florida) [See also
   pages 355-357]
Murphy, Dr. C. T.    Mariah Louisa Peake   2B    434-435    1861
                     (daughter of David D. Peake of Union
                     District)
Murphy, James        Elizabeth Mitchell    N     295-297    1844
   (in Edgefield District) (daughter of Daniel A. Mitchell)
Murphy, John B.      Eliza C. Byrd         I     178-179    1834
   (marriage contract 13 December 1834) (both of Richland
   District)
Murphy, John E.      Letty Lavender        O     310-311    1845
   (of Fairfield District)
Murphy, Oswald       Elizabeth Harris      2A    518-519    1858
   (of Washington County, Alabama) (daughter of David
   Harris of Edgefield District, S.C.)
Murphy, T. J. H.     Elna (Elnan) D.       2A    744-745    1859
                     Greer (daughter of Thomas S. Greer)
   (in Union District)
Murray, James        Frances Yarbrough     M     92-96      1842
Murray, James H.     Martha Glover         N     207-209    1843
   (marriage settlement 31 August 1843) (daughter of Jethro
   Glover of Edgefield District) (of Edgefield District)
Murray, John         Mary Spann            S     428-431    1848
   (marriage settlement 13 December 1848) (daughter of Col.
   James G. Spann) (both of Sumter District)

Implied South Carolina Marriages Volume IV 1787-1875

| MAN | WOMAN | VOL | PAGES | LIVED |
|---|---|---|---|---|
| Murray, Patrick T. | Ellen McKenna | 2B | 667-670 | 1863 |

(marriage settlement 16 July 1863) (widow) (she of Lancaster)

Murray, Samuel J.  Sarah Lang Robinson  K  338-340  1839
 (of Sumter District) (daughter of John Robinson of Charleston)
Murrell, James  Izett Long  2A  591-592  1859
 (of Edgefield District)
Muse, George W.  Elizabeth Edgerton  G  369-370  1831
 (marriage settlement 2 May 1831) (widow of Otis Edgerton) (both of Barnwell District)
Myers, _____  Ann Watson  S  279-280  1848
 (in Edgefield District)
Myers, _____  Ann C. Watson  U  66-67  1850
 (in Edgefield District)
Myers, George  Mary Benson  2B  164-166  1860
Mathew (of Marion District) (daughter of Willis Benson of Greenville District) (she died 12 August 1860)

(N)

Nance, Frederick  Tersea Ruff  G  371-372  1831
 (marriage settlement 26 March 1831) (widow) (of Newberry District)
Nance, Frederick A.  Susan A. Scurry  2A  54-56  1857
 (marriage settlement 2 July 1857) (in Newberry District)
Nance, Frederick A.  Sophia Wells  N  275-276  1843
 (daughter of David Wells) [See also Volume O, pages 204-205]
Nance, R. Drayton  Sally M. Campbell  Z  640-641  1857
 (in Laurens District) (daughter of Dr. Robert E. Campbell)
Napier, Robert  Caroline M. Killen  2B  658-659  1863
 (marriage settlement 26 June 1863) (widow of James F. Killen of Darlington District) (Napier of Marion District)
Nash, John  Mary Bolt  L  143-144  1840
 (marriage settlement 4 July 1840) (in Laurens District)
Nathans, _____  Matilda Nettles  E  535  1826
 (daughter of Samuel M. Nettles of Richland District)
Neal, John  Sarah Eaves  C  324-325  1811
 (marriage settlement 21 August 1811) (widow) (both if Chester District) [See also pages 438-439]

Implied South Carolina Marriages Volume IV 1787-1875

| MAN | WOMAN | VOL | PAGES | LIVED |
|---|---|---|---|---|
| Neal, W. M. | M. A. Lynam | 2A | 183-186 | 1857 |

(marriage settlement 22 December 1857) (he of Richland District) (she of Sumter District)

| | | | | |
|---|---|---|---|---|
| Neely, Jackson | Jane McAneer | S | 419-420 | 1848 |

(marriage settlement 8 September 1848)

| | | | | |
|---|---|---|---|---|
| Nelson, _____ | Emma C. Henry | 2B | 241-242 | 1860 |
| Nelson, _____ | Sarah Perry | C | 45 | 1817 |

(daughter of Lamuel Perry)

| | | | | |
|---|---|---|---|---|
| Nelson, _____ | Sarah Yarbrough | M | 92-96 | 1842 |
| Nelson, James M. | Sarah Robinson | K | 338-340 | 1839 |

Murray (daughter of Samuel J. Murray of Sumter District) (of Sumter District)

| | | | | |
|---|---|---|---|---|
| Nelson, Nathan O. | Susan (Susannah) Turner | X | 108-110 | 1853 |

(marriage settlement 20 October 1853) (widow) (both of Barnwell District)

| | | | | |
|---|---|---|---|---|
| Nettles, _____ | Hannah M. Gee | 2B | 358-361 | 1861 |

["Hannah M. Gee (now Hannah M. Nettles)"]

| | | | | |
|---|---|---|---|---|
| Nettles, J. Edward | Gertrude L. Sims | 2B | 342-345 | 1861 |

(marriage settlement 7 February 1861) (of Darlington District)

| | | | | |
|---|---|---|---|---|
| Nettles, John | Elizabeth J. Miller | L | 364-365 | 1840 |

(in Sumter District) (daughter of John B. Miller) (she died 24 May 1840)

| | | | | |
|---|---|---|---|---|
| Nettles, Jonadab | Rachel Goodwyn | H | 152-153 | 1831 |

(marriage settlement 17 October 1831) (widow)

| | | | | |
|---|---|---|---|---|
| Nettles, Joseph B. | Hannah M. Gee | H | 197-200 | 1832 |

(marriage settlement 5 October 1832) (widow of Edmund Gee) (both of Darlington District)

| | | | | |
|---|---|---|---|---|
| Nettles, Joseph B. | Hannah M. Gee | W | 529-531 | 1832 |

(reference to marriage settlement 5 October 1832) (in Darlington District)

| | | | | |
|---|---|---|---|---|
| Nettles, Joseph B. | Hannah M. Gee | Z | 773-776 | 1857 |

(of Darlington District)

| | | | | |
|---|---|---|---|---|
| Neuffer, Charles F. | Ann Caroline Geiger | N | 33-35 | 1843 |

(marriage settlement 25 January 1843)

| | | | | |
|---|---|---|---|---|
| Nevitt, Cornelius | Elisah (Elisha) Jenkins | W | 102 | 1852 |

(marriage agreement 5 August 1852) (in Fairfield District)

| | | | | |
|---|---|---|---|---|
| New, Martin Van Buren | Maria Blackburn | 2B | 671-673 | 1863 |

(marriage settlement 7 July 1863) (widow) (he of Barnwell District) (she of Edgefield District)

| | | | | |
|---|---|---|---|---|
| Newman, Wade W. | Susan McCoy | N | 170-171 | 1843 |

(marriage settlement 4 June 1843)

Implied South Carolina Marriages Volume IV 1787-1875

| MAN | WOMAN | VOL | PAGES | LIVED |
|---|---|---|---|---|

Newton, Willis　　Mary C. Dickson　　2B　515-517　1862
　　(marriage settlement 8 February 1862) (widow) (in
　　Anderson District)
Nicholson, Shemuel　Susan Adams　　X　208-211　1853
　W.　　　　　　　(daughter of James F. Adams of Edgefield
　　　　　　　　　District)
Nisbett, Douglass　Sarah Turner　　2B　585-586　1863
　　(of Charleston) (daughter of Franklin Turner of
　　Chesterfield District)
Noble, William A.　Frances E. Brady　Z　278-280　1856
　　(of Abbeville District) (daughter of Robert Brady of
　　Abbeville District)
Norman, Jesse　　Mary O. Dillard　　U　132-134　1850
　　(marriage contract 21 July 1850) (he was married before)
　　(widow of John A. Dillard) (both of Union District)
Norment, Dr.　　Hannah Louisa　　Z　772-776　1857
　Benjamin C.　　Nettles
　　(marriage settlement 7 May 1857) (he of Virginia) (she
　　of Darlington District, S.C.) [See also Volume 2A, page
　　590]
Norris, Alexander　Eliza Ann Merriman　Z　338-339　1855
　　(daughter of John Merriman Sr. of
　　Chesterfield District)
Norris, J. W.　　Anna L. Lesly　　Z　423-424　1856
　　(in Abbeville District) (daughter of William Lesly)
Norwood, James　　Ellenor Edward　　R　450-451　1847
　　　　　　　　　Lacoste (daughter of Stephen Lacoste of
　　　　　　　　　Sumter District)
Nott, Rufus A.　　Sally W. Whitaker　K　527-530　1840
　　(marriage settlement 1 January 1840)
Nunnery, Benjamin　Ann Wilson　　　N　7-8　　1843
　T.　(marriage settlement 18 January 1843) (in Sumter
　　District)

(O)

O'Conner, Bernard　Harriet P. Baker　2A　477-479　1858
　　(marriage settlement 27 December 1858) (both of
　　Abbeville District) [See also pages 606-608]
Odom, Samuel J.　　Hester C. Humphries　2A　547-549　1859
　　(marriage settlement 17 January 1859) (daughter of
　　Thomas Humphries) (Odom formerly of Union District, but
　　now of Darlington District)

Implied South Carolina Marriages Volume IV 1787-1875

| MAN | WOMAN | VOL | PAGES | LIVED |
|---|---|---|---|---|
| Oliver, Charles | Martha Green | C | 155-156 | 1814 |

(marriage settlement 29 September 1814) (of Richland District)

| Oliver, Peter Senr. | Ann B. Spigner | H | 225-229 | 1832 |
|---|---|---|---|---|

(marriage settlement 27 October 1832) (both of Orangeburgh District)

| Oliver, Robert C. | Frances Mary Thompson | 2C | 372-374 | 1860 |
|---|---|---|---|---|

(reference to marriage settlement 4 January 1860) (in Clarendon District)

| Oliver, Samuel | Mary Howell | C | 55 | 1813 |
|---|---|---|---|---|

(daughter of Matthew Howell of Richland District) (Oliver of Richland District)

| Oliver, William | Dorcas Ann Gassaway | Y | 454-457 | 1855 |
|---|---|---|---|---|

(marriage settlement 26 September 1855) (daughter of Thos. Gassaway) (both of Pickens District)

| O'Neale, Godfrey | Rebecca Francis Martin | S | 350-351 | 1848 |
|---|---|---|---|---|

(daughter of Robert Martin of Fairfield District) (of Fairfield District)

| OQuin, Daniel Junior | Sarah Adams | D | 105 | 1817 |
|---|---|---|---|---|

[daughter of Ephram (Ephraim) Adams of Sumter District] [See also page 164]

| Orr, _____ | Mary F. Robinson | M | 383-386 | 1843 |
|---|---|---|---|---|

(in Chester District) (daughter of James Robinson)

| Osborn, John S. | Jane G. _____ | P | 281-282 | 1846 |
|---|---|---|---|---|

(granddaughter of Charles Allen of Laurens District)

| Osteen, Thomas H. | Dolly Weeks | W | 496-499 | 1853 |
|---|---|---|---|---|

(marriage settlement 5 April 1853) (daughter of Chosel Weeks) (in Sumter District)

| Owens, _____ | Eliza Heath | P | 141-145 | 1845 |
|---|---|---|---|---|
| Owens, Doctr. Samuel H. | Alice Wyche Heath | K | 21-22 | 1838 |

(daughter of Thomas Heath of Richland District) [Must also see pages 271-272]

| Owens, George M. | Kesiah Toole | 2B | 276-277 | 1861 |
|---|---|---|---|---|

(daughter of Stephen Toole of Barnwell District)

| Owens, James W. | Sarah Ann Blackwell | W | 189-191 | 1852 |
|---|---|---|---|---|

(marriage settlement 6 December 1852) (widow) (both of Darlington District)

| Owens, James W. | Lucretia Ham | M | 187-189 | 1842 |
|---|---|---|---|---|

(marriage settlement 25 March 1842) (in Darlington District)

| Owens, Jesse T. | Sallie S. Woodward | X | 631-632 | 1854 |
|---|---|---|---|---|

(of Fairfield District) (daughter of Osmund Woodward of Fairfield District)

Implied South Carolina Marriages Volume IV 1787-1875

| MAN | WOMAN | VOL | PAGES | LIVED |
|---|---|---|---|---|

Owens, Mitchell L. Mary Ann Lemon V 227-228 1850
(of Fairfield District) (daughter of James Lemon of
Fairfield District)
Owens, Solomon Rachael Brown K 411-413 1839
(marriage contract 14 May 1839) (in Marion District)
Owens, William Eliz Furginson I 224-226 1835
(marriage settlement 5 February 1835) (widow of William
Furginson) (both of Barnwell District)
Owings, Richard M. Mary E. Hunter X 479-481 1853
(marriage settlement 22 December 1853) (in Edgefield
District)
Owings, William Malinda Thomas W 454-455 1853
(of Laurens District) (daughter of Reuben Thomas of
Laurens District)

(P)

Pace, William Elizabeth Susan 2A 785-788 1859
Bradford (daughter of William W. Bradford
of Sumter District)
Padget, John _____ Maddox L 181-185 1840
Padget, Peter Melinda Maddox L 181-185 1840
Paine, Nathaniel Elizabeth Mary M 21-24 1841
Russell Jumelle
(marriage settlement 4 November 1841) (daughter of Peter
L. Jumelle) (Paine of Charleston) (she of Camden) [Must
also see pages 1-4]
Painter, Jacob Zelime _____ 2A 178-179 1857
(in Greenville District) (granddaughter of Archibald
Lester)
Palmer, _____ Rebecca Foster P 28-29 1845
[daughter of Jariahr (Josiah?) Foster of
Union District]
Palmer, Benjamin M. Mary A. McConnell L 417-418 1841
Jr. (marriage contract 6 October 1841) (granddaughter of
Andrew Waltherer)
Parham, Casper Pamela Hardy K 15 1837
(daughter of William Hardy of Edgefield
District)
Parham, John Margaret _____ D 438-439 1822
(Purham) (bill for alimony) (settlement 4 May 1822) (in
Newberry District)
Park, Earnest G. Henrietta Hay 2C 186-187 1866
(of Union District, S.C.) (daughter of James Hay of
Scotland)

99

## Implied South Carolina Marriages Volume IV 1787-1875

| MAN | WOMAN | VOL | PAGES | LIVED |
|---|---|---|---|---|

Parker, William    Amelia A. Nott    R    138-139    1846
   McKenzie (marriage settlement 26 November 1846)
Parkinson, John    Sarah Crossle    A    286-289    1796
   (Crossbe)
   (marriage settlement 17 November 1796) (widow of George Crossle) (both of Winton County)
Parler, Samuel    Sophia Hare    D    237-239    1821
   (marriage agreement 20 March 1821) (daughter of Gunrod Hare) (both of St. Matthew's Parish)
Parr, _____    Mary Corben    I    413    1836
   (she of Columbia)
Parr, Richard    Eliza Faucett    2C    54-56    1865
   (marriage settlement 2 September 1865) (widow of Samuel Faucett) (both of Union District)
Parsons, Samuel    Elizabeth M.    G    226-227    1830
   Moncrieff (widow of Richard Moncrieff, her first husband) (in Orangeburgh District)
Pate, Levi    Gatsey Robinson    2C    356-358    1865
   (married 10 January 1865) (reference to marriage contract 10 January 1865) (both of Kershaw District)
Paterson, _____    Elizabeth Cowie    D    109-114    1818
   (Courie) (widow of Archibald Cowie of County of Stirling, Scotland)
Patterson, James    Emma L. Addison    2A    163-165    1857
   (marriage settlement 15 December 1857) (widow of Joseph Addison) (Patterson of Barnwell District) (she of Barnwell and Edgefield Districts)
Patterson, James    Nancy Smith    F    120-121    1827
   (his first marriage) (daughter of Robert Smith) (Patterson of Abbeville District)
Patton, John    Mary H. Bell    L    355-357    1841
   (marriage settlement 26 June 1841) (he was married before) (he of Tennessee) (she of S.C.)
Paul, William P.    Agnes Elvira _____    L    132-135    1840
   (separation agreement 16 September 1840)
Paulding, _____    Sarah Boulware    W    197-198    1852
   (daughter of Thomas Boulware)
Peach, Duren    Cynthia Jane Gaskins    W    528-529    1853
   (Gaskin) (daughter of Daniel Gaskins of Kershaw District) (of Kershaw District)
Pearce, Elijah L.    Charlotte C. Douglas    2C    93-96    1866
   (marriage settlement 17 January 1866) (in Marlborough District)
Pearson, George B.    _____ Alston    W    74-81    1845
   Sr (of Fairfield District) (daughter of James Alston of Fairfield District)

Implied South Carolina Marriages Volume IV 1787-1875

| MAN | WOMAN | VOL | PAGES | LIVED |
|---|---|---|---|---|
| Pearson, John (of Fairfield District) | Sarah Hill | G | 357-358 | 1831 |
| Pearson, John H. (of Richland District) | Ellen Wallace (daughter of Andrew Wallace of Richland District) | U | 269-271 | 1851 |
| Pelot, Charles M. [See also Volume H, pages 175-177] | Margaret Ann Ford | D | 69-70 | 1818 |
| Pendergrass, David (marriage settlement 16 June 1858) (both of Chester District) | Rebecca Worthy | 2A | 385-386 | 1858 |
| Penn, _____ | Louisiana J. Mims | S | 302-304 | 1848 |
| Perkins, Benjamin (marriage settlement 24 November 1841) (daughter of Peter L. Jumelle) (both of Camden) | Priscilla B. Jumelle | M | 1-4 | 1841 |
| Perritt, Perry Bryant | Frances America Rearden (daughter of Joseph Rearden) | W | 625-629 | 1853 |
| Perry, _____ | Mary Scott | N | 310 | 1844 |
| Perry, Lamuel (marriage contract 24 February 1817) | Rachel Wells | D | 187 | 1817 |
| Pester, John (separation 24 June 1814) (bill for alimony) (daughter of George Ruff) (of Newberry District) | Sarah Ruff | C | 141-143 | 1814 |
| Peterson, David | Polly Turner | F | 478 | 1829 |
| Peterson, James E. (marriage settlement 18 January 1853) (both of Newberry District) | Nancy Dalrymple | Z | 654-656 | 1853 |
| Pettigrew, William | Louisa Gibert | D | 130-133 | 1819 |
| Peurifoy, Tilghman D. (granddaughter of Col. Zachariah S. Brooks of Edgefield District, who died April 1848) (in Edgefield District) | Louisa A. Bird | T | 315-324 | 1848 |
| Pevy, John (in Sumter District) (daughter of William Deas) | Rosey Deas | L | 432 | 1841 |
| Peyton, John F. (marriage settlement 29 October 1834) (of Barnwell District) | Rebecca F. Wood | I | 110-111 | 1834 |
| Peyton, John F. (reference to marriage settlement 9 October 1834) | Rebecca F. Wood | K | 215-216 | 1838 |
| Philips, J. C. (marriage settlement 24 January 1854) (in York District) | Ann E. Bigger | X | 327-331 | 1854 |
| Phillips, J. C. (reference to marriage agreement 24 January 1854) (in York District) | Ann E. Bigger | Z | 445-447 | 1854 |
| Phillips, William T. | Mary Ables (daughter of John J. Ables of Lexington District) (of Orangeburgh District) | T | 255-256 | 1849 |

Implied South Carolina Marriages Volume IV 1787-1875

| MAN | WOMAN | VOL | PAGES | LIVED |
|---|---|---|---|---|

Pickens, Andrew C.   Mary Jones Boone      U    321-324    1850
   (marriage settlement 9 December 1850) (daughter of
   Thomas Boone who died 8 October 1830) (both of Pendleton
   District)
Pickens, Ezekiel      Eliza Barksdale       H    153-155    1832
   (daughter of George Barksdale)
Pickens, Thomas T.    Kezia Ann Miles       G    187-191    1830
   (marriage settlement 19 April 1830) (daughter of
   Jeremiah Miles of St. Paul's Parish, Colleton County)
   (Pickens of Pendleton District) [See also Volume H,
   pages 321-322, 381-383]
Pickett, Charles      Frances _____         E    266-267    1824
   (granddaughter of William Reynolds of
   Lincoln County, Georgia)
Pickett, Charles      Francis Griffin       E    45-46      1821
   (in Fairfield District)
Pickett, Reuben       Mary Jane Pegues      K    236-238    1838
Pickring, Samuel      Elizabeth Nelson      B    365-367    1804
   (Pickren) (marriage settlement 16 May 1804) (of Richland
   District)
Pierce, _____         Francis A. Nystrom    V    426-431    1852
                      ["Mrs. Francis A. Pierce (late Francis A.
                      Nystrom)"]
Pierce, _____         Frances A. Nythorn    W    37-41      1852
                      ["Mrs. Frances A. Nythorn (now Frances A.
                      Pierce)"] [See also pages 247-250]
Pinchback, David      Sarah Kennedy         Z    381-385    1856
   (marriage settlement 8 September 1856) (widow of Richard
   E. Kennedy) (both of Chester District)
Pinckney, Henry L.    Mary Ann _____        T    69-71      1849
   Jr. (reference to marriage settlement - no date given)
Pitts, _____          Amanda A. Diggs       K    28-29      1837
Pitts, James M.       Mary A. Mellett       M    196-197    1842
   (marriage settlement 3 May 1842) (daughter of Peter
   Mellett)
Pitts, Thomas         Irena Holston         N    186-187    1843
   (of Edgefield District)
Player, _____         Margaret Norton       O    180-183    1844
                      (widow of Allen Norton)
Player, Dr. William   Adela E. Dargan       2A   31-33      1857
   A. (in Darlington District) (daughter of Geo. W. Dargan)
Player, Joshua        Charlotte Elizabeth   I    150-173    1835
                      Thompson (Thomson)
   (reference to marriage settlement - no date given) (in
   Fairfield District)
Plowden, _____        Rachel Montgomery     M    270-272    1842
   (daughter of Samuel Montgomery)

Implied South Carolina Marriages Volume IV 1787-1875

| MAN | WOMAN | VOL | PAGES | LIVED |
|---|---|---|---|---|
| Plunkett, ____ | Cynthia Courtney | 2B | 524-525 | 1861 |

(daughter of Martin Courtney of Barnwell District)
Poellnitz, Edwin H.  Sallie E. Lyles  2A  754-755  1860
 (daughter of Thomas M. Lyles of Fairfield District)
Poellwitz, B. Bruno  Mary E. M. Rogers  2A  487-490  1858
 (marriage settlement 25 November 1858) (he of Marengo County, Alabama) (she of Darlington District, S.C.)
Poindexter, ____  Frances Lightfoot  C  111-117  1811
 (of Abbeville District)
Poole, H. Coleman  Eliza Dawkins  V  597-601  1852
 (of Union District) (Dankins) (widow of Col. Benjamin F. Dawkins) [See also Volume W, pages 128-132]
Poole, James Giles  Kezia J. Brockman  2C  175-177  1866
 (marriage settlement 10 April 1866) (widow) (both of Spartanburg District)
Poole, Martin P.  Elizabeth Martindale  H  444-445  1833
Pope, ____  Ellen M. Agnew  2A  580-581  1856
Porcher, Augustus H.  Eliza Marion DuBose  V  498-500  1852
 (daughter of Theodore S. DuBose)
Porcher, Octavius T.  Georgie M. Deveaux  W  509-511  1853
 (daughter of Stephen G. Deveaux of Charleston District)
Porter, ____  Emily Cooper  2A  231-233  1858
Porter, ____  Nancy A. Harris  G  36-37  1829
 (daughter of John Harris of Abbeville District)
Porter, Abner A.  Sarah E. Black  2B  799-801  1864
 (marriage agreement 12 March 1864) (widow of James A. Black) (Porter of Richland District) (she of York District)
Porter, Marion S.  Sarah A. Fant  2B  66-67  1860
 (daughter of David J. Fant of Union District)
Porter, Rev R. K.  Jane Johnston  W  557-562  1853
 (Johnson) (daughter of Samuel Johnston of Winnsborough, Fairfield District, who died 13 May 1853]
Postell, Wm G.  Mary Y. McCaslan  2B  441-442  1861
 (of Abbeville District) (daughter of William McCaslan of Abbeville District)
Powe, James H.  Josephine E. Robbins  2B  459-466  1862
 (marriage settlement 15 March 1862) (both of Chesterfield District)
Powel, Robert (Powell)  Matilda Barksdale  P  279-281  1846
 (daughter of Higgerson Barksdale of Laurens District)

Implied South Carolina Marriages Volume IV 1787-1875

| MAN | WOMAN | VOL | PAGES | LIVED |
|---|---|---|---|---|
| Powell, Richard T. | Margaret G. Whitaker | S | 338-342 | 1848 |

(postnuptial settlement 31 August 1848) (daughter of William Whitaker) (both of Cheraw)

| Powell, Sanford | Martha P. _____ | T | 300-303 | 1849 |
|---|---|---|---|---|

(separation agreement 31 July 1849) (of Laurens District)

| Powers, Nicholas | Catharine Fox | E | 200-201 | 1824 |
|---|---|---|---|---|

(marriage settlement 3 June 1824)

| Prator, Lerkin C. | Emiline Rhoden | 2A | 337-338 | 1858 |
|---|---|---|---|---|

(in Edgefield District) (daughter of Thomas Rhoden)

| Pratt, William | Louisa Robertson | T | 57-66 | 1848 |
|---|---|---|---|---|

(daughter of Andrew Robertson of Abbeville District)

| Prester, John | Sarah Sligh | H | 79-80 | 1832 |
|---|---|---|---|---|

(in Newberry District)

| Pressley, R. A. | Palmyra A. Hutchison | 2B | 754-755 | 1863 |
|---|---|---|---|---|

(both of Abbeville District) (daughter of Robert Hutchison of Abbeville District)

| Prewit, Andrew | Mary (Polly) D. Hawthorn | P | 87-91 | 1845 |
|---|---|---|---|---|
| Price, _____ | Hephzibah McCreless | F | 401 | 1829 |

(daughter of John McCreless of Richland District)

| Price, John | Martha Morgan | 2A | 712-713 | 1859 |
|---|---|---|---|---|

(of Barnwell District)

| Price, Joseph | Polly Jennings | I | 566-567 | 1837 |
|---|---|---|---|---|

(daughter of Joseph Jennings of Edgefield)

| Price, William | _____ Deason | Z | 693-694 | 1857 |
|---|---|---|---|---|

(of Edgefield District) (daughter of John Deason Sr. of Edgefield District)

| Pride, Dr. J. S. | Phoebe A. McLure | 2B | 74-77 | 1860 |
|---|---|---|---|---|

(marriage settlement 28 February 1860) (daughter of Thomas McLure) (both of Chester District)

| Prince, Clement L. | Ann E. Ellerbe | G | 112-113 | 1830 |
|---|---|---|---|---|

(marriage agreement 10 March 1830) (widow of William F. Ellerbe) (both of Chesterfield District)

| Pringle, _____ | Rebecca Frances Witherspoon (widow) | Z | 35-38 | 1856 |
|---|---|---|---|---|
| Prior, _____ | Elizabeth Hartly | B | 637-638 | 1810 |

(widow of Henry Hartly) (she of Lexington District)

| Prior, Richard D. | Mary Anna Nail | 2B | 715-716 | 1863 |
|---|---|---|---|---|

(to be married 17 December 1863) (marriage settlement 17 December 1863) (in Edgefield District)

| Proctor, _____ | Sarah Miles | 2B | 506-507 | 1862 |
|---|---|---|---|---|

Implied South Carolina Marriages Volume IV 1787-1875

| MAN | WOMAN | VOL | PAGES | LIVED |
|---|---|---|---|---|
| Proffitt, John R. | Mary Calhoun | 2B | 150 | 1860 |

(daughter of Nathan Calhoun of Abbeville District)

Profitt, John R.   Mary Calhoun   2A   443-444   1858
  (in Abbeville District) (daughter of Nathan Calhoun)
Pruit, Albert   Nancy Adams   X   470-472   1852
  (marriage settlement 8 May 1852) (widow of George Adams of Newberry District) (of Newberry District)
Pruit. See Prewit
Purlaskey, Thomas   Mary Copeland   X   351-352   1854
  (Pulaski) (of Barnwell District)
Purnall, Doctr.   Elizabeth Lark   B   487-488   1808
  Peter   (widow of John Lark)
  (of Barnwell District)
Pyles, Abner   Francis G. Stone   E   14-15   1822
  (marriage contract 10 May 1822) (widow) (both of Laurens District)
Pyles, S. M.   Nancy A. Rasor   2B   190-191   1860
  (of Cobb County, Georgia) (daughter of Ezekiel Rasor of Abbeville District, S.C.)

(Q)

Quarls, William G.   Elizabeth Sullivan   K   508-510   1839
  (marriage settlement 29 November 1839) (daughter of John Sullivan)
Quarls, William G.   Lucy Sullivan   K   508-510   1836
  (daughter of John Sullivan)
Quattlebum, _____   Sarah Johnston   X   22-27   1853
  (daughter of John K. Johnston of Edgefield District)
Quinn, John F.   Rose B. Wheeler   2A   658-659   1859
  (marriage contract 28 June 1859) (in Marion District)

(R)

Rabb, John Glazier   Nancy K. Watt   2C   299-300   1867
  (in Fairfield District)
Rabe, William   Pamela _____   P   146-148   1845
  (separated) (of Laurens District)

105

Implied South Carolina Marriages Volume IV 1787-1875

| MAN | WOMAN | VOL | PAGES | LIVED |
|---|---|---|---|---|
| Race, Ara | Sarah St. Johns Keeler | 2B | 553-556 | 1862 |

(marriage settlement 8 December 1862) (daughter of Samuel Keeler) (in Chesterfield District)

| | | | | |
|---|---|---|---|---|
| Ragin, Charles C. | Julia E. King | V | 580-582 | 1852 |

(her first marriage) (daughter of John G. King of Sumter District)

| | | | | |
|---|---|---|---|---|
| Ragin, John J. | Julia E. Ragin | V | 580-582 | 1852 |

(widow of Charles C. Ragin)

| | | | | |
|---|---|---|---|---|
| Ragsdale, _____ | Elizabeth Wall | R | 370-371 | 1847 |

(daughter of Charles Wall of Chester District)

| | | | | |
|---|---|---|---|---|
| Raiford, John D. | Sarah Watson | I | 524 | 1837 |

(in Edgefield District) (daughter of Elijah Watson Senr. of Edgefield District)

| | | | | |
|---|---|---|---|---|
| Raines, Littleton | Mary Cason | Y | 225-226 | 1855 |
| Rainsford, James | Esther Rainsford | H | 461-463 | 1833 |

(marriage settlement 26 October 1833) (in Edgefield District)

| | | | | |
|---|---|---|---|---|
| Ramsey, Josiah T. | Unity Jane Scott | 2A | 761-762 | 1860 |

(daughter of John Scott of Richland District)

| | | | | |
|---|---|---|---|---|
| Randall, Hollyman | Emily Haney | T | 42-44 | 1849 |

(daughter of Orashea Haney of Edgefield District)

| | | | | |
|---|---|---|---|---|
| Randall, Joseph | Caroline Walker | X | 493-494 | 1851 |
| Rantin, Alexander | Emmeline S. Dukes | U | 76-79 | 1850 |

(marriage settlement 4 April 1850) (widow of James T. Dukes)

| | | | | |
|---|---|---|---|---|
| Rawlinson, Richard | Sarah Jackson | A | 512 | 1801 |

(of Richland District)

| | | | | |
|---|---|---|---|---|
| Ray, _____ | Matilda Norman | U | 132-134 | 1850 |
| Ray, D. W. | Sally F. Weston | V | 103-105 | 1850 |

(marriage settlement 14 November 1850) (daughter of William Weston) (she of Richland District)

| | | | | |
|---|---|---|---|---|
| Reed, George J. | Rebecca H. Hartzog | O | 251-252 | 1844 |

(marriage settlement 23 October 1844) (widow of George F. Hartzog) (of Barnwell District)

| | | | | |
|---|---|---|---|---|
| Reed, James H. | Mary Weathersbe | Y | 378-379 | 1855 |

(of Barnwell District) (daughter of John Weathersbe of Barnwell District)

| | | | | |
|---|---|---|---|---|
| Reed, James W. | Ann R. Tyler | 2C | 450-451 | 1851 |
| Reed, Joseph | Nancy James | 2B | 222-224 | 1859 |

(daughter of Joseph James of Greenville District)

Implied South Carolina Marriages Volume IV 1787-1875

| MAN | WOMAN | VOL | PAGES | LIVED |
|---|---|---|---|---|

Reed, Samuel        Jane E. Still        2C     451-453      1868
    (marriage settlement 17 February 1868) (both of Barnwell
    District)
Reed, William A.    Elizabeth F. Cannon  2A     80-81        1857
    (daughter of David Cannon of Newberry
    District)
Reese, Jesse D.     Lucy Ellen McKinnon  2A     309-310      1858
    (marriage settlement 24 March 1858) (he of Richland
    District) (she of Marlborough District)
Reese, Thomas B.    Elizabeth T. Waldrum 2C     302-304      1866
    (marriage settlement 10 December 1866) (widow of William
    Waldrum) (both of Edgefield District)
Reid, Dr Jno S.     Anna E. Norris       G      239-240      1830
    (in Abbeville District)
Reid, Henry         Charlotte McDowell   O      335-337      1844
    (marriage settlement 21 December 1844) (in Abbeville
    District)
Reid, John          Harriet Hart         D      376-379      1821
    (marriage settlement 13 November 1821) (he of Columbia)
    (she of Orangeburgh District)
Rembert, Edward J.  Esther G. Gaillard   2A     584-586      1859
    (daughter of James Gaillard of Walnut
    Grove, St. John's Berkley Parish)
Reynolds, Larkin    Agnes W. Griffin     U      43-45        1850
    (marriage settlement 11 March 1850) (in Abbeville
    District)
Reynolds, Marcus    Julia E. Rees        X      274-276      1853
Reynolds, Marcus    Julia V. Rees        S      282-286      1848
    (marriage settlement 15 June 1848) (daughter of F. W.
    Rees) (both of Sumter District)
Rhame, Abel D.      Dorcas M. Boyd       N      112-113      1842
    (daughter of John Boyd of Sumter
    District)
Rhoderwits, John    Barbara Voss         D      339-341      1820
    (Rodewits) (marriage contract 27 April 1820) (of East
    Granby) [Must also see Volume E, pages 53-54]
Rhodes, James S.    Lydia G. Whittemore  2B     750-753      1863
    (marriage settlement 24 December 1863) (daughter of
    Cephas Whittemore of Orangeburg) (Rhodes of Charleston)
Rice, _____       Angaline Willis      X      22-27        1853
    (in Barnwell District)
Rice, David B.      Eliza Ann Beaty      I      466-468      1836
    (daughter of Jonathan Beaty)
Rich, Charles       Mary Charlotte       T      528-530      1849
    Augustus        Brumby
    (marriage settlement 20 December 1849) (both of Sumter
    District)

Implied South Carolina Marriages Volume IV 1787-1875

| MAN | WOMAN | VOL | PAGES | LIVED |
|---|---|---|---|---|

Rich, Dr. John S.   Lydia B. Richardson   T   415-416   1849
  (marriage settlement 1 November 1849) (in Sumter
  District)
Richardson, _____  _____ Eveleigh   F   338-339   1827
  (daughter of Thomas Eveleigh) [See also
  Volume G, pages 45-46]
Richardson, Charles Mary Ann _____   2A   612-614   1859
  M. (postnuptial settlement 30 April 1859) (in Clarendon
  District)
Richardson, James   Martha Redman   2B   491   1848
  M. (did not marry; had child only) (in Edgefield
  District)
Richardson, John S. Agness D. McDowell   U   302-304   1850
  (marriage settlement 10 December 1850) (daughter of
  Davidson McDowell) (both of Sumter District)
Richardson, John S. Agnes D. McDowell   Y   151-152   1855
  Jr. (in Sumter District)
Richardson, John T. Juliana Augusta   F   338-339   1827
              Richardson
  (marriage settlement 16 October 1827) (in Sumter
  District) [See also pages 397-399]
Richardson, Joseph  Caroline E. Stark   L   261-263   1840
  J. (marriage settlement 12 December 1840) (daughter of
  Eli Stark) (in Sumter District)
Richardson, William Sarah A. Mayrant   U   200-202   1843
  E. (reference to marriage settlement 23 March 1843) (in
  Sumter District)
Richardson, William Sarah Ann Mayrant   O   114-116   1843
  E. (marriage settlement 23 March 1843) (daughter of
  William Mayrant of Sumter District) (in Georgetown
  District)
Richardson, William Harriet Eveleigh   A   335-338   1798
  Guignard       [her first name torn]
  (marriage settlement 24 February 1798)
Richardson, William Dorothy A.   G   43-46   1829
  H. B.         Richardson
  (marriage settlement 4 November 1829) (daughter of
  Charles Richardson of Sumter District) (in Sumter
  District) [See also pages 161-170]
Richbourg, Isaac  _____ Gerald   R   383-385   1844
  (in Sumter District) [See also pages 386-388, 408-409]
Richbourg, James C. Eliza Bowman   2A   249-250   1857
              (daughter of John Bowman)
Richey, Isaac   Elizabeth Jane Razor Z   493-495   1857
Richey. See Ritchie
Richie, Wm H.   Matilda V. Lomax   2B   448-449   1846
  (in Abbeville District) (widow of Jas Lomax)

Implied South Carolina Marriages Volume IV 1787-1875

| MAN | WOMAN | VOL | PAGES | LIVED |
|---|---|---|---|---|

Richter, Edwin    Elizabeth Humphries  Y   596-598   1855
   (marriage settlement 23 October 1855) (both of Union
   District)
Ricks, John       Penelope Moore       K   57-58     1838
   (marriage settlement 11 January 1838) (widow of Moses
   Moore) (both of Sumter District)
Riddle, John G.   Susannah Hill        M   180-181   1842
   (marriage settlement 5 May 1842) (widow of John Hill)
   (both of Edgefield District)
Ridgway, John W.  Agness L. Richbourg  N   61-62     1843
   (marriage settlement 31 January 1843) (in Sumter
   District)
Ridgway, Robert   Harriett Richbourg   W   441-443   1853
   (marriage settlement 12 January 1853) (daughter of Eli
   Richbourg)
Riley, William G. E. M. Bryan          N   96-97     1843
   (marriage settlement 13 April 1843) (both of Barnwell
   District)
Rinehart, John    Sally Kinard         H   222-225   1832
Riser, William    Elizabeth Berly      I   396-397   1835
   (of Newberry District) (daughter of John Berly of
   Newberry District)
Ritchie, William H. Matilda V. Lomax   P   355-363   1846
   (separation agreement 13 February 1846) (of Abbeville
   District)
Ritchie. See Richey, Ritchie
Rizer, _____      Rebecca Ann Pricher  2C  177-179   1866
                  (daughter of Thomas Pricher)
Roach, _____      Frances W. Peterson  2B  762-764   1863
   (in Edgefield District) (daughter of Basil Peterson)
Roach, James M.   Leonora Haigood      S   421-422   1848
   (of Fairfield District) (daughter of Buckner Haigood of
   Fairfield District)
Roach, Nash       Elizabeth Ann Govan  C   62-65     1813
   (marriage settlement 24 April 1813) (of Charleston)
Roach, Nash       Elizabeth Ann Govan  F   292-293   1828
   (marriage contract 24 April 1828)
Roberts, Doctor   Martha A. G. Miller  E   35        1822
   John M. (reference to marriage settlement - no date
   given)
Roberts, Peter    Nancy Godfrey        D   158-159   1819
   (marriage settlement 4 July 1819) (in Laurens District)
Roberts, Reverend Martha Ann Glover    B   188-189   1802
   John Richard Miller
   (marriage settlement 29 October 1802) (both of Claremont
   County)

Implied South Carolina Marriages Volume IV 1787-1875

| MAN | WOMAN | VOL | PAGES | LIVED |
|---|---|---|---|---|
| Robertson, John H. | Joanna L. McDaniel | L | 58-61 | 1839 |

(marriage settlement 27 August 1839) (widow of John C. McDaniel) (both of Chester District)

Robertson, John J.    Sarah M. Robertson    2A    766    1859
   (of Richland District, S.C.) (daughter of John W.
   Robertson of Troup County, Georgia)
Robertson, Thomas    Martha Amanda Jones    2A    507-508    1859
G.
Robertson, Thomas    Mary Ophelia    W    506-507    1853
J.                   Caldwell (daughter of John Caldwell of
                     Richland District)
Robertson, William    Ann Haseltine    2B    690-695    1863
M.                    McBride
   (marriage settlement 8 September 1863) (widow of William
   McBride of Beaufort District) (Robertson of Charleston
   District)
Robertson, William    Elizabeth C. Rabb    O    318    1845
R. (of Fairfield District) (daughter of Thomas A. Rabb
   of Fairfield District)
Robeson, Samuel H.    Sarah Ann Evans    Z    194-196    1856
                     (daughter of John Evans of Chesterfield
                     District)
Robeson, William L.   Margaret Jane Samuel    S    453-454    1849
                     Sparks
   (he was married before) (of Chesterfield District)
Robinson, James M.    Eliza A. _____    2A    247-249    1858
                     (granddaughter of Archibald Lester)
Robinson, William     Patsey Drake    E    503-504    1826
   (Robertson) (marriage settlement 1 July 1826) (widow of
   Micajah Drake) (both of Edgefield District)
Robinson, William     Elvira C. Hagood    2C    252-256    1866
W.                   (daughter of Benjamin Hagood of Pickens
   District) [Must also see pages 259-262]
Robinson, Y. L.      Jane Brown             F    219-220    1828
                     Cunningham (daughter of Arthur Cunningham
                     of Kershaw District)
Robson, Thos.        Sarah Ann Cotchett     E    417-418    1828
                     (she of Columbia) [See also Volume F,
                     pages 5-11]
Rochell, John Senr.  Charlotte Cochran      N    56-58      1843
   (marriage settlement 9 April 1843) (both of Edgefield
   District) [See also pages 93-95]
Rochelle, John       Elizabeth Tomkins      F    65-67      1827
                     (Tompkins)
   (marriage settlement 13 April 1827) (widow of Samuel
   Tomkins of Edgefield District) (of Edgefield District)

110

Implied South Carolina Marriages Volume IV 1787-1875

| MAN | WOMAN | VOL | PAGES | LIVED |
|---|---|---|---|---|
| Rogers, _____ | Mary Swoford (daughter of John Swoford of Pickens District) | Y | 280-281 | 1855 |
| Rogers, J. Rice | Francis B. Mitchell | T | 93-94 | 1848 |

(married 26 October 1848) (both of Union District)

| Rogers, James L. | Emily A. Gray | V | 4-5 | 1851 |
|---|---|---|---|---|

(marriage settlement 3 May 1851) (daughter of John J. Gray of Beach Island, Edgefield District, S.C.) (Rogers of Burke County, Georgia)

| Rogers, James L. | Emily A. Gray | W | 465-466 | 1851 |
|---|---|---|---|---|
| Rogers, John | Ann Fincher | I | 460-462 | 1836 |

(marriage agreement 2 June 1836) (both of Union District)

| Rogers, John | Mary H. Rountree | P | 294-296 | 1845 |
|---|---|---|---|---|

(daughter of Dudley Rountree of Edgefield District)

| Rogers, Ledford | Eleonor VanLew (Vanlew) | U | 152-154 | 1850 |
|---|---|---|---|---|

(marriage contract 20 August 1850) (of Union District) [See also pages 150-152]

| Rogers, Patrick S. | Sarah L. Bussey | Y | 73-75 | 1855 |
|---|---|---|---|---|

(daughter of Demcy Bussey Sr.)

| Rolinson, Charles W. | Maria Melinda Scott | Z | 471-473 | 1857 |
|---|---|---|---|---|

(daughter of John Scott of Richland District)

| Rollins, Richard D. F. | Louanza Morris | 2A | 749 | 1860 |
|---|---|---|---|---|
| Roney, Edward | Nancy M. _____ | 2B | 103-104 | 1847 |

(reference to marriage settlement 16 September 1847) (she of Abbeville District)

| Roney, Edward | Nancy M. Sims | S | 22 | 1847 |
|---|---|---|---|---|

(marriage contract 16 September 1847) (in Abbeville District)

| Ross, _____ | Eliza Miles | 2B | 506-507 | 1862 |
|---|---|---|---|---|
| Ross, John | Olive Lee Thorn | M | 342-343 | 1842 |

(daughter of Charles Thorn)

| Rosser, William | Martha E. Bracey | K | 324-327 | 1839 |
|---|---|---|---|---|

(marriage settlement 3 January 1839) (widow of Philip Bracey) (Rosser of Kershaw District) (she of Sumter District) [See also Volume L, pages 416-417]

| Rouley, _____ | Mary R. L. B. Turpin | V | 385-389 | 1852 |
|---|---|---|---|---|
| Rountree, Capt. William | Elizabeth Bryant | G | 99-100 | 1830 |

(marriage settlement 26 January 1830) (widow) (both of Union District)

| Rountree, William | Martha Glover | T | 37-38 | 1848 |
|---|---|---|---|---|

(in Edgefield District)

Implied South Carolina Marriages Volume IV 1787-1875

| MAN | WOMAN | VOL | PAGES | LIVED |
|---|---|---|---|---|
| Rowan, James | Elizabeth (Eliza) Speigner | K | 370-371 | 1831 |

(marriage 16 February 1831) (widow of Samuel Speigner) (of Richland District)

| Rucker, Alexander R. | Aurelia Calhoun | 2A | 762-763 | 1860 |

(daughter of John A. Calhoun of Abbeville District, S.C.) (Rucker late of Louisiana, now of Abbeville District, S.C.)

| Rudulph, Michael J. | Louisa M. Hendrick | C | 375-376 | 1816 |

(marriage settlement 1 October 1816) (both of Columbia, Richland District)

| Ruff, _____ | Judy W. Elkins | X | 324-325 | 1854 |

(daughter of James Elkins of Fairfield District)

| Ruff, _____ | Barbara Priester (widow) | D | 365-367 | 1821 |
| Ruff, Henry | Maria Eve Summer | D | 118 | 1819 |

(daughter of George A. Summer Senr. of Lexington District) [See also pages 116-117]

| Ruff, Paul Monro | Julia Hasell Crouch | 2B | 765-766 | 1864 |

(marriage settlement 1 January 1864) (in Lexington District)

| Rumbough, James H. | Caroline T. Powell | Z | 421 | 1856 |

(of Greene County, Tennessee) (daughter of Joseph Powell of Greenville, S.C.)

| Runaman, James | Janet (Jennet) Hogg | E | 73-77 | 1820 |

(in County of Selkirk, Scotland)

| Rush, James (of Columbia) | Martha Ann Pearson (daughter of John Pearson of Fairfield District) | F | 408-409 | 1829 |
| Rush, James | Martha Ann Pearson (daughter of John Pearson of Fairfield District) | H | 105 | 1831 |
| Russell, Robert | Sarah Stewart | Y | 446-449 | 1855 |

(of Columbia, Richland District)

| Russell, Robert E. | Martha Taylor | D | 363-364 | 1821 |

(marriage settlement 16 May 1821) (separation agreement 27 May 1824) (of Columbia, Richland District) [Must also see Volume E, pages 191-193]

| Rutherford, James | Massy Mars | E | 73-77 | 1820 |

("Massy Mars alias Rutherford") (common-law marriage) (in Rutherford and Iredell Counties, North Carolina)

| Rutland, Abram | Dimcey Lott | 2B | 126-128 | 1860 |

(marriage contract __ February 1860) (widow) (both of Edgefield District)

Implied South Carolina Marriages Volume IV 1787-1875

| MAN | WOMAN | VOL | PAGES | LIVED |
|---|---|---|---|---|
| Ryan, \_\_\_\_\_ | Louisa Holston (daughter of Moses Holston Senr of Edgefield District) | X | 152-153 | 1852 |
| Ryan, \_\_\_\_\_ (in Edgefield District) | Sarah F. Mays | X | 599-601 | 1854 |
| Ryan, Benjamin G. (in Edgefield District) (Holstein) (daughter of Moses Holston Senr.) | Louisa Holston | Z | 117-118 | 1856 |

(S)

Sadler, \_\_\_\_\_   Margaret J. E.   M   192-193   1842
                 Witherspoon   (in Lancaster District)
Sallat, Max      Susan Gray      R   338-340   1847
   (marriage settlement 16 January 1847) (widow of William
   W. Gray of Edgefield District, S.C.) (Sallat of Augusta,
   Georgia, late from Germany)
Salley, \_\_\_\_\_   Marget Ann Corley   2A   418-419   1858
                 (daughter of Josiah Corley of Barnwell
                 District)
Salmon, David D.  Desdamonea Woodberry  I   599-600   1837
   (marriage settlement 17 May 1837) (he of Fayetteville,
   North Carolina) (she of Marion District, S.C.)
Salmond, Burwell  Nancy McWillie      O   133-134   1844
                 (daughter of William McWillie of Camden,
                 Kershaw District)
Salmond, Edward A.  Ann Cantey Cook   T   278-286   1847
   (in Kershaw District) (widow of Henry R. Cook)
Sampson, \_\_\_\_\_   Eliza. Marks        U   343-344   1851
                 (daughter of Alexander Marks) [See also
   pages 411-414; Volume V, pages 41-42]
Sampson, Emanuel  Leah Marks          O   110-111   1844
   (marriage contract - Hebrew date) (daughter of Alexander
   Marks and granddaughter of Mordecai Marks) (in Columbia,
   Richland District)
Samuel, Beverly   Susan S. Ford       H   315-316   1833
                 (daughter of Elijah Ford of Barnwell
                 District)
Samuels, Nathaniel  Fanny Lightfoot   C   111-117   1811
   (of Abbeville District) (daughter of Francis Lightfoot)
Sanders, Moses    Lydia (Lyddy) Bean  O   254-256   1844
                 (daughter of James Bean Senr. of
                 Edgefield District)

Implied South Carolina Marriages Volume IV 1787-1875

| MAN | WOMAN | VOL | PAGES | LIVED |
|---|---|---|---|---|
| Sanders, Moses R. | Mary Jane James (daughter of George C. James of Darlington District) | V | 203-205 | 1852 |
| Sanders, Samuel D. | Martha J. Pegues (marriage settlement 26 January 1848) (he of Chesterfield District) (she of Marlborough District) | S | 90-93 | 1848 |
| Sartor, Daniel R. | Alether Jeter (late of Union District, now of Newberry District) | Z | 481-484 | 1851 |
| Sartor, George W. | Julian Franklin Richard Farr (of Union District) (daughter of John P. Farr of Union District) | K | 172-173 | 1838 |
| Satcher, Henry | Sophronia Rutland (daughter of Abraham Rutland of Edgefield District) | 2A | 772-773 | 1860 |
| Satterwhite, Calvin | Margaret K. Cannon (daughter of David Cannon of Newberry District) | 2B | 365-366 | 1861 |
| Satterwhite, Richard | Susan C. Vance (marriage settlement 24 March 1854) (he of Newberry District) (she of Laurens District) | X | 452-454 | 1854 |
| Scarborough, Richard J. | Susan W. Cherry | Z | 426-430 | 1856 |
| Schmidt, John F. | Harriet M. Frazer (marriage agreement 18 October 1832) (widow of Joseph Frazer) (in Barnwell District) | H | 202-206 | 1832 |
| Scott, John A. | Sarah Slann Guignard (marriage settlement 25 February 1830) (daughter of James S. Guignard of Columbia, S.C.) (Scott of Mississippi) | G | 106-107 | 1830 |
| Scurry, Ridley M. | _____ Towels (of Edgefield District) (Towles) | Y | 600-601 | 1855 |
| Scurry, Ridley M. | Susan Elvira Towles (in Edgefield District) | X | 93-94 | 1853 |
| Seay, Thomas (Sea) | Jemima Sheppard (daughter of Abraham Sheppard Jr. of Richland District and granddaughter of Presley Garner of Richland District) | E | 421-422 | 1826 |
| Secrest, Andrew J. | Malissa A. McLure (in Chester District) (daughter of Hugh McLure) | 2A | 414 | 1858 |
| Seibels, _____ | Martha J. Lamar (she of Edgefield District) | K | 347-349 | 1839 |
| Self, Gamer | Lucy Seay (daughter of James Seay Sr of Spartanburg District) | I | 18 | 1834 |

Implied South Carolina Marriages Volume IV 1787-1875

| MAN | WOMAN | VOL | PAGES | LIVED |
|---|---|---|---|---|
| Seybt, Frederick | Ainre (Amie) Rimi Tierse (Turse) | Q | 96-97 | 1822 |

(he was born about 1769 in Bayreuth, Franconia) (she was born about 1775 in Paris) (arrived 19 July 1818, Alexandria, District of Columbia, then to S.C.)

| Shackelford, John | Ann Richardson | Y | 570-573 | 1852 |
|---|---|---|---|---|

(reference to marriage settlement 14 October 1852) (both of Marion District)

| Shackelford, Stephen J. | Malissa S. Lewis | 2B | 824-827 | 1843 |
|---|---|---|---|---|

(in Anderson District)

| Shannon, William | Henrietta McWillie | O | 134-135 | 1844 |
|---|---|---|---|---|

(daughter of William McWillie of Camden, Kershaw District)

| Shannon, William M. | Henrietta M. _____ | V | 420-421 | 1852 |
|---|---|---|---|---|

(of Camden, Kershaw District) (granddaughter of Joseph Cunningham of Liberty Hill, Kershaw District)

| Sharp, _____ | Martha Ann Elizabeth Lorick | N | 342-343 | 1844 |
|---|---|---|---|---|

(daughter of John Lorick) (she of Richland District)

| Sharp, Ebenezer | Sarah Lutcha Razor | Z | 493-495 | 1857 |
|---|---|---|---|---|
| Sharpton, Abel | Elizabeth Kilcrease | L | 397-398 | 1841 |

(of Edgefield District) (daughter of Lewis Kilcrease)

| Shaver, Jacob | Sarah Dunham | X | 672-674 | 1855 |
|---|---|---|---|---|

(of Greenville District)

| Shaw, David C. | Anna Jane McFaddin | 2B | 820-822 | 1864 |
|---|---|---|---|---|

(daughter of James D. McFaddin of Sumter District)

| Shaw, David Calvin | Anna J. McFaddin | 2B | 244-245 | 1860 |
|---|---|---|---|---|

(daughter of James D. McFaddin of Sumter District)

| Shealy, Ervin H. | Barbara C. Derrick | 2C | 77-78 | 1865 |
|---|---|---|---|---|

(marriage contract 28 September 1865) (both of Lexington District)

| Shelton, William J. | Cynthia C. Gibson | 2A | 707 | 1857 |
|---|---|---|---|---|

(of Fairfield District) (daughter of Jacob Gibson)

| Shepherd, John | Magdaline Burton | H | 30-31 | 1832 |
|---|---|---|---|---|

(daughter of Aaron Burton of Newberry District)

| Sheppard, _____ | Martha Lake | N | 151-152 | 1843 |
|---|---|---|---|---|

(daughter of Enoch Lake of Newberry District)

| Sheppard, Abraham | Elizabeth Garner | B | 734-735 | 1812 |
|---|---|---|---|---|

(daughter of Presly Garner) (in Richland District)

| Sheppard, Dr David | Kiziah J. _____ | X | 354-360 | 1851 |
|---|---|---|---|---|

(reference to separation agreement 18 November 1851) (formerly of Newberry, now of Edgefield District)

Implied South Carolina Marriages Volume IV 1787-1875

| MAN | WOMAN | VOL | PAGES | LIVED |
|---|---|---|---|---|
| Shermon, _____ | Mary Jones | 2B | 525-527 | 1862 |
| Shire, _____ | Selina Wannamaker (daughter of Henry Wannamaker) | G | 192 | 1830 |
| Shiver, William | Martha Bates (daughter of John Bates of Richland District) | 2A | 315 | 1857 |
| Shiver, William | Martha R. Beckham (marriage contract 2 June 1850) (widow of William M. Beckham) (both of Richland District) | U | 98-100 | 1850 |
| Shockley, Peter | Susan Waddill (marriage settlement 21 December 1847) (widow) (both of Greenville District) | S | 62-64 | 1847 |
| Shoemaker, James (or John) | Martha Beall (reference to marriage settlement - no date given) (widow of Duke Beall) | E | 449 | 1826 |
| Shoolbred, John S. | Fanny H. Adams (marriage settlement 4 September 1867) (he of Charleston District) (she of Richland District) | 2C | 384-389 | 1867 |
| Shrum, Jacob | Elvira G. Williams (marriage settlement 19 October 1859) (in Pickens District) | 2A | 795-796 | 1859 |
| Shuler, _____ | Elizabeth Kennerly (widow) (she of Lexington District) | 2B | 707-708 | 1863 |
| Shuler, George | Catherine Shuler (marriage settlement 27 January 1863) (both of Orangeburg District) | 2C | 184-186 | 1863 |
| Simkins, Arthur | Mary Ardis (daughter of Abram Ardis of Edgefield District) | C | 186 | 1815 |
| Simmons, Thomas A. | Mary S. _____ (reference to marriage settlement - no date given) | I | 1 | 1834 |
| Simons, John A. | Martha McCarty (marriage settlement 7 October 1867) (widow) (in Edgefield District) | 2C | 403-405 | 1867 |
| Simpson, Colo John | Sarah Hunter (marriage contract 22 January 1811) (in Laurens District) | C | 227-228 | 1811 |
| Simpson, Dr. John W. | Jane C. Clowney (marriage settlement 22 January 1856) (widow) (he of Laurens District) (she of Union District) | Z | 33-35 | 1856 |
| Simpson, J. B. | Elizabeth Martha Ann Cook (daughter of John Cook of Newberry District) | 2B | 298-300 | 1861 |
| Simpson. John R. | Sarah N. Belk (marriage contract 9 May 1867) (he of Union County, North Carolina) (she of Lancaster District, S.C.) | 2C | 338-340 | 1867 |

Implied South Carolina Marriages Volume IV 1787-1875

| MAN | WOMAN | VOL | PAGES | LIVED |
|---|---|---|---|---|
| Sims, C. E. | Mary Ann Tucker | 2B | 570-571 | 1863 |
| | (daughter of George B. Tucker) | | | |
| Sims, Charles E. | Harriet Jennings | Y | 532-533 | 1855 |
| | (daughter of Rev. John Jennings) | | | |
| Sims, Charles S. | Nancy Shelton | F | 229-230 | 1827 |
| Sims, John | Mahala McKey | K | 238-239 | 1838 |
| | (in Lancaster District) | | | |
| Sims, John D. | Mary E. Lyles | V | 554-557 | 1851 |
| Sims, John K. B. | Judah T. Shelton | F | 229-230 | 1827 |
| Sims, John S. | Sicily G. Farr | O | 308-309 | 1844 |
| | (both of Union District) (daughter of James Farr) | | | |
| Sims, Reuben | Mary T. N. Hopkins | H | 107-108 | 1832 |
| | (daughter of Newton Hopkins of Chester District) | | | |
| Sims, William H. | Elizabeth Ellis | N | 92-93 | 1843 |
| | (daughter of Benjamin Ellis of Union District) | | | |
| Singeltary, ____ | Elizabeth Hickson | X | 509-521 | 1853 |
| | (widow of Thomas J. Hickson) | | | |
| Singleton, John R. | Elizabeth James | M | 334-336 | 1839 |
| | (in Sumter District) | | | |
| Sitgreaves, John S. | Elizabeth J. Suber | Z | 220-223 | 1856 |
| | (marriage settlement 17 April 1856) (widow of Micajah Suber) (Sitgreaves formerly of York District) (she of Newberry District) | | | |
| Skinner, William | Jane Vermeille DuBose | P | 205-208 | 1845 |
| | (marriage settlement 10 December 1845) (both of Sumter District) | | | |
| Slagle, William | Julia Crawford | I | 312-313 | 1835 |
| | (Sleegle) (marriage settlement 8 October 1835) (widow) (of Chester District) | | | |
| Slawson, Levi | Elizabeth D. Spearman | 2A | 417 | 1858 |
| | (in Newberry District) | | | |
| Slia, ____ | Mary Koon | V | 270-273 | 1852 |
| Sligh, Jacob | Magdalina Summer | D | 18 | 1819 |
| | (daughter of George A. Summer Senr. of Lexington District) [See also pages 116-117] | | | |
| Sligh, William H. | Mary C. Fellers | 2A | 345-347 | 1857 |
| | (daughter of John Fellers) | | | |
| Sloan, Benjamin | Anna M. Maxwell | 2B | 624-626 | 1863 |
| | (daughter of John Maxwell of Pickens District) | | | |

117

Implied South Carolina Marriages Volume IV 1787-1875

| MAN | WOMAN | VOL | PAGES | LIVED |
|---|---|---|---|---|

Sloan, Hiram E.      Ulrica Leonora      X      428-430      1854
                     Ballard
   (marriage settlement 11 April 1854) (daughter of John
   Ballard) (she was born about 1835) (Sloan of Kershaw
   District) (she of Sumter District)
Sloan, Thomas M.     Cornelia A. Houston  2A     324-325      1858
   (marriage settlement 6 March 1858)
Smith, _____         Molsey Jordan        2B     390          1855
   (of Lexington District) (daughter of John Jordan Senr.
   of Orangeburgh District)
Smith, _____         Dorcas Miller        C      66           1813
   ("Dorcas Smith late Dorcas Miller")
   (she of North Carolina)
Smith, _____         _____ Reddle         2A     799-800      1860
   (sister of Napoleon B. Reddle, late of
   Louisiana)
Smith, A. T.         Mary Ann Faust       L      67-68        1840
   ["Mary Ann Smith (alias) Mary Ann Faust"]
Smith, Albert        Sarah Cantey Taylor  I      236-237      1835
   (marriage contract 13 May 1835) (he of Beaufort) (she of
   Columbia)
Smith, Alexander T.  Mary Ann Faust       G      109-110      1830
   (common-law marriage) (of Richland District) [See also
   pages 398-399]
Smith, Andrew K.     Minerva Littlejohn   2A     133          1857
   (daughter of Samuel Littlejohn of
   Spartanburg District)
Smith, Bryce         Clementine Helen     X      445-448      1854
                     Davis (daughter of Bushrod Washington
   Davis) (in Beaufort District)
Smith, Charles       Mary Smith           W      155-157      1852
   (of Abbeville District) (widow)
Smith, Christian H.  Sarah Eigleberger    F      177-178      1828
   (marriage settlement 21 January 1828) (both of Newberry
   District)
Smith, Christian     Sarah Eigleberger    I      20-22        1828
   Henry (married 22 January 1828) (marriage contract 31
   January 1828) (separation agreement 21 February 1834)
   (in Newberry District)
Smith, D. H. (Henry  Ellen Elizabeth      U      228-230      1850
   David)            Bossard
   (marriage settlement 24 October 1850) (he of Georgetown
   District) (she of Sumter District)
Smith, George P.     Sarah Gruber         G      77-78        1829
                     (daughter of John Gruber)

Implied South Carolina Marriages Volume IV 1787-1875

| MAN | WOMAN | VOL | PAGES | LIVED |
|---|---|---|---|---|
| Smith, Giles N. | Martha Holder | O | 420-421 | 1845 |

(to be married 19 April 1845) (marriage settlement 19 April 1845) (of Union District)

| Smith, Henry | Delila A. E. Hollis | Z | 559 | 1856 |

(of Fairfield District) (daughter of John Hollis of Fairfield District)

| Smith, Isaac H. | Sarah K. Munds | U | 305-306 | 1851 |

(marriage settlement 11 January 1851) (both of Columbia, Richland District)

| Smith, Isaac H. | Sarah K. Munds | Y | 381 | 1851 |

(reference to marriage articles 11 January 1851)

| Smith, James | Margaret Amanda Boyd | X | 261-263 | 1854 |

(marriage settlement 20 February 1854) (in York Dist.)

| Smith, James M. | Anna D. Boyle | 2A | 285-294 | 1857 |

(daughter of Cunningham Boyle)

| Smith, Jesse | Rebecca Rutland | 2A | 772-773 | 1860 |

(daughter of Abraham Rutland of Edgefield District)

| Smith, John | Sarah C. Walker | Z | 714-716 | 1857 |

(marriage settlement 17 March 1857) (both of Chester District)

| Smith, John Cheek | Jane Amanda Epps | 2A | 595-597 | 1859 |

(marriage settlement 24 February 1859) (in York District)

| Smith, John D. | Sarah Ann Hill | Y | 404-405 | 1855 |

(of Chester District) (daughter of Littleton Hill of Chester District)

| Smith, John D. | Emma C. Marshall | K | 284-286 | 1848 |

(marriage settlement 27 November 1848) (he of Winnsborough, Fairfield District) (she of Richland District)

| Smith, John W. | Hesky Clemens | 2B | 435-438 | 1861 |

(of Anderson District) (widow of C. W. Clemens)

| Smith, Josiah | Dorcas S. Miller | B | 610-611 | 1809 |

(widow of Benjamin Miller of York District)

| Smith, Reuben | Mary Ann Hornsby | Y | 71-73 | 1855 |

(in Richland District) (daughter of Daniel Hornsby)

| Smith, Thomas E. | Martha Marrs | S | 360-362 | 1848 |

(marriage settlement 23 October 1848) (both of Lexington District)

| Smith, Thomas L. | Mildred Watson | 2B | 170-171 | 1860 |

(of Edgefield District) (daughter of Elijah Watson Senior of Edgefield District)

| Smith, W. B. | Frances C. Bigger | 2C | 250-252 | 1866 |

(marriage settlement 18 December 1866) (daughter of A. B. Bigger) (in York District)

Implied South Carolina Marriages Volume IV 1787-1875

| MAN | WOMAN | VOL | PAGES | LIVED |
|---|---|---|---|---|
| Smith, Willard | Elizabeth Tomkins (Tompkins) | 2B | 598-599 | 1847 |

(marriage agreement 16 June 1847) (widow) (in Abbeville District)

Smith, William    Lucy W. Crosby    U    315-316    1851
(marriage settlement 21 January 1851) (he was married before) (widow of David Crosby of Fairfield District) (Smith of Union District)

Smith, William C.    Mary Cannon    Y    275-279    1855
(marriage settlement 14 June 1855) (widow) (he of Georgetown District) (she of Abbeville District)

Smith, William    Sarah North Smith    I    300-302    1834
Cuttino (of Abbeville) (daughter of Benjamin Smith of Anderson District) [See also pages 297-299]

Smoke, Samuel    Martha A. Huntt    2B    577-579    1862
(in Richland District)

Smyth, Bartlee    Caroline _____    B    205-211    1791
(Smith) (reference to marriage settlement 12 January 1791) (of Columbia)

Snead, John G.    Sarah B. Johnson    E    535-537    1826
(marriage agreement 3 July 1826) (he of Augusta, Georgia) (she of Barnwell District, S.C.)

Snelgrove, William    Eve Margaret Counts    V    270-273    1852
F. (marriage agreement 12 January 1852) (both of Lexington District)

Snider, William    Elizabeth E. Wells    2A    559-560    1859
(of Orangeburg District) (daughter of Henry H. Wells of Sumter District)

Sollee, Frederick    Floride P. Croft    G    22-24    1829
(daughter of Edward Croft of Greenville District)

Solomon, Abraham L.    Rebecca Polock    U    214-217    1850
(marriage settlement 18 December 1850) (daughter of Levi Polock) (in Richland District)

Souter, Daniel    Charlotte Turnipseed    U    148-150    1850
(of Richland District) (daughter of Felix Turnipseed of Richland District)

Southerland, _____    Eady Brown    N    218-219    1843
(daughter of Lewis Brown of Pickens District)

Southern, John P.    Abigail (Abby) C. Frean    2A    639-640    1859

Sowden, Joshua    Ann Henry    V    304-314    1852
(daughter of James Henry of Richland District)

Implied South Carolina Marriages Volume IV 1787-1875

| MAN | WOMAN | VOL | PAGES | LIVED |
|---|---|---|---|---|
| Spann, John R. | Anastasia McNamara | O | 14-17 | 1844 |

(marriage settlement 31 January 1844) (granddaughter of
General _____ Steele of North Carolina) (Spann of Sumter
District, S.C.) (she of Chesterfield District, S.C.)
[See also Volume R, pages 39-40]

| Spann, John Russell | Anastasia Macnamara | 2B | 291-293 | 1860 |
|---|---|---|---|---|

(of Texas)

| Spann, Richard R. | Mary E. Lee | M | 256-258 | 1839 |
|---|---|---|---|---|

(of Sumter District) [See also pages 73-74]

| Spann, S. Robert | Rosalie E. A. Moses | 2B | 633-634 | 1863 |
|---|---|---|---|---|

(in Sumter District) (daughter of Franklin J. Moses)

| Spann, Samuel Robert | Mary Emma McFaddin | Y | 605-606 | 1855 |
|---|---|---|---|---|

(daughter of James D. McFaddin of Sumter
District)

| Spann, Tyre D. | Maria E. Brockington | 2A | 351-352 | 1858 |
|---|---|---|---|---|

(in Sumter District) (widow of William T. Brockington)

| Spann, Tyre J. | _____ Gerald | R | 383-385 | 1844 |
|---|---|---|---|---|

(in Sumter District) [See also pages 386-388, 408-409]

| Spann, William T. | Elizabeth R. OQuin | I | 265-267 | 1830 |
|---|---|---|---|---|

(in Sumter District)

| Spearman, G. W. L. | Angeline Cannon | 2B | 508-509 | 1862 |
|---|---|---|---|---|

(daughter of George S. Cannon of Newberry
District)

| Spears, _____ | Margaret Foster | P | 28-29 | 1845 |
|---|---|---|---|---|

[daughter of Jariahr (Josiah?) Foster of
Union District]

| Spears, Isham | Gincy Ussery | Z | 15-18 | 1852 |
|---|---|---|---|---|

(both of Barnwell District)

| Spears, James Edwin | Emily E. Spears | 2A | 770-771 | 1860 |
|---|---|---|---|---|

(marriage settlement 9 February 1860) (daughter of
Joshua A. Spears) (James Edwin Spears of Marlborough
District) (she of Sumter District)

| Spears, Josiah | Martha McKissisck | Y | 187-188 | 1855 |
|---|---|---|---|---|

(formerly of Union District, S.C., now of Cherokee
County, Georgia)

| Speigner, Samuel | Elizabeth (Eliza) | K | 370-372 | 1831 |
|---|---|---|---|---|

Montgomery (daughter of John Montgomery)
(in Richland District)

| Spencer, Robert H. | Sarah T. S. F. Wadlington | K | 535-542 | 1835 |
|---|---|---|---|---|

| Spencer, Robert H. | Sarah T. Susannah F. Wadlington | I | 74-76 | 1834 |
|---|---|---|---|---|

[Must also see pages 107-108] [See also pages 7-8]

| Spruill, Simeon | Nancy Richey | H | 101-103 | 1832 |
|---|---|---|---|---|

(marriage settlement 31 January 1832) (both of Abbeville
District)

Implied South Carolina Marriages Volume IV 1787-1875

| MAN | WOMAN | VOL | PAGES | LIVED |
|---|---|---|---|---|
| Spurrier, Thomas J. | Eliza J. Thompson | W | 381-382 | 1852 |

(marriage settlement 28 December 1852) (in Kershaw District)

| | | | | |
|---|---|---|---|---|
| Staley, Lewis | Elizabeth M. Quattlebum | R | 224-226 | 1847 |

(marriage settlement 14 January 1847) (in Orangeburgh District)

| | | | | |
|---|---|---|---|---|
| Stall, Thomas H. | Drusilla A. P. Loveland | 2A | 371-373 | 1858 |

(marriage settlement 1 June 1858) (daughter of Roger Loveland) (in Greenville District)

| | | | | |
|---|---|---|---|---|
| Stallworth, William H. (Stallsworth) | Margaret R. Caldwell | 2B | 97-99 | 1860 |

(in Abbeville District)

| | | | | |
|---|---|---|---|---|
| Stark, _____ | Sarah Lamar | N | 293-295 | 1843 |

(she of Edgefield District)

| | | | | |
|---|---|---|---|---|
| Stark, _____ | Caroline R. Raoul | O | 326 | 1845 |

(in Richland District) (daughter of Dr. J. L. Raoul of Richland District)

| | | | | |
|---|---|---|---|---|
| Stark, _____ | Caroline R. Raoul | Y | 555-558 | 1855 |

(daughter of John L. Raoul)

| | | | | |
|---|---|---|---|---|
| Stark, Belfield | Emily M. Ray | G | 414-415 | 1831 |
| Stark, Jeremiah W. | Jane Cannon | E | 234 | 1824 |

(marriage settlement 25 October 1824) (both of Newberry District)

| | | | | |
|---|---|---|---|---|
| Starke, Reuben | Elizabeth G. _____ | H | 253-255 | 1827 |

(separation agreement __ August 1827)

| | | | | |
|---|---|---|---|---|
| Statham, Barnet | Caroline L. Seibels | K | 347-349 | 1839 |

(of Greenville District)

| | | | | |
|---|---|---|---|---|
| Stearn, Robert (Sterns) | Sarah Fewell (Fewel) | D | 411 | 1821 |

(marriage settlement 15 December 1821) (of York District)

| | | | | |
|---|---|---|---|---|
| Steen, James N. | Catherine Elizabeth Reilly | R | 12-13 | 1846 |

(daughter of Bernard Reilly of Columbia, Richland District)

| | | | | |
|---|---|---|---|---|
| Steen, William | Sarah Ann Palmer | 2B | 202-204 | 1860 |

(daughter of Ellis Palmer of Union District)

| | | | | |
|---|---|---|---|---|
| Stewart, _____ | _____ Harris | G | 36-37 | 1829 |

(daughter of John Harris of Abbeville District)

| | | | | |
|---|---|---|---|---|
| Stewart, Alexander | Eve Margarett Mayer | H | 61-62 | 1828 |

(widow of Major Adam Mayer)

| | | | | |
|---|---|---|---|---|
| Stewart, James S. | Clarissa (Clara) J. Mushatt | P | 341-342 | 1846 |

(marriage settlement 16 February 1846) (he of Winnsborough, Fairfield District) (she of Fairfield District)

Implied South Carolina Marriages Volume IV 1787-1875

| MAN | WOMAN | VOL | PAGES | LIVED |
|---|---|---|---|---|
| Stewart, William | Sarah Patterson (daughter of James Patterson) (of Feliciana Parish, Louisiana) | E | 64-65 | 1822 |
| Stiles, Copeland | Amelia Rosamond Rodgers (of Sumter District) | S | 411-412 | 1848 |
| Stitt, Thomas | Mary Ann Clark (reference to marriage settlement 16 February 1854) (in Fairfield District) | 2A | 68-69 | 1854 |
| Stitt, Thomas | Mary Ann B. Clark (marriage settlement 16 February 1854) (both of Fairfield District) | X | 529-531 | 1854 |
| Stivender, David T. | Jane F. E. _____ (he was married before) | 2A | 686 | 1859 |
| Stockman, Geo: | Elizabeth Kinard (of Newberry District) | E | 308-309 | 1816 |
| Stokes, Andrew J. | Margaret Shand Smith (married 8 September 1859 in Greenville) | 2A | 689-690 | 1859 |
| Stone, Charles | Sarah Tucker | C | 219-220 | 1803 |
| Strait, Richard | Mary C. McClain (marriage settlement 22 December 1858) (in York District) | 2A | 597 | 1858 |
| Strauss, Charles | Molly Levingston (marriage agreement 23 February 1857) (widow) (in Newberry District) | Z | 635-636 | 1857 |
| Streater, Drury | Esther W. Ganey (Gainey) (marriage settlement 24 December 1846) (both of Chesterfield District) | R | 164-166 | 1846 |
| Street, Simon P. | Unice _____ (reference to bill for alimony 14 May 1861) (in Edgefield District) | 2B | 355-357 | 1861 |
| Stribling, Perry C. | Elizabeth Francis Foote Farr (daughter of John P. Farr of Union District) (of Union District) | K | 171 | 1837 |
| Stringfellow, Edwin H. | Margaret L. Miller (marriage settlement 25 October 1859) (in York District) | 2A | 704-706 | 1859 |
| Stringfellow, Lee R. | Nancy Satcher (marriage settlement 18 January 1858) | 2A | 225-226 | 1858 |
| Strobel, _____ (Stroble) | Mary G. Beard | D | 239 | 1821 |
| Strother, George J. | Eloisa Bates (daughter of John Bates of Lexington District) | T | 544-547 | 1850 |
| Stroud, Leroy | Letty Jane Walker (daughter of Drury Walker) | 2A | 297-298 | 1858 |

Implied South Carolina Marriages Volume IV 1787-1875

| MAN | WOMAN | VOL | PAGES | LIVED |
|---|---|---|---|---|
| Stroud, Zachariah | Judith (Juda) C. Craddock | Z | 121 (of Laurens District) | 1856 |
| Stuart, Albert R. | Harriett Sophia Clarkson | 2C | 72-77 | 1865 |

(marriage settlement 5 December 1865) (daughter of William Clarkson who died __ July 1858) (she of Columbia) [Must also see pages 8-13]

| Stuart, Benjamin R. | Emma V. Thomson (Thompson) | 2B | 91-93 | 1860 |

(marriage settlement 1 May 1860) (he of Richland District) (she of St. Matthew's Parish) [Must also see pages 136-138] [See also pages 260-261]

| Stuart, Henry Middleton | Sarah Barnwell Fuller | 2B | 749-750 | 1863 |

(marriage settlement 2 December 1863) (widow) (both of Beaufort District)

| Stuart, William K. | Susan M. Heriott | P | 117-120 | 1845 |

(marriage settlement 11 November 1845) (in Sumter District)

| Stuckey, John J. | Laura A. Parnell | X | 559 | 1854 |

(marriage settlement 14 September 1854)

| Studdard, David | Rebecca Robinson | R | 479-481 | 1847 |

(marriage settlement 22 June 1847) (in Laurens District)

| Stukes, George | Margaret Ann Wells Washington | T | 413-415 | 1849 |

(marriage settlement 18 October 1849) (daughter of John W. Wells) (both of Sumter District)

| Sturgeon, Jacob P. | Elizabeth Ann Jane Norton | O | 180-183 | 1844 |

(marriage settlement 25 July 1844) (daughter of Allen Norton) (in Williamsburg District)

| Sturges, M. R. | Angerona J. Timmons | 2C | 117-118 | 1866 |

(marriage contract 2 January 1866) (widow of Luther R. Timmons) (in Marion District)

| Suber, Ephraim | Mariah Elizabeth Eigleberger | P | 472-474 | 1846 |

(marriage settlement 24 February 1846) (widow of Col. John Eigleberger) (in Newberry District)

| Suber, Henry | Susannah Darby | T | 84-87 | 1848 |

(marriage settlement 28 October 1848) (in Newberry District)

| Suber, Jefferson | Louisa M. N. Crooks | V | 223-225 | 1852 |

(of Newberry District) (daughter of John A. Crooks of Newberry District)

| Suber, Martin | Elizabeth Kinard | K | 64-65 | 1837 |

(marriage contract 19 December 1837) (both of Newberry District)

Implied South Carolina Marriages Volume IV 1787-1875

| MAN | WOMAN | VOL | PAGES | LIVED |
|---|---|---|---|---|

Suber, Micajah       Elizabeth J. _____       Z    220-223    1856
    (reference to marriage settlement - no date given)
Suber, Micajah       Elizabeth J. Noland      H    184-185    1832
    (marriage settlement 31 July 1832) (he of Columbia)
    (she of Newberry District)
Suber, Peter         Elizabeth Koon           T    309-312    1849
    (marriage contract 23 August 1849) (daughter of John
    Koon) (both of Newberry)
Sullivan, Dawson B.  Nancy Cheatham           F    227        1828
    (in Abbeville District) (daughter of Robert Cheatham)
    [See also pages 420-421]
Summer, Henry        Caroline Epting          2A   735-736    1859
    (of Newberry District) (daughter of John Epting Sr.)
Summit, Lawson       Margaret E. Speer        R    432        1847
    (daughter of William Speer of Abbeville
    District)
Sumter, Sebastian    Emma T. Bradley          2B   827-829    1864
    (marriage settlement 24 May 1864) (in Sumter District)
Sumter, Sebastian    Mary B. Waties           T    215-220    1849
    (marriage settlement 12 May 1849) (both of Stateburg,
    Sumter District)
Sumter, Sebastian    Mary B. Waties           V    489-491    1849
    D. (reference to marriage settlement 12 May 1849)
Sunday, Dr Francis   Mary _____               F    433-434    1828
    (separation agreement 7 February 1828) (in Edgefield
    District)
Surginer, John       Elizabeth Randol         C    171-177    1815
                     (Randell)
    (marriage settlement 18 March 1815) (widow of John Bond
    Randol) (of Richland District) [See also page 353]
Swinton, _____       Mary Ann Delorme         Y    419-421    1855
    (in Sumter District)
Switzer, Samuel      Sarah J. Miller          U    83-85      1850
    (Sweitzer) (marriage settlement 10 June 1850) (widow)
    (in Spartanburgh District)

(T)

Taggart, Oliver      Drusilla Yarborough      L    145-147    1840
    (in Abbeville District)
Taggart, Oliver      Drucilla Yarbrough       M    92-96      1842
Tait, Daniel         Margaret C. Denton       N    37-38      1843
    (Tate) (in Abbevile District)

125

Implied South Carolina Marriages Volume IV 1787-1875

| MAN | WOMAN | VOL | PAGES | LIVED |
|---|---|---|---|---|
| Talbert, _____ | Emeline D. Hollingsworth (daughter of John Hollingsworth) | 2A | 521-526 | 1858 |
| Tallon, Edward H. | Rebecca Ridgill | I | 295-297 | 1834 |

(marriage agreement 23 December 1834) (both of Sumter District)

| Tarrant, _____ | D. E. L. Turpin | V | 385-389 | 1852 |

(daughter of William Turpin of Greenville District)

| Tate, James | Nancy T. Tillman | L | 178-181 | 1840 |

(marriage settlement 7 November 1840) (widow of Hiram Tillman) (Tate of Mississippi) (she of Abbeville District, S.C.)

Tate. See Tait

| Tatum, Thomas | Ann Pou | I | 622-623 | 1837 |

(marriage settlement 18 July 1837) (both of Orangeburgh District)

| Taylor, _____ | Elizabeth Bird | T | 315-324 | 1848 |

(of Edgefield District)

| Taylor, _____ | Harriet P. Raoul | O | 327 | 1845 |

(daughter of Dr. J. L. Raoul of Richland District)

| Taylor, James | Jane Kirkpatrick | 2A | 63-65 | 1857 |

(marriage settlement 7 July 1857) (he of Laurens District) (she of Abbeville District)

| Taylor, James M. | Charlotte L. Boykin | O | 358-359 | 1845 |

(in Kershaw District)

| Taylor, John | Nancy J. Muse | 2B | 618-619 | 1863 |

(marriage settlement 26 March 1863) (both of Fairfield District)

| Taylor, John | Frances Steen | Y | 568-570 | 1855 |

(in Union District) (daughter of Col. Gideon Steen)

| Taylor, Mordecai Jr. | Sarah Ann Martindale | N | 22-23 | 1843 |

(daughter of William Martindale) (in Spartanburgh District)

| Taylor, Samuel S. | Ann Guphill | F | 468-469 | 1829 |

(marriage settlement 15 April 1829)

| Taylor, Thomas | Sally F. Elmore | 2B | 590-591 | 1863 |

(of Richland District) (daughter of F. H. Elmore)

| Taylor, William | Mary Clayton Miller | A | 361-363 | 1799 |

(marriage settlement 6 May 1799) (daughter of Andrew Miller) (Taylor of Savannah)

| Taylor, William | Martha C. Pearson | I | 459 | 1836 |
| Teague, _____ | Mary A. Wells | 2A | 678-680 | 1859 |

(daughter of Chesley Wells of Edgefield District)

| Teague, Dr Abner | Charlotte Teague | T | 398-400 | 1849 |

Implied South Carolina Marriages Volume IV 1787-1875

| MAN | WOMAN | VOL | PAGES | LIVED |
|---|---|---|---|---|
| Tennent, William | Harriet Eliza Gibert | 2A | 166-170 | 1857 |

(marriage settlement 15 December 1857) (both of Abbeville District)

| | | | | |
|---|---|---|---|---|
| Tennent, William | Patsy Middleton | N | 297-301 | 1795 |

(reference to marriage settlement 3 December 1795)

| | | | | |
|---|---|---|---|---|
| Terrell, John R. | Matilda A. Berry | W | 11-13 | 1852 |

(in Kershaw District) (daughter of James Berry)

| | | | | |
|---|---|---|---|---|
| Terry, Simon | Ann Moor | N | 209-210 | 1843 |

(marriage settlement 25 October 1843) (daughter of Moses Moor)

| | | | | |
|---|---|---|---|---|
| Terry, Stephen | Elizabeth Hill | G | 357-358 | 1831 |
| Terry, William S. | Mary Octavia Jones | Z | 532-533 | 1857 |

(daughter of Benjamin T. Jones of Laurens District)

| | | | | |
|---|---|---|---|---|
| Theus, Henry L. | Henrietta S. Anderson | H | 505-507 | 1833 |

(marriage agreement 22 December 1833) (he of Tennessee) (she of Sumter District, S.C.)

| | | | | |
|---|---|---|---|---|
| Thomas, _____ | Mary Y. Arthur | R | 65 | 1846 |

(she of Abbeville District)

| | | | | |
|---|---|---|---|---|
| Thomas, _____ | Elizabeth N. Bethune | 2B | 309-312 | 1861 |
| Thomas, Benjamin | Nancy M. Morris | Y | 145-147 | 1855 |

(in Edgefield District) (daughter of Thomas Morris of Edgefield District) [See also pages 490-492]

| | | | | |
|---|---|---|---|---|
| Thomas, Charles | Julia Hixon | W | 49-52 | 1852 |

(of Edgefield District)

| | | | | |
|---|---|---|---|---|
| Thomas, Eli | Francis Harrison | O | 161 | 1844 |

(marriage settlement 20 June 1844) (both of Marlborough District)

| | | | | |
|---|---|---|---|---|
| Thomas, F. G. | Mary Y. Arthur | S | 40-41 | 1848 |

(of Abbeville District) (widow of J. R. Arthur)

| | | | | |
|---|---|---|---|---|
| Thomas, James T. | Mary J. Halsey | Y | 134-135 | 1855 |

(of Coosa County, Alabama)

| | | | | |
|---|---|---|---|---|
| Thomas, John P. | Francis E. Kelly | T | 121-122 | 1848 |

(daughter of William Kelly of Union District)

| | | | | |
|---|---|---|---|---|
| Thomas, John Reese | Louisa Anderson | K | 217-219 | 1838 |

(marriage settlement 26 July 1838) (widow of Thomas Anderson) (in Sumter District)

| | | | | |
|---|---|---|---|---|
| Thomas, William A. | Mary Ann Louisa Kelly | L | 49-50 | 1839 |

(daughter of William Kelly of Union District)

| | | | | |
|---|---|---|---|---|
| Thomas, William Kelly | N. Udora Fant | 2B | 294-295 | 1861 |

(of Union District) (daughter of David J. Fant of Union District)

127

Implied South Carolina Marriages Volume IV 1787-1875

| MAN | WOMAN | VOL | PAGES | LIVED |
|---|---|---|---|---|
| Thompson, _____ | Eliza Gantt | K | 124 | 1838 |

(daughter of Richard Gantt of Greenville District)

Thompson, George F. Rachel E. Telford    N   278-279   1844
Thompson, Hilliard  M. L. Hudson          2B  95-97     1860
   L. (in Sumter District) (daughter of Robert Hudson)
Thompson, Hugh S.   Elizabeth Anderson    2A  355-356   1858
   Clarkson (daughter of Thomas B. Clarkson
   Senior of Richland District)
Thompson, Jas.      Rebecca Henrietta     H   491       1834
   (or Jos.) H.     Marshall [daughter of Martin (or A.)
   Marshall of Richland District]
Thompson, Robert    Mary Jane Cunningham  2C  295-298   1866
   (marriage settlement 20 December 1866) (daughter of
   Alexander Cunningham of Williamsburg District) (both of
   Williamsburg District)
Thomson, Charles R. Claudia S. Stuart     2B  85-86     1860
                    the Younger
   (marriage agreement 17 April 1860)
Thomson, Jonathan   Catharine Crosby      H   320-321   1832
   (marriage settlement 18 December 1832) (both of Barnwell
   District)
Thornley, John L.   Elizabeth M. McFall   2B  349-352   1861
   (of Anderson District) (daughter of Andrew N. McFall of
   Anderson District) [See also pages 347-349, 352-354]
Thornton, _____     Lucinda Ross          2B  647-648   1863
Thurmond, Pleasant  Sarah Quarles         D   97-100    1818
   (marriage settlement 15 December 1818) (of Edgefield
   District)
Tidwell, Henry H.   Lucinda Lavender      O   309-310   1845
   (of Fairfield District)
Tiller, James       Sarah Ellis           M   314-315   1842
   (marriage settlement 15 March 1842)
Tillman, Doctor     Cornelia M.           Z   270-275   1856
   James A.         Pettigrew
   (marriage settlement 27 May 1856) (he of North Carolina)
   (she of Darlington District, S.C.)
Tillman, Hiram      Nancy T. Baker        L   178-181   1840
Timmerman, William  Martha A. Doby        W   103-109   1852
   T. (marriage settlement 30 September 1852) (widow) (in
   Edgefield District)
Timmons, Francis R. Ann Elizabeth Adams   2A  22-23     1857
   (of Edgefield District) (daughter of Richard Wright
   Adams of Edgefield District)
Tims, Joseph        Winny Wood            K   31-33     1837
   (marriage settlement 2 December 1837) (he was married
   before) (both of Chester District)

Implied South Carolina Marriages Volume IV 1787-1875

| MAN | WOMAN | VOL | PAGES | LIVED |
|---|---|---|---|---|

Tindal, John B.     Mary E. Lynam     2A     183-186     1857
   (reference to marriage settlement - no date given)
   (widow)
Tindall, John     Lydia A. Wells     P     202-204     1845
   (marriage settlement 29 December 1845) (both of Sumter
   District)
Tindall, John B.     Mary E. Lynam     V     280-283     1852
   (marriage settlement 26 January 1852) (widow) (both of
   Chester District)
Tindall, John M.     Susan S. Lynam     2B     540-543     1862
   (marriage settlement 23 September 1862) (both of Sumter
   District)
Tisdale, _____     Ellen West     K     318-320     1830
   (in Sumter District)
Tobin, Cornelius     Lucia C. Duncan     K     121-124     1838
   (marriage settlement 17 February 1838) (daughter of
   Willis J. Duncan) (in Barnwell District)
Todd, Thomas H.     Burchet R. Roper     M     249-252     1842
   (marriage settlement 30 August 1842) (both of
   Mississippi) (in Greenville District, S.C.?)
Tolleson, William     Sarah L. Pratt     2A     660-662     1859
   (in Abbeville District)
Toney, Col. William     Servina Whiting     E     431-432     1826
   (marriage agreement 14 February 1826) (he was married
   before) (widow) (of Greenville District) [See also pages
   475-477; Volume F, pages 148-149]
Townes, Joseph H.     Rebeccah A. _____     G     103     1825
   (reference to marriage settlement 15 February 1825) (in
   Chesterfield District) [See also Volume F, pages
   446, 463]
Townes, Joseph H.     Rebecca Ann Halsey     E     516-518     1825
   (marriage settlement 15 February 1825) (she of
   Wilmington, North Carolina)
Towns, Dr. Henry H.     Lucretia Ann Calhoun     G     356     1831
                  (daughter of William Calhoun of Abbeville
                  District)
Townsend, Elias     Elizabeth Kirven     X     646-649     1854
   (marriage settlement 14 September 1854) (widow) (both of
   Marion District)
Tradewell, B. W.     Sarah Telford     N     278-279     1844
   (of Richland District)
Tradewell, Francis     Mary F. Freeman     K     468-471     1839
   A. (marriage settlement 23 September 1839) (widow) (both
   of Columbia)
Tradewell, Francis     Mary F. Freeman     Z     196-200     1839
   A. (reference to marriage settlement 23 September 1839)
   (of Columbia, Richland District)

Implied South Carolina Marriages Volume IV 1787-1875

| MAN | WOMAN | VOL | PAGES | LIVED |
|---|---|---|---|---|
| Tradewell, Francis | Ann Eliza Dingle | 2B | 449-451 | 1861 |

Asbury (marriage contract 10 December 1861) (daughter of Adam Dingle) (Tradewell of Richland District) (she of Clarendon District)

| | | | | |
|---|---|---|---|---|
| Trenholm, Frances H. | Mary Elizabeth Burroughs | 2C | 40-41 | 1865 |

(marriage settlement 1 June 1865)

| | | | | |
|---|---|---|---|---|
| Tresevant, Danl. H. | Epps G. Howell | T | 293-296 | 1849 |
| Trezvant, _____ | Epps G. Howell | U | 142-147 | 1850 |

(in Richland District) (daughter of Jesse M. Howell)

| | | | | |
|---|---|---|---|---|
| Tribble, Andrew K. | Nancy Floyd | X | 110-112 | 1853 |

(in Newberry District)

| | | | | |
|---|---|---|---|---|
| Trible, G. W. | Mary E. Barmore | 2B | 182-184 | 1860 |

(Tribble) (marriage settlement 12 September 1860) (both of Abbeville District)

| | | | | |
|---|---|---|---|---|
| Trotti, _____ | Sarah F. Means | 2A | 546-547 | 1858 |
| Trumble, James | Ellen Unity Bates | 2A | 314 | 1857 |

(daughter of John Bates of Richland District)

| | | | | |
|---|---|---|---|---|
| Tucker, _____ | Susan Jennings | I | 566-567 | 1837 |

(daughter of Joseph Jennings of Edgefield)

| | | | | |
|---|---|---|---|---|
| Tucker, George A. | Anna (Annie) L. Sanders | 2C | 194-196 | 1863 |
| Turner, Thomas E. | Harriet G. (or J.) Miles | 2B | 78-80 | 1860 |

(marriage settlement 18 February 1860) (both of Edgefield District)

| | | | | |
|---|---|---|---|---|
| Turner, William S. | Sarah Lenhardt | Z | 166-168 | 1856 |

(of Pickens District) (daughter of Lawrence Lenhardt of Greenville District)

| | | | | |
|---|---|---|---|---|
| Turnipseed, Felix | Anna C. Hendrix | 2A | 112-114 | 1857 |

(marriage settlement 24 September 1857) (he of Richland District) (she of Lexington District)

| | | | | |
|---|---|---|---|---|
| Turnipseed, Felix | Harriet E. Kennedy | S | 217-220 | 1848 |

(marriage settlement 27 April 1848) (he of Richland District) (she of Fairfield District)

| | | | | |
|---|---|---|---|---|
| Turpin, Alfred B. | Elizabeth S. Simkins | H | 1-2 | 1831 |

(marriage settlement 29 November 1831) (daughter of Jesse Simkins) (Turpin of Augusta, Georgia) (she of Edgefield District, S.C.)

| | | | | |
|---|---|---|---|---|
| Tustin, Samuel | Martha A. McKittrick | Y | 263-264 | 1855 |

(of Abbeville District) (daughter of Benjamin McKittrick of Abbeville District)

| | | | | |
|---|---|---|---|---|
| Twitchell, Isaiah | Sarah Egan | E | 194-195 | 1824 |

(marriage settlement 10 June 1824) (she of Columbia)

Implied South Carolina Marriages Volume IV 1787-1875

| MAN | WOMAN | VOL | PAGES | LIVED |
|---|---|---|---|---|
| Twitty, John C. | Mary Adeline Kilgore | X | 314-315 | 1854 |

(marriage contract 18 February 1854) (widow) (in Kershaw District)

(U)

Underwood, Enoch J.  Avalina Lancaster    L    444    1841
(marriage contract 9 November 1841) (both of
Spartanburgh District)

(V)

Vandiver, James M.    Malinda Ware    A    125-126    1856
  (of Abbeville District) (daughter of William Ware of
  Abbeville District)
Vandiver, William    Mary M. Clifton    U    356-358    1851
  M. (marriage settlement 25 January 1851)
Van Wert, Walter    Rebecca A. Jumper    P    10-12    1845
  (marriage settlement 15 May 1845) (of Richland District)
Vaughan, Drury T.    Ida Statira _____    2B    377    1858
  (reference to marriage settlement 8 January 1858) (in
  Edgefield District)
Vaughan, Thomas    Mary Harmon    C    291-292    1816
  (marriage settlement 28 February 1816) (daughter of
  Stephen Harmon) (both of Kershaw District)
Vaughn, Drury T.    Ida Statira Huiet    2A    223-225    1858
  (daughter of John Huiet)
Vermillion, J. N.    Frances E. Williams    Z    725-726    1857
  Whitner (married 12 March 1857) (of Anderson District)
Vernon, Jas. J.    Ann L. Oeland    N    367-368    1844
  (marriage contract 22 January 1844) (daughter of John
  Oeland) (in Spartanburgh District)

(W)

Wacter, George    Barbara Capplepower    B    659-670    1810
                  (widow)
Wadlington, _____    Dorothy Cates    I    107-108    1834
                  (daughter of Aaron Cates)

131

Implied South Carolina Marriages Volume IV 1787-1875

| MAN | WOMAN | VOL | PAGES | LIVED |
|---|---|---|---|---|
| Wait, L. G. | Alley Ann Dunn | 2A | 298-299 | 1858 |

(of Laurens District) (daughter of William Dunn of Abbeville District)

| Waldo, _____ | Elizabeth Lamar | N | 293-295 | 1843 |
|---|---|---|---|---|
| Waldrop, _____ | Hetty Davenport | F | 364-365 | 1828 |

(daughter of Isaac Davenport)

| Waldrop, Alfred B. | Eleonor _____ | 2C | 35-36 | 1864 |
|---|---|---|---|---|

(separation agreement 24 October 1864) (in Greenville District)

| Waldrop, Wilson W. | Bridget Honoria | U | 39-40 | 1850 |
|---|---|---|---|---|

Frean (daughter of Thomas Frean) [Must also see page 274]

| Waldrop, Wilson W. | Bridget Honoria Frean | 2A | 639-640 | 1859 |
|---|---|---|---|---|
| Walker, _____ | Eliza Ann Hollingsworth | 2A | 521-526 | 1858 |

(daughter of John Hollingsworth)

| Walker, Alexander | Eliza A. A. Freeman | 2B | 332-335 | 1861 |
|---|---|---|---|---|
| Walker, Coleman B. | Elizabeth S. McKenney | U | 417-418 | 1851 |
| Walker, Dr. John A. | Mary M. Crain | X | 537-538 | 1854 |

(marriage settlement 24 July 1854) (in Chester District)

| Walker, Isaac | Sheba Mason | G | 214-215 | 1830 |
|---|---|---|---|---|

(marriage settlement 11 February 1830) (widow) (both of Richland District)

| Walker, John C. | Victoria T. Wilks | W | 637-640 | 1853 |
|---|---|---|---|---|

(marriage settlement 23 July 1853) (of Columbia)

| Walker, Robert | Elizabeth _____ | V | 176-180 | 1851 |
|---|---|---|---|---|

(separation agreement 20 December 1851)

| Walker, William | Lovisa H. Bass | L | 168-169 | 1840 |
|---|---|---|---|---|

(marriage settlement __ September 1840) (in Orangeburgh District)

| Wallace, Bennett | Phebe Cannon | S | 245-247 | 1848 |
|---|---|---|---|---|

(marriage settlement 8 June 1848) (widow of Richard S. Cannon) (in Newberry District)

| Wallace, Dr. P. M. | Mary Eppes | L | 142-143 | 1840 |
|---|---|---|---|---|

(widow of Daniel Eppes of Newberry District)

| Wallace, John | Rebecca W. Witherspoon | T | 538-539 | 1850 |
|---|---|---|---|---|

(daughter of John D. Witherspoon of Darlington District)

| Wallace, William | Victoria McLemore | T | 2-4 | 1848 |
|---|---|---|---|---|

(marriage settlement 6 December 1848) (granddaughter of Majr. John McLemore)

| Wallace, William H. | Sarah Smith Dunlap | V | 25-30 | 1851 |
|---|---|---|---|---|

(marriage settlement 8 July 1851)

## Implied South Carolina Marriages Volume IV 1787-1875

| MAN | WOMAN | VOL | PAGES | LIVED |
|---|---|---|---|---|
| Wallace, William T. | Ann Love Adelade Bishop | 2B | 315-319 | 1861 |

(marriage settlement 19 February 1861) (daughter of Rev. P. E. Bishop) (in Marlboro District)

| Walsh, John H. | Sarah J. Spencer | 2C | 292-294 | 1867 |
|---|---|---|---|---|

(daughter of Oliver H. Spencer of Chesterfield District)

| Walter, H. W. | Sarah T. Timmerman | E | 260-263 | 1824 |
|---|---|---|---|---|

(marriage settlement 19 September 1824) (in Columbia, Richland District)

| Walter, Richard Charles | Mary Ford | A | 317-321 | 1797 |
|---|---|---|---|---|

(marriage settlement 15 May 1797) (daughter of George Ford) (both of Stateburgh)

| Walter, Richard Charles | Mary Ford | B | 391-398 | 1797 |
|---|---|---|---|---|

(married 15 May 1797) (daughter of George Ford) (Walter died 17___) (both of Stateburg)

| Wannamaker, Henry | Barbara _____ | G | 192 | 1830 |
|---|---|---|---|---|

(his first marriage)

| Wannamaker, Jacob G. | Ellen Seibles | 2C | 358-360 | 1867 |
|---|---|---|---|---|

(of Lexington District)

| Ward, Clinton | Martha Lott | 2B | 126-128 | 1860 |
| Ward, Dr James | Rebecca Pollard | L | 222-223 | 1841 |

(widow of James Pollard of Abbeville District)

| Ward, Joshua | Constantia Mortimer | 2C | 300-304 | 1866 |
|---|---|---|---|---|

(marriage settlement 6 September 1866) (he of Georgetown) (she of Newberry District)

| Ward, Richard | Feraby _____ | 2A | 47-49 | 1857 |
|---|---|---|---|---|

(separation agreement 6 April 1857) (in Edgefield District)

| Ward, Simon | Sarah P. Leach | 2B | 68-69 | 1860 |
|---|---|---|---|---|

(marriage settlement 6 March 1860) (in Darlington District)

| Ward, Solomon G. | Elizabeth Thurmond | E | 146 | 1821 |
|---|---|---|---|---|

(marriage agreement 25 September 1821) (he late of New York) (she of Greenville District, S.C.)

| Wardlaw, Hugh Marshall | Eliza Robertson | S | 356-358 | 1848 |
|---|---|---|---|---|

(marriage settlement 8 August 1848) (both of Abbeville District)

| Wardlaw, Joseph Junior | Elizabeth Davis | E | 419-420 | 1825 |
|---|---|---|---|---|

("sometimes called Joseph Hackett") (separation agreement 21 December 1825) (widow of William W. Davis) (both of Abbeville District)

| Ware, T. Edwin | _____ Williams | V | 564-567 | 1842 |
| Waring, _____ | Sarah E. Cooper | 2A | 231-233 | 1858 |

133

Implied South Carolina Marriages Volume IV 1787-1875

| MAN | WOMAN | VOL | PAGES | LIVED |
|---|---|---|---|---|

Waring, Archibald  Hannah E. Pawley      Y    182-185   1855
   H. (marriage settlement 18 April 1855) (he of Colleton
   District) (she of Darlington District)
Warren, Joseph     Harriot Moore         M     36-37    1842
   (in Sumter District) (daughter of Captain Matthew S.
   Moore Senr.)
Warren, Thos. J.   Maria Louisa Maxwell  Y    533-534   1855
   (of Camden)     (daughter of Robert A. Maxwell of
                   Anderson District)
Warren, William    Sarah E. Adger        2C   317-323   1866
   Dalton (of Anderson District) (daughter of Robert Adger
   of Charleston)
Waters, _____     Mariah Norman         U    132-134   1850
Waters, Henry W.   Elizabeth Dewalt      2A   327-332   1857
   (married 21 March 1857) (daughter of Daniel Dewalt Senr.
   of Newberry District, S.C., who died 6 November 1853)
   (Waters of Texas) [See also pages 364-368, 495-499, 541-
   544, 631-634, 673-677]
Waties, William    Eloisa Burgess        S    405-408   1829
   (reference to marriage settlement 8 January 1829) (he of
   Sumter District) (she of Williamsburg District)
Watkins, _____    Elizabeth Prior       W     217      1852
                   (daughter of Tobias Prior of Edgefield
   District, S.C.) (she in Richmond County, Georgia)
Watson, _____     Elizabeth Ferguson    U    67-68     1850
                   (daughter of Wade Ferguson of Newberry
                   District)
Watson, James      Mary R. Mathis        I    420-422   1836
   (marriage agreement 18 March 1836) (in Sumter District)
Watson, Samuel     Margaret Gardner      O    163-164   1844
   (marriage settlement __ May 1844) (both of Sumter
   District)
Watson, William    Sarah Simonton        M     4-6      1843
   (marriage settlement 21 February 1843) (he of York
   District) (she of Fairfield District)
Watt, James H.     Mary G. Brock         Z     557      1847
   (reference to marriage settlement 18 November 1847)
Watt, James H.     Mary Green Brock      S    25-26     1847
   (marriage settlement 18 November 1847) (daughter of
   William Brock) (both of Sumter District)
Watt, John         Louisa E. Irby        2B   805-806   1864
                   (daughter of Dr. Wm Irby) (she of
                   Fairfield District)
Watts, _____      Mary Brooks           Y    214-215   1855
   (in Abbeville District) ("Mrs. Mary Watts formerly Mary
   Brooks")

Implied South Carolina Marriages Volume IV 1787-1875

| MAN | WOMAN | VOL | PAGES | LIVED |
|---|---|---|---|---|

Wayne, Gabriel J.   Martha Ann Britt      Z    496-499    1856
   (marriage contract 8 November 1856) (widow of Daniel A.
   Britt) (Wayne of Marion District) (she of Sumter
   District)
Weatherall, Joseph   Cornelia Yarbrough   M     92-96    1842
Weathers, _____      _____ Bailey         D      371     1821
   (daughter of Thomas Bailey of York
   District) [See also page 373]
Weathersby, Lewis    Jane Bush            H    158-159   1832
   (marriage settlement 14 May 1832) (widow of Thomas Bush)
   (both of Barnwell District)
Weaver. See Wever
Webb, Elijah         Elizabeth R. S.      N     50-53    1843
                     Gaillard
   (marriage settlement __ February 1843) (in Anderson
   District)
Webb, Elijah         Rosa H. Waller       T     47-49    1849
   (marriage settlement 15 January 1849) (both of Anderson
   District)
Webb, William        Elizabeth Morse      2B   581-583   1863
   (daughter of Whitfield Morse of Edgefield
   District)
Weeks, Eli           Dorothy Sims         M    318-320   1842
   (marriage settlement 2 September 1842) (widow of James
   S. Sims) (in Sumter District)
Welch, William       Isabella Crosson     S     37-38    1847
   (in Newberry District) (widow)
Wells, _____         Susannah Singleton   D      46      1818
   (daughter of Thomas Singleton) (she of
   Charletown)
Wells, _____         Sarah K. Williamson  2B   707-708   1863
Wells, Thomas        Martha Betsel        R    438-440   1824
Wells, Warren S.     Mary E. M. Neal      2B   281-283   1845
   (postnuptial settlement 18 February 1861) (daughter of
   John Neal of Richland District) (Wells of Sumter
   District)
Welsh, Andrew        Elizabeth Brown      C    348-349   1816
   (daughter of Joseph Brown of Sumter
   District)
Werber, Frederick    _____ Bobo           2A     384     1858
   (of Newberry District) (daughter of John E. Bobo)
Werts, George Henry  Drusilla S. Spearman 2B   784-785   1864
   (daughter of Graves Spearman of Newberry
   District)
Werts, Jonathan      Mary C. H. Spearman  2A     777     1860
   (daughter of Graves Spearman of Newberry
   District)

Implied South Carolina Marriages Volume IV 1787-1875

| MAN | WOMAN | VOL | PAGES | LIVED |
|---|---|---|---|---|
| Wesber, Frederick | Maria Louisa _____ | Z | 420 | 1856 |

(of Newberry District) (natural daughter of John E. Bobo of Newberry District)

West, Jacob        Laura De Walt         Z    442-444    1856
(married 10 June 1856) (daughter of Daniel De Walt Senr. of Newberry District)

West, Jacob        Laura Dewalt          2A   673-677    1859
(daughter of Daniel Dewalt Senr. of Newberry District, who died 6 November 1853)

Weston, John M.    Elizabeth Geiger      O    282-284    1841
(in Alabama) (daughter of Abram Geiger) [See also pages 280-281, 329]

Weston, William    Caroline Woodward     2B   645-646    1863
(of Richland District) (daughter of Lewellen Woodward)

Wever, Pickens B.  Mary Catharine        Y    600-601    1855
                   Towels (Towles)
(of Emanuel County, Georgia)

Wever, Pickens B.  Mary C. Towles        X    93-94      1853
(in Edgefield District)

Weyman, _____     Emily (Emmala)        2A   200-201    1857
                   Maxwell (daughter of John Maxwell of
                   Pickens District)

Wharton, John      Eliza Penelope        V    1-3        1851
  Austin           Johnson (daughter of David Johnson of
(of Texas)         Union District, S.C.)

Wheeler, Morris J. Amanda F. Warren      G    485        1831
(daughter of Peter Warren of Camden, Kershaw District) (of Camden, Kershaw District)

Wheeler, Oliver    Susan W. Scarborough  Z    426-430    1856
  Perry (marriage contract 25 October 1856) (widow of Richard J. Scarborough) (in Marion District)

Wheeler, William   _____ Roach          L    325-326    1833

Whilden, R. Furman Martha E. Weaver      2C   492-493    1864
(reference to marriage settlement 24 August 1864) (in Greenville District)

Whilden, Richard   Martha E. Weaver      2C   18-21      1864
  Furman (marriage settlement 24 August 1864) (in Greenville District) [See also pages 492-493]

Whitaker, James    Mary Taylor Heath     E    107-109    1823
(daughter of Thomas Heath Senr. of Richland District) (of Fairfield District) [See also pages 187-188]

White, _____      Frankey Evans         G    482-483    1831
(daughter of William Evans of Abbeville District)

Implied South Carolina Marriages Volume IV 1787-1875

| MAN | WOMAN | VOL | PAGES | LIVED |
|---|---|---|---|---|
| White, Anthony Jr. | Elizabeth Ann S. Dick | X | 465-467 | 1854 |

(marriage settlement 11 May 1854) (granddaughter of Leonard White) (both of Sumter District)

| White, Anthony Junr. | Elizabeth Ann S. Dick | 2C | 96-98 | 1854 |

(reference to marriage settlement 11 May 1854) (granddaughter of Leonard White) (in Sumter District)

| White, James | Martha Rutland | 2A | 772-773 | 1860 |

(daughter of Abraham Rutland of Edgefield District)

| White, John B. | Eliza Allston | H | 7-8 | 1805 |

(reference to marriage settlement __ March 1805) (he of Charleston) (she of Georgetown)

| White, Joseph B. | Maria Lee | M | 73-74 | 1842 |

(widow of Timothy Lee)

| White, McCauley J. | Anna E. Thames | 2A | 788-789 | 1860 |

(in Sumter District) (daughter of John C. Thames)

| White, Newel T. | Georgiana A. Cochran | X | 186-187 | 1854 |

(of Edgefield District) (daughter of L. B. Cochran of Edgefield District)

| White, Noah | Mary F. Williams | 2C | 111-113 | 1866 |

(marriage settlement 8 March 1866) (both of Aiken, Barnwell District)

| White, R. B. H. | Catherine A. E. Coward | Y | 575-576 | 1855 |

(daughter of Solomon Coward of Williamsburgh District)

| White, Richard M. | Frances E. Mosely | 2B | 197-199 | 1860 |

(postnuptial settlement 5 September 1860) (in Abbeville District)

| White, Thomas M. | Sarah Calhoun | 2A | 444-445 | 1858 |

(of Anderson District) (daughter of Nathan Calhoun)

| White, William | Temperance Perkins | U | 193-195 | 1849 |

(in Chesterfield District) (daughter of Alfred Perkins)

| White, William R. | Mary M. Moseley | 2A | 680-681 | 1859 |

(daughter of John M. Moseley of Abbeville District)

| Whitehead, Jacob H. | Sarah E. Stukes | O | 17-18 | 1844 |

(marriage settlement 5 March 1844) (in Sumter District)

| Whiteside, Thomas L. | Margaret E. Brown | 2B | 473-474 | 1862 |

(marriage contract 30 January 1862) (widow of Wm C. Brown) (Whiteside of York District) (she of Union District)

| Whitesides, Thomas | Jane M. Patton | 2B | 806-809 | 1864 |

(marriage agreement 12 April 1864) (widow)

Implied South Carolina Marriages Volume IV 1787-1875

| MAN | WOMAN | VOL | PAGES | LIVED |
|---|---|---|---|---|
| Whitlaw, Nathaniel H. | Lucy S. Ware | H | 516-517 | 1834 |

(marriage settlement 1 January 1834) (he of Augusta, Georgia) (she of Edgefield District, S.C.)

| Whitlock, _____ | Nancy N. Mobley (widow) | Y | 294-296 | 1855 |
|---|---|---|---|---|
| Whitner, Joseph N. Jr | Amelia M. Howard | Y | 510-512 | 1855 |

(marriage settlement 13 November 1855) (daughter of Charles B. Howard) (she of Marion District)

| Whitney, _____ | Sarah Morris | Y | 490-492 | 1854 |
|---|---|---|---|---|

(daughter of Thomas Morris of Edgefield District) (she of Barnwell District)

| Wicker, Allen | Elizabeth Odom | X | 335-336 | 1854 |
|---|---|---|---|---|

(in Marlborough District)

| Wicker, Peter | Mary E. Muffett | L | 283-284 | 1841 |
|---|---|---|---|---|

(daughter of James Muffett of Newberry District)

| Wideman, Samuel Senr. | Mary _____ | Y | 635-637 | 1856 |
|---|---|---|---|---|

(separation agreement 1 February 1856)

| Wigfall, Levi Durand | Eliza _____ | G | 326-327 | 1830 |
|---|---|---|---|---|

(reference to marriage settlement - no date given)

| Wigg, William Hazzard | Letitia Maine | A | 145-147 | 1789 |
|---|---|---|---|---|

(marriage settlement 30 November 1789) (he of St. Helena's Parish, Beaufort District) (she of Prince William's Parish)

| Wiggins, _____ | Martha M. Russell | R | 438-440 | 1847 |
|---|---|---|---|---|
| Wightman, William J. | Ann McHarg | I | 103 | 1832 |

(married September 1832) (widow of William McHarg who died December 1824) (of Edgefield District) [See also pages 608-610]

| Wilber, J. Quincy | Martha G. Waldrop | 2C | 243-245 | 1866 |
|---|---|---|---|---|

(marriage settlement 8 October 1866) (in Laurens District)

| Wilder, Josiah | Mary S. Murrell | K | 55-57 | 1836 |
|---|---|---|---|---|

(of Sumter District)

| Wilder, Josiah M. | Frances Ann Thompson | 2B | 95-97 | 1860 |
|---|---|---|---|---|

(marriage settlement __ __ 1860 - proven 4 May 1860) (daughter of Hilliard L. Thompson and granddaughter of Robert Hudson) (in Sumter District)

| Wilder, Thomas J. | Amanda A. Pitts | K | 28-29 | 1837 |
|---|---|---|---|---|

(marriage settlement 26 July 1837) (widow) (in Sumter District)

| Wilder, William M. | Adelaide Z. P. Nettles | 2B | 101-102 | 1860 |
|---|---|---|---|---|

(daughter of Joseph M. Nettles of Sumter District)

Implied South Carolina Marriages Volume IV 1787-1875

| MAN | WOMAN | VOL | PAGES | LIVED |
|---|---|---|---|---|
| Wilder, William W. | Sarah Ricks | Y | 458-459 | 1855 |

(marriage settlement 11 October 1855) (in Sumter District)

| Wiley, \_\_\_\_\_ | Ann L. Harris | G | 36-37 | 1829 |

(daughter of John Harris of Abbeville District)

| Wilkinson, James G. O. | Martha Glover | L | 383-385 | 1841 |

(marriage settlement 16 July 1841) (both of Edgefield District)

| Williams, \_\_\_\_\_ | Harriet Carter | E | 81 | 1819 |

(daughter of Benjamin Carter of Richland District) [See also page 100]

| Williams, \_\_\_\_\_ | Anna S. D'Oyley | X | 501-502 | 1854 |

(in Greenville District)

| Williams, Benjamin W. | Rosa Ann Eliza Hadden | Y | 637-638 | 1856 |

(daughter of John T. Hadden of Abbeville District)

| Williams, Charles F. | Ibby Eliza Hunter | 2A | 105-106 | 1857 |

(daughter of John Hunter of Laurens District)

| Williams, David J. | Emily S. Earle | 2B | 371 | 1861 |

(his first marriage) (in Greenville District)

| Williams, Gustavus A. | Henrietta H. Cahusac | N | 25-30 | 1843 |

(marriage settlement 25 January 1843) (she of York District)

| Williams, Henry H. | Agnes N. Craig | M | 371-374 | 1842 |

(of Marlboro District) (widow of John H. Craig of Chesterfield District)

| Williams, James Pinckney | Elizabeth Ann Floyd | X | 110-112 | 1853 |
| Williams, John E. | Jane Wetherby | K | 33-34 | 1837 |

(of Spartanburgh District)

| Williams, Kindrick | Frances Lillis Bradford | 2A | 785-788 | 1859 |

(daughter of William W. Bradford of Sumter District)

| Williams, Richard H. | Laura Reed | G | 84-85 | 1828 |

(daughter of John Reed of Camden, who died 22 April 1821)

| Williams, S. M. | Carolina E. W. Freeman | 2B | 332-335 | 1861 |

(marriage settlement 14 May 1861) (granddaughter of John Hollingsworth) (both of Edgefield District)

| Williams, Stephen | Martha Diseker | F | 26 | 1827 |

(daughter of Jacob Diseker of Richland District)

139

Implied South Carolina Marriages Volume IV 1787-1875

| MAN | WOMAN | VOL | PAGES | LIVED |
|---|---|---|---|---|

Williams, Thomas B. Susan Caroline T 387-389 1849
    Lorick (daughter of John Lorick of
  Edgefield District) (Williams of Richland District)
Williamson, _____ Eliza A. Kennerly 2B 707-708 1863
Williamson, Masten Anna Wright S 358-360 1848
  (marriage settlement 8 August 1848) (widow) (both of
  Anderson District)
Willie, John M. Alice (Ailsey) F 78-80 1827
  (Willey) Woodward (Woodard)
  (marriage agreement 22 March 1827) (widow of Major John
  Woodward) (in Fairfield District)
Wilmore, _____ Eliza Barber H 351-354 1833
  (daughter of James Barber)
Wilson, _____ Ann J. How O 226-227 1840
  ("Ann J. Wilson late Ann J. How")
Wilson, Hugh Senr Matilda Durant X 362-364 1854
  (marriage settlement 7 January 1854) (in Sumter
  District)
Wilson, Isaac D. Margaret Jane Sparks R 517-520 1835
  (married 27 May 1835) (daughter of Alexander Sparks of
  Darlington District)
Wilson, James S. Margaret Hall T 335-336 1849
  (marriage settlement 23 August 1849) (granddaughter of
  Daniel Talbot) (both of Newberry District)
Wilson, Moultrie R. Susannah T. 2C 48-50 1865
  Montgomery (daughter of John W.
  Montgomery of Sumter District) (both of Sumter District)
Wilson, Reverend Ann Maria Eliza E 478-482 1826
Wm S. Blackburn
  (marriage settlement 24 June 1826) (he of Charleston)
  (she of Columbia)
Wilson, Samuel Franc_i_s Smith P 264-265 1828
  (reference to marriage settlement 18 December 1828) (she
  of Darlington District)
Wilson, Samuel Franc_i_s Smith R 460-461 1828
  (reference to marriage settlement 18 January 1828)
Wilson, Samuel J. Mary H. Robeson L 381-382 1841
  (Robison)
  (of Darlington District) (daughter of Peter L. Robeson
  of Chesterfield District)
Wilson, William Harriet Dewalt X 687-689 1855
  (in Newberry District) (daughter of Daniel Dewalt Senr.)
Wilson, William Littey Maddox L 181-185 1840
  (marriage settlement 17 November 1840) [widow of
  Augustus (Augustin) Maddox] (in Abbeville District)

Implied South Carolina Marriages Volume IV 1787-1875

| MAN | WOMAN | VOL | PAGES | LIVED |
|---|---|---|---|---|
| Wilson, William J. | Fathy (Faithey) L. Hambright | 2A | 599-602 | 1859 |

(marriage settlement 15 March 1859) (in York District)

| | | | | |
|---|---|---|---|---|
| Windham, Jesse H. | Sarah L. Lucas | 2B | 604-606 | 1863 |

(in Darlington District)

| | | | | |
|---|---|---|---|---|
| Windhorn, Dedrick | Caroline L. Becktler | 2B | 623-624 | 1863 |

(marriage settlement 29 May 1863)

| | | | | |
|---|---|---|---|---|
| Wingate, Benjamin F. | Sarah Ann Lewis | O | 5-7 | 1844 |

(marriage contract 3 April 1844) (daughter of James Lewis) (both of Darlington District)

| | | | | |
|---|---|---|---|---|
| Wingate, Edward | Sophenisba E. M. _____ [no last name] | F | 424-425 | 1829 |

(reference to marriage settlement - no date given) [See also pages 430-431]

| | | | | |
|---|---|---|---|---|
| Wingate, Joseph Edward | Ann Eugenia Pettigrew | Z | 411-412 | 1856 |

(marriage settlement 22 November 1856) (in Darlington District)

| | | | | |
|---|---|---|---|---|
| Wingate, William | Isabella Ann Blackwell | E | 152-153 | 1823 |

(marriage settlement 22 September 1823) (in Darlington District)

| | | | | |
|---|---|---|---|---|
| Wingate, William | Isabella Ann Blackwell | N | 304-306 | 1844 |

(of Darlington District)

| | | | | |
|---|---|---|---|---|
| Winn, Hinchey | Susan Watson | I | 606-607 | 1837 |

(marriage settlement 6 June 1837) (widow of John Watson of Edgefield District) (in Edgefield District)

| | | | | |
|---|---|---|---|---|
| Winningham, _____ | Mary Carson | L | 109-110 | 1840 |

(in Orangeburgh District) (widow of James Carson)

| | | | | |
|---|---|---|---|---|
| Wise, Frederic | Charlotte Ruff | S | 17-19 | 1847 |

(marriage settlement 9 December 1847) (widow) (both of Lexington District)

| | | | | |
|---|---|---|---|---|
| Wise, Henry | Caroline Harris | 2A | 723-724 | 1859 |

(of Barnwell District) (daughter of David Harris of Edgefield District)

| | | | | |
|---|---|---|---|---|
| Wise, John | Catharine Elizabeth Rinehart | G | 451-455 | 1831 |

(reference to marriage contract - no date given) (of Newberry District) [Must also see Volume H, pages 222-225]

| | | | | |
|---|---|---|---|---|
| Withers, Randall | Sarah Bailey | D | 372 | 1821 |

(daughter of Thomas Bailey of York District)

| | | | | |
|---|---|---|---|---|
| Witherspoon, _____ | Sarah Lane (widow) | 2A | 711-712 | 1859 |

(she in Williamsburg District)

Implied South Carolina Marriages Volume IV 1787-1875

| MAN | WOMAN | VOL | PAGES | LIVED |
|---|---|---|---|---|
| Witherspoon, Henry K. | Eliza A. Cameron | 2A | 6-8 | 1845 |

(marriage settlement 18 February 1845) (both of Orange County, North Carolina)

| Witherspoon, Isaac D. Junr. | Jannett A. Reese | Z | 231-233 | 1856 |

(of York District, S.C.) (daughter of George Reese of Chambers County, Alabama)

| Witherspoon, James H. | Frances E. H. McCaw | K | 103-107 | 1838 |

(marriage settlement 5 January 1838) (widow of Dr. William McCaw of Abbeville District) (of Lancaster District)

| Witherspoon, Robert | Elizabeth McFadden | H | 467-470 | 1833 |

(of Sumter District) (daughter of Col. Thomas McFadden of Sumter District)

| Witt, _____ | Emily M. Bland | X | 2-3 | 1853 |

["Emily Witt (otherwise known as Emily Bland)"] (in Newberry District)

| Witt, _____ | Mary M. Reddle | 2A | 799-800 | 1860 |
| Wolf, _____ | Mary Beard | D | 9-11 | 1818 |

(daughter of Joshua Beard) (she of Richland District)

| Wolfe, _____ | Ann Caroline Kaigler | O | 328-329 | 1845 |
| Wolfe, _____ | Caroline A. Kaigler | W | 81-83 | 1852 |

(in Lexington District)

| Wolfe, Jacob V. D. | Maria S. Rowe | M | 146-147 | 1842 |

(in Orangeburgh District)

| Wolff, Jacob M. | Ellen Graetz | Y | 201-202 | 1855 |

(marriage settlement 18 May 1855) (daughter of _____ Wolff Graetz)

| Wood, A. W. | Lydia L. Rooks | 2A | 656-657 | 1859 |

(marriage agreement 30 April 1859) (in Barnwell District)

| Wood, Jadaliah | Eliza Dixon | P | 101-102 | 1845 |

(of Gadsden County, Florida) (daughter of Abel Dixon of Sumter District, S.C.)

| Wood, James | Polly Motley | R | 372-374 | 1847 |

(daughter of John Motley of Kershaw District)

| Wood, Robert | Caroline James | 2B | 219-221 | 1859 |

(daughter of Joseph James of Greenville District)

| Woodward, _____ | Elizabeth McKenzie | V | 156-157 | 1846 |

(daughter of John McKenzie Junr. of Orangeburgh District and granddaughter of John McKenzie Senr.)

Implied South Carolina Marriages Volume IV 1787-1875

| MAN | WOMAN | VOL | PAGES | LIVED |
|---|---|---|---|---|

Woodward, Edward P.   Esther Caroline      X    607-610    1851
                      Woodward
    (marriage settlement 14 December 1851) (daughter of
    William T. Woodward of Fairfield District)
Woodward, Thomas      Louisa McBride       R    316-317    1847
    (daughter of William McBride of
    Chesterfield District)
Woodward, William     Eliza Henry          K    517-520    1839
F. (marriage settlement 14 October 1839) (widow of
    George Henry) (in Fairfield District)
Wooten, _____         Rachel Trapp         Z    293-295    1856
    (she of Fairfield District)
Worthington, Robert   Alse Summers         G    97-98      1830
    (marriage settlement 4 January 1830) (both of Newberry
    District)
Worthy, Martin        Agness Cornwell      X    676-677    1848
    Senr. (marriage settlement 28 October 1848) (widow) (in
    Chester District)
Wright, J. D.         Ann Moore Maxwell    2B   248-249    1861
    (of Spartanburg District) (daughter of Robert A. Maxwell
    of Anderson District)
Wright, Thomas        Elizabeth McGehee    G    258        1830
Wright, William       Jane Youngblood      M    459-461    1843
    (of Yorkville, York District)
Wright, Z. C.         Sarah Chalmers       O    138-140    1844
    (marriage settlement 2 April 1844) (widow of Thomas B.
    Chalmers) (both of Newberry District)
Wright, Zachariah     Sarah Chalmers       T    449-452    1844
C. (reference to marriage settlement 2 April 1844)
    (widow of Thomas B. Chalmers) (both of Newberry
    District)
Wyatt, Wesley         Adeline A. McDowell  Z    218        1856
    (in Spartanburg District)
Wyett, Redmond        Nancy Ophelia Razor  Z    493-495    1857
Wylie, _____          Martha M. Robinson   M    383-386    1843
    (in Chester District) (daughter of James Robinson)

(Y)

Yancey, John          Anne Wood Delane     C    297-299    1816
    (marriage agreement 20 May 1816) (both of Columbia,
    Richland District)
Yarbrough, Beaufort   Louisa M. Adams      Z    12-14      1856
T.                    (daughter of Jesse S. Adams)

Implied South Carolina Marriages Volume IV 1787-1875

| MAN | WOMAN | VOL | PAGES | LIVED |
|---|---|---|---|---|
| Yates, David S. | Martha Ann Taylor | K | 546-552 | 1840 |

(married 23 January 1840) (marriage settlement 22 January 1840) (daughter of Henry P. Taylor and granddaughter of Col. Thomas Taylor) (Yates of Charleston) (she of Columbia)

| Yates, William | Jane Taylor | I | 306-309 | 1835 |
|---|---|---|---|---|

Black (marriage contract 28 October 1835) (widow) (he of Charleston) (she of Columbia)

| Yongue, _____ | Sarah Miller | 2B | 649-651 | 1863 |
|---|---|---|---|---|

(daughter of Robert Miller)

| Yongue, John L. | Sarah Miller | 2A | 468-469 | 1858 |
|---|---|---|---|---|

(marriage settlement 18 October 1858) (he of Fairfield District) (she of Chester District)

| Yongue, O. W. | Jane M. Lemon | V | 225-226 | 1850 |
|---|---|---|---|---|

(of Fairfield District) (daughter of James Lemon of Fairfield District)

| Yongue, Robert A. | Margaret R. Logan | U | 126-128 | 1850 |
|---|---|---|---|---|

(marriage settlement 10 July 1850) (granddaughter of Judge John S. Richardson) (of Fairfield District)

| Young, _____ | Mary Bryce | Y | 583 | 1856 |
|---|---|---|---|---|
| Young, _____ | Betsey Harris | G | 36-37 | 1829 |

(daughter of John Harris of Abbeville District)

| Young, James | Kitty Griffin | D | 388-389 | 1822 |
|---|---|---|---|---|

(marriage settlement 28 March 1822) (daughter of Reuben Griffin) (of Laurens District)

| Young, John D. | Sarah K. Johnson | X | 141-144 | 1853 |
|---|---|---|---|---|

(marriage settlement 4 December 1853) (daughter of Alexander Johnson) (both of Kershaw District)

| Young, Robert A. | Mary Riley Kershaw | H | 138-139 | 1832 |
|---|---|---|---|---|

(in Kershaw District)

| Young, Thompson | Martha Hawkins | 2B | 147-148 | 1860 |
|---|---|---|---|---|

(in Newberry District)

| Young, Thompson | Patsey Hawkins | T | 174-180 | 1849 |
|---|---|---|---|---|

Senr. (in Newberry District)

| Youngblood, _____ | Isabella Deen | E | 439 | 1826 |
|---|---|---|---|---|

(daughter of William Deen Senior of Edgefield District)

| Youngblood, Erasmus J. | Eliza Wigfall | G | 326-327 | 1831 |
|---|---|---|---|---|
| Youngblood, Lewis W. | Florella Holstein | 2A | 305-306 | 1858 |

(daughter of Wade Holstein of Edgefield District)

| Youngblood, William | Brunetta Lightfoot | T | 71 | 1847 |
|---|---|---|---|---|

(marriage contract 22 December 1847) (he of Abbeville District) (she of Edgefield District)

Implied South Carolina Marriages Volume IV 1787-1875

| MAN | WOMAN | VOL | PAGES | LIVED |
|---|---|---|---|---|

(Z)

Zeagler, Coonrod   Sarah Smith   G   77-78   1829
(marriage settlement 23 November 1830) (he was married before) (widow of George P. Smith) (in Barnwell District)
Zimmerman, Charles   Hannah Green   X   629-630   1855
Zimmerman, Charles C. H.   Hannah Green   2A   338-339   1858
Zuill, William   Mary Ann McClockin   F   107-110   1803
(reference to marriage settlement - no date given) (of Sumter District)

Implied South Carolina Marriages Volume IV 1787-1875

| WOMAN | MAN | VOL | PAGES | LIVED |
|---|---|---|---|---|

(A)

Ables, Dorothy		Daniel Garvin		T	255-256		1849
	(daughter of John J. Ables of Lexington District) (of
	Orangeburgh District)
Ables, Mary		William T. Phillips	T	255-256		1849
	(daughter of John J. Ables of Lexington District) (of
	Orangeburgh District)
Adams, Amy G.		John P. Adams		2C	206-208		1866
	(marriage settlement 17 November 1866)
Adams, Ann		Frances R. Timmons	2A	22-23		1857
	Elizabeth (daughter of Richard Wright Adams of Edgefield
	District) (of Edgefield District)
Adams, Elizabeth	Archibald C.		2A	670-673		1859
	Pringle		Campbell
	(marriage settlement 12 July 1859) (she of Pickens
	District) (he of Anderson District)
Adams, Fanny H.		John S. Shoolbred	2C	384-389		1867
	(marriage settlement 4 September 1867) (she of Richland
	District) (he of Charleston District)
Adams, Frances		Joseph Adams		X	208-211		1853
	(daughter of James F. Adams of Edgefield District)
Adams, Louisa M.	Beaufort T.		Z	12-14		1856
			Yarbrough
	(daughter of Jesse S. Adams)
Adams, Nancy		Albert Pruit		X	470-472		1852
	(marriage settlement 8 May 1852) (widow of George Adams
	of Newberry District) (of Newberry District)
Adams, Sarah		William Deen Sr		F	359-360		1828
	(marriage settlement 12 September 1828) (widow)
Adams, Sarah		Daniel OQuin Junior	D	105		1817
	[daughter of Ephram (Ephraim) Adams of Sumter District]
	[See also page 164]
Adams, Susan		Shemuel W. Nicholson	X	208-211		1853
	(daughter of James F. Adams of Edgefield District)
Adamson, Sarah A.	Zachariah Cantey	T	139-148		1848
	(in Kershaw District) [See also Volume W, pages 247-250,
	619-620]
Addison, Emma L.	James Patterson		2A	163-165		1857
	(marriage settlement 15 December 1857) (widow of Joseph
	Addison) (she of Barnwell and Edgefield Districts)
	(Patterson of Barnwell District)
Addison, Matilda	John Gaskins		T	232-233		1849
	(marriage settlement 14 June 1849) (in Edgefield
	District)

Implied South Carolina Marriages Volume IV 1787-1875

| WOMAN | MAN | VOL | PAGES | LIVED |
|---|---|---|---|---|
| Adger, Margaret | _____ Ellison | X | 144-145 | 1850 |
| Adger, Sarah E. | William Dalton Warren | 2C | 317-323 | 1866 |

(daughter of Robert Adger of Charleston) (of Anderson District)

| Adkinson, Tabitha | James Cammer | I | 474-476 | 1836 |

(marriage agreement 31 October 1836) (of Newberry District)

| Agnew, Ellen M. | _____ Pope | 2A | 580-581 | 1856 |
| Aiken, Harriet | John McK. Milling | 2B | 474-475 | 1862 |

Lowndes (daughter of James Aiken of Fairfield District) (of Fairfield District)

| Aiken, Henrietta W. | Joseph Clowney | Z | 660-661 | 1857 |

(daughter of James Aiken of Fairfield District)

| Aiken, Martha K. | David R. Evans | 2A | 746-747 | 1859 |

(daughter of James Aiken of Fairfield District, S.C.) (Evans late of Fairfield District, S.C., now of Louisiana)

| Albert, Ann | O. R. Bell | V | 570-571 | 1852 |
| Aldrich, Rosa | Darling P. Duncan | 2B | 761-762 | 1864 |

(daughter of Alfred P. Aldrich) (in Barnwell District)

| Allen, C. W. | E. Bellinger Jr. | Y | 401-404 | 1855 |

(daughter of John C. Allen) (of Barnwell District)

| Allen, Elizabeth C. | _____ Colzy | F | 369 | 1828 |

(daughter of Francis Allen of Camden)

| Allen, H. S. | R. C. Fowke | Z | 527-528 | 1857 |

(daughter of John C. Allen)

| Allen, Jane T. | W. H. Burns | X | 506 | 1854 |

(daughter of Thomas Allen) (of Greenville District)

| Allen, Juanda A. | J. H. Barksdale | S | 177-178 | 1848 |

(daughter of Bannister Allen of Abbeville District)

| Allen, Mary Lucia | John R. Allen | G | 33-35 | 1823 |

(marriage settlement __ June 1823) (widow of George Allen of Richmond County, Georgia) (John R. Allen of Richmond County, Georgia)

| Allen, Rebecca W. | Joseph Brown | I | 200-201 | 1835 |

(daughter of Francis Allen of Camden) (of Sumter District)

| Allen, Sarah E. | Joseph Allen | N | 191 | 1826 |

(reference to marriage settlement recorded 12 April 1826)

| Allen, Sarah E. | Joseph Allen Junr. | E | 439-441 | 1826 |

(marriage settlement 19 January 1826) (widow of Josiah G. Allen) (both of Barnwell District)

| Allen, Zilphia Z. | Paul H. Allen | 2B | 831-834 | 1864 |

(marriage contract 7 July 1864) (both of Barnwell District)

Implied South Carolina Marriages Volume IV 1787-1875

WOMAN              MAN                    VOL    PAGES      LIVED

Allston, Eliza     John B. White          H      7-8        1805
  (reference to marriage settlement __ March 1805) (she
  of Georgetown) (he of Charleston)
Alston, _____      George B. Pearson Sr   W      74-81      1845
  (daughter of James Alston of Fairfield District) (of
  Fairfield District)
Anderson, Ann      David B. Marten        K      146-147    1838
  (marriage settlement 13 April 1838) (both of Chester
  District)
Anderson, Henrietta Henry L. Theus        H      505-507    1833
  S. (marriage agreement 22 December 1833) (she of Sumter
  District, S.C.) (he of Tennessee)
Anderson, Louisa   John Reese Thomas      K      217-219    1838
  (marriage settlement 26 July 1838) (widow of Thomas
  Anderson) (in Sumter District)
Anderson, Margaret Samuel D. Carter       G      89-90      1830
  (marriage settlement 5 January 1830) (daughter of John
  Anderson Junr. and granddaughter of John Anderson Senr.)
  (both of Sumter District)
Anderson, Mildred  Thomas C. Ivey         Z      283        1856
  (marriage contract 5 June 1856) (in Lancaster District)
Anderson, Nancy    Daniel Gent            F      265-266    1828
  (marriage settlement 15 April 1828) (widow of James
  Anderson) (in Edgefield District)
Anderson, Sarah F. William S. Allgary     2A     581-584    1859
  (marriage settlement 1 March 1859) (widow of Richard L.
  Anderson) (both of Abbeville District)
Andrews, Mary      Andrew Hunter Senr.    D      119-122    1819
  (married 10 February 1819) (of Darlington District)
Ardis, Ann J.      John C. G. Key         M      283-285    1842
  (marriage settlement 31 August 1842) (both of Edgefield
  District)
Ardis, Mary        Arthur Simkins         C      186        1815
  (daughter of Abram Ardis of Edgefield District)
Ardis, Sarah       Henry Laurens Mayson   L      368-370    1841
  (widow of Abram Ardis of Be_a_ch Island, Edgefield
  District) (Mayson of Aiken)
Arledge, Charlotte Lucus A. Broom         L      463        1841
  (Arlege) (daughter of Isaac Arledge Senr. of Fairfield
  District) (of Fairfield District)
Arledge, Sarah     Lee D. Arick           K      169-170    1838
  (marriage settlement 28 June 1838) (widow) (both of
  Fairfield District)
Arnold, Elizabeth  Thomas J. Heard        2C     6-7        1864
  Y. (marriage settlement 28 July 1864) (she of Abbeville
  District, S.C.) (he of Elbert County, Georgia)

Implied South Carolina Marriages Volume IV 1787-1875

| WOMAN | MAN | VOL | PAGES | LIVED |
|---|---|---|---|---|
| Arnold, Frances | _____ Madden | 2B | 366-367 | 1861 |

(in Laurens District)

Arnold, Mary          Isaac L. Henning      S     391-393     1844
   (married 30 November 1844) (in Greenville District)
Arthur, Mary A.       Anderson Holmes       Z     776-778     1857
   (marriage settlement 5 March 1857) (widow) (she of
   Columbia, S.C.) (he of Alabama)
Arthur, Mary A.       _____ Homes           2B    52-61       1860
   (widow)
Arthur, Mary Ann      William E. Chambers   S     222-225     1848
   (marriage settlement 30 May 1848) (both of Columbia,
   Richland District)
Arthur, Mary Y.       _____ Thomas          R     65          1846
   (she of Abbeville District)
Arthur, Mary Y.       F. G. Thomas          S     40-41       1848
   (widow of J. R. Arthur) (of Abbeville District)
Ash, Eleanor S.       Newton E. Crawford    W     124-125     1852
   (daughter of Samuel Ash) (Cranford)
Ashley, Caroline      John Henry Anderson   Z     619-621     1856
   (marriage settlement 31 December 1856) (widow of Barnett
   Ashley)
Ashmore, Mary Jane    William Harris        X     605-607     1855
   (daughter of William H. Ashmore of Greenville District)
Atkin, Elizabeth C.   _____ Boozer          I     564         1837
   (Akin) (daughter of David Atkin of Newberry District)
Atkinson, Hannah      Lansden Fraser        E     277-279     1824
   (marriage settlement 8 December 1824) (both of Sumter
   District)
Atkinson, Sarah A.    Joseph J. Exum        I     26-27       1834
   (marriage agreement 19 February 1834) (she of Sumter
   District) (he of Kershaw District)
Atkinson. See Adkinson
Aul, Margaret         Jacob Cook            E     27-30       1822
   (marriage settlement 22 August 1822) (of Newberry
   District)
Autry, Sarah. See Sarah Rowe
Aveilhe, Clara        Eugene Durbec Sr.     M     281-283     1842
                      (of Aiken, Barnwell District)
Ayer, Elizabeth B.    _____ Breeden         Y     524-526     1855
Ayer, Elizabeth B.    James B. Breeden      Y     371-372     1854
   (both of Marlborough District)
Ayer, Mary A.         _____ Long            Y     524-526     1855
Ayer, Sarah H.        Thomas Marshall       Y     524-526     1855
   (marriage settlement 19 November 1855) (daughter of
   Hutwell Ayer) (in Marlborough District)

Implied South Carolina Marriages Volume IV 1787-1875

| WOMAN | MAN | VOL | PAGES | LIVED |
|---|---|---|---|---|

(B)

Bacot, Ada W.     Lieut. Thomas A. G.    2B    728-732    1863
Clark
(marriage settlement 10 November 1863) (widow) (she of Darlington District)
Bacot, Elizabeth E.    George B. Bealer    W    200-203    1852
(marriage settlement 14 December 1852) (daughter of Samuel Bacot) (she of Darlington District) (he now of Chesterfield District)
Bacot, Hannah S.    Archibald S. Dyson    2A    415-417    1858
(marriage settlement 15 July 1858) (both of Darlington District)
Bacot, Maria Louisa    Theodore A. Dargan    O    236-238    1844
(marriage settlement 5 November 1844) (both of Darlington District)
Bacot, Serena L.    Charles A. Dargan    2A    721-722    1859
(marriage settlement 24 August 1859)
Bailey, \_\_\_\_\_    \_\_\_\_\_ Weathers    D    371    1821
(daughter of Thomas Bailey of York District) [See also page 373]
Bailey, Catharine L.    Benjamin Clifford    H    4-5    1831
(of Edgefield District)
Bailey, Cynthia    George Foster    L    351    1841
(in Union District)
Bailey, Sarah    Randall Withers    D    372    1821
(daughter of Thomas Bailey of York District)
Bailey. See Bayly
Baker, Harriet P.    Bernard O'Conner    2A    477-479    1858
(marriage settlement 27 December 1858) (both of Abbeville District) [See also pages 606-608]
Baker, Nancy T.    Hiram Tillman    L    178-181    1840
Baker, Sarah E.    Charles W. Doyley    G    107-109    1817
(Doyly)
(reference to marriage settlement 14 April 1817) (in Greenville District)
Baker, Sarah Jane    William Harris    2B    118-119    1860
(in Abbeville District)
Ballard, Ulrica    Hiram E. Sloan    X    428-430    1854
Leonora (marriage settlement 11 April 1854) (daughter of John Ballard) (she was born about 1835) (she of Sumter District) (Sloan of Kershaw District)
Bane, Martha    \_\_\_\_\_ Holman    2B    770-771    1863
Barber, Eliza    \_\_\_\_\_ Wilmore    H    351-354    1833
(daughter of James Barber)

Implied South Carolina Marriages Volume IV 1787-1875

| WOMAN | MAN | VOL | PAGES | LIVED |
|---|---|---|---|---|
| Barber, Jane | Hugh Barkley | H | 351-354 | 1833 |
| Barker, Sheba | ____ Mason | G | 214-215 | 1830 |
| Barksdale, Eliza | Ezekiel Pickens | H | 153-155 | 1832 |

(daughter of George Barksdale)

| Barksdale, Matilda | Robert Powel (Powell) | P | 279-281 | 1846 |

(daughter of Higgerson Barksdale of Laurens District)

| Barmore, Elzira | David L. Donald | X | 677-679 | 1854 |

(in Abbeville District)

| Barmore, Mary | James Kay | U | 410-411 | 1851 |

(marriage settlement 4 February 1851) (in Abbeville District)

| Barmore, Mary E. | G. W. Trible (Tribble) | 2B | 182-184 | 1860 |

(marriage settlement 12 September 1860) (both of Abbeville District)

| Barnard, Ann | ____ Jervis (Bernard) | B | 566-569 | 1808 |

(daughter of Robert Barnard of Horse Creek, Edgefield District)

| Barnard, Jane (Jean) | John Heard | B | 589-593 | 1809 |

(married 16 July 1809) (marriage contract 15 July 1809) (she of Horse Creek, Edgefield District) (he of Pine Grove, Barnwell District)

| Barnett, Jane Ann | Thomas C. Brady | Z | 646-648 | 1857 |

(daughter of Jorial Barnett) (both of Spartanburg District)

| Barr, Margaret R. | Edwin Cater | 2A | 539-540 | 1859 |

(marriage settlement 15 February 1859) (daughter of William H. Barr)

| Barsh, Catharine M. | Abner Lewis Hammond | I | 131-135 | 1834 |

(marriage settlement 19 November 1834) [See also Volume K, pages 87-90]

| Bartley, Mahala | Samuel Lott | Y | 519-521 | 1855 |

(daughter of Thomas Bartley of Edgefield District)

| Baskerville, Susannah (widow) | ____ Farrow | F | 367 | 1828 |

| Bass, Lovisa H. | William Walker | L | 168-169 | 1840 |

(marriage settlement __ September 1840) (in Orangeburgh District)

| Bates, Ellen Unity | James Trumble | 2A | 314 | 1857 |

(daughter of John Bates of Richland District)

| Bates, Eloisa | George J. Strother | T | 544-547 | 1850 |

(daughter of John Bates of Lexington District)

| Bates, Georgiana | Robert Baugh | T | 544-547 | 1850 |

(daughter of John Bates of Lexington District)

Implied South Carolina Marriages Volume IV 1787-1875

| WOMAN | MAN | VOL | PAGES | LIVED |
|---|---|---|---|---|
| Bates, Gracia (Gracie) Ann (daughter of John Bates of Richland District) | Albert James | V | 214-215 | 1852 |
| Bates, Martha (daughter of John Bates of Richland District) | William Shiver | 2A | 315 | 1857 |
| Bates, Martha R. | William M. Beckham | U | 98-100 | 1850 |
| Bates, Mary Hannah (daughter of John Bates of Richland District) | Dr. Francis M. Beckham | 2A | 312 | 1857 |
| Bates, Phoebe (daughter of William Bates) | Francis Morgan | X | 449-450 | 1854 |
| Bates, Sarah Adeline (daughter of John Bates Sr.) (Griffin of Buncombe County, North Carolina) | Horatio Griffin | 2A | 278-279 | 1858 |
| Bauskett, Susan Ann (daughter of John Bauskett of Columbia, Richland District) | David M. Clarke | Z | 791-792 | 1857 |
| Baxter, Violet (marriage settlement 4 October 1847) (both of York District) | A. F. Branch | S | 139-141 | 1847 |
| Beacham, Elizabeth (daughter of Daniel S. Beacham of Abbeville District) (Mays of Abbeville District) | Larkin Mays | X | 665-667 | 1855 |
| Beall, Martha (reference to marriage settlement - no date given) (widow of Duke Beall) | James (or John) Shoemaker | E | 449 | 1826 |
| Bean, Lydia (Lyddy) (daughter of James Bean Senr. of Edgefield District) | Moses Sanders | O | 254-256 | 1844 |
| Beard, Anne (daughter of Joshua Beard) (she of Richland District) | ____ Mardney | D | 9-11 | 1818 |
| Beard, Mary (daughter of Joshua Beard) (she of Richland District) | ____ Wolf | D | 9-11 | 1818 |
| Beard, Mary G. | ____ Strobel (Stroble) | D | 239 | 1821 |
| Beard, Sarah E. (daughter of James Beard) (in Fairfield District) | John W. Lawhon | V | 30-31 | 1851 |
| Beatty, Margarett L. (daughter of Jonathan Beatty) (of Union District) | Robert G. H. Farr | H | 213-215 | 1828 |
| Beaty, Eliza Ann (daughter of Jonathan Beaty) | David B. Rice | I | 466-468 | 1836 |
| Beckham, Martha R. (marriage contract 2 June 1850) (widow of William M. Beckham) (both of Richland District) | William Shiver | U | 98-100 | 1850 |
| Beckham, Rebecca (widow) (in Lancaster District) | Thomas Gibbons | H | 208-209 | 1832 |

Implied South Carolina Marriages Volume IV 1787-1875

| WOMAN | MAN | VOL | PAGES | LIVED |
|---|---|---|---|---|
| Becktler, Caroline L. | Dedrick Windhorn | 2B | 623-624 | 1863 |

(marriage settlement 29 May 1863)

Bedgegood,      John B. Billingsley    Z    170-182    1851
Catharine (widow of Malachi N. Bedgegood of Marlborough District)

Bedgegood,      John B. Billingsley    F    73-78    1827
Catharine (marriage settlement 7 July 1827) (widow of Malachi N. Bedgegood) (in Marlborough District)

Bee, Mary Eliza    Robert Lebby the    2C    363-368    1867
                          Younger
(daughter of Robert R. Bee)

Belk, Sarah N.     John R. Simpson     2C    338-340    1867
(marriage contract 9 May 1867) (she of Lancaster District, S.C.) (he of Union County, North Carolina)

Bell, Emily E.     Lewis M. Hatch      2C    417-419    1837
(reference to marriage settlement 24 November 1837) (of Charleston) [See also pages 426-428]

Bell, Mary H.      John Patton         L    355-357    1841
(marriage settlement 26 June 1841) (he was married before) (she of S.C.) (he of Tennessee)

Bellinger, Mary E.  Joseph Edward Glover 2B    651-654    1863
(marriage settlement 7 July 1863) (daughter of Edmund C. Bellinger) (she of Charleston) (Glover of Colleton District) (in Barnwell District) [See also pages 720-721, 724, 772-773]

Belton, Martha    Joseph Mickle      B    180-183    1802
(marriage settlement 16 August 1802) (daughter of John Belton) (of Camden)

Bender, Sarah R. M.  Abram Ardis         B    594-595    1809
(marriage agreement 24 April 1809) (widow of George Bender) (Ardis was married before) (of Edgefield District)

Benson, Elizabeth L.  _____ Butler         2C    429-430    1868

Benson, Esther    _____ Moore          W    460-462    1853
Westfield (daughter of E. B. Benson of Anderson District)

Benson, Francis   Joseph Green        N    71        1843
(marriage contract 3 January 1843) (both of Greenville District)

Benson, Mary      George Mathew Myers 2B    164-166    1860
(daughter of Willis Benson of Greenville District) (she died 12 August 1860) (of Marion District)

Benson, Nancy G.   Hugh Dickson        2B    335-337    1861
(widow of William P. Benson) (in Pickens District)

Implied South Carolina Marriages Volume IV 1787-1875

| WOMAN | MAN | VOL | PAGES | LIVED |
|---|---|---|---|---|

Bently, Sarah　　　William A. H. Bevill　O　357-358　1822
　(marriage 2 September 1822) (daughter of Joel Bently)
　(both of Union District)
Berly, Elizabeth　　William Riser　　　I　396-397　1835
　(daughter of John Berly of Newberry District) (of
　Newberry District)
Berry, Eliza V.　　　Pressly Brown　　　2A　513-514　1859
　(of Columbia, Richland District)
Berry, Matilda A.　　John R. Terrell　　W　11-13　　1852
　(daughter of James Berry) (in Kershaw District)
Bethea, Rebecca　　　Simeon P. McCormic_　2B　159-161　1860
　(marriage settlement 21 August 1860) (widow of Francis
　Bethea) (both of Marion District)
Bethea, S. A.　　　　C. J. Fladger　　　2A　694-695　1859
　(marriage settlement 16 August 1859) (widow of W. S.
　Bethea) (both of Marion District)
Bethune, Elizabeth _____ Thomas　　　2B　309-312　1861
　N.
Betsel, Martha　　　Thomas Wells　　　　R　438-440　1824
Bigger, Ann E.　　　J. C. Philips　　　X　327-331　1854
　(marriage settlement 24 January 1854) (in York District)
Bigger, Ann E.　　　J. C. Phillips　　　Z　445-447　1854
　(reference to marriage agreement 24 January 1854) (in
　York District)
Bigger, Frances C.　W. B. Smith　　　　2C　250-252　1866
　(marriage settlement 18 December 1866) (daughter of A.
　B. Bigger) (in York District)
Bird, Cornelia L. _____ Cross　　　　　T　315-324　1848
　(in Edgefield District)
Bird, Elizabeth _____ Taylor　　　　　T　315-324　1848
　(in Edgefield District)
Bird, Louisa A.　　　Tilghman D. Peurifoy T　315-324　1848
　(granddaughter of Col. Zachariah S. Brooks of Edgefield
　District, who died April 1848) (in Edgefield District)
Bird. See Byrd
Bishop, Ann Love　　William T. Wallace　2B　315-319　1861
　Adelade (marriage settlement 19 February 1861) (daughter
　of Rev. P. E. Bishop) (in Marlboro District)
Black, Jane Ann _____ Cline　　　　　　G　181-185　1830
　(daughter of John Black of Columbia, Richland District)
Black, Mary P.　　　John L. Black　　　2A　35-38　　1857
Black, Sarah E.　　　Abner A. Porter　　2B　799-801　1864
　(marriage agreement 12 March 1864) (widow of James A.
　Black) (she of York District) (Porter of Richland
　District)

Implied South Carolina Marriages Volume IV 1787-1875

| WOMAN | MAN | VOL | PAGES | LIVED |
|---|---|---|---|---|
| Blackburn, Ann Maria Eliza | Reverend Wm S. Wilson | E | 478-482 | 1826 |

(marriage settlement 24 June 1826) (she of Columbia) (he of Charleston)

| Blackburn, Maria | Martin Van Buren New | 2B | 671-673 | 1863 |

(marriage settlement 7 July 1863) (widow) (she of Edgefield District) (he of Barnwell District)

| Blackwell, Isabella Ann | William Wingate | E | 152-153 | 1823 |

(marriage settlement 22 September 1823) (in Darlington District)

| Blackwell, Isabella Ann | William Wingate | N | 304-306 | 1844 |

(of Darlington District)

| Blackwell, Sarah Ann | James W. Owens | W | 189-191 | 1852 |

(marriage settlement 6 December 1852) (widow) (both of Darlington District)

| Bland, Emily M. | ____ Witt | X | 2-3 | 1853 |

["Emily Witt (otherwise known as Emily Bland)"] (in Newberry District)

| Blasingame, Caroline C. | Thomas T. Brown | Y | 232-234 | 1855 |

(in Anderson District)

| Bledsoe, Elizabeth | ____ Addison | 2A | 571 | 1857 |

(daughter of Lewis Bledsoe of Edgefield District)

| Blewer, Elizabeth M. | James B. Coleman | K | 221-224 | 1838 |

(marriage settlement 9 August 1838) (widow of John G. Blewer of Lexington District) (Coleman was married before) (of Edgefield District)

| Blocker, Caroline S. | Matthew W. Abney | 2B | 161-164 | 1860 |

(daughter of James Blocker) (in Edgefield District)

| Blount, Elizabeth | Andrew Miller | A | 224-240 | 1793 |

(daughter of Charles Blount)

| Boatwright, ____ | ____ Hutchinson | Y | 436-437 | 1855 |

(daughter of James Boatwright)

| Boatwright, Lavica | Obediah Gulledge | L | 128-131 | 1840 |

(Levica) (marriage settlement 25 June 1840) (widow of Drury Boatwright) (both of Chesterfield District)

| Bobo, ____ | Frederick Werber | 2A | 384 | 1858 |

(daughter of John E. Bobo) (of Newberry District)

| Bogan, Elizabeth | William H. Green | I | 400 | 1835 |

Jr. (marriage settlement 31 December 1835) (daughter of William Bogan) (in Union District)

| Bolt, Mary | John Nash | L | 143-144 | 1840 |

(marriage settlement 4 July 1840) (in Laurens District)

| Bones, Martha | ____ Hughes | N | 15 | 1842 |
| Bookter, Judith | Judah Barrett | B | 446-449 | 1806 |

(marriage settlement 19 November 1806) (widow of Jacob Bookter and a prior marriage with ____ Frost) (of Columbia, Richland District)

Implied South Carolina Marriages Volume IV 1787-1875

| WOMAN | MAN | VOL | PAGES | LIVED |
|---|---|---|---|---|

Boone, Hannah J. H. Thomas M. McCutchen 2A 783-784 1860
(marriage settlement 1 February 1860) (she of Sumter District) (he of Williamsburg District)
Boone, Mary Jones Andrew C. Pickens U 321-324 1850
(marriage settlement 9 December 1850) (daughter of Thomas Boone who died 8 October 1830) (both of Pendleton District)
Boozer, Mary E. G. Fairbarn 2A 50-51 1857
(daughter of George Boozer of Newberry District) (of Laurens District)
Bossard, Ellen D. H. (Henry David) U 228-230 1850
Elizabeth Smith
(marriage settlement 24 October 1850) (she of Sumter District) (he of Georgetown District)
Bossard, Sarah Andrew H. Buchanan P 326-328 1846
Howell (in Sumter District)
Bostick, Nancy John C. Mayson E 306 1817
(of Abbeville District)
Boucher, Mary William Elders C 222-223 1816
(marriage agreement 13 January 1816) (widow)
Boulware, Sarah _____ Paulding W 197-198 1852
(daughter of Thomas Boulware)
Bowers, Martha Angus P. Brown R 513-516 1847
Teresa (marriage contract 24 September 1847) (she of Edgefield District) (he of Barnwell District)
Bowie, Alathea James J. Gilmer L 126-127 1840
(in Abbeville District)
Bowman, Eliza James C. Richbourg 2A 249-250 1857
(daughter of John Bowman)
Bowman, Sarah William F. Butler 2A 249-250 1857
(daughter of John A. Bowman)
Box, Mary John Buford C 147-150 1814
(marriage settlement 1 December 1814) (widow of Thomas Box) (both of Beaufort District, S.C.) (Buford late of Screven County, Georgia)
Boyce, Martha John Boyce O 195-197 1844
Elizabeth Rosanna (marriage contract 10 July 1844) (both of Union District)
Boyd, Dorcas M. Abel D. Rhame N 112-113 1842
(daughter of John Boyd of Sumter District)
Boyd, Margaret James Smith X 261-263 1854
Amanda (marriage settlement 20 February 1854) (in York District)
Boyd, Sarah George Davis E 484-486 1826
(marriage settlement 25 April 1826) (both of York District)

Implied South Carolina Marriages Volume IV 1787-1875

| WOMAN | MAN | VOL | PAGES | LIVED |
|---|---|---|---|---|
| Boyett, Margaret | Elijah J. Beck | U | 160-161 | 1850 |

(marriage settlement 9 September 1850) (in Barnwell District)

| | | | | |
|---|---|---|---|---|
| Boykin, Charlotte L. | James M. Taylor | O | 358-359 | 1845 |

(in Kershaw District)

| | | | | |
|---|---|---|---|---|
| Boykin, Kitty L. | Thomas Savage Heyward | 2B | 329-331 | 1861 |

(marriage settlement 9 April 1861)

| | | | | |
|---|---|---|---|---|
| Boykin, Mahazra | ____ Bradley | U | 208-210 | 1850 |

(Mahaza) R. (she of Sumter District)

| | | | | |
|---|---|---|---|---|
| Boykin, Mary | Major Edward B. Cantey | 2B | 706-707 | 1863 |

(daughter of Alexander Hamilton Boykin of Kershaw District)

| | | | | |
|---|---|---|---|---|
| Boykin, Mary Whitaker | Edward B. Cantey | 2C | 85-87 | 1866 |

(daughter of A. Hamilton Boykin of Kershaw District)

| | | | | |
|---|---|---|---|---|
| Boyle, Anna D. | James M. Smith | 2A | 285-294 | 1857 |

(daughter of Cunningham Boyle)

| | | | | |
|---|---|---|---|---|
| Boyle, Mary | ____ Jones | 2A | 285-294 | 1857 |

(widow of Cunningham Boyle)

| | | | | |
|---|---|---|---|---|
| Bracey, Martha E. | William Rosser | K | 324-327 | 1839 |

(marriage settlement 3 January 1839) (widow of Philip Bracey) (she of Sumter District) (Rosser of Kershaw District) [See also Volume L, pages 416-417]

| | | | | |
|---|---|---|---|---|
| Bracy, Maria | Jonathan Boykin | G | 92-93 | 1830 |

(marriage settlement 24 January 1830)

| | | | | |
|---|---|---|---|---|
| Bracy, Maria | William Mathias | D | 187-188 | 1820 |

(Mariah) (reference to marriage articles 7 March 1820) (widow of Solly Bracy) (Mathias of Camden)

| | | | | |
|---|---|---|---|---|
| Bradford, ____ | John R. Jayroe | 2A | 586-587 | 1859 |

(daughter of William W. Bradford)

| | | | | |
|---|---|---|---|---|
| Bradford, Elizabeth Susan | William Pace | 2A | 785-788 | 1859 |

(daughter of William W. Bradford of Sumter District)

| | | | | |
|---|---|---|---|---|
| Bradford, Frances Lillis | Kindrick Williams | 2A | 785-788 | 1859 |

(daughter of William W. Bradford of Sumter District)

| | | | | |
|---|---|---|---|---|
| Bradham, Sarah | William O. W. Dorithy | U | 329-331 | 1851 |

(marriage settlement 9 January 1851) (in Sumter District)

| | | | | |
|---|---|---|---|---|
| Bradley, Elizabeth Lang | Dr John D. McLeod | T | 30 | 1849 |

(daughter of John Bradley of Sumter District)

| | | | | |
|---|---|---|---|---|
| Bradley, Emma T. | Sebastian Sumter | 2B | 827-829 | 1864 |

(marriage settlement 24 May 1864) (in Sumter District)

Implied South Carolina Marriages Volume IV 1787-1875

| WOMAN | MAN | VOL | PAGES | LIVED |
|---|---|---|---|---|

Bradley, Margaret   Richard Harrison     R    391-393    1847
   Isabella (marriage settlement 18 February 1847)
   (daughter of John Bradley of Sumter District, S.C.)
   (Harrison of Florida)
Bradley, Sarah      William Bowen        Y    256-258    1855
   (marriage settlement 5 July 1855) (widow of Isaac
   Bradley) (she of Greenville District) (Bowen of Pickens
   District)
Brady, Frances E.   William A. Noble     Z    278-280    1856
   (daughter of Robert Brady of Abbeville District) (of
   Abbeville District)
Bratten, Mary C.    William R. Loury     U    1-4        1850
   (daughter of Dr. John S. Bratten of York District) (of
   York District)
Breithaupt, Ann     Ossian (Osmund)      I    610-612    1837
   Elizabeth        Gregory
   (daughter of Christian Breithaupt of Edgefield District,
   S.C., who died 4 December 1835) (Gregory of Macon and
   Savannah, Georgia)
Brewer, Clarissa    Alfred Lewis         S    47-48      1847
   (daughter of John Brewer) (of Anderson District)
Bright, Anna C.     Andrew J. Counts     2B   208-210    1860
   (marriage settlement 13 November 1860) (in Lexington
   District)
Bright, Elizabeth   Smith W. Dozier      G    370-371    1831
Bright, Polly       Jonathan Adams       G    370-371    1831
Britt, Martha Ann   Gabriel J. Wayne     Z    496-499    1856
   (marriage contract 8 November 1856) (widow of Daniel A.
   Britt) (she of Sumter District) (Wayne of Marion
   District)
Britton, Elizabeth  Charles Delorme      N    73-75      1843
   (in Sumter District)
Brock, Mary G.      James H. Watt        Z    557        1847
   (reference to marriage settlement 18 November 1847)
Brock, Mary Green   James H. Watt        S    25-26      1847
   (marriage settlement 18 November 1847) (daughter of
   William Brock) (both of Sumter District)
Brockington, Maria  Tyre D. Spann        2A   351-352    1858
   E. (widow of William T. Brockington) (in Sumter
   District)
Brockman, Kezia J.  James Giles Poole    2C   175-177    1866
   (marriage settlement 10 April 1866) (widow) (both of
   Spartanburg District)
Brogdon, Martha Ann David E. Hoyle       2B   247-248    1860
   Ellen Tindal (widow of Isaac B. Brogdon)

Implied South Carolina Marriages Volume IV 1787-1875

| WOMAN | MAN | VOL | PAGES | LIVED |
|---|---|---|---|---|

Brooks, Behithland _____ Bird          T    315-324   1848
    (daughter of Col. Zachariah S. Brooks of Edgefield
    District, who died April 1848)
Brooks, Ellen S.     R. G. M. Dunovant  T    468-469   1849
    (daughter of Whitfield Brooks of Edgefield District)
Brooks, Lucinda      _____ Bird         T    315-324   1848
    (daughter of Col. Zachariah S. Brooks of Edgefield
    District, who died April 1848)
Brooks, Mary         _____ Watts        Y    214-215   1855
    ("Mrs. Mary Watts formerly Mary Brooks") (in Abbeville
    District)
Brooks, Nancy        Barkley M. Blocker H    212-213   1832
    (daughter of Col. Zachariah Smith Brooks of Edgefield
    District, who died April 1848) [Must also see pages 315-
    324]] [See also Volume T, pages 10-11]
Brough, Frances A.   Thomas M. Ard      2A   81-82     1857
    (both of Abbeville District)
Brough, Jane E.      Albert A. Humphries W  632-633    1853
    (daughter of Thomas Brough of Abbeville District) (of
    Abbeville District)
Brown, _____         _____ Ervin        R    398-400   1847
    (daughter of James Brown of Darlington District)
Brown, Anna H.       Cyrus Bacot        F    152-153   1827
    (marriage settlement 20 September 1827) (widow of Wm.
    Brown) (she of Marlborough District) (Bacot of
    Darlington District)
Brown, Antoinette    William E. Black   Y    195-197   1855
    E. (marriage settlement __ February 1855) (widow)
Brown, Eady          _____ Southerland  N    218-219   1843
    (daughter of Lewis Brown of Pickens District)
Brown, Elizabeth     James Jones        E    390-391   1825
    (marriage settlement 23 November 1825) (widow) (in
    Colleton District)
Brown, Elizabeth     Andrew Welsh       C    348-349   1816
    (daughter of Joseph Brown of Sumter District)
Brown, Margaret E.   Thomas L. Whiteside 2B  473-474   1862
    (marriage contract 30 January 1862) (widow of Wm C.
    Brown) (she of Union District) (Whiteside of York
    District)
Brown, Martha P.     Jno: C. Livingston G    354-356   1830
    (daughter of Peter Brown of Abbeville District)
Brown, Nancy         Jesse Brown        P    243-244   1845
    (marriage contract 30 November 1845) (she of Laurens
    District) (he of Spartanburgh District)
Brown, Rachael       Solomon Owens      K    411-413   1839
    (marriage contract 14 May 1839) (in Marion District)
Brown, Sally C.      John T. Goodwyn    R    22-23     1846

Implied South Carolina Marriages Volume IV 1787-1875

| WOMAN | MAN | VOL | PAGES | LIVED |
|---|---|---|---|---|
| Brumby, Anna E. | Ravenel S. Bradwell | W | 536-539 | 1853 |

(marriage settlement 5 April 1853) (both of Sumter District)

Brumby, Anna E.   Ravenel S. Bradwell   2A   587-589   1853
(reference to marriage settlement 5 April 1853) (in Sumter District)

Brumby, Mary Charlotte   Charles Augustus Rich   T   528-530   1849
(marriage settlement 20 December 1849) (both of Sumter District)

Brumby, Mary Elvira   James Denson   E   447-448   1826
(marriage settlement 28 February 1826) (both of Sumter District)

Brunson, Amanda C.   Laurence S. Johnson   Z   690-691   1857
(daughter of Daniel D. Brunson of Edgefield District) (of Edgefield District)

Brunson, Caroline Macon   Edwin D. Felder   X   548   1854
(daughter of William L. Brunson) (in Sumter District)

Brunson, Caroline Macon   Erwin D. Felder   2B   225-228   1860
(daughter of William L. Brunson of Sumter District)

Brunson, Elizabeth   John O. Holladay   F   383-384   1828
(marriage settlement 27 November 1828) (daughter of Daniel Brunson) (in Sumter District)

Brunson, Mary Marsena   Capt. Lucius P. Loring   2C   498-501   1868
(daughter of William L. Brunson of Sumter District) (in Sumter District)

Brunson, Mary Marsena   Lucius P. Loring   2C   157-166   1846
(daughter of William L. Brunson of Sumter District) (in Sumter District)

Brunson, Rebecca   Elihu Hodge   I   601-602   1837
(marriage agreement 13 July 1837) (daughter of Daniel Brunson) (both of Sumter District)

Brunson, Susan   Advil Davis   W   252-254   1852
(Susannah) (marriage settlement __ December 1852) (in Sumter District)

Bryan, Ann M.   William B. Jennings   X   145-147   1854
(daughter of Allen Bryan of Russell County, Alabama) (of Sumter District, S.C.)

Bryan, E. M.   William G. Riley   N   96-97   1843
(marriage settlement 13 April 1843) (both of Barnwell District)

Bryan, Elizabeth   John Ball the Younger   C   321-323   1810
(daughter of John Bryan)

Implied South Carolina Marriages Volume IV 1787-1875

| WOMAN | MAN | VOL | PAGES | LIVED |
|---|---|---|---|---|
| Bryan, Sarah E. (daughter of Joseph Bryan) | Josiah G. Allen | E | 439-441 | 1826 |
| Bryant, Elizabeth (widow) (marriage settlement 26 January 1830) (both of Union District) | Capt. William Rountree | G | 99-100 | 1830 |
| Bryce, Mary | ____ Young | Y | 583 | 1856 |
| Bryson, Kezia J. | ____ Brockman | 2C | 175-177 | 1866 |
| Burgess, Eloisa (reference to marriage settlement 8 January 1829) (she of Williamsburg District) (he of Sumter District) | William Waties | S | 405-408 | 1829 |
| Burroughs, Mary Elizabeth (marriage settlement 1 June 1865) | Francis H. Trenholm | 2C | 40-41 | 1865 |
| Burton, Amelia (widow of Peter Burton of Columbia, Richland District) (Boozer of Newberry District) | David Boozer | S | 413-414 | 1848 |
| Burton, Bethaniah (daughter of Aaron Burton of Newberry District) | John B. Cole | G | 348 | 1831 |
| Burton, Magdaline (daughter of Aaron Burton of Newberry District) | John Shepherd | H | 30-31 | 1832 |
| Burton, Susannah (daughter of Aaron Burton of Newberry District) | Lorunzey Holsten | H | 30-31 | 1832 |
| Bush, Caroline A. (marriage settlement 4 February 1852) (widow) (both of Barnwell District) | Hansford A. Cochran | V | 392-395 | 1852 |
| Bush, Elizabeth Sapp (daughter of George Bush of Barnwell District) | James M. Bowers | O | 427-428 | 1845 |
| Bush, Jane (marriage settlement 14 May 1832) (widow of Thomas Bush) (both of Barnwell District) | Lewis Weathersby | H | 158-159 | 1832 |
| Bussey, Polly (daughter of Demcy Bussey Sr.) | ____ Edmunds | Y | 73-75 | 1855 |
| Bussey, Sarah L. (daughter of Demcy Bussey Sr.) | Patrick S. Rogers | Y | 73-75 | 1855 |
| Butler, Eloise Brevard (marriage settlement 20 November 1854) (of Barnwell) | Johnson Hagood | X | 596-597 | 1854 |
| Butler, Lucy T. (marriage settlement 16 January 1834) (widow) (in Edgefield District) | Joseph Moore | H | 485-487 | 1834 |
| Butler, Martha Ann Ellen Tindal (daughter of Peter M. Butler of Clarendon District) | Isaac B. Brogdon | 2B | 247-248 | 1860 |
| Butler, Mary (daughter of Seth Butler of Edgefield District) (of Edgefield District) | ____ Anderson | Z | 298 | 1856 |

Implied South Carolina Marriages Volume IV 1787-1875

| WOMAN | MAN | VOL | PAGES | LIVED |
|---|---|---|---|---|

Butler, Sarah Elizabeth   J. L. Dixon   U   221   1850
(daughter of Peter M. Butler of Sumter District)
Buzzard, Sarah   James J. Jones   Z   637-638   1857
(marriage contract 14 February 1857) (daughter of Jacob Buzzard) (both of Newberry District)
Bynum, Eugenia A.   Andrew J. Mobley   2B   679-680   1863
(daughter of Nathaniel Bynum of Richland District) (of Fairfield District)
Byrd, Elizabeth   Christopher Flinn   R   94-96   1846
(marriage settlement 13 October 1846) (widow of Miller Byrd) (both of Darlington District)
Byrd, Eliza C.   John B. Murphy   I   178-179   1834
(marriage contract 13 December 1834) (both of Richland District)
Byrd, Mary L.   Julius A. Mims   2B   180-181   1860
(postnuptial settlement 2 October 1860) (daughter of Reddin Byrd) (of Sumter District)
Byrd. See Bird

(C)

Cahusac, Henrietta H.   Gustavus A. Williams   N   25-30   1843
(marriage settlement 25 January 1843) (she of York District)
Caldwell, Catharine E.   Dr. John C. Mobley   2B   280-281   1860
(daughter of James E. Caldwell of Fairfield District) (of Fairfield District)
Caldwell, Elizabeth   Robert Hadden   U   119-122   1850
(of Spartanburgh District)
Caldwell, Elizabeth T.   David O. McLin   M   166   1842
(daughter of James Caldwell of Abbeville District)
Caldwell, Margaret R.   William H. Stallworth (Stallsworth)   2B   97-99   1860
(in Abbeville District)
Caldwell, Mary A.   Gabriel Cannon   2A   131   1857
(marriage settlement 21 October 1857) (in Spartanburg District)
Caldwell, Mary Ophelia   Thomas J. Robertson   W   506-507   1853
(daughter of John Caldwell of Richland District)
Caldwell, Nancy   Revd. L. W. Curtis   U   283-285   1850
(reference to antenuptial agreement 29 July 1850) (in Union District)

Implied South Carolina Marriages Volume IV 1787-1875

| WOMAN | MAN | VOL | PAGES | LIVED |
|---|---|---|---|---|
| Caldwell, Rosannah | James Brown | G | 202-204 | 1828 |

(marriage settlement 23 July 1828) (in Newberry District)

Caldwell, Sarah Coger  \_\_\_\_\_ Kenner   X   122-123   1849

Calhoun, Aurelia   Alexander R. Rucker   2A   762-763   1860
(daughter of John A. Calhoun of Abbeville District)
(Rucker late of Louisiana, now of Abbeville District, S.C.)

Calhoun, Lucretia   Dr. Henry H. Towns   G   356   1831
Ann (daughter of William Calhoun of Abbeville District, S.C.)

Calhoun, Martha C.   A. Burt   G   357   1831
(daughter of William Calhoun of Abbeville District)

Calhoun, Mary   John R. Proffitt   2B   150   1860
(daughter of Nathan Calhoun of Abbeville District)

Calhoun, Mary   John R. Profitt   2A   443-444   1858
(daughter of Nathan Calhoun) (in Abbeville District)

Calhoun, Sarah   Thomas M. White   2A   444-445   1858
(daughter of Nathan Calhoun) (of Anderson District)

Calhoun, Sarah A.   John Archer   L   329-331   1841
(marriage settlement 15 April 1841) (both of Abbeville District)

Calvert, Nancy C.   \_\_\_\_\_ Dunn   L   426-428   1841
(daughter of Jesse Calvert)

Cameron, Eliza A.   Henry K. Witherspoon   2A   6-8   1845
(marriage settlement 18 February 1845) (both of Orange County, North Carolina)

Cameron, Jane   William P. Hall   P   48-49   1845
(daughter of Joseph Cameron of Fairfield District, S.C.)
(of Pickens County, Alabama)

Cammer, Susan   \_\_\_\_\_ Debruhl   H   169   1832
(daughter of James Cammer of Richland District)

Campbell, Sally M.   R. Drayton Nance   Z   640-641   1857
(daughter of Dr. Robert E. Campbell) (in Laurens District)

Cannon, Angeline   G. W. L. Spearman   2B   508-509   1862
(daughter of George S. Cannon of Newberry District)

Cannon, Christena   John A. Folk   L   103-104   1840
(marriage settlement 27 June 1840) (widow) (he was married before) (both of Newberry District)

Cannon, Elizabeth F.   William A. Reed   2A   80-81   1857
(daughter of David Cannon of Newberry District)

Cannon, Jane   John Jennings   H   211   1832
(marriage agreement 5 August 1832) (widow of Wm Cannon of Orangeburgh District) (of Orangeburgh District)

Implied South Carolina Marriages Volume IV 1787-1875

| WOMAN | MAN | VOL | PAGES | LIVED |
|---|---|---|---|---|

Cannon, Jane　　　Jeremiah W. Stark　　E　234　　　1824
　　(marriage settlement 25 October 1824) (both of Newberry
　　District)
Cannon, Laura E.　　David M. H. Langston　2A　696　　1859
　　(daughter of David M. Cannon of Newberry District)
　　(Langston of Laurens District)
Cannon, Margaret K. Calvin Satterwhite　2B　365-366　1861
　　(daughter of David Cannon of Newberry District)
Cannon, Martha A.　Spencer L. Glasgow　2A　120-121　1857
　　(daughter of George S. Cannon of Newberry District)
Cannon, Mary　　　William C. Smith　　Y　275-279　　1855
　　(marriage settlement 14 June 1855) (widow) (she of
　　Abbeville District) (he of Georgetown District)
Cannon, Mary L.　　Jared S. Johnson　　2A　119-120　1857
　　(daughter of George S. Cannon of Newberry District)
Cannon, Phebe　　　Bennet Wallace　　　S　245-247　　1848
　　(marriage settlement 8 June 1848) (widow of Richard S.
　　Cannon) (in Newberry District)
Cantelou, Martha　Robert Burt　　　　F　378-379　　1828
　　(marriage agreement 30 December 1828) (widow of Lemuel
　　Cantelou) (of Edgefield District)
Cantey, Martha　　William Ransom Davis A　202-211　　1792
　　(marriage settlement 19/20 June 1792) (she of Camden
　　District) (he of Stateburgh, Camden District)
Capplepower,　　　George Wacter　　　　B　659-670　　1810
　　Barbara (widow)
Capplepower, Katy　Andrew Kaigler　　　B　659-670　　1810
　　[See also pages 654-656]
Caps, Sarah　　　　William Cox　　　　　R　420　　　　1847
　　(marriage contract 16 February 1847) (in Greenville
　　District)
Carey, Martha L.　William M. Bobo　　　N　196-197　　1841
　　(married 21 July 1841) (daughter of W. H. Carey) (she of
　　Edgefield District) (he of Union District)
Carr, Mary　　　　Augustus McNeal　　　F　261　　　　1828
　　(marriage settlement 3 May 1828) (both of Columbia,
　　Richland District)
Carruth, Louisa L. Genl. James Gillam　U　242-245　　1850
　　(marriage settlement 17 October 1850) (she of Anderson
　　District) (he of Abbeville District)
Carson, Julia A.　William R. Bull　　　L　109-110　　1840
　　(in Orangeburgh District)
Carson, Mary　　　_____ Winningham　　L　109-110　　1840
　　(widow of James Carson) (in Orangeburgh District)

Implied South Carolina Marriages Volume IV 1787-1875

| WOMAN | MAN | VOL | PAGES | LIVED |
|---|---|---|---|---|

Carter, Caroline E. James Jenkins Y 238-241 1855
(or M.) (Jinkins)
(marriage settlement 30 May 1855) (in Darlington District)

Carter, Cora E. William J. Gayer 2A 709-711 1859
(daughter of Larkin G. Carter of Abbeville District) (Gayer of Charleston)

Carter, Harriet _____ Williams E 81 1819
(daughter of Benjamin Carter of Richland District) [See also page 100]

Carter, Sophia _____ Joyner E 9 1820
(daughter of Benjamin Carter) (she in Richland District) [See also pages 10-11]

Cartledge, _____ Jennings H 448-449 1825
Elizabeth (daughter of Edmund Cartledge of Edgefield District)

Cartledge, Mary _____ Hardy H 449-450 1825
(daughter of Edmund Cartledge of Edgefield District)

Cartledge, Nancy _____ Martin H 450-451 1825
(daughter of Edmund Cartledge of Edgefield District)

Cartledge, Sarah John Addison E 433-434 1825
(marriage contract 26 June 1825) (both of Edgefield District)

Cary, Ann M. Joseph Hightower M 26-27 1841
(marriage settlement 16 August 1841) (widow of William H. Cary) (both of Edgefield District)

Cason, Isabella A. W. Gibson R 213-214 1847
(of Fairfield District)

Cason, Mary Littleton Raines Y 225-226 1855

Cason, Sarah Moses Knighton G 205 1830
(daughter of Cannon Cason of Fairfield District) (of Fairfield District)

Cassety, Patience John Havis K 142-143 1838
(marriage agreement 13 May 1838) (she of Fairfield District, S.C.) (he of Leon County, Florida)

Cater, Sarah Dr. Nathaniel Harris Z 233-237 1854
(Sally) P. (married 14 December 1854) (marriage agreement 13 December 1854) (she of Anderson District) (he of Abbeville District)

Cates, Dorothy _____ Wadlington I 107-108 1834
(daughter of Aaron Cates)

Cathey, Mary John Cathey R 354-356 1847
(marriage settlement 8 February 1847) (in York District)

Chalmers, Sarah Z. C. Wright O 138-140 1844
(marriage settlement 2 April 1844) (widow of Thomas B. Chalmers) (both of Newberry District)

Implied South Carolina Marriages Volume IV 1787-1875

| WOMAN | MAN | VOL | PAGES | LIVED |
|---|---|---|---|---|

Chalmers, Sarah      Zachariah C. Wright      T      449-452      1844
　　(reference to marriage settlement 2 April 1844) (widow
　　of Thomas B. Chalmers) (both of Newberry District)
Chandler, Agnes D.     Daniel B. McLaurin     I     372-373     1836
　　(marriage settlement 6 January 1836) (daughter of Samuel
　　Chandler) (both of Sumter District)
Chandler, Agness D.    Dan<u>el</u> B. McLauren    2A    512-513    1836
　　(reference to marriage settlement 6 January 1836) (in
　　Sumter District)
Chandler,           Charles R. F. Baker    2C    113-115    1866
　　Jacqueline (marriage settlement 19 January 1866) (widow
　　of Genl. Samuel R. Chandler) (she of Sumter District)
　　(Baker of Clarendon District)
Chandler, Margaret _____ Gordon      E     190-191      1824
　　(widow of George Chandler, her first husband)
Chapman, Margaret    Archibald Blue      Z     82-86      1855
　　C. (daughter of Allen Chapman Sr. of Chesterfield
　　District) (Blue of Cheraw, Chesterfield District)
Charles, Caroline    George W. Caldwell    2B    539-540    1862
　　Elizabeth    (of Hempstead County, Arkansas) (in
　　Greenville District, S.C.)
Charles, Frances  _____ Mostello      2B    538-539    1862
　　(she of Hall County, Georgia) (in Greenville District,
　　S.C.)
Charles, Mary L.     William F. B.       2A     410-412     1858
　　　　　　　　　　 Haynsworth
　　(marriage settlement 13 July 1858) (daughter of Edgar W.
　　Charles of Darlington District and granddaughter of Hugh
　　Lide) (Haynsworth of Sumter District) [Must also see
　　pages 529-530] [See also pages 686-687]
Chatham, Mary        Thomas J. Adams      Z     444-445     1856
　　Jemima (daughter of Thomas Chatham of Abbeville
　　District) (Adams of Edgefield District)
Cheatham, Mary Ann   Samuel A. Dyke    2B    530-531    1862
　　Elizabeth (daughter of Guthredge Cheatham of Edgefield
　　District) (Dyke of Abbeville District)
Cheatham, Nancy      Dawson B. Sullivan    F     227      1828
　　(daughter of Robert Cheatham) (in Abbeville District)
　　[See also pages 420-421]
Cherry, Mary         Andrew Hickey       C     397-398     1816
　　(marriage settlement 26 December 1816) (both of
　　Orangeburgh District)
Cherry, Susan W.     Richard J           Z     426-430     1856
　　　　　　　　　　 Scarborough
Chesnut, Esther      Thomas E. Haile     V     582-585     1852
　　Lerena (daughter of John Chesnut) (of Kershaw District)

166

Implied South Carolina Marriages Volume IV 1787-1875

| WOMAN | MAN | VOL | PAGES | LIVED |
|---|---|---|---|---|
| Chesnut, Mary Whitaker | Edward Haile | V | 585-588 | 1852 |

(daughter of John Chesnut) (of Kershaw District)

| Cheves, Ann M. (Chivers) | Wade H. Gaulden | C | 392-394 | 1816 |

(marriage settlement 25 November 1816) (both of Sumter District)

| Cheves, Anna Maria | Thomas Pinckney Huger | M | 296-299 | 1842 |

(daughter of Langdon Cheves of Anderson District) (of Abbeville District)

| Cheves, Louisa S. | David J. McCord | L | 88-93 | 1840 |

(marriage settlement 20 May 1840) (she of St. Matthew's Parish) (he of Columbia) [See also page 414]

| China, Sarah Elizabeth | W. W. Jenkins | W | 169-172 | 1852 |

(marriage settlement 29 October 1852) (in Sumter District)

| Chollet, Sophia | Lawrence D. Hallonquist | W | 420-422 | 1853 |

(of Barnwell District) [See also page 206; Volume X, pages 338-340; Volume 2A, pages 479-485]

| Clark, Elizabeth H. | Joseph E. Graham | 2B | 124-125 | 1860 |

(marriage settlement 1 April 1860) (both of Clarendon District)

| Clark, Julia O. | Samuel D. Hodge | 2B | 229-230 | 1860 |

(marriage settlement 21 October 1860) (in Clarendon District)

| Clark, Maria (widow) | _____ Blackburn | 2B | 671-673 | 1863 |

| Clark, Mary Ann | Thomas Stitt | 2A | 68-69 | 1854 |

(reference to marriage settlement 16 February 1854) (in Fairfield District)

| Clark, Mary Ann B. | Thomas Stitt | X | 529-531 | 1854 |

(marriage settlement 16 February 1854) (both of Fairfield District)

| Clark, Rebecca R. A. | Hamilton Husbands | S | 286-288 | 1848 |

(marriage settlement 10 June 1848) (daughter of William Clark) (in Sumter District)

| Clark, Sarah Eliza | John E. B. Evans | Z | 406-407 | 1856 |

(daughter of J. W. Clark of Columbia, Richland District) (of Richland District)

| Clarke, Anna C. | William Clarke | V | 266-270 | 1851 |

(marriage settlement 1 December 1851) (daughter of Caleb Clarke) (in Fairfield District)

| Clarke, Harriet Ann | Harmon Holleyman | K | 296-298 | 1838 |

(marriage settlement 28 November 1838) (daughter of George Clarke) (she of Newberry District) (Holleyman of Kershaw District)

Implied South Carolina Marriages Volume IV 1787-1875

| WOMAN | MAN | VOL | PAGES | LIVED |
|---|---|---|---|---|

Clarkson, Caroline    Lemuel Clarence      2A    300-301    1858
    Beaumont          Clarke
    (daughter of Thomas B. Clarkson Senior of Richland
    District)
Clarkson, Elizabeth   Hugh S. Thompson     2A    355-356    1858
    Anderson (daughter of Thomas B. Clarkson Senior of
    Richland District)
Clarkson, Harriett    Albert R. Stuart     2C    72-77      1865
    Sophia (marriage settlement 5 December 1865) (daughter
    of William Clarkson who died __ July 1858) (she of
    Columbia) [Must also see pages 8-13]
Clawson, Lucie H.     Sample Alexander     2A    758-760    1860
    (marriage settlement 16 January 1860) (in York District)
Clayton, Ann          John W. Fraser       X     15-18      1853
                      (Frasier)
    (marriage settlement 9 July 1853) (widow of Edmond
    Clayton) (in Barnwell District)
Cleckly, Elizabeth    William M. Bell      Z     594-596    1857
    A. (marriage settlement 13 January 1857) (widow of D. F.
    Cleckly) (in Abbeville District)
Clemens, Hesky        John W. Smith        2B    435-438    1861
    (widow of C. W. Clemens) (of Anderson District)
Cleveland, Adaline    William S. Keese     2A    602-605    1859
    (marriage settlement 11 April 1859) (widow of Benjamin
    Milton Cleveland) (both of Pickens District)
Clifton, Mary M.      William M. Vandiver  U     356-358    1851
    (marriage settlement 25 January 1851)
Clinch, Katherine     Edward Barnwell      2B    588-590    1863
    (Catharine) Maria         Heyward
    (marriage settlement 17 February 1863)
Cloud, Elizabeth      Archibald Kemp       P     123-125    1845
    (marriage settlement 7 September 1845) (of Edgefield
    District)
Cloud, Elizabeth      Archibald Kemp       2A    377-378    1845
    (reference to marriage settlement 27 September 1845)
    (widow) (in Edgefield District)
Cloud, Margaret W.    W. L. Calhoun        Z     105-106    1853
    (daughter of William Cloud of Chester District)
Cloud, Martha C.      ___ Hogan            2B    278-280    1860
    (daughter of Austin N. Cloud)
Clowney, Jane C.      Dr. John W. Simpson  Z     33-35      1856
    (marriage settlement 22 January 1856) (widow) (she of
    Union District) (he of Laurens District)
Cochran, Charlotte    John Rochell Senr.   N     56-58      1843
    (marriage settlement 9 April 1843) (both of Edgefield
    District) [See also pages 93-95]

Implied South Carolina Marriages Volume IV 1787-1875

| WOMAN | MAN | VOL | PAGES | LIVED |
|---|---|---|---|---|

Cochran, Georgiana Newel T. White      X      186-187    1854
   A. (daughter of L. B. Cochran of Edgefield District) (of
   Edgefield District)
Cockran, Fanny       Daniel Cook Jr.    2A     325-327    1858
   (of Barnwell District)
Coggeshall, Hannah   William Jas. Dargan X    178-181    1853
   E. (marriage settlement 22 December 1853) (daughter of
   Peter C. Coggeshall) (in Darlington District)
Coggeshall, M.       Jilson B. Douglas  2A     516-518    1859
   Carolina (marriage settlement 19 January 1859) (both of
   Darlington District)
Coggeshall, Sarah    Samuel J. Ervin    X      7-11       1853
   A. (marriage settlement 8 August 1853) (daughter of
   Peter C. Coggeshall) (both of Darlington District)
Cohen, C. Alice      Dr. Franklin J.    2C     33-35      1864
                     Moses
   (marriage settlement 1 December 1864) (daughter of John
   J. Cohen of Columbia, Richland District)
Colclough, Leonora   Hugh McDonald      H      429-434    1833
   G. (marriage contract 10 July 1833) (widow of William A.
   Colclough) (she of Sumter District) (McDonald of
   Charleston District)
Colclough, Leonora   Leonard W. Dick    2B     263-265    1860
   Ida (marriage settlement 20 December 1860) (daughter of
   John A. Colclough) (both of Sumter District)
Cole, Amanda         John B. Good       2A     369-371    1858
   (daughter of William Cole of Union District)
Cole, Bethniah       Elbert Lindsey     V      260-262    1851
   (both of Laurens District)
Cole, Narry          James W. Good      2A     369-371    1858
   (daughter of William Cole of Union District) (Good of
   York District)
Coleman, Permelia    Nathan Glenn       M      392-393    1843
                     (of Union District)
Collins, Martha S.   James Lambright    C      139-141    1814
   (marriage settlement 23 June 1814) (of Barnwell
   District)
Colter, Elizabeth    _____ Humphreyville Z    780        1857
   (she of Mobile, Alabama)
Connell, Susannah    John Good          C      281-283    1816
   (marriage settlement 6 March 1816) (in Darlington
   District)
Converse, Catharine John N. Frierson    S      205-208    1845
   K. (granddaughter of Daniel Kellogg) (Frierson of
   Claremont County, Sumter District)

Implied South Carolina Marriages Volume IV 1787-1875

| WOMAN | MAN | VOL | PAGES | LIVED |
|---|---|---|---|---|

Converse, Catherine John N. Frierson    O    423-424    1845
  K. (daughter of Augustus L. Converse of Sumter District)
  (Frierson of Claremont County, Sumter District) [Must
  also see pages 445-448]
Cook, Ann Cantey     Edward A. Salmond     T    278-286    1847
  (widow of Henry R. Cook) (in Kershaw District)
Cook, Barbary        Samuel Kirkland       S    170-171    1846
  (marriage settlement 25 March 1846) (both of Kershaw
  District)
Cook, Elizabeth M.   Marshall McGraw       Y    43-44      1855
  D. (marriage settlement 20 February 1855) (she of
  Kershaw District) (he of Fairfield District)
Cook, Elizabeth      J. B. Simpson         2B   298-300    1861
  Martha Ann (daughter of John Cook of Newberry District)
Cook, Mary A. W.     John E. Cannon        F    419        1829
  (marriage settlement 2 April 1829) (both of Darlington
  District)
Cook, Rosannah       J. T. P. Crosson      2B   298-300    1861
  Catherine (daughter of John Cook of Newberry District)
Cook, Sarah          John L. Gregory       Z    409-411    1856
  Elizabeth (daughter of Nathaniel Cook of Lancaster
  District) (of Lancaster District)
Cooper, Emily        _____ Porter          2A   231-233    1858
Cooper, Sarah E.     _____ Waring          2A   231-233    1858
Copeland, Mary       Thomas Purlaskey      X    351-352    1854
  (of Barnwell District) (Pulaski)
Corben, Mary         _____ Parr            I    413        1836
  (she of Columbia)
Corley, Marget Ann   _____ Salley          2A   418-419    1858
  (daughter of Josiah Corley of Barnwell District)
Cornwell, Agness     Martin Worthy Senr.   X    676-677    1848
  (marriage settlement 28 October 1848) (widow) (in
  Chester District)
Cotchett, Sarah Ann Thos. Robson           E    417-418    1828
  (she of Columbia) [See also Volume F, pages 5-11]
Counts, Eve          William F. Snelgrove  V    270-273    1852
  Margaret (marriage agreement 12 January 1852) (both of
  Lexington District)
Counts, Rebecca      Charles P. Harward    U    69-71      1850
  (marriage settlement 29 April 1850) (widow) (in
  Lexington District)
Courtney, Cynthia    _____ Plunkett        2B   524-525    1861
  (daughter of Martin Courtney of Barnwell District)
Courtney, Eliza H.   Alpheus Baker         D    208-210    1820
  (marriage contract 9 April 1820) (she of Wilkes County,
  Georgia) (he of Abbeville District, S.C.)

Implied South Carolina Marriages Volume IV 1787-1875

| WOMAN | MAN | VOL | PAGES | LIVED |
|---|---|---|---|---|
| Covington, Sarah | William Mudd | R | 314-315 | 1847 |

(marriage contract 5 January 1847) (both of Marlborough District)

Cowan, Anna (Anny)  Joseph J. Hawthorn  P  87-91  1845
(daughter of Col. Isaac Cowan) (in Abbeville District)

Coward, Catherine  R. B. H. White  Y  575-576  1855
A. E. (daughter of Solomon Coward of Williamsburgh District)

Cowie, Elizabeth  _____ Paterson  O  109-114  1818
(Courie) (widow of Archibald Cowie of County of Stirling, Scotland)

Cox, Agnes  Micajah A. Lane  2B  236-238  1860
(marriage settlement 15 December 1860) (she of Abbeville District, S.C.) (he of Lincoln County, Georgia)

Craddock, Judith  Zachariah Stroud  Z  121  1856
(Juda) C.  (of Laurens District)

Craig, Agnes N.  Henry H. Williams  M  371-374  1842
(widow of John H. Craig of Chesterfield District) (Williams of Marlboro District)

Crain, Mary M.  Dr. John A. Walker  X  537-538  1854
(marriage settlement 24 July 1854) (in Chester District)

Crankfield,  _____ Hogan  R  478-479  1846
Margaret Jane (daughter of Littleton Crankfield of Fairfield District)

Crankfield, Mary  Samuel Laughon  S  130-132  1846
Ann (daughter of Littleton Crankfield of Fairfield District)

Crankfield,  _____ Miller  S  130-131  1846
Temperance (daughter of Littleton Crankfield of Fairfield District)

Crawford, Hessy  Revr. M. D. Fraser  N  271-272  1843

Crawford, Julia  William Slagle  I  312-313  1835
(widow)  (Sleegle)
(marriage settlement 8 October 1835) (of Chester District)

Crawford, Mary H.  Dr. William M. Hill  2B  272-273  1861
(daughter of Andrew Crawford of Columbia, Richland District) (Hill of Edgefield District)

Crawley, Mary E.  James King  2B  811-812  1864
(daughter of John Crawley) (in Darlington District)

Crenshaw, Margaret  Jehu Bailey Sr.  2C  214-216  1856
(reference to marriage contract 7 October 1856)

Creswell, Alethea  C. L. Gailliard  R  433-435  1847
L. (marriage settlement 1 March 1847) (widow) (in Anderson District)

Croft, Floride P.  Frederick Sollee  G  22-24  1829
(daughter of Edward Croft of Greenville District)

Implied South Carolina Marriages Volume IV 1787-1875

| WOMAN | MAN | VOL | PAGES | LIVED |
|---|---|---|---|---|
| Crook, Sarah Hoke | William F. Lester | 2C | 247-250 | 1866 |

(marriage settlement 21 December 1866) (daughter of Dr. A. B. Crook and granddaughter of John Hoke) (both of Greenville District)

| | | | | |
|---|---|---|---|---|
| Crooks, Louisa M. | Jefferson Suber | V | 223-225 | 1852 |

N. (daughter of John A. Crooks of Newberry District) (of Newberry District)

| | | | | |
|---|---|---|---|---|
| Crooks, Mary A. B. | James B. Hutchison | Z | 508 | 1857 |

(daughter of Thomas C. Crooks of Newberry District)

| | | | | |
|---|---|---|---|---|
| Crosby, Catharine | Jonathan Thomson | H | 320-321 | 1832 |

(marriage settlement 18 December 1832) (both of Barnwell District)

| | | | | |
|---|---|---|---|---|
| Crosby, Lucy W. | William Smith | U | 315-316 | 1851 |

(marriage settlement 21 January 1851) (widow of David Crosby of Fairfield District) (Smith was married before) (Smith of Union District)

| | | | | |
|---|---|---|---|---|
| Cross, Maria P. | James F. Chunn | 2B | 337-338 | 1861 |

(marriage settlement 25 April 1861) (in Richland District)

| | | | | |
|---|---|---|---|---|
| Crossle, Sarah | John Parkinson | A | 286-289 | 1796 |

(Crossbe) (marriage settlement 17 November 1796) (widow of George Crossle) (both of Winton County)

| | | | | |
|---|---|---|---|---|
| Crosson, Isabella | William Welch | S | 37-38 | 1847 |

(widow) (in Newberry District)

| | | | | |
|---|---|---|---|---|
| Crosswell, Amanda | Peter DuBose | Y | 553-555 | 1855 |

(marriage settlement 18 December 1855) (both of Darlington District)

| | | | | |
|---|---|---|---|---|
| Crouch, Julia | Paul Monro Ruff | 2B | 765-766 | 1864 |

Hasell (marriage settlement 1 January 1864) (in Lexington District)

| | | | | |
|---|---|---|---|---|
| Crumpton, Elizabeth | William C. Harrison | F | 396-397 | 1828 |

E. (marriage settlement 18 December 1828) (daughter of David Crumpton of Twiggs County, Georgia)

| | | | | |
|---|---|---|---|---|
| Culler, Sarah E. | John L. Carroll | 2B | 88-89 | 1860 |

(marriage settlement 14 February 1860) (widow of Jacob Culler of Orangeburg District)

| | | | | |
|---|---|---|---|---|
| Cunningham, Isabella F. | _____ McDow | Z | 499-501 | 1856 |
| Cunningham, Jane Brown | Y. L. Robinson | F | 219-220 | 1828 |

(daughter of Arthur Cunningham of Kershaw District)

| | | | | |
|---|---|---|---|---|
| Cunningham, Jane Missori | Mahalaleel Lindsey | O | 385-387 | 1845 |

(in Newberry District)

| | | | | |
|---|---|---|---|---|
| Cunningham, Margaret | _____ Cartledge | F | 357-358 | 1825 |

(in Edgefield District)

| | | | | |
|---|---|---|---|---|
| Cunningham, Mary (widow) | _____ Barnes | 2B | 213-217 | 1860 |

Implied South Carolina Marriages Volume IV 1787-1875

| WOMAN | MAN | VOL | PAGES | LIVED |
|---|---|---|---|---|

Cunningham, Mary Robert Thompson 2C 295-298 1866
Jane (marriage settlement 20 December 1866) (daughter of Alexander Cunningham of Williamsburg District) (both of Williamsburg District)
Cunningham, Mary S. Dennis Lindsey 2A 227-229 1858
(marriage settlement 2 January 1858) (widow of O. H. P. Cunningham) (Lindsey of Hamburg, Edgefield District)
Cunningham, Nancy Cunningham B. Z 499-501 1856
Cureton
(marriage settlement 16 December 1856) (daughter of John S. Cunningham) (both of Kershaw District)
Cureton, Elizabeth Sidney P. Durant 2A 502-504 1859
M. (daughter of Jere Cureton Jr. and granddaughter of Jere Cureton Sr.) (of Sumter District)

(D)

Dain, Julia Richard S. Bedon Y 515-516 1855
(daughter of Hyder A. Dain) (of Colleton District)
Dalrymple, Nancy James E. Peterson Z 654-656 1853
(marriage settlement 18 January 1853) (both of Newberry District)
Daniel, Asceneth William Hunt P 164-171 1845
Daniel, Aseemath William Hunt H 480-481 1833
(daughter of Richard Daniel Senr.)
Dantzler, John Hill E 452-453 1826
Christiana (marriage settlement 4 February 1826) (in Orangeburgh District)
Darby, Eliza Dr. Thomas J. 2A 743-744 1859
Elliott Goodwyn
Darby, Sarah Robert Hamilton S 351-352 1848
(daughter of James Darby of Chester District)
Darby, Susannah Henry Suber T 84-87 1848
(marriage settlement 28 October 1848) (in Newberry District)
Dargan, Adela E. Dr. William A. 2A 31-33 1857
Player
(daughter of Geo. W. Dargan) (in Darlington District)
Dargan, Clara Timothy George 2B 211-214 1866
Louise Dargan
(marriage settlement 15 November 1866)
Dargan, Leonora Edward P. Montgomery 2C 209-211 1866
Addie (or Addie L.) (marriage settlement 15 November 1866) (in Darlington District)

Implied South Carolina Marriages Volume IV 1787-1875

| WOMAN | MAN | VOL | PAGES | LIVED |
|---|---|---|---|---|
| Darlington, Elizabeth (daughter of John Darlington of Barnwell District) | John Lark | B | 487-488 | 1808 |
| Darrington, Maria (Mariah) [her last name illegible] (daughter of Robert Darrington) (in Kershaw District) | Solly Bracy | D | 187-188 | 1820 |
| Dart, A. A. R. | Zephaniah W. Barnes | Y | 32-33 | 1855 |
| Dart, Mary Louisa | John N. Barnes (in Pickens District) | Y | 32-33 | 1855 |
| Davenport, Anna (marriage settlement 6 March 1838) (widow of William Davenport) (she of Newberry District) | James McCann | K | 118-119 | 1838 |
| Davenport, Hetty (daughter of Isaac Davenport) | _____ Waldrop | F | 364-365 | 1828 |
| Davenport, Jane | James Caldwell | K | 118-119 | 1838 |
| Davenport, Matilda | _____ Murdock | K | 118-119 | 1838 |
| Davidson, Ann (daughter of Robert Davidson of York District) | _____ Galbreath | E | 171-172 | 1824 |
| Davis, Clementine Helen (daughter of Bushrod Washington Davis) (in Beaufort District) | Bryce Smith | X | 445-448 | 1854 |
| Davis, Elizabeth Hackett") (separation agreement 21 December 1825) (widow of William W. Davis) (both of Abbeville District) | Joseph Wardlaw Junior ("sometimes called Joseph | E | 419-420 | 1825 |
| Davis, Hannah (marriage settlement 19 December 1855) (both of Newberry District) | Thomas Montgomery | Y | 577-579 | 1855 |
| Dawkins, Eliza (Dankins) (widow of Col. Benjamin F. Dawkins) (of Union District) [See also Volume W, pages 128-132] | H. Coleman Poole | V | 597-601 | 1852 |
| Dean, Cassandra Lucy (daughter of John Dean of Spartanburgh District) | _____ Folger | S | 226-227 | 1848 |
| Dean, Frances C. (daughter of Alfred Dean of Spartanburgh District) | Major William Hoy | U | 355-356 | 1851 |
| Deas, Rosey (daughter of William Deas) (in Sumter District) | John Pevy | L | 432 | 1841 |
| Deason, _____ (daughter of John Deason Sr. of Edgefield District) (of Edgefield District) | William Price | Z | 693-694 | 1857 |
| DeBruhl, Elizabeth A. (daughter of Jesse DeBruhl of Richland District) (Marshall of Abbeville District) | J. Foster Marshall | W | 412-415 | 1853 |
| DeBruhl, Mary D. (daughter of Jesse DeBruhl of Richland District) (Fair of Richland District) | Samuel Fair | W | 412-415 | 1853 |

174

Implied South Carolina Marriages Volume IV 1787-1875

| WOMAN | MAN | VOL | PAGES | LIVED |
|---|---|---|---|---|
| Deen, Isabella | _____ Youngblood | E | 439 | 1826 |

(daughter of William Deen Senior of Edgefield District)

De Graffenreid, Sarah | Richard E. Kennedy | Z | 381-385 | 1856

(daughter of Allen De Graffenreid)

Delane, Anne Wood | John Yancey | C | 297-299 | 1816

(marriage agreement 20 May 1816) (both of Columbia, Richland District)

Delaughter, Catherine | _____ Harvey | U | 274-276 | 1850

de Lein, Jeanne Marie Odette | Joseph Marie Legrunio Kerblay | Q | 63 | 1805

(she was born about 1763 in Toulouse, France) (he was born about 1755 in Sarzeau, France) (to Georgia, then S.C.)

Delorme, Mary Ann | _____ Swinton | Y | 419-421 | 1855

(in Sumter District)

Denton, Margaret C. | Daniel Tait (Tate) | N | 37-38 | 1843

(in Abbeville District)

Derrick, Barbara C. | Ervin H. Shealy | 2C | 77-78 | 1865

(marriage contract 28 September 1865) (both of Lexington District)

DeVeaux, Annie Peyre | John Burchell Moore | 2B | 496-502 | 1855

(married 3 July 1855) (reference to marriage settlement 3 July 1855) (daughter of Robert Marion DeVeaux and granddaughter of S. G. DeVeaux) (in Sumter District)

Deveaux, Georgie M. | Octavius T. Porcher | W | 509-511 | 1853

(daughter of Stephen G. Deveaux of Charleston District)

Deveaux, Elizabeth Ann | Manning Brown | 2A | 360-362 | 1848

(reference to marriage settlement 28 November 1848)

Deveaux, Lizzie A. | Manning Brown | W | 33-36 | 1852

(marriage settlement 3 June 1852) (daughter of Stephen G. Deveaux of Charleston District) (Brown of Richland District)

Deveaux, Silina G. | Paul G. Chappell | W | 486-487 | 1853

(of Richland District)

Deveaux, Videau Marion | Reverend Augustus L. T. Converse | T | 156-160 | 1849

(marriage settlement 27 March 1849) (in Sumter District) [See also page 252; Volume U, pages 178-180]

Dew, Martha Ann | B. F. Hays | 2A | 780-781 | 1860

(marriage settlement 24 January 1860) (daughter of Wilson Dew) (in Marion District)

Implied South Carolina Marriages Volume IV 1787-1875

| WOMAN | MAN | VOL | PAGES | LIVED |
|---|---|---|---|---|

Dewalt, Elizabeth   Henry W. Waters      2A   327-332   1857
   (married 21 March 1857) (daughter of Daniel Dewalt
   Senr. of Newberry District, S.C., who died 6 November
   1853) (Waters of Texas) [See also pages 364-368, 495-
   499, 541-544, 631-634, 673-677]
Dewalt, Harriet     William Wilson       X    687-689   1855
   (daughter of Daniel Dewalt Senr.) (in Newberry
   District)
De Walt, Laura      Jacob West           Z    442-444   1856
   (married 10 June 1856) (daughter of Daniel De Walt
   Senr. of Newberry District)
Dewalt, Laura       Jacob West           2A   673-677   1859
   (daughter of Daniel Dewalt Senr. of Newberry District,
   who died 6 November 1853)
Dewalt, Liberty     OBrien S. Hughs      2A   327-332   1857
   (daughter of Daniel Dewalt Senr. of Newberry District,
   who died 6 November 1853) (of Texas) [See also pages
   364-368, 495-499, 541-544, 631-634, 673-677]
Dewalt, Nancy       J. R. Adams          2A   327-332   1858
   (daughter of Daniel Dewalt Senr. of Newberry District,
   who died 6 November 1853) [See also pages 364-368, 495-
   499, 541-544, 631-634, 673-677]
Dick, Elizabeth Ann Anthony White Jr.    X    465-467   1854
   S. (marriage settlement 11 May 1854) (granddaughter of
   Leonard White) (both of Sumter District)
Dick, Elizabeth Ann Anthony White Junr.  2C   96-98     1854
   S. (reference to marriage settlement 11 May 1854)
   (granddaughter of Leonard White) (in Sumter District)
Dicker, Sarah J.    Thomas (or Willis)   2A   458-460   1858
                    J. Johnson
   (marriage settlement 4 November 1858) (both of
   Williamsburgh District)
Dickson, Mary C.    Willis Newton        2B   515-517   1862
   (marriage settlement 8 February 1862) (widow) (in
   Anderson District)
Diggs, Amanda A.    ____ Pitts           K    28-29     1837
Dillard, Mary A. E. Isaac Calmes Jacks   2B   758-760   1863
   (widow)
Dillard, Mary O.    Jesse Norman         U    132-134   1850
   (marriage contract 21 July 1850) (widow of John A.
   Dillard) (Norman was married before) (both of Union
   District)
Dingle, Ann Eliza   Francis Asbury       2B   449-451   1861
                    Tradewell
   (marriage contract 10 December 1861) (daughter of Adam
   Dingle) (she of Clarendon District) (Tradewell of
   Richland District)

Implied South Carolina Marriages Volume IV 1787-1875

| WOMAN | MAN | VOL | PAGES | LIVED |
|---|---|---|---|---|
| Dinkins, Leonora H. T. W. Lenoir Z 806-808 1857 (marriage settlement 16 April 1857) (daughter of L. T. Dinkins) | | | | |
| Diseker, Martha | Stephen Williams | F | 26 | 1827 |
| (daughter of Jacob Diseker of Richland District) | | | | |
| Diseker, Wilmoth M. | William Jones | E | 472-473 | 1825 |
| (daughter of Jacob Diseker of Richland District) | | | | |
| Dixon, Eliza | Jadaliah Wood | P | 101-102 | 1845 |
| (daughter of Abel Dixon of Sumter District, S.C.) (of Gadsden County, Florida) | | | | |
| Dixon, Nancy | Jefferson McDaniel | X | 121-122 | 1853 |
| (daughter of Benjamin Dixon of Barnwell District) | | | | |
| Dobbs, Margaret | Augustin Bumpass | A | 303 | 1796 |
| (did not marry; had child only) | | | | |
| Doby, Martha A. | William T. Timmerman | W | 103-109 | 1852 |
| (marriage settlement 30 September 1852) (widow) (in Edgefield District) | | | | |
| Dogan, Ann E. | Benjamin F. Arthur | X | 163-166 | 1854 |
| (daughter of Joseph H. Dogan of Union District) | | | | |
| Doggett, Sarah M. | John B. Goudelock | H | 87-88 | 1832 |
| (marriage settlement 4 February 1832) (she of Rutherford County, North Carolina) (he of Union District, S.C.) | | | | |
| Donaldson, Elizabeth | Richard G. Jenkins | O | 316-317 | 1845 |
| (marriage settlement 4 February 1845) (in Kershaw District) | | | | |
| Douglas, Charlotte C. | Elijah L. Pearce | 2C | 93-96 | 1866 |
| (marriage settlement 17 January 1866) (in Marlborough District) | | | | |
| Douglas, Charlotte E. | William A. Ancrum | T | 429-430 | 1850 |
| (daughter of James K. Douglas of Kershaw District) | | | | |
| Douglass, Elizabeth | Eli Harrison | Y | 485-486 | 1855 |
| (daughter of Dr. John Douglass of Chester District) (Harrison of Fairfield District) | | | | |
| Douglass, Sarah B. | William Anderson | F | 451-452 | 1829 |
| (daughter of James K. Douglass of Camden, Kershaw District) | | | | |
| Douglass, Sarah Rebecca | Dr. James C. Hecklin | Y | 484-485 | 1855 |
| (daughter of Dr. John Douglass of Chester District) (of York District) | | | | |
| Dove, Anna Jane | Charles H. DeLorme | Z | 307-313 | 1856 |
| (marriage settlement 25 June 1856) (daughter of Daniel Dove of Darlington District) (both of Darlington District) | | | | |
| D'Oyley, Anna S. | _____ Williams | X | 501-502 | 1854 |
| (in Greenville District) | | | | |

Implied South Carolina Marriages Volume IV 1787-1875

| WOMAN | MAN | VOL | PAGES | LIVED |
|---|---|---|---|---|
| Drake, Laura A. | J. P. Harrall | V | 146-149 | 1851 |

(daughter of Lemuel S. Drake of Chesterfield District)

| Drake, Patsey | William Robinson | E | 503-504 | 1826 |

(Robertson) (marriage settlement 1 July 1826) (widow of Micajah Drake) (both of Edgefield District)

| Dreher, Caroline | Henry Meetze | X | 310-312 | 1854 |

(daughter of Godfrey Dreher of Lexington District) (of Lexington District)

| DuBose, Betsey | Dr. John Bratton | 2B | 186-187 | 1860 |

Porcher (daughter of Theodore S. DuBose of Fairfield District) (of Fairfield District)

| Dubose, Catharine | Isaac Dubose | A | 311-315 | 1797 |

(marriage settlement 6 July 1797) (both of Camden, Kershaw County)

| Dubose, Elizabeth | Samuel Dwyer | D | 198-201 | 1820 |

(marriage settlement 3 June 1820) (both of Sumter District)

| DuBose, Eliza Marion | Augustus H. Porcher | V | 498-500 | 1852 |

(daughter of Theodore S. DuBose)

| DuBose, Harriet | ____ Kershaw | T | 422-423 | 1850 |

(daughter of Isaac DuBose) (in Williamsburg and Georgetown Districts)

| DuBose, Jane | William Skinner | P | 205-208 | 1845 |

Vermeille (marriage settlement 10 December 1845) (both of Sumter District)

| DuBose, Margaret C. | Samuel Cordes Boylston | 2B | 663-665 | 1863 |

(marriage settlement 15 September 1863) (daughter of Samuel DuBose of Fairfield District) (Boylston of Charleston) (to Florida?)

| Dubose, Mary S. | ____ Cannon | W | 529-531 | 1851 |
| Duke, Elizabeth A. | Henry S. Gill | O | 387-389 | 1845 |

(marriage settlement 10 March 1845) (of Richland District)

| Duke, Harriet | Mason G. Cole | C | 442-445 | 1817 |

(marriage settlement 6 October 1817)

| Dukes, Emmeline S. | Alexander Rantin | U | 76-79 | 1850 |

(marriage settlement 4 April 1850) (widow of James T. Dukes)

| Duncan, Lucia C. | Cornelius Tobin | K | 121-124 | 1838 |

(marriage settlement 17 February 1838) (daughter of Willis J. Duncan) (in Barnwell District)

| Dunham, Sarah | Jacob Shaver | X | 672-674 | 1855 |

(of Greenville District)

| Dunlap, Nancy | Ewel Black | I | 31 | 1834 |

(daughter of William Dunlap)

Implied South Carolina Marriages Volume IV 1787-1875

| WOMAN | MAN | VOL | PAGES | LIVED |
|---|---|---|---|---|
| Dunlap, Sarah Smith | William H. Wallace | V | 25-30 | 1851 |

(marriage settlement 8 July 1851)

| Dunn, Alley Ann | L. G. Wait | 2A | 298-299 | 1858 |

(daughter of William Dunn of Abbeville District) (Wait of Laurens District)

| Dunn, Nancy C. | James L. Anderson | L | 426-428 | 1841 |

(marriage settlement 7 September 1841) (widow) (both of Abbeville District)

| Durant, Matilda | Hugh Wilson Senr | X | 362-364 | 1854 |

(marriage settlement 7 January 1854) (in Sumter District)

| Duren, Eleanor | William Beckham | G | 406 | 1831 |

(daughter of Thomas Duren)

(E)

| Eagerton, Charlotte | William Jackson | H | 313-315 | 1833 |

(marriage settlement 16 January 1833) (of Marion District)

| Earle, Elizabeth Eugenia | J. Edward Bomar | 2A | 736-737 | 1859 |

(daughter of James W. Earle) (in Anderson District)

| Earle, Emily S. | David J. Williams | 2B | 371 | 1861 |

(in Greenville District) (his first marriage)

| Earle, Susan Haynsworth | William F. B. Haynsworth | X | 112-118 | 1853 |

(marriage settlement 1 December 1853) (daughter of Elias Drayton Earle who died in Greenville District) (she late of Greenville District, now of Sumter District) (Haynsworth of Sumter District)

| Eaves, Sarah | John Neal | C | 324-325 | 1811 |

(marriage settlement 21 August 1811) (widow) (both of Chester District) [See also pages 438-439]

| Ebney, Amanda | Charles M. Hurst | Z | 487-489 | 1851 |

(married 1851) (postnuptial settlement 9 December 1856) (in Sumter District) [her last name illegible]

| Eckhard, Ann Margaret | Peter L. Jumelle | M | 1-4 | 1841 |

(daughter of Jacob Eckhard Senr.) [See also pages 21-24]

| Eddins, Mary | Thomas Chiles | E | 437-438 | 1826 |

(marriage settlement 6 March 1826) (widow) (both of Edgefield District)

| Edgerton, Elizabeth | George W. Muse | G | 369-370 | 1831 |

(marriage settlement 2 May 1831) (widow of Otis Edgerton) (both of Barnwell District)

Implied South Carolina Marriages Volume IV 1787-1875

| WOMAN | MAN | VOL | PAGES | LIVED |
|---|---|---|---|---|
| Edgeworth, Harriet | Thomas Huntley | 2A | 598-599 | 1859 |

A. (daughter of Richard L. Edgeworth Senr. of Chesterfield District, S.C.) (Huntley now of Anson County, North Carolina)

| Edwards, A. M. | James S. Guignard | 2A | 171 | 1857 |
|---|---|---|---|---|

(widow) (in Richland District)

| Edwards, Anna | James S. Guignard | 2B | 716-717 | 1860 |
|---|---|---|---|---|

Margaret (widow of Philip Gadsden Edwards of Charleston) (Guignard of Columbia)

| Egan, Sarah | Daniel Colvin | D | 383-384 | 1822 |
|---|---|---|---|---|

("Sarah Colvin otherwise called Sarah Egan") (separation agreement 17 January 1822)

| Egan, Sarah | Isaiah Twitchell | E | 194-195 | 1824 |
|---|---|---|---|---|

(marriage settlement 10 June 1824) (she of Columbia)

| Eigleberger, Anna | John Kibler Jr. | T | 31-33 | 1848 |
|---|---|---|---|---|

Mary (she of Newberry District) (he died about 1835)

| Eigleberger, Mariah | Ephraim Suber | P | 472-474 | 1846 |
|---|---|---|---|---|

Elizabeth (marriage settlement 24 February 1846) (widow of Col. John Eigleberger) (in Newberry District)

| Eigleberger, Sarah | Christian H. Smith | F | 177-178 | 1828 |
|---|---|---|---|---|

(marriage settlement 21 January 1828) (both of Newberry District)

| Eigleberger, Sarah | Christian Henry Smith | I | 20-22 | 1828 |
|---|---|---|---|---|

(married 22 January 1828) (marriage contract 31 January 1828) (separation agreement 21 February 1834) (in Newberry District)

| Elder, Jane | Robert Cathcart | N | 133-135 | 1843 |
|---|---|---|---|---|

(marriage settlement 19 May 1843) (both of Winnsborough, Fairfield District)

| Elkins, Judy W. | _____ Ruff | X | 324-325 | 1854 |
|---|---|---|---|---|

(daughter of James Elkins of Fairfield District)

| Ellerbe, Allan Eunice | Ellerbe Boggan Crawford Cash | V | 57-62 | 1848 |
|---|---|---|---|---|

(married 28 November 1848) (daughter of William C. Ellerbe) (she of Kershaw District) (Cash of Chester District)

| Ellerbe, Ann E. | Clement L. Prince | G | 112-113 | 1830 |
|---|---|---|---|---|

(marriage agreement 10 March 1830) (widow of William F. Ellerbe) (both of Chesterfield District)

| Ellerbe, Caroline | Gideon Duvall | L | 441-444 | 1841 |
|---|---|---|---|---|

(marriage settlement 20 November 1841) (widow of Thomas G. Ellerbe)

| Ellerbe, Elizabeth | Joseph Ellerbe | H | 81-83 | 1832 |
|---|---|---|---|---|

(daughter of William Ellerbe) (of Chesterfield District)

Implied South Carolina Marriages Volume IV 1787-1875

| WOMAN | MAN | VOL | PAGES | LIVED |
|---|---|---|---|---|
| Ellerbe, Margaret A. | John H. McIver | 2B | 367-371 | 1861 |

(marriage settlement 22 July 1861) (of Cheraw, Chesterfield District)

| | | | | |
|---|---|---|---|---|
| Ellington, Biddy | Col. Wm. H. Caldwell | G | 367-369 | 1831 |

(marriage contract 10 February 1831) (widow) (he was married before) (both of Abbeville District)

| | | | | |
|---|---|---|---|---|
| Ellis, Elizabeth | William H. Sims | N | 92-93 | 1843 |

(daughter of Benjamin Ellis of Union District)

| | | | | |
|---|---|---|---|---|
| Ellis, Sarah | James Tiller | M | 314-315 | 1842 |

(marriage settlement 15 March 1842)

| | | | | |
|---|---|---|---|---|
| Ellison, Mary Ann | William B. Browning | W | 54-56 | 1851 |

(in Laurens District)

| | | | | |
|---|---|---|---|---|
| Elmore, Hannah | Thomas Frean | D | 152-154 | 1819 |

(daughter of Mathias Elmore) (Frean of Charleston, formerly of Newberry District) [See also Volume V, page 163; Volume 2A, pages 639-640]

| | | | | |
|---|---|---|---|---|
| Elmore, Sally F. | Thomas Taylor | 2B | 590-591 | 1863 |

(daughter of F. H. Elmore) (of Richland District)

| | | | | |
|---|---|---|---|---|
| Elrod, Elizabeth | Thomas McCarthy | R | 77-79 | 1846 |

(marriage settlement 31 August 1846) (daughter of Jeremiah Elrod) (in Anderson District)

| | | | | |
|---|---|---|---|---|
| Eppes, Eliza | ___ Huson | G | 290 | 1831 |

(daughter of William Eppes of Newberry District)

| | | | | |
|---|---|---|---|---|
| Eppes, Mary | Dr. P. M. Wallace | L | 142-143 | 1840 |

(widow of Daniel Eppes of Newberry District)

| | | | | |
|---|---|---|---|---|
| Epps, Jane Amanda | John Cheek Smith | 2A | 595-597 | 1859 |

(marriage settlement 24 February 1859) (in York District)

| | | | | |
|---|---|---|---|---|
| Epting, Caroline | Henry Summer | 2A | 735-736 | 1859 |

(daughter of John Epting Sr.) (of Newberry District)

| | | | | |
|---|---|---|---|---|
| Ervin, Ann D. | Henry K. W. Flinn | V | 16-18 | 1851 |

(marriage settlement 26 July 1851) (in Darlington District)

| | | | | |
|---|---|---|---|---|
| Ervin, Margaret Jane | Wm M. Cannon | M | 68-70 | 1842 |
| Ervins, Mary E. | Francis M. Baxter | R | 90-91 | 1809 |

(reference to marriage settlement 24 November 1809)

| | | | | |
|---|---|---|---|---|
| Eubanks, Rosinna | Robert W. Matthews | Z | 614-618 | 1857 |

(daughter of James J. Eubanks of Barnwell District) (of Barnwell District)

| | | | | |
|---|---|---|---|---|
| Evans, Frankey | ___ White | G | 482-483 | 1831 |

(daughter of William Evans of Abbeville District)

| | | | | |
|---|---|---|---|---|
| Evans, Martha E. | Milledge T. Holly | 2B | 383-384 | 1861 |

(daughter of Gideon Evans of Barnwell District) (of Barnwell District)

| | | | | |
|---|---|---|---|---|
| Evans, Mary G. | Henry Adams | G | 216-217 | 1830 |

(marriage settlement 12 October 1830)

Implied South Carolina Marriages Volume IV 1787-1875

| WOMAN | MAN | VOL | PAGES | LIVED |
|---|---|---|---|---|
| Evans, Sarah Ann | Samuel H. Robeson | Z | 194-196 | 1856 |

(daughter of John Evans of Chesterfield District)
Evans. See Evins
Eveleigh, _____    _____ Richardson    F    338-339    1827
 (daughter of Thomas Eveleigh) [See also Volume G, pages 45-46]
Eveleigh, Harriet    William Guignard    A    335-338    1798
 Richardson
 (marriage settlement 24 February 1798) [her first name torn]
Evins, Margaret    William McNeely    2C    180-182    1866
 (marriage settlement 4 June 1866) (widow of M. P. Evins of Laurens District) (of Greenville)
Ewart, Mary R.    Samuel Donnelly    K    155-157    1838
 (marriage settlement 11 June 1838)
Ewart, Mary R.    Samuel Donnelly    2B    217-219    1860
 (reference to marriage settlement - no date given)

(F)

Fair, Josephine P.    John G. Caldwell    Y    36-39    1854
 (separation agreement 28 December 1854) (daughter of James Fair) (in Abbeville District)
Falls, Sarah    Daniel Plympton    2B    626-629    1863
 Elizabeth    Kelley
 (marriage settlement 14 May 1863) (widow of Alexander Falls) (in Richland District)
Fant, N. Udora    William Kelly Thomas    2B    294-295    1861
 (daughter of David J. Fant of Union District) (of Union District)
Fant, Sarah A.    Marion S. Porter    2B    66-67    1860
 (daughter of David J. Fant of Union District)
Faries, Catherine    Joseph Kendrick    2A    148-152    1857
 E. (marriage settlement 5 November 1857) (she of Mecklenburg County, North Carolina) (he of York District, S.C.)
Farr, Elizabeth    Perry C. Stribling    K    171    1837
 Francis Foote (daughter of John P. Farr of Union District) (of Union District)
Farr, Julian    George W. Sartor    K    172-173    1838
 Franklin Richard (daughter of John P. Farr of Union District) (of Union District)
Farr, Nancy K.    Eli Gordon    K    398-399    1839
 (daughter of John P. Farr of Union District) (of Newberry District)

Implied South Carolina Marriages Volume IV 1787-1875

| WOMAN | MAN | VOL | PAGES | LIVED |
|---|---|---|---|---|
| Farr, Sicily G. | John S. Sims | O | 308-309 | 1844 |

(daughter of James Farr) (both of Union District)

| Faster, Mary | Samuel Howell | P | 242-243 | 1845 |
|---|---|---|---|---|

(Foster) (daughter of Robert Faster) (in Union District)

| Faucett, Eliza | Richard Parr | 2C | 54-56 | 1865 |
|---|---|---|---|---|

(marriage settlement 2 September 1865) (widow of Samuel Faucett) (both of Union District)

| Faust, Mary Ann | A. T. Smith | L | 67-68 | 1840 |
|---|---|---|---|---|

["Mary Ann Smith (alias) Mary Ann Faust"]

| Faust, Mary Ann | Alexander T. Smith | G | 109-110 | 1830 |
|---|---|---|---|---|

(common-law marriage) (of Richland District) [See also pages 398-399]

| Felder, Eugenia M. | John M. Buchanan | 2B | 469-471 | 1862 |
|---|---|---|---|---|

(daughter of John H. Felder of Orangeburg District)

| Fellers, Mary C. | William H. Sligh | 2A | 345-347 | 1857 |
|---|---|---|---|---|

(daughter of John Fellers)

| Ferguson, Elizabeth | _____ Watson | U | 67-68 | 1850 |
|---|---|---|---|---|

(daughter of Wade Ferguson of Newberry District)

| Ferguson, Mary D. | B. W. Chambers | X | 580-581 | 1854 |
|---|---|---|---|---|

(marriage settlement 16 November 1854) (she of Darlington District) (he of Charleston)

| Fewell, Sarah | Robert Stearn | D | 411 | 1821 |
|---|---|---|---|---|

(Fewel) (Sterns) (of York District) (marriage settlement 15 December 1821)

| Fincher, Ann | John Rogers | I | 460-462 | 1836 |
|---|---|---|---|---|

(marriage agreement 2 June 1836) (both of Union District)

| Flemming, Rebecca | Thomas Cauthen Senr. | U | 172-176 | 1850 |
|---|---|---|---|---|

(marriage settlement 26 September 1850) (in Lancaster District)

| Floyd, Elizabeth Ann | James Pinckney Williams | X | 110-112 | 1853 |
|---|---|---|---|---|
| Floyd, Eustatia | John A. Coleman | X | 110-112 | 1853 |
| Floyd, Lavalette | George Frederick Holmes | O | 353-355 | 1845 |

(marriage settlement 3 February 1845) (she of Tazewell County, Virginia) (he of S.C.)

| Floyd, Nancy | Andrew K. Tribble | X | 110-112 | 1853 |
|---|---|---|---|---|

(in Newberry District)

| Folk, Mary Magdalena | David Cannon | H | 440-442 | 1833 |
|---|---|---|---|---|

(in Newberry District)

| Ford, Elizabeth Sanders | James Sanders Guignard | D | 69-70 (of Columbia) | 1818 |
|---|---|---|---|---|
| Ford, Margaret | William Hollis | 2C | 430-433 | 1867 |

(daughter of William Ford) (of Chester District)

| Ford, Margaret Ann | Charles M. Pelot | D | 69-70 | 1818 |
|---|---|---|---|---|

[See also Volume H, pages 175-177]

Implied South Carolina Marriages Volume IV 1787-1875

| WOMAN | MAN | VOL | PAGES | LIVED |
|---|---|---|---|---|
| Ford, Mary | Richard Charles Walter | A | 317-321 | 1797 |

(marriage settlement 15 May 1797) (daughter of George Ford) (both of Stateburgh)

| Ford, Mary | Richard Charles Walter | B | 391-398 | 1797 |

(married 15 May 1797) (daughter of George Ford) (Walter died 17__) (both of Stateburg)

| Ford, Sarah A. | Thomas J. Johnsey | 2B | 265-267 | 1860 |

(marriage agreement 19 December 1860) (both of Chester District)

| Ford, Sarah B. | Robert D. Kellin | N | 167-169 | 1843 |

(marriage settlement 8 August 1843) (she in Chesterfield District) (he of Darlington District)

| Ford, Susan S. | Beverly Samuel | H | 315-316 | 1833 |

(daughter of Elijah Ford of Barnwell District)

| Foreman, Caroline A. | _____ Bush | V | 392-395 | 1852 |
| Foster, Malinda | _____ Bailey | P | 28-29 | 1845 |

[daughter of Jariahr (Josiah?) Foster of Union District]

| Foster, Margaret | _____ Spears | P | 28-29 | 1845 |

[daughter of Jariahr (Josiah?) Foster of Union District]

| Foster, Rebecca | _____ Palmer | P | 28-29 | 1845 |

[daughter of Jariahr (Josiah?) Foster of Union District]

| Foster, Sarah G. | _____ Hunt | O | 315-316 | 1843 |

Foster. See Faster

| Fountain, Martha Amanda | Washington Murphy Bacot | 2A | 432-435 | 1858 |

(marriage settlement 7 October 1858) (daughter of George Fountain) (both of Darlington District)

| Fountain, Mary Ann | R. Brockington Bacot Jr. | 2A | 560-564 | 1859 |

(marriage settlement 24 February 1859) (daughter of George H. Fountain) (both of Darlington District)

| Fountain, Sarah J. | Peter S. A. Bacot | 2A | 796-799 | 1860 |

(marriage settlement 23 February 1860) (daughter of George H. Fountain) (both of Darlington District)

| Fox, Catharine | Nicholas Powers | E | 200-201 | 1824 |

(marriage settlement 3 June 1824)

| Fraser, Harriet I. (or J.) B. | John I. (or J.) Miller | W | 239-243 | 1852 |

(marriage settlement 7 December 1852) (daughter of Ladson L. Fraser and granddaughter of John B. Fraser) (both of Sumter District)

Implied South Carolina Marriages Volume IV 1787-1875

| WOMAN | MAN | VOL | PAGES | LIVED |
|---|---|---|---|---|
| Fraser, Laura Ann | Horatio N. Brown | Z | 794-799 | 1857 |

(marriage settlement 25 April 1857) (daughter of Ladson L. Fraser and granddaughter of John Baxter Fraser) (both of Sumter District)

| Fraser, Laura Ann | Horatio N. Browne | 2A | 311 | 1858 |
|---|---|---|---|---|

(daughter of Ladson L. Fraser of Sumter District)

| Frazer, Harriet M. | John F. Schmidt | H | 202-206 | 1832 |
|---|---|---|---|---|

(marriage settlement 18 October 1832) (widow of Joseph Frazer) (in Barnwell District)

| Frean, Abigail (Abby) C. | John P. Southern | 2A | 639-640 | 1859 |
|---|---|---|---|---|
| Frean, Bridget Honoria | Wilson W. Waldrop | U | 39-40 | 1850 |

(daughter of Thomas Frean) [Must also see page 274]

| Frean, Bridget Honoria | Wilson W. Waldrop | 2A | 639-640 | 1859 |
|---|---|---|---|---|
| Frean, Hannah | John Belton | 2A | 639-640 | 1859 |
| Freeman, Carolina E. W. | S. M. Williams | 2B | 332-335 | 1861 |

(marriage settlement 14 May 1861) (granddaughter of John Hollingsworth) (both of Edgefield District)

| Freeman, Eliza A. | Alexander Walker | 2B | 332-335 | 1861 |
|---|---|---|---|---|
| Freeman, Mary F. | Francis A. Tradewell | K | 468-471 | 1839 |

(marriage settlement 23 September 1839) (widow) (both of Columbia)

| Freeman, Mary F. | Francis A. Tradewell | Z | 196-200 | 1839 |
|---|---|---|---|---|

(reference to marriage settlement 23 September 1839) (of Columbia, Richland District)

| Friedeberg, Mary Ann | Capt. James R. Malcom | 2C | 193-194 | 1866 |
|---|---|---|---|---|

(marriage settlement 11 October 1866) (widow) (she of Columbia) (he in Richland District)

| Frierson, Margaret (widow) | William J. Anderson (of Sumter District) | Z | 404-406 | 1856 |
|---|---|---|---|---|
| Fuller, Ann | John H. Middleton | D | 412-414 | 1822 |

(marriage settlement 21 March 1822) (both of Edgefield District) [See also Volume E, pages 70-71]

| Fuller, Mary | Robt. Knight | Z | 356 | 1856 |
|---|---|---|---|---|

(married 10 June 1856) (daughter of Messer Fuller)

| Fuller, Sarah Barnwell | Henry Middleton Stuart | 2B | 749-750 | 1863 |
|---|---|---|---|---|

(marriage settlement 2 December 1863) (widow) (both of Beaufort District)

| Fullwood, Martha J. | Cunningham Boyle | 2A | 472-473 | 1858 |
|---|---|---|---|---|

(marriage settlement __ December 1858) (widow of Robert Fullwood) (she of Sumter District) (Boyle of Richland District)

Implied South Carolina Marriages Volume IV 1787-1875

| WOMAN | MAN | VOL | PAGES | LIVED |
|---|---|---|---|---|

Fulmer, Amanda L.    William P. Fulmer    2B    814-815    1864
(marriage settlement 19 May 1864) (widow of John H. Fulmer) (both of Newberry District)
Furginson, Eliz      William Owens        I     224-226    1835
(marriage settlement 5 February 1835) (widow of William Furginson) (both of Barnwell District)

(G)

Gahagan, Elizabeth   Doctor John Hughes   C     44-47      1810
(Eliza) (separation agreement 29 August 1810) (widow of John Gahagan) (of Columbia, Richland District)
Gaillard, Elizabeth William Moultrie      2B    254-255    1861
P.                   Dwight
(marriage settlement 30 January 1861) (she of Fairfield District) (he of Abbeville District)
Gaillard, Elizabeth Elijah Webb           N     50-53      1843
R. S. (marriage settlement __ February 1843) (in Anderson District)
Gaillard, Esther G.  Edward J. Rembert    2A    584-586    1859
(daughter of James Gaillard of Walnut Grove, St. John's Berkley Parish)
Gaillard, Jane       William L. Jenkins   K     360-364    1839
Harvey (marriage settlement 27 April 1839) (daughter of David Gaillard) (in Anderson District)
Gaillard, Marion     _____ Allen         2A    608-612    1859
Gourdine
Gaillard, Rebecca    Samuel Brown         2A    608-612    1859
Scott (marriage settlement 26 April 1859) (in Anderson District)
Gallagher, Mary E.   John Cureton         T     430-433    1849
(marriage settlement 30 October 1849) (daughter of Mack Lamar of Edgefield District) (of Edgefield District)
Gallman, Angelina    Thomas G. Bacon      L     36-37      1839
(daughter of Harmon Gallman)
Galluchat, Virginia William C. Kirkland   M     462        1843
(in Sumter District)
Ganey, Esther W.     Drury Streater       R     164-166    1846
(Gainey) (marriage settlement 24 December 1846) (both of Chesterfield District)
Gantt, Eliza         _____ Thompson      K     124        1838
(daughter of Richard Gantt of Greenville District)
Gardner, Margaret    Samuel Watson        O     163-164    1844
(marriage settlement __ May 1844) (both of Sumter District)

Implied South Carolina Marriages Volume IV 1787-1875

| WOMAN | MAN | VOL | PAGES | LIVED |
|---|---|---|---|---|
| Gardner, Martha | _____ Bouchillon | G | 345-346 | 1831 |
| Gardner, Martha F. | _____ Bouchillon | K | 66 | 1837 |

(daughter of Jeremiah Gardner of Abbeville District)

Garner, Elizabeth    Abraham Sheppard    B    734-735    1812
(daughter of Presly Garner) (in Richland District)

Garrett, Elizabeth    Richard M. Johnson    L    14-16    1840
C. (marriage settlement 6 January 1840) (daughter of Henry W. Garrett and granddaughter of John C. Garrett) (of Edgefield District)

Garrot, Ellen    William T. DeLoach    P    122-123    1845
(marriage settlement 7 December 1845) (in Sumter District)

Garvin, Adela    Ephraim Barnes    X    472-474    1853
(daughter of David Garvin of Hall County, Georgia)

Garvin, Elizabeth    Anthony Lishness    E    212-213    1824
(Eliza) (marriage settlement 28 June 1824) (widow of James Garvin of Barnwell District)

Gaskins, Cynthia    Duren Peach    W    528-529    1853
Jane (Gaskin) (daughter of Daniel Gaskins of Kershaw District) (of Kershaw District)

Gaskins, Margaret    John C. Baskin    W    493-496    1853
(daughter of Daniel Gaskins Sr. of Kershaw District) (of Kershaw District)

Gaskins, Matilda    Wiley Glover    2A    622-625    1859
(marriage settlement 16 June 1859) (both of Edgefield District)

Gaskins, Sarah L.    John W. McKellar    W    469-472    1853
(daughter of John Gaskins of Edgefield District)

Gassaway, Dorcas    William Oliver    Y    454-457    1855
Ann (marriage settlement 26 September 1855) (daughter of Thos. Gassaway) (both of Pickens District)

Gause, Maria T.    James H. Lane    T    82-84    1849
(marriage settlement 27 January 1849) (in Marlborough District)

Gause, Sarah B.    Thomas Jefferson Dozier    T    351-355    1849
(marriage settlement 5 November 1849) (both of Marion District)

Gay, Mourning    William H. Clay    E    196    1824
(of Caswell County, North Carolina)

Gee, Hannah M.    _____ Nettles    2B    358-361    1861
["Hannah M. Gee (now Hannah M. Nettles)"]

Gee, Hannah M.    Joseph B. Nettles    H    197-200    1832
(marriage settlement 5 October 1832) (widow of Edmund Gee) (both of Darlington District)

Implied South Carolina Marriages Volume IV 1787-1875

| WOMAN | MAN | VOL | PAGES | LIVED |
|---|---|---|---|---|
| Gee, Hannah M. | Joseph B. Nettles | W | 529-531 | 1832 |

(reference to marriage settlement 5 October 1832) (in Darlington District)

| Gee, Hannah M. | Joseph B. Nettles | Z | 773-776 | 1857 |
|---|---|---|---|---|

(of Darlington District)

| Geiger, Ann | Joseph Culpepper | D | 57-58 | 1818 |
|---|---|---|---|---|

(of Abbeville District)

| Geiger, Ann | Charles F. Neuffer | N | 33-35 | 1843 |
|---|---|---|---|---|

Caroline (marriage settlement 25 January 1843)

| Geiger, Elizabeth | John M. Weston | O | 282-284 | 1841 |
|---|---|---|---|---|

(daughter of Abram Geiger) (in Alabama) [See also pages 280-281, 329]

| Geiger, Mary | John Henry Gardner | 2A | 635-637 | 1859 |
|---|---|---|---|---|

Caroline (marriage settlement 22 June 1859) (daughter of Godfrey H. Geiger and granddaughter of Michael Lorick)

| Gentry, Sarah | John McComb | T | 383-384 | 1849 |
|---|---|---|---|---|

(of Richland District)

| Gerald, _____ | Isaac Richbourg | R | 383-385 | 1844 |
|---|---|---|---|---|

(in Sumter District) [See also pages 386-388, 408-409]

| Gerald, _____ | Tyre J. Spann | R | 383-385 | 1844 |
|---|---|---|---|---|

(in Sumter District) [See also pages 386-388, 408-409]

| Gerald, Emma | Lewis W. Ballard | R | 383-385 | 1844 |
|---|---|---|---|---|

(in Sumter District) [See also pages 386-388, 408-409]

| Gerald, Martha | J. W. Doby | R | 383-385 | 1844 |
|---|---|---|---|---|

(in Sumter District) [See also pages 386-388, 408-409]

| Gerald, Rebecca | Lawrington R. Jennings | R | 383-385 | 1844 |
|---|---|---|---|---|

(in Sumter District) [See also pages 386-388, 408-409]

| Gibbes, Eliza | J. Gadsden Edwards | 2B | 317-319 | 1861 |
|---|---|---|---|---|

Gabriella (marriage settlement 29 April 1861) (both of Columbia)

| Gibbs, Martha Ann | Adolphus Gregory | W | 451-452 | 1853 |
|---|---|---|---|---|

(daughter of Churchill Gibbs of Union District) (of Union District)

| Gibert, Harriet | William Tennent | 2A | 166-170 | 1857 |
|---|---|---|---|---|

Eliza (marriage settlement 15 December 1857) (both of Abbeville District)

| Gibert, Louisa | William Pettigrew | D | 130-133 | 1819 |
|---|---|---|---|---|
| Gibson, _____ | _____ Capehart | 2B | 73 | 1860 |

(daughter of Absolom Gibson) (in Pickens District)

| Gibson, Cynthia C. | William J. Shelton | 2A | 707 | 1857 |
|---|---|---|---|---|

(daughter of Jacob Gibson) (of Fairfield District)

| Gibson, Desdamona | Charles C. Law | Z | 621-625 | 1857 |
|---|---|---|---|---|

S. A. (marriage settlement 15 January 1857) (daughter of John C. Gibson) (she of Marion District) (Law of Darlington District)

Implied South Carolina Marriages Volume IV 1787-1875

| WOMAN | MAN | VOL | PAGES | LIVED |
|---|---|---|---|---|
| Giles, Sarah C. | Thomas A. Cater | 2B | 104-106 | 1860 |

(marriage settlement 3 May 1860) (in Abbeville District)

| Gill, Mary E. | ___ Lindsay | W | 598 | 1853 |

(daughter of Robert Gill of Laurens District)

| Gill, Rebecca M. | Joseph Galluchat | R | 131-132 | 1846 |

(to be married 22 October 1846) (marriage settlement 19 October 1846) (daughter of Lewis Gill) (in Lancaster District)

| Gilliam, Drusilla M. E. | Wilson P. Gee | R | 220-222 | 1847 |

(daughter of Reuben Gilliam of Union District)

| Gilmore, Julia | ___ Cureton | 2B | 561 | 1862 |

(in Chester District)

| Gladney, Nancy | Thomas Black | Y | 561-562 | 1855 |

(of Fairfield District)

| Glenn, ___ | Patrick F. Herndon | H | 107-108 | 1832 |
| Glover, Caroline | Lewis Jervey | 2B | 775-777 | 1864 |

Howard (marriage settlement 9 March 1864) (in Greenville District)

| Glover, Elizabeth S. | Aaron A. Clark | T | 37-38 | 1848 |

(marriage contract 16 December 1848) (widow) (both of Edgefield District)

| Glover, Elizabeth S. | Aaron A. Clark | Z | 808-811 | 1857 |

(reference to marriage settlement - no date given) (widow) (in Edgefield District)

| Glover, Elizabeth S. | Aaron A. Clark | 2A | 85-86 | 1857 |

(reference to marriage settlement - no date given) (in Edgefield District)

| Glover, Martha | James H. Murray | N | 207-209 | 1843 |

(marriage settlement 31 August 1843) (daughter of Jethro Glover of Edgefield District) (of Edgefield District)

| Glover, Martha | William Rountree | T | 37-38 | 1848 |

(in Edgefield District)

| Glover, Martha | James G. O. Wilkinson | L | 383-385 | 1841 |

(marriage settlement 16 July 1841) (both of Edgefield District)

| Godfrey, Nancy | Peter Roberts | D | 158-159 | 1819 |

(marriage settlement 4 July 1819) (in Laurens District)

| Gomillion, Margaret M. | M. E. Hollingsworth | U | 48-49 | 1850 |

(of Edgefield District)

| Gomillion, Mary A. | Samuel F. Good | U | 49-50 | 1850 |

(of Edgefield District)

| Goode, Nancy P. | John M. Caldwell | 2A | 152-153 | 1857 |

(marriage settlement 4 November 1857) (widow of George M. Goode) (in York District)

| Goodlett, Eliza E. | ___ Hunt | M | 323 | 1842 |

(daughter of Spartan Goodlett)

Implied South Carolina Marriages Volume IV 1787-1875

| WOMAN | MAN | VOL | PAGES | LIVED |
|---|---|---|---|---|

Goodman, Lena  Charles Hamburg  2C  304-307  1867
 (reference to marriage settlement 26 March 1867) (she of Charleston) (he of Columbia, Richland District)
Goodwyn, Keziah  James Hopkins  B  638-650  1804
 (Goodwin) (widow of Jesse Goodwyn who died September 1792)
Goodwyn, Rachel  Jonadab Nettles  H  152-153  1831
 (marriage settlement 17 October 1831) (widow)
Gordon, Elizabeth  Samuel L. Love  2A  592-594  1858
 Ann (reference to marriage agreement - no date given) (daughter of Mansfield Gordon) (in York District)
Gordon, Elizabeth  Samuel Lucian Love  Z  431-432  1855
 Ann (marriage settlement 17 April 1855) (both of York District)
Gordon, Jane  Alexander Hopper  D  3-5  1813
 (marriage settlement 29 December 1813) (both of Newberry District)
Gordon, Margaret  William Lee  E  190-191  1824
 (marriage agreement 18 March 1824) (widow) (widower) (both of Sumter District)
Gordon, Nancy F.  Samuel Chandler  E  304-305  1825
 (daughter of Charles F. Gordon) (in Sumter District)
Goree, Ann  Robert Kelly  L  23-24  1839
 ("otherwise Robert Kelly Goree")
 (marriage contract 23 October 1839) (of Newberry District)
Gossett, Francis  G. Luwiler Glazener  2B  468-469  1859
 Elizabeth (daughter of John T. Gossett) (in Greenville District)
Govan, Elizabeth  Nash Roach  C  62-65  1813
 Ann (marriage settlement 24 April 1813) (of Charleston)
Govan, Elizabeth  Nash Roach  F  292-293  1828
 Ann (marriage contract 24 April 1828)
Gowen, Catharine  Moses Evans  D  191-194  1820
 (marriage settlement 24 April 1820) (widow of John Gowen of York District) (of York District)
Graetz, Ellen  Jacob M. Wolff  Y  201-202  1855
 (marriage settlement 18 May 1855) (daughter of _____ Wolff Graetz)
Graham, Mary  Berry W. Jeans  N  200-202  1843
  (Jeanes)
 (daughter of John Graham of Newberry District) (of Union District)
Graham, Sarah Ann  James L. Bowers  M  426-427  1842
 (daughter of James Graham of Newberry District)
Gramling, Margaret  William Austin  I  451-452  1836
 (marriage settlement 7 May 1836)

Implied South Carolina Marriages Volume IV 1787-1875

| WOMAN | MAN | VOL | PAGES | LIVED |
|---|---|---|---|---|
| Grant, Susan P. | Marcus Dendy | Z | 477 | 1856 |

(marriage settlement 23 December 1856) (he was married before) (both of Laurens District)

| | | | | |
|---|---|---|---|---|
| Gray, C. Louisa | William Miller | W | 465-467 | 1851 |
| Gray, Carolina A. | John A. Mays | 2A | 103-105 | 1856 |

(marriage settlement 13 February 1856) (widow of M. M. Gray) (granddaughter of Archibald Lester) (both of Edgefield District)

| | | | | |
|---|---|---|---|---|
| Gray, Eliza. C. | David Ardis | W | 465-466 | 1851 |
| Gray, Eliza Corby | David Ardis | F | 43-45 | 1827 |

(marriage settlement 1 February 1827) (daughter of John J. Gray of Be<u>a</u>ch Island, Edgefield District) (in Edgefield District)

| | | | | |
|---|---|---|---|---|
| Gray, Emily A. | James L. Rogers | V | 4-5 | 1851 |

(marriage settlement 3 May 1851) (daughter of John J. Gray of Be<u>a</u>ch Island, Edgefield District, S.C.) (Rogers of Burke County, Georgia)

| | | | | |
|---|---|---|---|---|
| Gray, Emily A. | James L. Rogers | W | 465-466 | 1851 |
| Gray, Julia H. | John F. Lanneau (Lennau) | W | 465-466 | 1851 |
| Gray, Julia Helena | John Francis Lanneau | M | 130-131 | 1842 |

(marriage settlement 17 March 1842) (daughter of John J. Gray) (in Edgefield District)

| | | | | |
|---|---|---|---|---|
| Gray, Susan | Max Sallat | R | 338-340 | 1847 |

(marriage settlement 16 January 1847) (widow of William W. Gray of Edgefield District, S.C.) (Sallat of Augusta, Georgia, late from Germany)

| | | | | |
|---|---|---|---|---|
| Greaves, Elizabeth | Alexander McWhite | N | 219-221 | 1843 |

(marriage settlement 20 November 1843) (both of Marion District)

| | | | | |
|---|---|---|---|---|
| Green, Agnes | Michael Hefferon | X | 279-280 | 1854 |

(marriage settlement 7 February 1854) (widow of Henry C. Green)

| | | | | |
|---|---|---|---|---|
| Green, Elizabeth Jane | Charles Henry Green | 2A | 511-512 | 1858 |

(marriage settlement 29 December 1858) (she in Sumter District, S.C.) (he of Georgia)

| | | | | |
|---|---|---|---|---|
| Green, Emilia E. | George T. Hughes | 2B | 559-561 | 1862 |

(marriage settlement 15 December 1862) (widow) (she of Greenville District)

| | | | | |
|---|---|---|---|---|
| Green, Hannah | Wyatt Lipscomb | F | 18 | 1821 |

(widow) (she of York District) (he of Spartanburgh District)

| | | | | |
|---|---|---|---|---|
| Green, Hannah | Charles Zimmerman | X | 629-630 | 1855 |
| Green, Hannah | Charles C. H. Zimmerman | 2A | 338-339 | 1858 |
| Green, Harriet | William Gray | D | 364-365 | 1821 |

(marriage agreement 9 June 1821) (in Richland District)

Implied South Carolina Marriages Volume IV 1787-1875

| WOMAN | MAN | VOL | PAGES | LIVED |
|---|---|---|---|---|
| Green, Malinda (widow) | ____ Huskerson | 2C | 440-444 | 1868 |
| Green, Martha | Charles Oliver | C | 155-156 | 1814 |

(marriage settlement 29 September 1814) (of Richland District)

| Greenland, Elizabeth | Cornelius Brown | 3A | 290 | 1791 |
|---|---|---|---|---|
| Greer, Elna (Elnan) | T. J. H. Murphy | 2A | 744-745 | 1859 |

D. (daughter of Thomas S. Greer) (in Union District)

Greer. See Grier

| Gregg, Julia R. | John J. McIver | Z | 244-248 | 1856 |
|---|---|---|---|---|

(marriage settlement 4 June 1856) (both of Darlington District)

| Gregory, Miriam | Samuel D. Kennington | 2A | 703 | 1859 |
|---|---|---|---|---|

(marriage agreement 5 November 1859) (widow) (both of Lancaster District)

| Gregory, Sarah Elvira | Doctr. James Gregory | V | 246-247 | 1852 |
|---|---|---|---|---|

(daughter of Benjamin J. Gregory of Union District)

| Grier, Mary Ann | Henry Britton | N | 73-75 | 1843 |
|---|---|---|---|---|

(reference to marriage settlement - no date given) (his first marriage)

Grier. See Greer

| Griffin, Agnes W. | Larkin Reynolds | U | 43-45 | 1850 |
|---|---|---|---|---|

(marriage settlement 11 March 1850) (in Abbeville District)

| Griffin, Avarilla | ____ Anthony | 2A | 728-729 | 1859 |
|---|---|---|---|---|

(in Pickens District)

| Griffin, Elener (Eleanor) | Edwin Garlington | C | 231-233 | 1815 |
|---|---|---|---|---|

(marriage settlement 23 November 1815) (in Laurens District)

| Griffin, Eliza A. | ____ Hollingsworth | 2A | 521-526 | 1858 |
|---|---|---|---|---|
| Griffin, Francis | Charles Pickett | E | 45-46 | 1821 |

(in Fairfield District)

| Griffin, Kitty | James Young | D | 388-389 | 1822 |
|---|---|---|---|---|

(marriage settlement 28 March 1822) (daughter of Reuben Griffin) (of Laurens District)

| Griffin, Margaret | John Davis | E | 45-46 | 1821 |
|---|---|---|---|---|

(in Fairfield District)

| Griffin, Martha Ann | William C. Black | I | 35-36 | 1834 |
|---|---|---|---|---|

(daughter of Ira Griffin) (in Abbeville District)

| Griffin, Phebe | Richard S. Cannon | S | 245-247 | 1848 |
|---|---|---|---|---|
| Griffis, Elizabeth R. | Philip W. Fairey | 2C | 351-353 | 1867 |

(marriage settlement 14 May 1867) (she of Colleton District) (he of Orangeburg District)

Implied South Carolina Marriages Volume IV 1787-1875

| WOMAN | MAN | VOL | PAGES | LIVED |
|---|---|---|---|---|
| Griffith, Pernecy C. | David Q. Anderson | 2B | 565-566 | 1856 |

(married about 1856) (separation agreement 12 January 1863) (daughter of Stephen Griffith) (in Laurens District)

| Groves, Elizabeth Yancey | _____ Arnold | S | 293-294 | 1848 |
|---|---|---|---|---|

(daughter of Joseph Groves of Abbeville District)

| Groves, Emma Francis | _____ Gantt | S | 293-294 | 1848 |
|---|---|---|---|---|

(daughter of Joseph Groves of Abbeville District)

| Groves, Francis Emala | Thomas W. Gantt | V | 522-524 | 1852 |
|---|---|---|---|---|

(in Abbeville District)

| Gruber, Sarah | George P. Smith | G | 77-78 | 1829 |
|---|---|---|---|---|

(daughter of John Gruber)

| Guignard, Anna Margaret | Philip Gadsden Edwards | 2B | 716-717 | 1840 |
|---|---|---|---|---|

(reference to postnuptial settlement 4 May 1840) (he died 1847) (of Charleston)

| Guignard, Frances Ann Margaret Horry | Robert Pringle Mayrant | G | 364-365 | 1831 |
|---|---|---|---|---|

(marriage settlement 12 May 1831) (daughter of James S. Guignard of Columbia) (Mayrant of Sumter District) [See also Volume H, pages 193-194]

| Guignard, Mary Margaret | Peter Horry | C | 287-289 | 1793 |
|---|---|---|---|---|

(marriage bond 9 February 1793) (of Richland District)

| Guignard, Sarah Slann | John A. Scott | G | 106-107 | 1830 |
|---|---|---|---|---|

(marriage settlement 25 February 1830) (daughter of James S. Guignard of Columbia, S.C.) (Scott of Mississippi)

| Guphill, Ann | Samuel S. Taylor | F | 468-469 | 1829 |
|---|---|---|---|---|

(marriage settlement 15 April 1829)

(H)

| Hadden, Rosa Ann Eliza | Benjamin W. Williams | Y | 637-638 | 1856 |
|---|---|---|---|---|

(daughter of John T. Hadden of Abbeville District)

| Hagood, Eliza M. | Francis A. Miles | 2C | 252-256 | 1866 |
|---|---|---|---|---|

(daughter of Benjamin Hagood of Pickens District) [Must also see pages 259-262]

| Hagood, Elmina E. | Philip B. Martin | 2C | 259-262 | 1866 |
|---|---|---|---|---|

(daughter of Benjamin Hagood of Pickens District) [See also pages 252-256]

| Hagood, Elvira C. | William W. Robinson | 2C | 252-256 | 1866 |
|---|---|---|---|---|

(daughter of Benjamin Hagood of Pickens District) [Must also see pages 259-262]

Implied South Carolina Marriages Volume IV 1787-1875

| WOMAN | MAN | VOL | PAGES | LIVED |
|---|---|---|---|---|

Haigood, Leonora    James M. Roach         S   421-422   1848
   (daughter of Buckner Haigood of Fairfield District) (of
   Fairfield District)
Haile, Catharine    Christopher Matheson   I   433       1836
   (daughter of Benjamin Haile of Camden, Kershaw District)
   (of Camden, Kershaw District)
Haile, Mary W.      William Kennedy        I   433-434   1836
   (daughter of Benjamin Haile of Camden, Kershaw District)
   (of Camden, Kershaw District)
Hails, Sarah B.     Carnot Bellinger       H   28-29     1832
   (marriage settlement 1 February 1832) (daughter of Capt.
   Robert Hails)
Hair, Narcissa H.   Dr. William S.         V   69-71     1851
   (Hare)           Johnson
   (marriage contract 8 November 1851) (widow) (both of
   Barnwell District)
Hall, Margaret      James S. Wilson        T   335-336   1849
   (marriage settlement 23 August 1849) (granddaughter of
   Daniel Talbot) (both of Newberry District)
Halsey, Mary J.     James T. Thomas        Y   134-135   1855
   (of Coosa County, Alabama)
Halsey, Rebecca Ann Joseph H. Townes       E   516-518   1825
   (marriage settlement 15 February 1825) (she of
   Wilmington, North Carolina)
Ham, Lucretia       James W. Owens         M   187-189   1842
   (marriage settlement 25 March 1842) (in Darlington
   District)
Hambright, Fathy    William J. Wilson      2A  599-602   1859
   (Faithey) L. (marriage settlement 15 March 1859) (in
   York District)
Hamer, Emily        Thomas C. Bristow      2C  182-183   1866
   (marriage settlement 31 July 1866) (widow of Thomas C.
   Hamer) (in Marlboro District)
Hamer, Mary E.      Wilson Conger          G   39-42     1829
   (of Warren County, Mississippi)
Hamilton, Jane      John Bowie             I   371       1836
   Eliza (daughter of Alexander C. Hamilton) (of Aiken,
   Barnwell District) [See also Volume K, pages 166-168]
Hammond, Margaret   Samuel Kingman         G   441-443   1831
   Ellen            (of Edgefield District)
Hammond, Talitha    ____ Hall              C   51-52     1813
Haney, Emily        Hollyman Randall       T   42-44     1849
   (daughter of Orashea Haney of Edgefield District)
Hankinson, Martha   John Darlington        F   23-24     1826
                    (in Barnwell District)

Implied South Carolina Marriages Volume IV 1787-1875

| WOMAN | MAN | VOL | PAGES | LIVED |
|---|---|---|---|---|
| Hannon, Emily C. | Archibald Chaplis Campbell | K | 96-98 | 1836 |

(marriage settlement 8 September 1836) (in Anderson District)

| Harden, Sarah M. | Richard J. Gladney | W | 550-552 | 1853 |
|---|---|---|---|---|

(marriage settlement 4 May 1853) (daughter of Silas Harden) (both of Fairfield District)

| Harden, Sarah M. | Richard J. Gladney | 2B | 187-190 | 1853 |
|---|---|---|---|---|

(reference to marriage settlement 4 May 1853) (in Fairfield District)

| Hardy, Pamela | Casper Parham | K | 15 | 1837 |
|---|---|---|---|---|

(daughter of William Hardy of Edgefield District)

| Hare, Sophia | Samuel Parler | D | 237-239 | 1821 |
|---|---|---|---|---|

(marriage agreement 20 March 1821) (daughter of Gunrod Hare) (both of St. Matthew's Parish)

Hare. See Hair

| Harker, Ann | William McHarg | I | 103 | 1817 |
|---|---|---|---|---|

(married 1817) (she was born about 1790 in Cumberland, England) (he died December 1824) (she arrived at Savannah, Georgia from Liverpool, November 1815) (of Edgefield District, S.C.) (to Augusta, Georgia, June 1820)

| Harkness, Eliza Jane | Lewis C. Gaillard | S | 414-415 | 1848 |
|---|---|---|---|---|

(daughter of John Harkness) (in Anderson District)

| Harley, Sarah R. | Christopher H. Langley | P | 102-105 | 1838 |
|---|---|---|---|---|

(both of Barnwell District)

| Harmon, Maria | John P. Mays | E | 196-197 | 1824 |
|---|---|---|---|---|

(marriage settlement 26 May 1824) (both of Edgefield District)

| Harmon, Mary | Thomas Vaughan | C | 291-292 | 1816 |
|---|---|---|---|---|

(marriage settlement 28 February 1816) (daughter of Stephen Harmon) (both of Kershaw District)

| Harper, Ann M. | John Augustus Gibson | V | 608-609 | 1852 |
|---|---|---|---|---|

(marriage settlement 24 June 1852) (widow) (both of Richland District)

| Harper, Sarah C. | Dr. James A. McGehee | W | 213-214 | 1853 |
|---|---|---|---|---|

(of Paulding County, Georgia) [See also pages 311-312]

| Harper, Sarah H. | James A. McGehee | Y | 218 | 1855 |
|---|---|---|---|---|

(of Paulding County, Georgia)

| Harrell, Sarah Ann | _____ Blackwell | W | 189-191 | 1852 |
|---|---|---|---|---|

(daughter of James Harrell)

| Harris, _____ | _____ Stewart | G | 36-37 | 1829 |
|---|---|---|---|---|

(daughter of John Harris of Abbeville District)

| Harris, Ann L. | _____ Wiley | G | 36-37 | 1829 |
|---|---|---|---|---|

(daughter of John Harris of Abbeville District)

| Harris, Betsey | _____ Young | G | 36-37 | 1829 |
|---|---|---|---|---|

(daughter of John Harris of Abbeville District)

Implied South Carolina Marriages Volume IV 1787-1875

| WOMAN | MAN | VOL | PAGES | LIVED |
|---|---|---|---|---|
| Harris, Caroline | Henry Wise | 2A | 723-724 | 1859 |

(daughter of David Harris of Edgefield District) (Wise of Barnwell District)

Harris, Elizabeth   Oswald Murphy   2A   518-519   1858
(daughter of David Harris of Edgefield District, S.C.) (of Washington County, Alabama)

Harris, Frances C. _____ Alexander   G   36-37   1829
(daughter of John Harris of Abbeville District)

Harris, Margaretta _____ Cowen   G   36-37   1829
(daughter of John Harris of Abbeville District)

Harris, Nancy A. _____ Porter   G   36-37   1829
(daughter of John Harris of Abbeville District)

Harrison, Francis   Eli Thomas   O   161   1844
(marriage settlement 20 June 1844) (both of Marlborough District)

Hart, Elizabeth S.   Augustus F. Edwards   2A   708-709   1859
(in Darlington District)

Hart, Harriet   John Reid   D   376-379   1821
(marriage settlement 13 November 1821) (she of Orangeburgh District) (he of Columbia)

Hart, Mary W. _____ Law   2A   708-709   1859

Hartly, Elizabeth _____ Prior   B   637-638   1810
(widow of Henry Hartly) (she of Lexington District)

Hartzog, Rebecca H.   George J. Reed   O   251-252   1844
(marriage settlement 23 October 1844) (widow of George F. Hartzog) (of Barnwell District)

Harvey, Catherine   Joseph Morris   U   274-276   1850
(marriage settlement 26 December 1850) (widow) (in Edgefield District)

Harvin, Alice C.   John J. Hodge   2B   307-308   1861
(marriage settlement 27 February 1861) (in Clarendon District)

Haseldon, Caroline M.   James F. Killen   2B   658-659   1863
(of Darlington District)

Haseldon, Elizabeth _____ James   2B   658-659   1863

Haskew, Margaret A.   John R. Donaldson   N   314-317   1844
(marriage settlement 22 February 1844) (daughter of Zacheus Haskew of Marlboro District) (of Marlboro District)

Hatcher, Elizabeth   Amos Landrum   K   305-306   1838
(marriage agreement 21 August 1838) (daughter of John Hatcher Senr.) (both of Edgefield District)

Havird, Jane M.   James T. Haney   O   213-215   1844
(marriage settlement 26 July 1844) (both of Edgefield District)

Havis, Elizabeth   Joseph Evans   E   139-145   1823
(daughter of Jesse Havis Senior) (in Fairfield District)

196

Implied South Carolina Marriages Volume IV 1787-1875

| WOMAN | MAN | VOL | PAGES | LIVED |
|---|---|---|---|---|
| Havis, Martha | John Graham | E | 139-145 | 1823 |

(daughter of Jesse Havis Senior) (in Fairfield District)

| | | | | |
|---|---|---|---|---|
| Hawkins, Martha | Thompson Young | 2B | 147-148 | 1860 |

(in Newberry District)

| | | | | |
|---|---|---|---|---|
| Hawkins, Patsey | Thompson Young Senr. | T | 174-180 | 1849 |

(in Newberry District)

| | | | | |
|---|---|---|---|---|
| Hawthorn, Amasillas | James F. Crawford | P | 87-91 | 1845 |
| Hawthorn, Elizabeth A. | Alexander H. Miller | P | 87-91 | 1845 |
| Hawthorn, Jane J. | Toliver Johnson | P | 87-91 | 1845 |
| Hawthorn, Lavinia | Hardy Gilstrap | 2C | 56-59 | 1865 |

(postnuptial settlement/separation agreement 9 October 1865) (widow of Jasper N. Hawthorn) (Gilstrap was married before) (in Pickens District)

| | | | | |
|---|---|---|---|---|
| Hawthorn, Mary (Polly) D. | Andrew Prewit | P | 87-91 | 1845 |
| Hawthorn, Susan | William Martin | P | 87-91 | 1845 |
| Hay, Henrietta | Earnest G. Park | 2C | 186-187 | 1866 |

(daughter of James Hay of Scotland) (of Union District, S.C.)

| | | | | |
|---|---|---|---|---|
| Haynsworth, E. H. | _____ Miller | T | 304-306 | 1849 |

(daughter of Dr. James Haynsworth) (in Marion District)

| | | | | |
|---|---|---|---|---|
| Haynsworth, Elizabeth H. | C. W. Miller | 2A | 621-622 | 1859 |

(daughter of Doctor James Haynsworth) (in Marion District)

| | | | | |
|---|---|---|---|---|
| Haywood, Elizabeth | Charles W. Miller | V | 237-238 | 1837 |

(daughter of James Haywood of Sumter District) (of Sumter District)

| | | | | |
|---|---|---|---|---|
| Hearst, Jane | William S. Ansly (Ansley) | O | 66-68 | 1844 |

(daughter of John Hearst of Abbeville District)

| | | | | |
|---|---|---|---|---|
| Heath, Alice Wyche | Doctr. Samuel H. Owens | K | 21-22 | 1838 |

(daughter of Thomas Heath of Richland District) [Must also see pages 271-272]

| | | | | |
|---|---|---|---|---|
| Heath, Drusillar | James Jackson | B | 561-563 | 1808 |

(of Dinwiddie County, Virginia)

| | | | | |
|---|---|---|---|---|
| Heath, Eliza | _____ Owens | P | 141-145 | 1845 |
| Heath, Mary Taylor | James Whitaker | E | 107-109 | 1823 |

(daughter of Thomas Heath Senr. of Richland District) (of Fairfield District) [See also pages 187-188]

| | | | | |
|---|---|---|---|---|
| Heath, Rebecca | _____ Kirkland | P | 141-145 | 1845 |
| Heatly, Ann | James Lovell | E | 397-400 | 1825 |

(of Orangeburgh District) [See also pages 395-397]

| | | | | |
|---|---|---|---|---|
| Henderson, Jane | Nesbit Cochran | W | 21-24 | 1852 |

Implied South Carolina Marriages Volume IV 1787-1875

| WOMAN | MAN | VOL | PAGES | LIVED |
|---|---|---|---|---|
| Henderson, Sarah P. | John F. Fowler | 2A | 552-554 | 1859 |

(marriage settlement 31 January 1859) (widow of Hugh L. Henderson) (in Laurens District)

Hendrick, Louisa M. Michael J. Rudulph C 375-376 1816
(marriage settlement 1 October 1816) (both of Columbia, Richland District)

Hendrix, Anna C. Felix Turnipseed 2A 112-114 1857
(marriage settlement 24 September 1857) (she of Lexington District) (he of Richland District)

Henry, Ann Joshua Sowden V 304-314 1852
(daughter of James Henry of Richland District)

Henry, Barbara E. Jesse Collins V 304-314 1852
(daughter of James Henry of Richland District)

Henry, Eliza William F. Woodward K 517-520 1839
(marriage settlement 14 October 1839) (widow of George Henry) (in Fairfield District)

Henry, Emma C. _____ Nelson 2B 241-242 1860

Henry, Jane William B. Creber V 304-314 1852
(daughter of James Henry of Richland District)

Henry, Margaret John Levingston V 304-314 1852
(daughter of James Henry of Richland District)

Henry, Martha Jonathan Melton V 304-314 1852
(daughter of James Henry of Richland District)

Henstiss, Venetta James Husbands U 318-319 1851
(marriage settlement 9 January 1851) (in Marlborough District)

Heriot, Sarah Caroline Thomas Boston Clarkson 2C 78-83 1830
(reference to marriage settlement 25 February 1830)

Heron, Mary Doctr William Ley H 219 1832
(Herron) (marriage contract 6 September 1832) (both of Columbia)

Herrington, Susannah Joseph Cantey Junr B 368-369 1805
(marriage settlement 10 May 1805) (of Sumter District)

Herriot, Agnes Warren H. Burgess I 85-88 1834
(marriage contract 6 November 1834)

Herriott, Susan M. William K. Stuart P 117-120 1845
(marriage settlement 11 November 1845) (in Sumter District)

Hewitt, Janette L. David J. Andrews Z 131-133 1856
(marriage settlement 28 February 1856) (widow of Francȩs M. Hewitt of Darlington District) (of Darlington District)

Hibben, Mary Hays Alexander Greenfield 2A 281-282 1858
(marriage settlement __ January 1858) (of Greenville District)

Implied South Carolina Marriages Volume IV 1787-1875

| WOMAN | MAN | VOL | PAGES | LIVED |
|---|---|---|---|---|
| Hickson, Caroline | ____ Johnson | W | 109-111 | 1852 |

(daughter of Levi Hickson of Barnwell District)

Hickson, Elizabeth ____ Singeltary X 509-521 1853
    (widow of Thomas J. Hickson)
Hickson, Martha M. ____ Hagood T 357-359 1849
    (daughter of Levi Hickson of Barnwell District)
Hickson, Sarah A. George Washington 2C 93-108 1866
    Hicks
    (marriage settlement 13 January 1866) (widow of John
    Hickson) (both of Barnwell District)
Hickson. See Hixon
Hightower, Ann ____ Goodin 2A 90-91 1851
Hightower, ____ Barton 2A 90-91 1851
    Catharine
Hightower, Darius Holcombe 2A 90-91 1851
    Charlotte (marriage agreement 1 February 1851) (both of
    Greenville District)
Hightower, Harriet Jeremiah Bussey D 415 1811
    (marriage settlement 12 October 1811) (of Edgefield
    District)
Hightower, Louisa ____ Barton 2A 90-91 1851
Hightower, Lucy T. Thomas E. Hitt S 373-374 1848
    (of Edgefield District)
Hill, Elizabeth Stephen Terry G 357-358 1831
Hill, Harriet W. Edward P. Mobley G 357-358 1831
Hill, Rebecca Doct Trezevant G 357-358 1831
    DeGraffenreid
Hill, Sarah John Pearson G 357-358 1831
    (of Fairfield District)
Hill, Sarah Ann John D. Smith Y 404-405 1855
    (daughter of Littleton Hill of Chester District) (of
    Chester District)
Hill, Susannah John G. Riddle M 180-181 1842
    (marriage settlement 5 May 1842) (widow of John Hill)
    (both of Edgefield District)
Hinton, Patsey ____ Hays E 290-291 1824
    (daughter of William Hinton)
Hiron, Ann Lemuel Cary C 433-435 1807
    (marriage agreement 30 July 1807) (widow of John Hiron)
    (both of Columbia)
Hirons, Ann Freeman Delane B 214-217 1803
    (marriage settlement 22 March 1803) (widow of John
    Hirons) (both of Columbia, Richland District) [See also
    Volume C, pages 102, 433-435]
Hix, Julia Ann John Joiner H 475-477 1833
    (marriage settlement 18 September 1833) (of Union
    District)

Implied South Carolina Marriages Volume IV 1787-1875

| WOMAN | MAN | VOL | PAGES | LIVED |
|---|---|---|---|---|
| Hixon, Julia | Charles Thomas (of Edgefield District) | W | 49-52 | 1852 |

Hixon. See Hickson
Hodges, Rebecca   Richard C. Bowen   W   258-259   1852
(daughter of Gabriel Hodges of Abbeville District, S.C.)
(Bowen of Mississippi)
Hodges, Susan L.   Thomas C. Jones   2B   439-440   1861
(daughter of Robert H. W. Hodges of Abbeville District)
Hogg, Janet   James Runaman   E   73-77   1820
(Jennet) (in County of Selkirk, Scotland)
Holder, Martha   Giles N. Smith   O   420-421   1845
(to be married 19 April 1845) (marriage settlement 19 April 1845) (of Union District)
Holder, Rutha   William Little   R   57-58   1846
(marriage settlement 7 September 1846) (daughter of Daniel Holder) (of Union District)
Holland, Elisabeth   Charles Humphries   F   421-422   1829
(marriage settlement 17 February 1829) (in Union District)
Hollingsworth, Eliza A.   William H. Harrington   2A   521-526   1858
(marriage settlement 1 December 1858) (widow) (in Edgefield District)
Hollingsworth, Eliza A. A.   _____ Freeman   2B   332-335   1861
Hollingsworth, Eliza Ann   _____ Walker   2A   521-526   1858
(daughter of John Hollingsworth)
Hollingsworth, Emeline D.   _____ Talbert   2   521-526   1858
(daughter of John Hollingsworth)
Hollingsworth, Laura Ann   Burrell E. Hobbs   I   289-290   1835
(marriage settlement 18 July 1835) (of Edgefield District)
Hollingsworth, Margaret C.   Robert D. Brunson   2C   170-174   1866
(marriage settlement 9 May 1866) (granddaughter of John Hollingsworth) (she of Abbeville District) (Brunson of Edgefield District) [See also page 263]
Hollis, Delila A. E.   Henry Smith   Z   559   1856
(daughter of John Hollis of Fairfield District) (of Fairfield District)
Hollis, Sarah   Jesse Bailey   W   606-607   1853
(marriage settlement 28 April 1853) (in Union District)
Holman, Mary M.   Henry D. Grimes   2A   12-13   1855
(in Barnwell District)
Holstein, Florella   Lewis W. Youngblood   2A   305-306   1858
(daughter of Wade Holstein of Edgefield District)

Implied South Carolina Marriages Volume IV 1787-1875

| WOMAN | MAN | VOL | PAGES | LIVED |
|---|---|---|---|---|
| Holstein, Louisa | A. W. Kennerly | 2A | 305-306 | 1858 |

(daughter of Wade Holstein of Edgefield District)

| Holston, Cusdrado | Jacob Long Junr. | N | 186-187 | 1843 |

(of Edgefield District)

| Holston, Irena | Thomas Pitts | N | 186-187 | 1843 |

(of Edgefield District)

| Holston, Louisa | _____ Ryan | X | 152-153 | 1852 |

(daughter of Moses Holston Senr of Edgefield District)

| Holston, Louisa | Benjamin G. Ryan | Z | 117-118 | 1856 |

(Holstein) (daughter of Moses Holston Senr.) (in Edgefield District)

| Hood, Elizabeth R. | Thomas M. Belk | 2A | 619-621 | 1859 |

(marriage settlement 9 May 1859) (widow) (both of Lancaster District)

| Hope, Mary Ann C. | Dr. Lewellen P. Hobbs | Y | 584-585 | 1856 |

(daughter of John C. Hope of Lexington District) (Hobbs of Lexington District)

| Hopkins, _____ | Theodorus W. Brevard | G | 338-339 | 1828 |

(daughter of James Hopkins of Richland District)

| Hopkins, Mary T. N. | Reuben Sims | H | 107-108 | 1832 |

(daughter of Newton Hopkins of Chester District)

| Hornsby, Christina | Peter Dent | Y | 125-126 | 1855 |

(in Richland District)

| Hornsby, Christina W. | James Dent | Y | 71-73 | 1855 |

(daughter of Daniel Hornsby) (in Richland District)

| Hornsby, Mary Ann | Reuben Smith | Y | 71-73 | 1855 |

(daughter of Daniel Hornsby) (in Richland District)

| Horton, Elizabeth N. | _____ Bethune | 2B | 309-312 | 1861 |
| Horton, Mary Jane | William H. McKnight | 2B | 309-312 | 1861 |

(daughter of Joseph Horton) (in Clarendon District)

| Houston, Cornelia A. | Thomas M. Sloan | 2A | 324-325 | 1858 |

(marriage settlement 6 March 1858)

| How, Ann J. | _____ Wilson | O | 226-227 | 1840 |

("Ann J. Wilson late Ann J. How")

| How, Mary | Robert W. Gibbes Junior | Y | 8-10 | 1855 |

(marriage settlement 6 February 1855)

| Howard, Amelia M. | _____ Harllee | Y | 510-512 | 1855 |

(widow of Charles B. Howard)

| Howard, Amelia M. | Joseph N. Whitner Jr | Y | 510-512 | 1855 |

(marriage settlement 13 November 1855) (daughter of Charles B. Howard) (she of Marion District)

| Howard, Roxana | Holloway James | D | 107 | 1819 |

(marriage contract 15 March 1819)

| Howell, Epps G. | Danl. H. Tresevant | T | 293-296 | 1849 |

Implied South Carolina Marriages Volume IV 1787-1875

| WOMAN | MAN | VOL | PAGES | LIVED |
|---|---|---|---|---|

Howell, Epps G.　　　＿＿＿ Trezvant　　U　142-147　1850
　(daughter of Jesse M. Howell) (in Richland District)
Howell, Mary　　Samuel Oliver　　C　55　1813
　(daughter of Matthew Howell of Richland District)
　(Oliver of Richland District)
Howell, Mary Eliza　Thomas Dickson　2A　270-271　1857
　(marriage contract 8 December 1857) (daughter of Joseph
　Howell) (both of York District)
Hubbard, Eliza Ann　Allen Chapman　Y　209-212　1855
　(marriage settlement 25 April 1855) (daughter of William
　Hubbard) (both of Chesterfield District)
Huckabee, Mary P.　Franklin Dupree　Z　518-519　1857
　(daughter of G. W. Huckabee)
Hudson, M. L.　　Hilliard L. Thompson 2B　95-97　1860
　(daughter of Robert Hudson) (in Sumter District)
Hughes, Susan W.　William D. Allen　2B　571-572　1862
　(married 27 April 1862) (she of Barnwell District, S.C.)
　(he of Houston County, Georgia)
Hughey, Effie　　William Eigleberger　U　5-7　1850
　(daughter of Daniel Hughey of Fairfield District)
Huiet, Ida Statira　Drury T. Vaughn　2A　223-225　1858
　(daughter of John Huiet)
Humphries,　　　Edwin Richter　　Y　596-598　1855
　Elizabeth (marriage settlement 23 August 1855) (both of
　Union District)
Humphries, Hester　Samuel J. Odom　2A　547-549　1859
　C. (marriage settlement 17 January 1859) (daughter of
　Thomas Humphries) (Odom formerly of Union District, but
　now of Darlington District)
Hunt. See Huntt
Hunter, Ibby Eliza　Charles F. Williams 2A　105-106　1857
　(daughter of John Hunter of Laurens District)
Hunter, Ida L.　　George W. Dargan　2B　250-253　1861
　(marriage settlement 2 January 1861) (in Darlington
　District)
Hunter, Mary E.　Richard M. Owings　X　479-481　1853
　(marriage settlement 22 December 1853) (in Edgefield
　District)
Hunter, Sarah　　Colo John Simpson　C　227-228　1811
　(marriage contract 22 January 1811) (in Laurens
　District)
Hunter, Susan E.　William H. Eddy　2A　531　1859
　(daughter of Joseph Y. Hunter of Newberry District)
Huntt, Martha A.　Samuel Smoke　　2B　577-579　1862
　(in Richland District)

Implied South Carolina Marriages Volume IV 1787-1875

| WOMAN | MAN | VOL | PAGES | LIVED |
|---|---|---|---|---|
| Huskerson, Malinda | Samuel Morris | 2C | 440-444 | 1868 |

(married about 1868) (separation agreement 4 March 1868) (widow) (he was married before) (in Anderson District)

| Huson, Hannah Ann | John Flowers | H | 461 | 1833 |
|---|---|---|---|---|
| Hutchinson, Martha | Joseph Cook | Y | 436-437 | 1855 |

(granddaughter of James Boatwright)

| Hutchinson, Martha | George L. Martindale | Z | 183-184 | 1856 |
|---|---|---|---|---|

Minerva (daughter of A. S. Hutchinson of Laurens District)

| Hutchison, Palmyra | R. A. Pressley | 2B | 754-755 | 1863 |
|---|---|---|---|---|

A. (daughter of Robert Hutchison of Abbeville Distirict) (both of Abbeville District)

(I)

| Ingram, Dorcas | Green B. Montgomery | Y | 422-423 | 1855 |
|---|---|---|---|---|

(marriage settlement 9 October 1855) (widow) (both of Chester District)

| Ioor, Emily H. | William Brown | M | 410-412 | 1842 |
|---|---|---|---|---|

(marriage settlement 22 December 1842) (she of Edgefield District, S.C.) (he of Richmond County, Georgia)

| Ioor, Julia S. | Absalom T. Hodges | I | 560-561 | 1837 |
|---|---|---|---|---|

(marriage agreement 9 March 1837) (she in Edgefield) (he of Abbeville District)

| Irby, Louisa E. | John Watt | 2B | 805-806 | 1864 |
|---|---|---|---|---|

(daughter of Dr. Wm Irby) (she of Fairfield District)

(J)

| Jacks, Mary A. E. | Simpson Malone | 2B | 758-760 | 1863 |
|---|---|---|---|---|

(marriage settlement 10 December 1863) (widow of Isaac Calmes Jacks) (she of Laurens District) (Malone of Union District)

| Jackson, Jane | Josiah Jordan | X | 269-272 | 1854 |
|---|---|---|---|---|

(marriage contract 3 January 1854) (both of Chester District)

| Jackson, Sarah | Richard Rawlinson | A | 512 | 1801 |
|---|---|---|---|---|

(of Richland District)

| Jaffray, Janet | Revd. James Lister | C | 326-338 | 1798 |
|---|---|---|---|---|

(daughter of Henry Jaffray of County of Stirling, Scotland) [See also pages 340-344]

Implied South Carolina Marriages Volume IV 1787-1875

| WOMAN | MAN | VOL | PAGES | LIVED |
|---|---|---|---|---|

Jaffray, Jean     Richard Hinksman    C    326-338    1798
(daughter of Henry Jaffray of County of Stirling, Scotland) [See also pages 340-344]
James, Alice      Benjamin Gerald     B    194-196    1802
(marriage settlement 26 June 1802) (of Claremont County, Sumter District)
James, Amanthes    Tyre J. Dinkins     M    334-336    1839
(in Sumter District)
James, Caroline    Robert Wood          2B    219-221    1859
(daughter of Joseph James of Greenville District)
James, Charlotte   Edward Coxe         C    456-457    1818
Victoria (daughter of Matthew James of Sumter District, S.C.) (Coxe of Wilkes County, Georgia)
James, Elizabeth   Robert Brailsford    A    228-238    1803
(marriage settlement 14 April 1803) (daughter of John James) (she of St. Mark's Parish, Clarendon County) (Brailsford of Charleston)
James, Elizabeth   John R. Singleton    M    334-336    1839
(in Sumter District)
James, Esther      Tyre J. Dinkins      H    325-328    1833
Amanthus (marriage settlement 8 March 1833) (daughter of Walter James) (both of Sumter District)
James, Frances     Langdon H. Dinkins    M    334-336    1839
(in Sumter District)
James, Francis L.   Langdon H. Dinkins    K    303-305    1838
(marriage settlement 22 December 1838) (daughter of Walter James) (in Sumter District)
James, Julia Ann   Henry W. Bacon      G    59-61      1829
(Julian) (marriage settlement 8 October 1829) (daughter of Walter James) (she of Sumter District, S.C.) (Bacon of Georgia)
James, Julian      William H. Bacon     M    334-336    1839
(in Sumter District)
James, Juliana     _____ Bacon          H    325-328    1833
(daughter of Walter James)
James, Mary Jane   Moses R. Sanders     V    203-205    1852
(daughter of George C. James of Darlington District)
James, Nancy       Joseph Reed          2B    222-224    1859
(daughter of Joseph James of Greenville District)
Jeffrey. See Jaffray
Jenkins, Elisah    Cornelius Nevitt     W     102       1852
(Elisha) (marriage agreement 5 August 1852) (in Fairfield District)
Jennings, Elizabeth Washington Johnson    I    566-567    1837
(daughter of Joseph Jennings of Edgefield)
Jennings, Francis   Aurelius Martin      I    566-567    1837
(daughter of Joseph Jennings of Edgefield)

Implied South Carolina Marriages Volume IV 1787-1875

| WOMAN | MAN | VOL | PAGES | LIVED |
|---|---|---|---|---|
| Jennings, Harriet (daughter of Rev. John Jennings) | Charles E. Sims | Y | 532-533 | 1855 |
| Jennings, Harriet L. (marriage settlement 3 July 1861) (both of Orangeburg District) | James D. Cleckley | 2B | 381-383 | 1861 |
| Jennings, Polly (daughter of Joseph Jennings of Edgefield) | Joseph Price | I | 566-567 | 1837 |
| Jennings, Rachael (marriage settlement 27 July 1826) (in Orangeburgh District) [See also pages 544-545] | James Bell | E | 499-500 | 1826 |
| Jennings, Sarah E. (daughter of Larkin Jennings) (both of Sumter District) | Alexander J. McFarland | O | 313-315 | 1845 |
| Jennings, Susan (daughter of Joseph Jennings of Edgefield) | ____ Tucker | I | 566-567 | 1837 |
| Jeter, Alether (late of Union District, now of Newberry District) | Daniel R. Sartor | Z | 481-484 | 1851 |
| Jeter, Angelina (daughter of Thomas C. Jeter) | ____ Hamilton | 2C | 715-716 | 1875 |
| Jeter, Antoinette (daughter of James R. Jeter of Union District) | James P. Knight | 2A | 284-285 | 1858 |
| Jeter, Arsinoe M. (marriage settlement 17 October 1860) (in Union District) | Dr. Pierce P. Butler | 2B | 210-213 | 1860 |
| Jeter, Mary P. (daughter of William Jeter) (in Edgefield District) | Christopher W. Mantz | G | 237-238 | 1827 |
| Jeter, Sarah R. (widow) | Vincent E. Collum | L | 99-100 | 1840 |
| Johnson, Eliza Catherine (marriage settlement 12 July 1860) (she in Anderson District) (he of Chester District) | John Anderson Bradley | 2B | 152-154 | 1860 |
| Johnson, Eliza Penelope (daughter of David Johnson of Union District, S.C.) (Wharton of Texas) | John Austin Wharton | V | 1-3 | 1851 |
| Johnson, Ellen Susan (marriage settlement __ July 1848) (both of Sumter District) | Adam Logram Kobb | S | 290-291 | 1848 |
| Johnson, Frances (marriage settlement 3 February 1824) (widow of Taley Johnson) (both of Edgefield District) | Col. Zachariah S. Brooks | E | 174-175 | 1824 |
| Johnson, Jane | ____ McCrady | G | 329-332 | 1831 |
| Johnson, M. E. (marriage settlement 27 January 1857) (in Clarendon District) | D. O. Brunson | Z | 695-696 | 1857 |

Implied South Carolina Marriages Volume IV 1787-1875

| WOMAN | MAN | VOL | PAGES | LIVED |
|---|---|---|---|---|
| Johnson, Margaret Ann | David St. Piere DuBose | G | 329-332 | 1831 |

(marriage contract 3 January 1831) (both of Sumter District)

| Johnson, Sarah B. | John G. Snead | E | 535-537 | 1826 |

(marriage agreement 3 July 1826) (she of Barnwell District, S.C.) (he of Augusta, Georgia)

| Johnson, Sarah K. | John D. Young | X | 141-144 | 1853 |

(marriage settlement 4 December 1853) (daughter of Alexander Johnson) (both of Kershaw District)

| Johnson, Sofey | Elza Bland the Elder | N | 285-287 | 1844 |

(in Edgefield District)

| Johnston, Caroline | Sylvanus Chambers | U | 237-238 | 1850 |

(daughter of Samuel Johnston of Fairfield District)

| Johnston, Jane | Rev R. K. Porter | W | 557-562 | 1853 |

(Johnson) (daughter of Samuel Johnston of Winnsborough, Fairfield District, who died 13 May 1853)

| Johnston, Margaret | _____ Adams | W | 557-559 | 1853 |

(Johnson) (daughter of Samuel Johnston of Winnsborough, Fairfield District, who died 13 May 1853)

| Johnston, Margaret C. | James P. Adams | U | 7-9 | 1850 |

(daughter of Samuel Johnston of Winnsborough, Fairfield District) (Adams of Richland District)

| Johnston, Rebecca | _____ Harrison | X | 22-27 | 1853 |

(daughter of John K. Johnston of Edgefield District)

| Johnston, Rebecca S. | Harry W. Adams | O | 418-420 | 1845 |

(daughter of Samuel Johnston of Winnsborough, Fairfield District) (Adams of Richland District)

| Johnston, Rebecca S. | Harry W. Adams | P | 339-340 | 1846 |

(daughter of Samuel Johnston of Winnsborough, Fairfield District)

| Johnston, Sarah | James Farnandis | H | 103 | 1832 |

(Johnson) (daughter of John Johnston of Fairfield District)

| Johnston, Sarah | _____ Quattlebum | X | 22-27 | 1853 |

(daughter of John K. Johnston of Edgefield District)

| Jones, Anne | John Cole | F | 434-435 | 1818 |

(widow of Elijah Jones) (both of Newberry District)

| Jones, Clara Ann | Dr. Moses M. Long | Y | 469-470 | 1855 |

(daughter of Abraham Jones of Edgefield District) (of Edgefield District)

| Jones, Elizabeth | Smith Lipscomb | H | 474-475 | 1833 |

(marriage settlement 18 September 1833) (he was married before) (of Spartanburgh District)

| Jones, Elizabeth C. | Joseph A. C. Jones | 2B | 809-810 | 1864 |

(daughter of Lewis Jones of Edgefield District)

Implied South Carolina Marriages Volume IV 1787-1875

| WOMAN | MAN | VOL | PAGES | LIVED |
|---|---|---|---|---|
| Jones, Henrietta | Dr. Jacob G. McMeekin | V | 562-563 | 1852 |

(daughter of Abraham Jones of Edgefield District) (McMeekin of Fairfield District)

| | | | | |
|---|---|---|---|---|
| Jones, Isabella G. | Leonard J. Cross | H | 143-144 | 1832 |

(marriage settlement 16 June 1832) (daughter of Samuel P. Jones)

| | | | | |
|---|---|---|---|---|
| Jones, Martha Amanda | Thomas G. Robertson | 2A | 507-508 | 1859 |
| Jones, Mary | ____ Shermon | 2B | 525-527 | 1862 |
| Jones, Mary Elizabeth | Joseph E. Lee | Z | 462-463 | 1856 |

(daughter of Abraham Jones of Edgefield District) (Lee of Lexington District)

| | | | | |
|---|---|---|---|---|
| Jones, Mary Octavia | William S. Terry | Z | 532-533 | 1857 |

(daughter of Benjamin T. Jones of Laurens District)

| | | | | |
|---|---|---|---|---|
| Jones, Narcissa C. | Joseph H. Morgan | 2A | 716-719 | 1859 |

(marriage settlement 3 November 1859) (both of Orangeburg District)

| | | | | |
|---|---|---|---|---|
| Jones, Rebecca (widow) | ____ Beckham | H | 208-209 | 1831 |
| Jones, Sarah H. | Wiley (Wylie) J. Davis | 2A | 252-255 | 1858 |

(marriage settlement 12 January 1858) (widow of Ralph Jones of Fairfield District) [Must also see pages 504-508]

| | | | | |
|---|---|---|---|---|
| Jones, Susannah | John Cook | I | 615 | 1837 |

(marriage agreement 1 August 1837) (he was married before) (in Laurens District)

| | | | | |
|---|---|---|---|---|
| Jordan, Molsey | ____ Smith | 2B | 390 | 1855 |

(daughter of John Jordan Senr. of Orangeburgh District) (of Lexington District)

| | | | | |
|---|---|---|---|---|
| Jumelle, Elizabeth Mary | Nathaniel Russell Paine | M | 21-24 | 1841 |

(marriage settlement 4 November 1841) (daughter of Peter L. Jumelle) (she of Camden) (Paine of Charleston) [Must also see pages 1-4]

| | | | | |
|---|---|---|---|---|
| Jumelle, Priscilla B. | Benjamin Perkins | M | 1-4 | 1841 |

(marriage settlement 24 November 1841) (daughter of Peter L. Jumelle) (both of Camden)

| | | | | |
|---|---|---|---|---|
| Jumper, Rebecca A. | Walter Van Wert | P | 10-12 | 1845 |

(marriage settlement 15 May 1845) (of Richland District)

Implied South Carolina Marriages Volume IV 1787-1875

| WOMAN | MAN | VOL | PAGES | LIVED |
|---|---|---|---|---|

(K)

Kaigler, Ann Caroline  ___ Wolfe  O  328-329  1845
Kaigler, Caroline A.  ___ Wolfe  W  81-83  1852
   (in Lexington District)
Keeler, Sarah  Ara Race  2B  553-556  1862
   St. Johns (marriage settlement 8 December 1862)
   (daughter of Samuel Keeler) (in Chesterfield District)
Keitt, Mary W.  James McCauley  2B  477-478  1861
   (marriage settlement 14 August 1861) (in Orangeburg District)
Kellogg, Mary Ann  Augustus L. Converse  O  445-448  1845
   (daughter of Daniel Kellogg)
Kellogg, Mary S.  ___ Converse  S  205-208  1845
   (daughter of Daniel Kellogg) (Converse of Claremont County, Sumter District)
Kelly, ___  ___ Haltiwanger  E  521  1826
   (daughter of Frederick Kelly of Lexington District)
Kelly, Caroline  Major William McJunkin  U  440-441  1850
   (daughter of William Kelly of Union District)
Kelly, Elizabeth  ___ Brown  E  390-391  1825
   (daughter of John Kelly)
Kelly, Francis E.  John P. Thomas  T  121-122  1848
   (daughter of William Kelly of Union District)
Kelly, Harriet S.  Dr. Charles W. Hodges  R  353-354  1847
   (daughter of William Kelly of Union District)
Kelly, Mary Ann Louisa  William A. Thomas  L  49-50  1839
   (daughter of William Kelly of Union District)
Kelly, Susan E.  John Hopkins  M  98-99  1842
   (daughter of William Kelly of Union District)
Kemble, Emily H.  Thomas B. Lockhart  N  15-17  1843
   (marriage settlement 30 March 1843) (she of Columbia, Richland District) (he of Laurens District)
Kennedy, Clementina Sarah  George W. H. Legg  M  383-386  1842
   (daughter of Lionel H. Kennedy of Spartanburgh District) (of Spartanburgh District)
Kennedy, Harriet E.  Felix Turnipseed  S  217-220  1848
   (marriage settlement 27 April 1848) (she of Fairfield District) (he of Richland District)
Kennedy, Martha Jane  William Brand  H  100-101  1832
   (marriage settlement 24 January 1832) (widow of John M. Kennedy) (in Sumter District)

208

Implied South Carolina Marriages Volume IV 1787-1875

| WOMAN | MAN | VOL | PAGES | LIVED |
|---|---|---|---|---|
| Kennedy, Nancy A. | Robert W. Kennedy | 2A | 189 | 1857 |

(daughter of William Kennedy of Fairfield District)

| Kennedy, Sarah | David Pinchback | Z | 381-385 | 1856 |

(marriage settlement 8 September 1856) (widow of Richard E. Kennedy) (both of Chester District)

| Kenner, Mary L. | Robert Moorman | M | 285-286 | 1842 |

(daughter of Samuel E. Kenner of Newberry District)

| Kennerly, Amelia B. | _____ Kinsler | 2B | 707-708 | 1863 |
| Kennerly, Ann | Amos L. Jenkins | K | 149-150 | 1838 |

(she of Lexington District)

| Kennerly, Eliza A. | _____ Williamson | 2B | 707-708 | 1863 |
| Kennerly, Elizabeth | _____ Shuler | 2B | 707-708 | 1863 |

(widow) (she of Lexington District)

| Kennerly, Julia S. | James B. Glass | 2B | 62-63 | 1852 |

(daughter of Eli Kennerly) (both of Richland District)

| Kershaw, Ann | George Gilman | B | 736-738 | 1812 |

(marriage settlement 7 April 1812) (widow of George Kershaw of Camden) (Gilman late of Camden, now of Black River)

| Kershaw, Mary Riley | Robert A. Young | H | 138-139 | 1832 |

(in Kershaw District)

| Kervick, Ellen | William McGuinnis | 2B | 790-793 | 1864 |

(marriage settlement 4 February 1864) (she formerly of Charleston, now of Columbia) (he of Columbia)

| Kibler, Celina Louisa | George Moffett | X | 102-103 | 1853 |

(daughter of John Adam Kibler of Newberry District)

| Kibler, Christiana Barbara | George H. Dickert | T | 31-33 | 1848 |
| Kibler, Elizabeth | Claiborne Dickert | T | 31-33 | 1848 |
| Kibler, Pirmelia Angeline | David Folk | T | 31-33 | 1848 |
| Kilcrease, Elizabeth | Abel Sharpton | L | 397-398 | 1841 |

(daughter of Lewis Kilcrease) (of Edgefield District)

| Kilgore, Mary Adeline | John C. Twitty | X | 314-315 | 1854 |

(marriage contract 18 February 1854) (widow) (in Kershaw District)

| Killen, Caroline M. | Robert Napier | 2B | 658-659 | 1863 |

(marriage settlement 26 June 1863) (widow of James F. Killen of Darlington District) (Napier of Marion District)

| Killingsworth, Caroline | Gilbert Garner | 2B | 274-275 | 1861 |

(marriage settlement 30 January 1861) (widow) (both of Richland District)

Implied South Carolina Marriages Volume IV 1787-1875

| WOMAN | MAN | VOL | PAGES | LIVED |
|---|---|---|---|---|
| Killingsworth, Sarah (daughter of Mark Killingsworth of Abbeville District) (of Abbeville District) | Samuel Lockhart | K | 273 | 1838 |
| Kilpatrick, Clara (marriage settlement 29 April 1858) (she of Pendleton District) (he of Abbeville, Abbeville District) | James W. Livingston | 2A | 340-345 | 1858 |
| Kilpatrick, E. Amanda (widow) | _____ Lorton | 2A | 340-345 | 1858 |
| Kimbrel, Selenah (Kembrell) (marriage contract 5 February 1858) (widow of G. W. Kimbrel) | John McGuire | 2A | 500-502 | 1858 |
| Kinard, Elizabeth | Geo: Stockman (of Newberry District) | E | 308-309 | 1816 |
| Kinard, Elizabeth (marriage contract 19 December 1837) (both of Newberry District) | Martin Suber | K | 64-65 | 1837 |
| Kinard, Milley (widow) (she of Edgefield District) | _____ Medlock | K | 165 | 1838 |
| Kinard, Sally | John Rinehart | H | 222-225 | 1832 |
| Kincaid, Elizabeth K. | Edward K. Anderson (in Fairfield District) | T | 234-237 | 1849 |
| King, Ellen M. (marriage settlement 5 November 1862) (daughter of Mitchell King of Charleston, S.C.) (Campbell of Henderson County, North Carolina) | Francis L. Campbell | 2B | 533-537 | 1862 |
| King, Ellen S. (daughter of William King of Darlington District) | Benjamin S. Lucas | 2C | 495-497 | 1867 |
| King, Julia E. (her first marriage) (daughter of John G. King of Sumter District) | Charles C. Ragin | V | 580-582 | 1852 |
| King, Margaret (daughter of Gillam King of Chesterfield District) (McLean of Darlington District) | John D. McLean | X | 27-28 | 1853 |
| Kinsler, Catharine | _____ Kaigler | 2B | 52-61 | 1859 |
| Kinsler, Elizabeth | _____ Fenly | 2B | 52-61 | 1859 |
| Kinsler, Mary A. | _____ Arthur | 2B | 52-61 | 1859 |
| Kirk, Mary Bryce (daughter of Alexander Kirk of Columbia, Richland District) (of Columbia, Richland District) | Charles Hoagland | T | 126-129 | 1849 |
| Kirkland, Martha A. (marriage settlement 13 June 1846) (daughter of John D. Kirkland) | Samuel R. Black | R | 16-19 | 1846 |
| Kirkland, Martha Ann | Sam R. Black (in Fairfield District) | Z | 123-124 | 1856 |
| Kirkland, Mary Louisa (daughter of George Kirkland of Barnwell District) | Elijah G. Allen | P | 85-86 | 1845 |

Implied South Carolina Marriages Volume IV 1787-1875

| WOMAN | MAN | VOL | PAGES | LIVED |
|---|---|---|---|---|
| Kirkpatrick, Jane | James Taylor | 2A | 63-65 | 1857 |

(marriage settlement 7 July 1857) (she of Abbeville District) (he of Laurens District)

| Kirksey, Nancy | David Garvin | X | 472-474 | 1853 |

(daughter of William Kirksey Senr. of Pickens District, S.C.) (Garvin of Hall County, Georgia)

| Kirksey, Penelope | _____ Holland | M | 167-168 | 1842 |

(daughter of William Kirksey of Pickens District)

| Kirven, Elizabeth | Elias Townsend | X | 646-649 | 1854 |

(marriage settlement 14 September 1854) (widow) (both of Marion District)

| Kirven, Jane F. | John M. Davis | K | 498-501 | 1839 |

(marriage settlement 9 September 1839)

| Klugh, Eliza C. | W. L. Hudgins | 2B | 290-291 | 1860 |

(in Abbeville District)

| Knight, Frances | Capt. John Evans | F | 411 | 1828 |

Anna Augusta Jane (marriage settlement 24 June 1828) (both of Hamburg, Edgefield District)

| Knighton, Milly | Jourdan Morris | L | 93-94 | 1840 |

(daughter of Moses Knighton of Fairfield District) (of Fairfield District)

| Knighton, Nancy | Henry Maybin | L | 94-95 | 1839 |

(daughter of Moses Knighton of Fairfield District) (of Fairfield District)

| Koon, Elizabeth | Michael Kibler Jr | H | 163-164 | 1828 |

(of Newberry District) [See also pages 298-304]

| Koon, Elizabeth | Peter Suber | T | 309-312 | 1849 |

(marriage contract 23 August 1849) (daughter of John Koon) (both of Newberry)

| Koon, Mary | _____ Slia | V | 270-273 | 1852 |
| Koppel, Frederica | Abraham Harris | 2B | 385-386 | 1862 |

(married 13 August 1862) (daughter of Jacob Koppel) (she of Unionville) (Harris of Newberry)

(L)

| Lacoste, Anna | James Bradley | R | 450-451 | 1847 |

Adeline (daughter of Stephen Lacoste of Sumter District)

| Lacoste, Eleanor | James Norwood | R | 450-451 | 1847 |

Edward (daughter of Stephen Lacoste of Sumter District)

| Lacoste, Mary | Charles Crane | R | 450-451 | 1847 |

Margaret (daughter of Stephen Lacoste of Sumter District)

Implied South Carolina Marriages Volume IV 1787-1875

| WOMAN | MAN | VOL | PAGES | LIVED |
|---|---|---|---|---|

Lagrone, Mary M.　　Silas Marchant　　H　354-355　1832
 (marriage settlement 25 October 1832) (widow of John
 Lagrone) (of Newberry District)
Lake, Martha　　_____ Sheppard　　N　151-152　1843
 (daughter of Enoch Lake of Newberry District)
Lamar, Ann　　Melines Conkling　　B　222-228　1803
 (La Mar)　　Leavensworth
 (marriage settlement 4 June 1803) (widow of Thomas Lamar
 of Horse Creek, Edgefield District) (both of Edgefield
 District)
Lamar, Ann　　_____ Milledge　　N　293-295　1843
Lamar, Elizabeth　_____ Waldo　　N　293-295　1843
Lamar, Martha J.　_____ Seibels　　K　347-349　1839
 (she of Edgefield District)
Lamar, Mary E.　　_____ Gallagher　　T　430-433　1849
 (daughter of Mack Lamar of Edgefield District)
Lamar, Sarah　　_____ Stark　　N　293-295　1843
 (she of Edgefield District)
Lamb, Ellen L.　　Thomson B. Brown　2C　420-423　1868
 (reference to antenuptial settlement 15 January 1868)
Lancaster, Avalina　Enoch J. Underwood　L　444　1841
 (marriage contract 9 November 1841) (both of
 Spartanburgh District)
Lane, Sarah　　_____ Witherspoon　　2A　711-712　1859
 (widow) (she in Williamsburg District)
Langley, Frances　John Cox　　Q　60　1803
 (she was born 27 June 1778 in Dewsberry, Yorkshire,
 England) (he was born 28 February 1777 in Portsmouth,
 Hampshire, England) (arrived Charleston, S.C., 16
 February 1800) (to Columbia, S.C.)
Lark, Elizabeth　　Doctr. Peter Purnall　B　487-488　1808
 (widow of John Lark) (of Barnwell District)
LaRoche, Sophia M.　Griffin McDonald　　2B　636-642　1863
 (marriage settlement 17 April 1863) (reference to
 marriage settlement in Macon, Georgia) (widow of J. J.
 LaRoche) (of Aiken, Barnwell District, S.C.)
Latimer, Sarah Ann　Edmund Peyton　　V　38-41　1851
　　　　　　　　　　　Halleman
 (marriage settlement 13 April 1851) (both of Abbeville
 District)
Latta, Cecelia　　Rufus M. Johnston　2A　643-656　1856
 (married 29 May 1856) (daughter of Robert Latta who
 died 25 August 1852)
Lavender, Letty　　John E. Murphy　　O　310-311　1845
 (of Fairfield District)
Lavender, Lucinda　Henry H. Tidwell　　O　309-310　1845
 (of Fairfield District)

212

Implied South Carolina Marriages Volume IV 1787-1875

| WOMAN | MAN | VOL | PAGES | LIVED |
|---|---|---|---|---|
| Law, Rosannah S. | John B. F. McMorries | X | 484-486 | 1854 |

(marriage settlement 6 April 1854) (widow) (she of Abbeville District) (he of Newberry District)

| Leach, Sarah P. | Simon Ward | 2B | 68-69 | 1860 |

(marriage settlement 6 March 1860) (in Darlington District)

| Leaman, Mary Ann | James A. Jones | W | 60-62 | 1852 |

(Leeman) (daughter of Hugh Leaman of Laurens District)

| Leapheart, Margaret Godfrey Dreher | | S | 450-452 | 1848 |

(marriage settlement 20 November 1848) (widow of William Leapheart) (in Lexington District)

| Ledingham, Anna Frances | Dr. Michael R. Clark | Y | 437-439 | 1855 |

(daughter of John Ledingham of Richland District, S.C.) (of Richland District) (to Franklin County, Mississippi)

| Lee, Maria | Joseph B. White | M | 73-74 | 1842 |

(widow of Timothy Lee)

| Lee, Mary A. | Sebastian Kraft | 2A | 208-209 | 1857 |

(marriage contract 22 December 1857) (widow of Horace Lee) (both of Union District)

| Lee, Mary Ann | Wm. J. McMillan | I | 397-398 | 1835 |

(of Lexington District, S.C.) (to Columbus, Georgia?)

| Lee, Mary E. | Richard R. Spann | M | 256-258 | 1839 |

(of Sumter District) [See also pages 73-74]

| Leever, Catharina | John Drehr | A | 308-311 | 1797 |

(marriage settlement 21 July 1797) (widow of Jacob Leever) (both of Orangeburgh District)

| Leister, Elizabeth | Miller Byrd | R | 93-96 | 1846 |

(widow of Craven Leister) (she of Darlington District)

| Leitner, Mary Ann | David Gradick F. | 2B | 661-662 | 1863 |

(daughter of Daniel W. Leitner)

| Lemon, Jane M. | O. W. Yongue | V | 225-226 | 1850 |

(daughter of James Lemon of Fairfield District) (of Fairfield District)

| Lemon, Mary Ann | Mitchell L. Owens | V | 227-228 | 1850 |

(daughter of James Lemon of Fairfield District) (of Fairfield District)

| Lemon, Sarah J. | Ezekiel Chandler | X | 495 | 1854 |

(in Sumter District)

| Lenhardt, Mary | Colbert Barrett | Z | 461-462 | 1856 |

(daughter of Lawrence Lenhardt of Greenville District) (of Greenville District)

| Lenhardt, Sarah | William S. Turner | Z | 166-168 | 1856 |

(daughter of Lawrence Lenhardt of Greenville District) (Turner of Pickens District)

| Lenoir, Jane Ingram | Israel G. Mathis | E | 166-167 | 1810 |

(daughter of John Lenoir Senior) (of Lancaster District)

Implied South Carolina Marriages Volume IV 1787-1875

| WOMAN | MAN | VOL | PAGES | LIVED |
|---|---|---|---|---|
| Lequeux, Mary | Revd. John P. Cooke | R | 442-446 | 1847 |

(marriage settlement 29 May 1847) (she of Winnsborough, Fairfield District) (he of Columbia, Richland District)

| Lesesne, Margaret Ann Mary | Theodore W. Brailsford | P | 192-194 | 1845 |

(marriage settlement 29 November 1845) (daughter of Charles Lesesne of Sumter District) (both of Sumter District)

| Lesly, Anna L. | J. W. Norris | Z | 423-424 | 1856 |

(daughter of William Lesly) (in Abbeville District)

| Lesly, Jane | _____ Armstrong | W | 21-24 | 1852 |

("Jane Lesly, afterwards Jane Armstrong")

| Lesly, Jane A. | _____ Fraser | Z | 422-423 | 1856 |

(she in Abbeville District)

| Lesly, Virginia E. | James A. Montgomery | Z | 423-424 | 1856 |

(daughter of William Lesly) (in Abbeville District)

| Lester, Ermin | Thomas Green | 2A | 178-179 | 1857 |

(daughter of Archibald Lester)

| Levingston, Molly | Charles Strauss | Z | 635-636 | 1857 |

(marriage agreement 23 February 1857) (widow) (in Newberry District)

| Levy, Eliza R. | _____ Anderson | K | 522 | 1839 |
| Lewis, Caroline Elizabeth | John W. Cook | U | 426-427 | 1851 |

(daughter of Joseph Lewis of Chester District) (Cook of Fairfield District)

| Lewis, Caroline Matilda | William H. Campbell | U | 224-226 | 1850 |

(marriage settlement 12 December 1850) (both of Greenville District)

| Lewis, Louisa D. | James Crawford Keys | 2B | 824-827 | 1843 |

(in Anderson District)

| Lewis, Malissa S. | Stephen J. Shackelford | 2B | 824-827 | 1843 |

(in Anderson District)

| Lewis, Martha E. | Wallace B. Ioor | V | 143-146 | 1851 |

(marriage settlement 30 December 1851) (both of Greenville District)

| Lewis, Mary | Wiley Kemp | F | 401-402 | 1828 |

(marriage settlement 17 November 1828) (of Edgefield District)

| Lewis, Narcass | Moses Dean | 2B | 824-827 | 1843 |

(in Anderson District)

| Lewis, Sarah Ann | Benjamin F. Wingate | O | 5-7 | 1844 |

(marriage contract 3 April 1844) (daughter of James Lewis) (both of Darlington District)

| Lightfoot, Betsey | George Johnson | C | 111-117 | 1811 |

(daughter of Francis Lightfoot) (of Abbeville District)

Implied South Carolina Marriages Volume IV 1787-1875

| WOMAN | MAN | VOL | PAGES | LIVED |
|---|---|---|---|---|
| Lightfoot, Brunetta | William Youngblood | T | 71 | 1847 |

(marriage contract 22 December 1847) (she of Edgefield District) (he of Abbeville District)

| Lightfoot, Fanny | Nathaniel Samuels | C | 111-117 | 1811 |

(daughter of Francis Lightfoot) (of Abbeville District)

| Lightfoot, Frances | ____ Poindexter | C | 111-117 | 1811 |

(of Abbeville District)

| Lightfoot, Polly | John McAllister | C | 111-117 | 1811 |

(daughter of Francis Lightfoot) (of Abbeville District)

| Lightfoot, Sukey | John Johnson | C | 111-117 | 1811 |

(of Abbeville District)

| Lindsey, ____ | ____ Hixon | W | 49-52 | 1852 |

(daughter of Benjamin Lindsey of Edgefield District)

| Lipscomb, Taphenis B. | ____ Brooks | F | 263 | 1828 |

(in Abbeville District)

| Little, Susan R. | John M. Askew | 2A | 429-430 | 1858 |

(marriage contract 24 September 1858) (in Union District)

| Littlejohn, Minerva | Andrew K. Smith | 2A | 133 | 1857 |

(daughter of Samuel Littlejohn of Spartanburg District)

Livingston. See Levingston

| Logan, Elizabeth S. | James A. Black | M | 70-71 | 1841 |

(of York District)

| Logan, Huldah | Robert Crawford | G | 28 | 1829 |

(daughter of Andrew Logan of Abbeville District) (of Abbeville District)

| Logan, Margaret R. | Robert A. Yongue | U | 126-128 | 1850 |

(marriage settlement 10 July 1850) (granddaughter of Judge John S. Richardson) (of Fairfield District)

| Lomax, Cynthia | ____ Keller | L | 57-58 | 1836 |

(daughter of G. Lomax of Abbeville District)

| Lomax, Matilda C. | ____ Douglass | L | 57-58 | 1836 |

(daughter of G. Lomax of Abbeville District)

| Lomax, Matilda V. | Wm H. Richie | 2B | 448-449 | 1846 |

(widow of Jas Lomax) (in Abbeville District)

| Lomax, Matilda V. | William H. Ritchie | P | 355-363 | 1846 |

(separation agreement 13 February 1846) (of Abbeville District)

| Long, Ann (Anny) | James Herron | K | 514-516 | 1839 |

(marriage settlement 5 November 1839) (both of Anderson District)

| Long, Elizabeth A. | Benjamin W. Hatcher | 2A | 591-592 | 1858 |

(of Edgefield District)

| Long, Izett | James Murrell | 2A | 591-592 | 1859 |

(of Edgefield District)

Implied South Carolina Marriages Volume IV 1787-1875

| WOMAN | MAN | VOL | PAGES | LIVED |
|---|---|---|---|---|
| Long, Mary | ___ Hall | 2B | 267-268 | 1861 |

Elizabeth (daughter of Jacob S. Long of Newberry District)

| | | | | |
|---|---|---|---|---|
| Long, Vary L. | Benjamin G. Kinny (of Louisiana) | 2A | 591-592 | 1859 |
| Looper, Sarah | G. W. Julin | 2B | 178-179 | 1860 |

(daughter of Jeremiah Looper Sr. of Pickens District) (of Pickens District)

| | | | | |
|---|---|---|---|---|
| Lorick, ___ | Jesse Drafts | T | 387-389 | 1849 |

(widow of John Lorick)

| | | | | |
|---|---|---|---|---|
| Lorick, Frances Stack | William W. Dunsford | Z | 369-372 | 1856 |

(daughter of John Lorick of Richland District and stepdaughter of Jesse Drafts) (Dunsford of Richland District)

| | | | | |
|---|---|---|---|---|
| Lorick, Martha Ann Elizabeth | ___ Sharp | N | 342-343 | 1844 |

(daughter of John Lorick) (she of Richland District)

| | | | | |
|---|---|---|---|---|
| Lorick, Susan Caroline | Thomas B. Williams | T | 387-389 | 1849 |

(daughter of John Lorick of Edgefield District) (Williams of Richland District)

| | | | | |
|---|---|---|---|---|
| Loring, Rebecca | ___ McLane | G | 90-91 | 1830 |

(widow)

| | | | | |
|---|---|---|---|---|
| Lott, Dimcey | Abram Rutland | 2B | 126-128 | 1860 |

(marriage contract __ February 1860) (widow) (both of Edgefield District)

| | | | | |
|---|---|---|---|---|
| Lott, Elizabeth | William Morgan | D | 167-168 | 1819 |

(marriage agreement 10 June 1819) (both of Chester District)

| | | | | |
|---|---|---|---|---|
| Lott, Martha | Clinton Ward | 2B | 126-128 | 1860 |
| Loveland, Drusilla A. P. | Thomas H. Stall | 2A | 371-373 | 1858 |

(marriage settlement 1 June 1858) (daughter of Roger Loveland) (in Greenville District)

| | | | | |
|---|---|---|---|---|
| Lowe, Martha C. | Graville Grimes | L | 271 | 1841 |

(in Richland District)

| | | | | |
|---|---|---|---|---|
| Lucas, Margaret J. | George H. Caraway | 2B | 392-394 | 1861 |

(marriage settlement 30 November 1861) (daughter of Benjamin Lucas) (both of Darlington District)

| | | | | |
|---|---|---|---|---|
| Lucas, Sarah L. | Jesse H. Windham | 2B | 604-606 | 1863 |

(in Darlington District)

| | | | | |
|---|---|---|---|---|
| Lunsford, Rebecca | Michael Moore | B | 239-243 | 1803 |

(marriage settlement 8 May 1803) (widow of Swanson Lunsford) (both of Columbia, Richland District) [See also pages 315-316]

| | | | | |
|---|---|---|---|---|
| Lyles, Mary E. | John D. Sims | V | 554-557 | 1851 |
| Lyles, Orrah E. | James H. Irby | 2A | 190 | 1858 |

(daughter of Reuben S. Lyles of Newberry District)

Implied South Carolina Marriages Volume IV 1787-1875

| WOMAN | MAN | VOL | PAGES | LIVED |
|---|---|---|---|---|
| Lyles, Sallie E. | Edwin H. Poellnitz | 2A | 754-755 | 1860 |

(daughter of Thomas M. Lyles of Fairfield District)

| | | | | |
|---|---|---|---|---|
| Lynam, M. A. | W. M. Neal | 2A | 183-186 | 1857 |

(marriage settlement 22 December 1857) (she of Sumter District) (he of Richland District)

| | | | | |
|---|---|---|---|---|
| Lynam, Mary E. | John B. Tindal | 2A | 183-186 | 1857 |

(reference to marriage settlement - no date given) (widow)

| | | | | |
|---|---|---|---|---|
| Lynam, Mary E. | John B. Tindall | V | 280-283 | 1852 |

(marriage settlement 26 January 1852) (widow) (both of Chester District)

| | | | | |
|---|---|---|---|---|
| Lynam, Susan S. | John M. Tindall | 2B | 540-543 | 1862 |

(marriage settlement 23 September 1862) (both of Sumter District)

| | | | | |
|---|---|---|---|---|
| Lynch, Sarah Ann | John H. Goodwin (Goodwyn) | 2C | 342-344 | 1867 |

(marriage settlement 17 June 1867)

| | | | | |
|---|---|---|---|---|
| Lyons, Isabella R. | M. C. Mordecai | H | 521-522 | 1834 |

(daughter of Isaac Lyons of Columbia, Richland District) (Mordecai of Charleston)

| | | | | |
|---|---|---|---|---|
| Lyons, Loudia L. | Frederick C. Jacobs | 2C | 242-243 | 1867 |

(daughter of Jacob C. Lyons of Columbia, Richland District)

(Mc)

| | | | | |
|---|---|---|---|---|
| McAdams, Mary J. | Charles H. Davis | I | 481 | 1836 |

(widow of Hiram A. McAdams) (she of Camden, Kershaw District) (Davis of Newberry District)

| | | | | |
|---|---|---|---|---|
| McAneer, Jane | Jackson Neely | S | 419-420 | 1848 |

(marriage settlement 8 September 1848)

| | | | | |
|---|---|---|---|---|
| McArn, Christian | Malcom Buchanan | O | 442-444 | 1833 |

(married 1833) (of Cheraw, Chesterfield District)

| | | | | |
|---|---|---|---|---|
| McBride, Ann Haseltine | William M. Robertson | 2B | 690-695 | 1863 |

(marriage settlement 8 September 1863) (widow of William McBride of Beaufort District) (Robertson of Charleston District)

| | | | | |
|---|---|---|---|---|
| McBride, E. Lauretta | David Gulledge | R | 316-317 | 1847 |

(daughter of William McBride of Chesterfield District)

| | | | | |
|---|---|---|---|---|
| McBride, Louisa | Thomas Woodward | R | 316-317 | 1847 |

(daughter of William McBride of Chesterfield District)

| | | | | |
|---|---|---|---|---|
| McBride, Martha M. | Matthew P. Mayes | V | 85-88 | 1851 |

(marriage settlement 12 September 1851) (widow of Samuel McBride) (both of Sumter District)

Implied South Carolina Marriages Volume IV 1787-1875

| WOMAN | MAN | VOL | PAGES | LIVED |
|---|---|---|---|---|
| McCall, Ann Eliza | George W. Earle | 2B | 167-168 | 1860 |

(daughter of James S. McCall Senr. of Darlington District)

McCall, Elizabeth    Thomas B. Haynsworth    N    214-216    1843
H. (marriage settlement 5 September 1843) (in Darlington District)
McCarty, Martha    John A. Simons    2C    403-405    1867
(marriage settlement 7 October 1867) (widow) (in Edgefield District)
McCaslan, Mary Y.    Wm G. Postell    2B    441-442    1861
(daughter of William McCaslan of Abbeville District) (of Abbeville District)
McCaw, Elizabeth    William T. Bailey    Z    467-469    1856
(marriage settlement 27 November 1856) (widow) (she of Abbeville District, S.C.) (he of Oglethorpe County, Georgia)
McCaw, Elizabeth    William T. Bailey    2A    186-187    1856
(reference to marriage settlement 7 November 1856)
McCaw, Frances E.    James H. Witherspoon    K    103-107    1838
H. (marriage settlement 5 January 1838) (widow of Dr. William McCaw of Abbeville District) (Witherspoon of Lancaster District)
McClain, Mary C.    Richard Strait    2A    597    1858
(marriage settlement 22 December 1858) (in York District)
McClanahan, Annette    Nathan Andrew    2B    144-145    1860
C.            Feaster
(daughter of Samuel G. McClanahan) (of Greenville District)
McClanahan, Laura    Thomas Decature Gwin    2B    146-147    1860
M. (daughter of Samuel G. McClanahan) (of Greenville District)
McClary, Lenora    Lemuel B. Davis    I    302    1835
(marriage settlement 15 August 1835) (widow) (both of Sumter District)
McClockin, Mary Ann    William Zuill    F    107-110    1803
(reference to marriage settlement - no date given) (of Sumter District)
McComb, Margaret P.    William Jackson    2A    514-516    1858
                     Hammond         (of Abbeville District)
McConnell, Mary A.    Benjamin M. Palmer    L    417-418    1841
                     Jr.
(marriage contract 6 October 1841) (granddaughter of Andrew Waltherer)
McCoy, Lavinia    Willburn Clark    M    205-206    1842
(marriage settlement 9 April 1842) (both of Sumter District)

Implied South Carolina Marriages Volume IV 1787-1875

| WOMAN | MAN | VOL | PAGES | LIVED |
|---|---|---|---|---|
| McCoy, Mary Caroline | Wilburn D. Clark | S | 458-459 | 1848 |

(marriage contract 30 November 1848) (daughter of Joseph McCoy) (of Sumter District)

| McCoy, Susan | Wade W. Newman | N | 170-171 | 1843 |

(marriage settlement 4 June 1843)

| McCreary, Sarah | James B. McCully | M | 132-134 | 1842 |

(marriage contract 5 February 1842) (widow of John McCreary) (both of Chester District)

| McCreless, Hephzibah | _____ Price | F | 401 | 1829 |

(daughter of John McCreless of Richland District)

| McCutchen, Martha A. | William W. Fraser | 2B | 566-568 | 1862 |

(in Sumter District)

| McDaniel, Francis | Jesse Bailey | 2A | 144-146 | 1857 |

(marriage contract 13 November 1857) (both of Edgefield District)

| McDaniel, Jane E. | Mansel Hall | R | 482-484 | 1847 |

(marriage contract 14 April 1847) (in Chester District)

| McDaniel, Joanna L. | John H. Robertson | L | 58-61 | 1839 |

(marriage settlement 27 August 1839) (widow of John C. McDaniel) (both of Chester District)

| McDonald, Frances E. | Alexander Y. Lee | 2C | 4-6 | 1864 |

(daughter of William McDonald) (of Kershaw District)

| McDonald, Sarah E. | J. W. McCurry | 2C | 169-170 | 1866 |

(daughter of Charles A. McDonald of Kershaw District) (of Kershaw District)

| McDowall, Nancy Narcissa | Irvin Hutchison | Z | 511-512 | 1856 |

(of Abbeville District)

| McDowell, Adeline A. | Wesley Wyatt | Z | 218 | 1856 |

(in Spartanburg District)

| McDowell, Agnes D. | John S. Richardson Jr. | Y | 151-152 | 1855 |

(in Sumter District)

| McDowell, Agness D. | John S. Richardson | U | 302-304 | 1850 |

(marriage settlement 10 December 1850) (daughter of Davidson McDowell) (both of Sumter District)

| McDowell, Catherine M. | Robert J. Dick | 2B | 93-95 | 1860 |

(marriage settlement 30 March 1860) (in Sumter District)

| McDowell, Charlotte | Henry Reid | O | 335-337 | 1844 |

(marriage settlement 21 December 1844) (in Abbeville District)

| McDowell, Sarah (McDowall) | Thomas Herron (Heron) | E | 37-38 | 1822 |

(marriage contract 24 July 1822) (widow of William McDowell) (both of Abbeville District)

| McDuffie, Mary Singleton | Wade Hampton, Jr. | 2A | 217-218 | 1858 |

(marriage settlement 28 January 1858)

Implied South Carolina Marriages Volume IV 1787-1875

| WOMAN | MAN | VOL | PAGES | LIVED |
|---|---|---|---|---|
| McElroy, Mary | John Doyle | E | 281-282 | 1824 |

(marriage settlement 26 December 1824)

| McFadden, Elizabeth | Robert Witherspoon | H | 467-470 | 1833 |

(daughter of Col. Thomas McFadden of Sumter District)
(of Sumter District)

| McFadden, Melinda | Templar S. Fayssoux | Y | 34 | 1855 |

A. (daughter of Isaac McFadden of Chester District)

| McFadden, Susan E. | Solomon W. Givens | 2A | 537 | 1858 |

(in Chester District)

| McFaddin, Anna J. | David Calvin Shaw | 2B | 244-245 | 1860 |

(daughter of James D. McFaddin of Sumter District)

| McFaddin, Anna Jane | David C. Shaw | 2B | 820-822 | 1864 |

(daughter of James D. McFaddin of Sumter District)

| McFaddin, Leonora | James D. Blanding | Y | 606-607 | 1855 |

A. (daughter of James D. McFaddin of Sumter District)

| McFaddin, Leonora | _____ Blanding | 2B | 823-824 | 1864 |

M. (daughter of James D. McFaddin of Sumter District)

| McFaddin, Mary Emma | Samuel Robert Spann | Y | 605-606 | 1855 |

(daughter of James D. McFaddin of Sumter District)

| McFaddin, Sallie A. | James Caldwell | 2B | 529-530 | 1862 |

(daughter of James D. McFaddin of Sumter District)

| McFall, Elizabeth | John L. Thornley | 2B | 349-352 | 1861 |

M. (daughter of Andrew N. McFall of Anderson District)
(of Anderson District) [See also pages 347-349, 352-354]

| McFie, Catharine | William James Lomax | 2B | 603-604 | 1861 |

(of Abbeville District)

| McGehee, Elizabeth | Thomas Wright | G | 258 | 1830 |
| McGregor, Catharine | _____ Macfie | W | 519-522 | 1853 |
| McHarg, Ann | William J. Wightman | I | 103 | 1832 |

(married September 1832) (widow of William McHarg who died December 1824) (of Edgefield District) [See also pages 608-610]

| McIver, Cornelia J. | Zimmerman Davis | 2A | 179-182 | 1857 |

(marriage settlement 9 November 1857) (in Darlington District)

| McIver, Sarah | Thomas B. Fraser | V | 422-426 | 1852 |

Margaret (marriage settlement 24 March 1852) (she of Yorkville) (he of Sumterville)

| McKellar, Elizabeth | _____ Boozer | 2A | 188-189 | 1858 |

A. (daughter of John W. McKellar)

| McKelvey, Elizabeth | Caleb Clarke | M | 368-369 | 1842 |

(marriage settlement 18 September 1842) (widow) (in Fairfield District)

| McKenna, Ellen | Patrick T. Murray | 2B | 667-670 | 1863 |

(marriage settlement 16 July 1863) (widow) (she of Lancaster)

Implied South Carolina Marriages Volume IV 1787-1875

| WOMAN | MAN | VOL | PAGES | LIVED |
|---|---|---|---|---|
| McKenney, Elizabeth S. | Coleman B. Walker | U | 417-418 | 1851 |
| McKenney, Hetty | Patrick Flyn | U | 417-418 | 1851 |
| McKenney, Mary Ellen | John W. Mangum | U | 417-418 | 1851 |
| McKenzie, Elizabeth | _____ Hickson | X | 509-521 | 1853 |

(daughter of William McKenzie of Sumter District)

| McKenzie, Elizabeth | _____ Woodward | V | 156-157 | 1846 |

(daughter of John McKenzie Junr. of Orangeburgh District and granddaughter of John McKenzie Senr.)

| McKey, Mahala | John Sims | K | 238-239 | 1838 |

(in Lancaster District)

| McKie, Francis | Caleb A. Arp | M | 255-256 | 1842 |

(daughter of Daniel McKie of Edgefield District)

| McKie, Mary | Seaburn Doulittle | M | 255-256 | 1842 |

(daughter of Daniel McKie of Edgefield District)

| McKinnon, Lucy Ellen | Jesse D. Reese | 2A | 309-310 | 1858 |

(marriage settlement 24 March 1858) (she of Marlborough District) (he of Richland District)

| McKissick, Martha | Josiah Spears | Y | 187-188 | 1855 |

(formerly of Union District, S.C., now of Cherokee County, Georgia)

| McKittrick, Martha A. | Samuel Tustin | Y | 263-264 | 1855 |

(daughter of Benjamin McKittrick of Abbeville District) (of Abbeville District)

| McKnight, Sallie H. | R. Rutledge Dingle | W | 219-221 | 1852 |

(marriage settlement 4 November 1852) (both of Sumter District)

| McKnight, Susan Rebecca | Robert J. Anderson | Z | 686-688 | 1857 |

(marriage settlement 5 February 1857) (she of Williamsburg District) (he of Sumter District)

| McLane, Rebecca | Lemuel B. Davis | G | 90-91 | 1830 |

(widow) (in Sumter District)

| McLarin, Elizabeth (McLaurin) | John Calhoun | 2A | 422-423 | 1858 |

(marriage settlement 19 July 1858) (both of Marlboro District)

| McLemore, Victoria | William Wallace | T | 2-4 | 1848 |

(marriage settlement 6 December 1848) (granddaughter of Majr. John McLemore)

| McLeod, Isabella J. H. | Daniel A. Horn | Y | 104-110 | 1855 |

(marriage settlement 13 February 1855) (she of Marlborough District) (he of Cheraw, Chesterfield District)

| McLeod, Joana Catherine | Peter A. Brunson | P | 15-21 | 1845 |

(marriage settlement 8 May 1845) (widow of James Henry McLeod) (in Sumter District)

Implied South Carolina Marriages Volume IV 1787-1875

| WOMAN | MAN | VOL | PAGES | LIVED |
|---|---|---|---|---|

McLucas, Effee   James R. McLaurin   N   283-285   1844
(Effy) Ann (marriage contract 22 January 1844) (she of
Marlborough District, S.C.) (he of Richmond County,
North Carolina)
McLure, Eliza J.   Abraham H. Davega   2A   465-466   1858
(daughter of Hugh McLure) (in Chester District)
McLure, Malissa A.   Andrew J. Secrest   2A   414   1858
(daughter of Hugh McLure) (in Chester District)
McLure, Phoebe A.   Dr. J. S. Pride   2B   74-77   1860
(marriage settlement 28 February 1860) (daughter of
Thomas McLure) (both of Chester District)
McMakin, Isabella   John R. McElwee Jr   R   496-498   1847
(daughter of Thomas McMakin) (of York District)
McMorries, Harriet   Robert A. Johnston   Z   357-358   1856
M. F. (marriage contract 22 October 1856) (in Newberry
District)
McMullin, Martha J.   Wm J. Gardener   Y   124-125   1855
(separation agreement 19 February 1855) (daughter of
Cullin McMullin) (in Spartanburg District)
McNamara, Anastasia   John R. Spann   O   14-17   1844
(marriage settlement 31 January 1844) (granddaughter of
General ____ Steele of North Carolina) (she of
Chesterfield District, S.C.) (Spann of Sumter District,
S.C.) [See also Volume R, pages 39-40]
McNamara.   See Macnamara
McNeel, Jane A.   James F. Bowden   W   138-139   1852
(to be married 5 October 1852) (marriage settlement 5
October 1852) (she of Chester District, S.C.) (he of
Talladega County, formerly Shelby County, Alabama)
McPherson, Mary   James Bell   2A   550-552   1859
Eleanor (daughter of James McPherson)
McRae, Catharine F.   Moses S. McColl   R   422-424   1847
(marriage settlement 26 May 1847 recorded in Darlington
and Marlborough Districts)
McRae, Catharine F.   Moses S. McColl   X   32   1847
(reference to marriage settlement 26 May 1847) (in
Darlington and Marlborough Districts)
McRae, Isabel Scota   John McRae   Y   280-281   1855
(McRa) (marriage settlement 17 July 1855) (daughter of
Duncan McRae) (she of Camden)
McWillie, Henrietta   William Shannon   O   134-135   1844
(daughter of William McWillie of Camden, Kershaw
District)
McWillie, Margaret   John Mackey   E   69   1820
D. (daughter of Adam McWillie of Beaver Dam, Kershaw
District) (Mackey of Fairfield District)

Implied South Carolina Marriages Volume IV 1787-1875

| WOMAN | MAN | VOL | PAGES | LIVED |
|---|---|---|---|---|
| McWillie, Nancy | Burwell Salmond | O | 133-134 | 1844 |

(daughter of William McWillie of Camden, Kershaw District)

(M)

Mace, Drucilla    James DuPre (Dupree)   Y   128-129   1855
    (marriage settlement 6 March 1855) (in Marion District)
Mace, Drucilla    James DuPre            Z   478-480   1855
    (reference to marriage settlement 6 March 1855) (in
    Marion District)
Mace, Mary E.     H. P. Adams            2B  607-608   1863
    (marriage agreement 11 March 1863) (in Marion District)
Macfarlan,        Randle McKay           W   259-265   1852
    Catharine Taylor (marriage settlement 28 December 1852)
    (daughter of John Macfarlan) (she of Chesterfield
    District, S.C.) (McKay of Anson County, North Carolina)
Macfarlan, Marjory ____ McQueen          W   259-265   1852
Macnamara,        John Russell Spann     2B  291-293   1860
    Anastasia     (of Texas)
Macnamara, Eliza  Dr. John Lynch         2B  291-294   1860
                  (of Columbia)
Maddon, Jannet    William T. Holland     Z   779       1857
    Elizabeth (daughter of Samuel L. Maddon) (in Laurens
    District)
Maddox, ____      John Padget            L   181-185   1840
Maddox, Littey    William Wilson         L   181-185   1840
    (marriage settlement 17 November 1840) [widow of
    Augustus (Augustin) Maddox] (in Abbeville District)
Maddox, Melinda   Peter Padget           L   181-185   1840
Maddox, Polly     William Mosely         L   181-185   1840
Maine, Letitia    William Hazzard Wigg   A   145-147   1789
    (marriage settlement 30 November 1789) (she of Prince
    William's Parish) (he of St. Helena's Parish, Beaufort
    District)
Marion, Julie     Armand Godefroy        H   131       1831
    (Julia) (marriage agreement 12 December 1831) (both of
    Columbia) [See also pages 80-81]
Marks, Eliza.     ____ Sampson           U   343-344   1851
    (daughter of Alexander Marks) [See also pages 411-414;
    Volume V, pages 41-42]
Marks, Leah       Emanuel Sampson        O   110-111   1844
    (marriage contract - Hebrew date) (daughter of Alexander
    Marks and granddaughter of Mordecai Marks) (in Columbia,
    Richland District)

Implied South Carolina Marriages Volume IV 1787-1875

| WOMAN | MAN | VOL | PAGES | LIVED |
|---|---|---|---|---|
| Marks, Rebecca J. | ___ Hawley | U | 4 | 1851 |

[See also Volume V, pages 41-42]

Marrs, E. Martha    Thomas Smith    S    360-362    1848
 (marriage settlement 23 October 1848) (both of Lexington District)
Mars, Frances C.    Lovezinski Anderson    2B    782-783    1864
 (daughter of John A. Mars of Abbeville District)
 (Anderson of Newberry District)
Mars, Frances    Lovinski Anderson    Z    793-794    1857
 Cornelia (daughter of John A. Mars of Abbeville
 District) (of Newberry District)
Mars, Massy    James Rutherford    E    73-77    1820
 ("Massy Mars alias Rutherford") (common-law marriage)
 (in Rutherford and Iredell Counties, North Carolina)
Marsh, Laura M.    Gustavus Ingraham    T    373-375    1849
 (daughter of John Marsh of Edgefield District)
Marshall, Emma C.    John D. Smith    K    284-286    1848
 (marriage settlement 27 November 1848) (she of Richland
 District) (he of Winnsborough, Fairfield District)
Marshall, Nancy    ___ McDowall    Z    511-512    1856
 Narcissa (daughter of George Marshall of Abbeville
 District)
Marshall, Rebecca    Jas. (or Jos.) H.    H    491    1834
 Henrietta    Thompson
 [daughter of Martin (or A.) Marshall of Richland
 District]
Martin, Elizabeth    Nathan Busby    P    310-311    1846
 T.    (in Fairfield District)
Martin, Jane    James McCullough    U    439-440    1851
 (separation agreement 10 March 1851) (both of Greenville
 District) (he late of Ireland)
Martin, Mary M.    William W. Belcher    2A    774-775    1860
 (of Abbeville District)
Martin, Rebecca    Godfrey O'Neale    S    350-351    1848
 Francis (daughter of Robert Martin of Fairfield
 District) (of Fairfield District)
Martindale,    Martin P. Poole    H    444-445    1833
 Elizabeth
Martindale, Sarah    Mordecai Taylor Jr.    N    22-23    1843
 Ann (daughter of William Martindale) (in Spartanburgh
 District)
Mason, Sheba    Isaac Walker    G    214-215    1830
 (marriage settlement 11 February 1830) (widow) (both of
 Richland District)
Mason. See Mayson
Massey, Charlotte    ___ Jones    2B    213-217    1860

Implied South Carolina Marriages Volume IV 1787-1875

| WOMAN | MAN | VOL | PAGES | LIVED |
|---|---|---|---|---|
| Massey, Elizabeth | William H. Beckham | 2B | 213-217 | 1860 |

(marriage agreement 22 November 1860) (daughter of James R. Massey of Lancaster District) (Beckham of Chester District)

| | | | | |
|---|---|---|---|---|
| Massey, Mary | _____ Cunningham | 2B | 213-217 | 1860 |
| Massey, Sarah | _____ Jones | 2B | 213-217 | 1860 |
| Matheson, Mary C. | Dr Thomas W. McCaa | V | 516-518 | 1852 |

(daughter of Christopher Matheson of Camden, Kershaw District)

| | | | | |
|---|---|---|---|---|
| Mathis, Mary R. | James Watson | I | 420-422 | 1836 |

(marriage agreement 18 March 1836) (in Sumter District)

| | | | | |
|---|---|---|---|---|
| Mauldin, Mary C. | John Alexander Chambliss | 2B | 397-398 | 1861 |

(marriage contract 22 October 1861) (daughter of Samuel Mauldin) (she of Greenville) (Chambliss of Sumter) [See also pages 568-569]

| | | | | |
|---|---|---|---|---|
| Maxwell, Anna M. | Benjamin Sloan | 2B | 624-626 | 1863 |

(daughter of John Maxwell of Pickens District)

| | | | | |
|---|---|---|---|---|
| Maxwell, Ann Moore | J. D. Wright | 2B | 248-249 | 1861 |

(daughter of Robert A. Maxwell of Anderson District) (Wright of Spartanburgh District)

| | | | | |
|---|---|---|---|---|
| Maxwell, Eliza | _____ Lewis | S | 448-449 | 1848 |

(daughter of John Maxwell of Anderson District)

| | | | | |
|---|---|---|---|---|
| Maxwell, Emily | _____ Weyman | 2A | 200-201 | 1857 |

(Emmala) (daughter of John Maxwell of Pickens District)

| | | | | |
|---|---|---|---|---|
| Maxwell, Harriet H. | Dr M. B. Earle | V | 23-24 | 1851 |

(daughter of John Maxwell of Anderson District) (Earle of Greenville)

| | | | | |
|---|---|---|---|---|
| Maxwell, Maria | Thos. J. Warren | Y | 533-534 | 1855 |

Louisa (daughter of Robert A. Maxwell of Anderson District) (Warren of Camden)

| | | | | |
|---|---|---|---|---|
| Maxwell, Martha P. | Jno. A. Keels | Z | 373-374 | 1856 |

(daughter of John Maxwell of Pickens District) (Keels of Williamsburg District)

| | | | | |
|---|---|---|---|---|
| Mayer, Eve Margaret | Alexander Stewart | H | 61-62 | 1828 |

(widow of Major Adam Mayer)

| | | | | |
|---|---|---|---|---|
| Mayo, Sarah Elizabeth | David Curry | V | 75-79 | 1851 |

(marriage settlement 27 October 1851) (she of Fairfield District, S.C.) (he of Oktibbeha County, Mississippi)

| | | | | |
|---|---|---|---|---|
| Mayrant, Sarah A. | William E. Richardson | U | 200-202 | 1843 |

(reference to marriage settlement 23 March 1843) (in Sumter District)

Implied South Carolina Marriages Volume IV 1787-1875

| WOMAN | MAN | VOL | PAGES | LIVED |
|---|---|---|---|---|
| Mayrant, Sarah Ann | William E. Richardson | O | 114-116 | 1843 |

(marriage settlement 23 March 1843) (daughter of William Mayrant of Sumter District) (in Georgetown District)

| Mays, Evalina V. | Dr. Grenville Hord | W | 377-378 | 1853 |
|---|---|---|---|---|

(marriage settlement 7 February 1853) (widow of Sampson B. Mays) (both of Edgefield District)

| Mays, Sarah F. | ____ Ryan | X | 599-601 | 1854 |
|---|---|---|---|---|

(in Edgefield District)

| Mays, Susan E. | Dr. Grenville Hord | 2B | 635-636 | 1863 |
|---|---|---|---|---|

(daughter of Stephen W. Mays of Edgefield District)

| Mayson, Elizabeth | John McBryde | F | 340-342 | 1828 |
|---|---|---|---|---|

(marriage settlement 23 July 1828) (widow of Archy Mayson of Edgefield District) (McBryde of Hamburgh, Edgefield District)

Mayson. See Mason

| Meachem, Martha R. | Snowden G. Meriwether | Y | 143-144 | 1855 |
|---|---|---|---|---|

(of Edgefield District)

| Means, Maria | John English | 2A | 546-547 | 1858 |
| Means, Sarah F. | ____ Trotti | 2A | 546-547 | 1858 |
| Mellett, Frances H. | Andrew J. McElveen | Y | 412-416 | 1855 |

(marriage settlement 29 September 1855) (widow of Dr. James L. Mellett) (in Sumter District)

| Mellett, Mary A. | James M. Pitts | M | 196-197 | 1842 |
|---|---|---|---|---|

(marriage settlement 3 May 1842) (daughter of Peter Mellett)

| Mellett, Sarah P. | William Lewis | U | 203-206 | 1850 |
|---|---|---|---|---|

(marriage settlement 3 September 1850) (both of Sumter District) [See also pages 207-208]

| Mellett, Susan V. | Augustus Conway | M | 240-242 | 1842 |
|---|---|---|---|---|

(marriage settlement 20 July 1842) (both of Sumter District)

| Melton, Aley | Jesse McClendon | Y | 154-155 | 1843 |
|---|---|---|---|---|

(widow of Elisha Melton)

| Melton, Rosena | James Cumming | Y | 154-155 | 1843 |
|---|---|---|---|---|

(married 1 July 1843) (daughter of Elisha Melton) (of Edgefield District)

| Mercer, Zilpah | James Davis | 2A | 147-148 | 1844 |
|---|---|---|---|---|

(daughter of Thomas Mercer of Darlington District) (in Darlington District)

| Meriner, Jane | Alexander Kincaid | H | 512-514 | 1834 |
|---|---|---|---|---|

(Mamar) (marriage settlement 15 January 1834) (in Fairfield District)

| Merriman, Eliza Ann | Alexander Norris | Z | 338-339 | 1855 |
|---|---|---|---|---|

(daughter of John Merriman Sr. of Chesterfield District)

Implied South Carolina Marriages Volume IV 1787-1875

| WOMAN | MAN | VOL | PAGES | LIVED |
|---|---|---|---|---|
| Meyer, Betsy M. | William E. Barnes | 2A | 282-284 | 1857 |

(marriage settlement 16 April 1857) (daughter of David Meyer) (she of Barnwell District, S.C.) (Barnes of Augusta, Georgia)

| Michau, Mary W. | Benjamin Mitchell | I | 374-375 | 1835 |
|---|---|---|---|---|

(marriage settlement 13 December 1835) (widow of Manasseth Michau) (in Sumter District) [See also page 404]

| Mickle, Martha B. | Rice Dulin | I | 569 | 1837 |
|---|---|---|---|---|

(daughter of Joseph Mickle of Kershaw District) (of Columbia)

| Mickle, Mary Ann | James V. Lyles | L | 150-161 | 1840 |
|---|---|---|---|---|

(marriage settlement 9 September 1840) (daughter of Joseph Mickle) (she in Kershaw District) (Lyles of Columbia)

| Middleton, Caroline | John W. Garrett | M | 15 | 1841 |
|---|---|---|---|---|

(daughter of John Middleton of Edgefield District) (of Edgefield District)

| Middleton, Patsy | William Tennent | N | 297-301 | 1795 |
|---|---|---|---|---|

(reference to marriage settlement 3 December 1795)

Middleton. See Myddleton

| Miles, Agnes | _____ Futrell | 2B | 506-507 | 1862 |
|---|---|---|---|---|
| Miles, Eliza | _____ Ross | 2B | 506-507 | 1862 |
| Miles, Harriet G. | Thomas E. Turner | 2B | 78-80 | 1860 |

(or J.) (marriage settlement 18 February 1860) (both of Edgefield District)

| Miles, Kezia Ann | Thomas T. Pickens | G | 187-191 | 1830 |
|---|---|---|---|---|

(marriage settlement 19 April 1830) (daughter of Jeremiah Miles of St. Paul's Parish, Colleton District) (Pickens of Pendleton District) [See also Volume H, pages 321-322, 381-383]

| Miles, Mary | _____ Garner | 2B | 506-507 | 1862 |
|---|---|---|---|---|
| Miles, Sarah | _____ Proctor | 2B | 506-507 | 1862 |
| Miles, Susan | _____ Cook | 2B | 506-507 | 1862 |
| Miller, _____ | _____ Lide | Y | 155-156 | 1847 |

("Mrs. Miller now Lide") (reference to marriage settlement - no date given) (widow) (she to Alabama)

| Miller, Ann | William Keitt | F | 224-225 | 1828 |
|---|---|---|---|---|

(marriage agreement 10 March 1828) (widow) (widower) (she of Orange Parish, Orangeburgh District) (he of St. Matthew's Parish, Orangeburgh District)

| Miller, Dorcas | _____ Smith | C | 66 | 1813 |
|---|---|---|---|---|

("Dorcas Smith late Dorcas Miller") (she of North Carolina)

| Miller, Dorcas S. | Josiah Smith | B | 610-611 | 1809 |
|---|---|---|---|---|

(widow of Benjamin Miller of York District)

Implied South Carolina Marriages Volume IV 1787-1875

| WOMAN | MAN | VOL | PAGES | LIVED |
|---|---|---|---|---|
| Miller, Elizabeth | John Macnair | A | 224-240 | 1793 |

(widow of Andrew Miller)

Miller, Elizabeth  John Nettles  L  364-365  1840
J. (daughter of John B. Miller) (she died 24 May 1840)
(in Sumter District)

Miller, Hannah  Benjamin Lawrence  Q  62  1801
(she was born about 1748 in County of Gloucester,
England) (he was born November 1757 in County of
Gloucester, England) (arrived Charleston, S.C., 4
September 1801) (to Columbia, S.C.)

Miller, Helena H.  Dr Horatio R. Cook  S  469-472  1849
M. (daughter of John Miller) (Cook of Edgefield
District)

Miller, Jane  Washington C. Hall  U  436-437  1851
(marriage settlement 5 April 1851) (widow) (both of
Edgefield District)

Miller, Margaret  Samuel Mathis  A  224-240  1793
Cathcart (marriage settlement 22 January 1793) (daughter
of Andrew Miller) (she of Claremont County) (Mathis of
Camden)

Miller, Margaret L.  Edwin H.  2A  704-706  1859
                    Stringfellow
(marriage settlement 25 October 1859) (in York District)

Miller, Martha A.  Doctor John M.  E  35  1822
G.                 Roberts
(reference to marriage settlement - no date given)

Miller, Martha Ann  Reverend John  B  188-189  1802
Glover              Richard Roberts
(marriage settlement 29 October 1802) (both of Claremont
County)

Miller, Mary Ann  Thomas R. Anderson  P  316-317  1846
(daughter of James Miller of Edgefield District) [See
also Volume U, pages 60-61]

Miller, Mary  William Taylor  A  361-363  1799
Clayton (marriage settlement 6 May 1799) (daughter of
Andrew Miller) (Taylor of Savannah)

Miller, Rachel  David G. Leigh  L  123-124  1840
(marriage agreement 25 June 1840) (in Kershaw District)

Miller, Sarah  _____ Yongue  2B  649-651  1863
(daughter of Robert Miller)

Miller, Sarah  John L. Yongue  2A  468-469  1858
(marriage settlement 18 October 1858) (she of Chester
District) (he of Fairfield District)

Miller, Sarah J.  Samuel Switzer  U  83-85  1850
                  (Sweitzer)
(marriage settlement 10 June 1850) (widow) (in
Spartanburgh District)

Implied South Carolina Marriages Volume IV 1787-1875

| WOMAN | MAN | VOL | PAGES | LIVED |
|---|---|---|---|---|
| Milling, Mary | Dr. James S. Milling | 2A | 454-455 | 1858 |

Whitaker (daughter of John Milling of Kershaw District) (of Fairfield District)

Milling, Matilda W.  Joseph T. Mickle   2C   30-32   1864
   (marriage settlement __ November 1864) (she of Kershaw
   District, S.C.) (he late of Mobile, Alabama)
Milling, Sarah      John Belton Mickle   R   141-143   1846
   (marriage settlement 21 October 1846) (both of Kershaw
   District)
Milling, Sarah      John Belton Mickle   Y   41-42   1855
   (daughter of John Milling of Kershaw District) (of
   Kershaw District)
Mills, Sarah        Joshua Hendrix       G   304-305   1831
   (daughter of Thomas Mills) (in Newberry District)
Mims, Louisiana J.  _____ Penn          S   302-304   1848
Mitchell, Elizabeth James Murphy         N   295-297   1844
   (daughter of Daniel A. Mitchell) (in Edgefield District)
Mitchell, Elizabeth Richard Birchette    G   327-328   1831
   T. (marriage settlement 1 January 1831) (in Union
   District)
Mitchell, Francis   J. Rice Rogers       T   93-94   1848
   B. (married 26 October 1848) (both of Union District)
Mixson, Eliza A.    John S. Daniel       W   613-617   1853
   (marriage settlement 28 June 1853) (daughter of William
   J. Mixson) (Daniel late of Barnwell District, now of
   Edgefield District)
Mobley, _____      J. T. Hill           2A  668-669   1859
   (daughter of Edward P. Mobley of Fairfield District)
   (Hill of Union District)
Mobley, Elizabeth   John T. Hill         M   338-339   1842
   (daughter of Edward P. Mobley)
Mobley, Harriet R.  Dr. J. R. McMaster   Y   563-564   1856
   (daughter of Edward P. Mobley of Fairfield District) (of
   Fairfield District)
Mobley, Lucretia    James McCrory        2A  763-764   1860
   (daughter of John Mobley Senr. of Fairfield District)
   (of Fairfield District)
Mobley, Marion R.   Edward P. Mobley     2A  134-135   1857
   (daughter of John Mobley Sr. of Fairfield District)
Mobley, Mary M.     Williams Dunovant    Y   294-296   1855
   (marriage settlement 30 May 1855) (daughter of John M.
   Mobley) (in Chester District)
Mobley, Mary Wagner John Woodward Durham 2B  756-757   1863
   (daughter of Dr. Isaiah Mobley) (of Fairfield District)
Mobley, Nancy N.    _____ Whitlock      Y   294-296   1855
   (widow)
Moffatt. See Muffett

Implied South Carolina Marriages Volume IV 1787-1875

| WOMAN | MAN | VOL | PAGES | LIVED |
|---|---|---|---|---|
| Moncrieff, Elizabeth M. | Samuel Parsons | G | 226-227 | 1830 |

(widow of Richard Moncrieff, her first husband) (in Orangeburgh District)

| Montgomery, Ann | ____ Duke | N | 102 | 1836 |

(daughter of David Montgomery of Kershaw District)

| Montgomery, Elizabeth (Eliza) | Samuel Speigner | K | 370-372 | 1831 |

(daughter of John Montgomery) (in Richland District)

| Montgomery, Martha | James Conyers | B | 341-342 | 1804 |

(marriage settlement 24 August 1804) (widow of William Montgomery) (both of Sumter District)

| Montgomery, Rachel | ____ Plowden | M | 270-272 | 1842 |

(daughter of Samuel Montgomery)

| Montgomery, Susannah T. | Moultrie R. Wilson | 2C | 48-50 | 1865 |

(daughter of John W. Montgomery of Sumter District) (both of Sumter District)

| Moon, Octavia R. | Dr. William K. Griffin | 2A | 449-451 | 1858 |

(daughter of Peter Moon of Newberry District)

| Moor, Ann | Simon Terry | N | 209-210 | 1843 |

(marriage settlement 25 October 1843) (daughter of Moses Moor)

| Moore, Cyntha L. | ____ Bynum | R | 117-118 | 1846 |

(daughter of James Moore) (in York District)

| Moore, Harriot | Joseph Warren | M | 36-37 | 1842 |

(daughter of Captain Matthew S. Moore Senr.) (in Sumter District)

| Moore, Leontina | Henry S. Kerr | Z | 712-714 | 1857 |

(of Abbeville District)

| Moore, Mary Honoria | Charles D. Hunter | M | 36-37 | 1842 |

(daughter of Captain Matthew S. Moore Senr.) (in Sumter District)

| Moore, Mary Jane | Edwin R. Mills | Z | 596-598 | 1857 |

(marriage settlement 5 February 1857) (she of York District) (he of Chester District)

| Moore, Mary M. | George Pleasant Cocke | H | 503-505 | 1834 |

(marriage agreement 16 January 1834) (widow of Col. Richard Moore)

| Moore, Penelope | John Ricks | K | 57-58 | 1838 |

(marriage settlement 11 January 1838) (widow of Moses Moore) (both of Sumter District)

| Moore, Rachel | Jedediah Coulter | F | 403-404 | 1828 |

(marriage settlement 28 November 1828) (in York District)

Implied South Carolina Marriages Volume IV 1787-1875

| WOMAN | MAN | VOL | PAGES | LIVED |
|---|---|---|---|---|
| Moorman, Mary Ann | Zaddock Hooker | G | 358-362 | 1830 |

(marriage settlement 30 December 1830) (both of Union District)

Mordecai, Julia    Jacob Levin    U    117-119    1850
(Judith) (marriage settlement 14 August 1850) (he was married before) (in Richland District)

Morgan, Harriet Ann    William Glaze    I    511-512    1836
(marriage settement 19 October 1836) (she of Columbia)

Morgan, Martha    John Price    2A    712-713    1859
(of Barnwell District)

Morgan, Matilda    Henry Griffeth    2B    373-374    1861
(Griffith)
(marriage contract 8 August 1861) (widow of Mark Morgan) (both of Newberry District)

Morgan, Nancy C.    Joseph Bussey    2B    619-620    1863
(marriage contract 21 May 1863) (both of Edgefield District)

Morris, Louanza    Richard D. F. Rollins    2A    749    1860

Morris, Nancy M.    Benjamin Thomas    Y    145-147    1855
(daughter of Thomas Morris of Edgefield District) (in Edgefield District) [See also pages 490-492]

Morris, Sarah    ___ Whitney    Y    490-492    1854
(daughter of Thomas Morris of Edgefield District) (she of Barnwell District)

Morse, Elizabeth    William Webb    2B    581-583    1863
(daughter of Whitfield Morse of Edgefield District)

Morse, Rebecca    Ransom L. Motley    2A    778-779    1858
(marriage agreement __ September 1858) (in Richland District)

Mortimer, Constantia    Joshua Ward    2C    300-304    1866
(marriage settlement 6 September 1866) (she of Newberry District) (he of Georgetown)

Moseley, Anna M.    James Huckbee    2A    681-682    1859
(daughter of John M. Moseley of Abbeville District)

Moseley, Eliza W.    ___ Caldwell    2B    596    1862
(daughter of Henry Moseley of Coosa County, Alabama)

Moseley, Emila Josephine    James T. Barnes    2A    682-683    1859
(daughter of John M. Moseley of Abbeville District)

Moseley, Mary M.    William R. White    2A    680-681    1859
(daughter of John M. Moseley of Abbeville District)

Mosely, Frances E.    Richard M. White    2B    197-199    1860
(postnuptial settlement 5 September 1860) (in Abbeville District)

Moses, Eliza Jane P.    ___ Baker    W    479-480    1853
(daughter of Franklin J. Moses of Sumter District)

Implied South Carolina Marriages Volume IV 1787-1875

| WOMAN | MAN | VOL | PAGES | LIVED |
|---|---|---|---|---|
| Moses, Rebecca R. | _____ Mikell | 2A | 84-85 | 1857 |

(daughter of Franklin J. Moses of Sumter District)
| Moses, Rebecca R. | Thomas P. Mikell | Z | 723-724 | 1857 |

(daughter of Franklin J. Moses of Sumter District)
| Moses, Rebecca R. | Thomas P. Mikell | 2B | 66 | 1860 |

(daughter of Franklin J. Moses of Sumter District)
| Moses, Rosalie E. S. | Robert Spann | 2B | 633-634 | 1863 |

A. (daughter of Franklin J. Moses) (in Sumter District)
| Mosley, Amanda | George W. Mathis | Y | 253-255 | 1855 |
| Mosley, Martha G. | Luellen O. Loveless | Y | 253-255 | 1855 |
| Mosley, Susan M. | John A. Addison | Y | 253-255 | 1855 |

(marriage settlement 2 June 1855) (daughter of John Mosley) (both of Edgefield District)
| Motley, Polly | James Wood | R | 372-374 | 1847 |

(daughter of John Motley of Kershaw District)
| Moye, Anna Maria | George H. Moye | M | 178-180 | 1842 |

(daughter of George W. Moye) (she of Chesterfield District) (George H. of Darlington District)
| Moye, Martha A. | W. J. Bailey | M | 178-180 | 1842 |
| Moye, Martha A. | William J. Bailey | I | 612-614 | 1837 |

(marriage settlement 22 May 1837) (in Darlington District)
| Muffett, Mary E. | Peter Wicker | L | 283-284 | 1841 |

(daughter of James Muffett of Newberry District)
| Muldrow, Harriet A. | John F. Haynesworth | S | 457 | 1848 |

(daughter of Matthew E. Muldrow of Salem County, Sumter District) (of Sumter District) [See also page 416]
| Muldrow, Harriet A. | John F. Haynsworth | I | 388-389 | 1836 |

(daughter of Matthew D. Muldrow of Salem County, Sumter District) (of Sumter District)
| Muldrow, Jane C. | Joseph C. Haynsworth | W | 243-246 | 1852 |

(marriage settlement 17 December 1852) (both of Sumter District)
| Muldrow, Louisa Amanda | Augustus Washington Moye | P | 260-264 | 1845 |

(marriage settlement 18 December 1845) (in Darlington District)
| Muldrow, Margaret | _____ Frierson | Z | 404-406 | 1856 |

(daughter of Matthew E. Muldrow of Salem County, Sumter District)
| Muldrow, Margaret | Joseph S. Durant | 2B | 732-735 | 1864 |

E. (marriage settlement 13 January 1864) (daughter of Robert B. Muldrow of Sumter District) (she of Sumter District) (Durant of Clarendon District)
| Muldrow, Mary Francis | Junius A. Mayes | P | 98-100 | 1845 |

(daughter of Matthew E. Muldrow of Salem County, Sumter District) (of Sumter District)

Implied South Carolina Marriages Volume IV 1787-1875

| WOMAN | MAN | VOL | PAGES | LIVED |
|---|---|---|---|---|
| Mullen, Sarah (Mellen) | Adam Costner | E | 168-169 | 1824 |

("Sarah Mullen sometimes called Sarah Ware") (marriage settlement 25 March 1824) (of Lincoln County, North Carolina)

| Munds, Sarah K. | Isaac H. Smith | U | 305-306 | 1851 |

(marriage settlement 11 January 1851) (both of Columbia, Richland District)

| Munds, Sarah K. | Isaac H. Smith | Y | 381 | 1851 |

(reference to marriage articles 11 January 1851)

| Murdock, Jacqueline H. | James McDaniel | F | 51 | 1827 |

(marriage agreement 23 May 1827)

| Murph, Ann | Andrew B. Fleming | 2B | 135-136 | 1854 |

(marriage contract 16 August 1854) (in Spartanburg District)

| Murphy, Aroline | Thomas Moneyhan | 2B | 140-142 | 1860 |

(marriage settlement 21 July 1860) (in Marion District)

| Murphy, Elizabeth | Robert H. Brumley | E | 81-82 | 1822 |

(reference to marriage contract 25 December 1822) (of Sumter District)

| Murray, Catherine A. | Thomas Marsh | H | 120-121 | 1832 |

(marriage settlement 1 March 1832) (in Edgefield District)

| Murray, Sarah Robinson | James M. Nelson | K | 338-340 | 1839 |

(daughter of Samuel J. Murray of Sumter District) (of Sumter District)

| Murrell, Mary S. | Josiah Wilder | K | 55-57 | 1836 |

(of Sumter District)

| Muse, Nancy J. | John Taylor | 2B | 618-619 | 1863 |

(marriage settlement 26 March 1863) (both of Fairfield District)

| Mushatt, Clarissa (Clara) J. | James S. Stewart | P | 341-342 | 1846 |

(marriage settlement 16 February 1846) (she of Fairfield District) (he of Winnsborough, Fairfield District)

| Mushatt, Margaret C. | Kemp S. Dargan | Z | 700-702 | 1857 |
| Myddleton, Sarah (Middleton) | William Dunbar | A | 259-262 | 1794 |

(marriage settlement 7 July 1794) (she of Orangeburgh District) (he of Winton County)

| Myers, Ann Louisa | Joseph Duncan Allen | K | 258 | 1838 |

(daughter of Col. David Myers) (of Richland District)

| Myers, Jane Sophia | Robert Carter | 2A | 176-177 | 1858 |

Implied South Carolina Marriages Volume IV 1787-1875

| WOMAN | MAN | VOL | PAGES | LIVED |
|---|---|---|---|---|

(N)

Nail, Mary Anna   Richard D. Prior   2B   715-716   1863
  (to be married 17 December 1863) (marriage settlement 17
  December 1863) (in Edgefield District)
Nail, Rebecca   James T. Gardner   Z   275-278   1856
  (separation agreement 10 June 1856) (daughter of Casper
  Nail) (in Edgefield District)
Nail, Sarah   Henry L. Mayson   M   378-380   1843
  (daughter of Casper Nail of Edgefield District)
Nail, Sarah Ann   John Marsh   E   545-547   1826
  (marriage settlement 10 October 1826) (widow of John
  Nail) (both of Edgefield District)
Nail, Sarah Ann   John Marsh   T   373-375   1826
  (reference to marriage settlement 10 October 1826)
  (widow of John Nail) (both of Edgefield District)
Nance, Patsey   Philip Littlefield   E   422-423   1825
  (daughter of Zachariah Nance of Union District)
Neal, Mary E. M.   Warren S. Wells   2B   281-283   1845
  (postnuptial settlement 18 February 1861) (daughter of
  John Neal of Richland District) (Wells of Sumter
  District)
Neel, Elizabeth A.   Jonathan McMorries   X   522-524   1854
  (in Newberry District)
Neely, Elizabeth   Eli P. Moore   2A   438-441   1858
  Ann (marriage agreement 30 September 1858)
Neil, Eliza. A.   John McCully   Z   415   1852
  (marriage settlement 9 October 1852) (both of Fairfield
  District)
Neil, Sarah   Daniel House   F   439   1829
Nelson, Elizabeth   Samuel Pickring   B   365-367   1804
        (Pickren)
  (marriage settlement 16 May 1804) (of Richland District)
Nelson, Emily C.   Charles M. Calhoun   2B   112-117   1858
  (married 19 October 1858)
Nesbett, Mary   _____ Anderson   I   398-399   1836
Nettles, Adaline O.   John F. DeLorme   X   603-605   1855
        (of Darlington District)
Nettles, Adelaide   William M. Wilder   2B   101-102   1860
  Z. P. (daughter of Joseph M. Nettles of Sumter District)
Nettles, Hannah   Dr. Benjamin C.   Z   772-776   1857
  Louisa      Norment
  (marriage settlement 7 May 1857) (she of Darlington
  District, S.C.) (he of Virginia) [See also Volume 2A,
  page 590]

Implied South Carolina Marriages Volume IV 1787-1875

| WOMAN | MAN | VOL | PAGES | LIVED |
|---|---|---|---|---|

Nettles, Hannah M.    Peter K. McIver    R    521-524    1847
  (marriage settlement 29 September 1847) (widow of James
  Nettles) (in Darlington District)
Nettles, Henrietta    James Kelly    2A    684    1859
  A. (daughter of Amos A. Nettles of Sumter District)
  (of Clarendon District)
Nettles, Jane    Thomas Crimm    G    363-364    1809
  (married 23 June 1809) (daughter of Zachariah Nettles)
Nettles, Martha    Joseph J. McCown    2B    358-361    1861
  Emma (marriage settlement __ June 1861) (both of
  Darlington District)
Nettles, Mary Ann    George Morse    X    303-306    1854
  (marriage settlement 18 January 1854) (in Darlington
  District)
Nettles, Mary Anna    John W. Harrington    2B    684-687    1863
  (marriage settlement 19 September 1863) (daughter of
  Joseph B. Nettles) (both of Darlington District)
Nettles, Matilda    _____ Nathans    E    535    1826
  (daughter of Samuel M. Nettles of Richland District)
Neuffer, Sallie C.    James C. Kenneth    2C    45-48    1865
  (marriage settlement 8 September 1865) (daughter of
  Charles Neuffer) (in Richland District)
Newman, Ann C.    Robert H. McElmurray    E    169-171    1824
  (marriage settlement 14 February 1824) (both of Barnwell
  District)
Nicholas, Emely    William King    I    406    1836
  (Emala) (marriage settlement 21 January 1836) (of
  Edgefield District)
Nicholson, Anna B.    James C. Brooks    2B    550-552    1862
  (marriage settlement 20 November 1862) (in Edgefield
  District)
Nickels, Catherine    Zelatus Holmes    O    329-330    1844
  N. (daughter of John Nickels of Laurens District) (in
  Spartanburg District)
Nickels, Mary    Dr David L. Anderson    R    404-405    1846
  Elizabeth (daughter of John Nickels of Laurens District)
  (of Laurens District)
Niles, Esther    Joseph Cunningham    L    385-386    1841
  (Hester) A. (marriage contract 20 July 1841) (she of
  Camden) (he of Liberty Hill)
Nixon, Martha A.    George T. Mason    U    40-42    1850
  (marriage settlement 2 May 1850) (daughter of Washington
  F. Nixon) (she of Richland District, S.C.) (Mason of
  North Carolina) [Must also see pages 4-5]
Noble, Elizabeth    _____ Cloud    2A    375-378    1845
  (daughter of William Noble)

Implied South Carolina Marriages Volume IV 1787-1875

| WOMAN | MAN | VOL | PAGES | LIVED |
|---|---|---|---|---|
| Nobles, Nancy | George Jones | M | 316-317 | 1842 |

(marriage settlement 10 September 1842) (daughter of
William Nobles) (she of Edgefield District, S.C.) (Jones
of Kentucky)

| Noland, Elizabeth | Micajah Suber | H | 184-185 | 1832 |

J. (marriage settlement 31 July 1832) (she of Newberry
District) (he of Columbia)

| Norman, Elizabeth | _____ Bailey | U | 132-134 | 1850 |
| Norman, Eliza Jane | _____ Harris | U | 132-134 | 1850 |
| Norman, Mariah | _____ Waters | U | 132-134 | 1850 |
| Norman, Martha W. | _____ Dillard | U | 132-134 | 1850 |
| Norman, Matilda | _____ Ray | U | 132-134 | 1850 |
| Norman, Susahan | _____ Cooper | U | 132-134 | 1850 |
| Norris, Anna E. | Dr Jno S. Reid | G | 239-240 | 1830 |

(in Abbeville District)

| Norton, Elizabeth | John B. Benson | 2C | 208-209 | 1866 |

A. (daughter of Jeptha Norton of Pickens District, S.C.)
(Benson of Hart County, Georgia)

| Norton, Elizabeth | Jacob P. Sturgeon | O | 180-183 | 1844 |

Ann Jane (marriage settlement 25 July 1844) (daughter of
Allen Norton) (in Williamsburg District)

| Norton, Margaret | _____ Player | O | 180-183 | 1844 |

(widow of Allen Norton)

| Norton, Milby Ann | Thomas P. McQueen | Z | 401-402 | 1856 |

(of Sumter District)

| Nott, Amelia A. | William McKenzie Parker | R | 138-139 | 1846 |

(marriage settlement 26 November 1846)

| Nystrom, Francis A. | _____ Pierce | V | 426-431 | 1852 |

["Mrs. Francis A. Pierce (late Francis A. Nystrom")]

| Nythorn, Frances A. | _____ Pierce | W | 37-41 | 1852 |

["Mrs. Francis A. Nythorn (now Francis A. Pierce)"]
[See also pages 247-250]

(O)

| O'Brien, Mary | Hubert Croghan | U | 30-35 | 1850 |

(marriage settlement 23 February 1850) (widow of William
O'Brien) (both of Sumter District)

| OCain, Elizabeth | William Hickey | H | 273-274 | 1832 |

(marriage settlement 5 December 1832) (daughter of
Daniel OCain of Orangeburgh District) (both of
Orangeburgh District)

| Odom, Elizabeth | Allen Wicker | X | 335-336 | 1854 |

(in Marlborough District)

Implied South Carolina Marriages Volume IV 1787-1875

| WOMAN | MAN | VOL | PAGES | LIVED |
|---|---|---|---|---|
| Oeland, Ann L. | Jas J. Vernon | N | 367-368 | 1844 |

(marriage contract 22 January 1844) (daughter of John Oeland) (in Spartanburgh District)

| O'Hanlon, Hannah | _____ Jones | F | 153-154 | 1827 |
|---|---|---|---|---|

[See also page 287]

| O'Hanlon, Margaret | Joshua Leon Lumsden | 2A | 508-510 | 1859 |
|---|---|---|---|---|

D. (marriage settlement 9 February 1859) (she of Columbia) (he now of Columbia)

| O'Keefe, Eliza | Samuel Hammond | B | 176-180 | 1802 |
|---|---|---|---|---|

Amelia (marriage settlement 25 May 1802) (he of Georgia)

| OKeiff, Eliza | Col. Saml. Hammond | G | 442-443 | 1831 |
|---|---|---|---|---|

Amelia (reference to marriage settlement - no date given)

| Oneal, Adeline | Ephraim H. Atkinson | W | 621-622 | 1853 |
|---|---|---|---|---|

(daughter of Richard Oneal of Columbia, Richland District) (of Chester District)

| OQuin, Elizabeth R. | William T. Spann | I | 265-267 | 1830 |
|---|---|---|---|---|

(in Sumter District)

| Orr, Eliza | Robert H. Fulwood | S | 438-441 | 1848 |
|---|---|---|---|---|

(marriage settlement 13 September 1848) (widow of Joab Orr) (she of Mecklenburg County, North Carolina) (Fullwood of York District, S.C.)

| Osborn, Catharine | Thomas D. Gerald | L | 464-465 | 1841 |
|---|---|---|---|---|

(marriage settlement 8 November 1841) (in Sumter District)

| Ostman, Barbara | _____ Capplepower | B | 659-670 | 1810 |
|---|---|---|---|---|
| Otterson, Amelia Ann | _____ Cavens | Y | 224-225 | 1855 |
| Otterson, Mary | _____ McCarter | Y | 224-225 | 1855 |
| Owens, Eliza C. | John F. Crawley | X | 59-62 | 1846 |

(reference to marriage settlement 22 December 1846) (widow) (in Barnwell District)

(P)

| Palmer, Amanda | Robert A. McKnight | 2A | 15-17 | 1857 |
|---|---|---|---|---|

(daughter of Ellis Palmer of Union District) (of Union District)

| Palmer, Charlotte | Ellison Capers | 2A | 568-570 | 1859 |
|---|---|---|---|---|

R. (marriage settlement 24 February 1859) (she of St. John's Berkley Parish) (he now of Winnsboro)

| Palmer, Eliza | William Harlan | 2A | 14-15 | 1857 |
|---|---|---|---|---|

(daughter of Ellis Palmer of Union District) (of Union District)

Implied South Carolina Marriages Volume IV 1787-1875

| WOMAN | MAN | VOL | PAGES | LIVED |
|---|---|---|---|---|

Palmer, Martha H. Thomas B. Darracott 2B 207-208 1860 (daughter of Champion D. Palmer of Abbeville District, S.C.) (she of Brooks County, Georgia)
Palmer, Sarah Ann William Steen 2B 202-204 1860 (daughter of Ellis Palmer of Union District)
Paris, Mary J. James Laurence V 504-505 1852 (in Sumter District)
Parker, Elcy A. Laban Hall N 301-302 1844 (marriage settlement 21 February 1844) (she in Kershaw District) (he of Chesterfield District)
Parker, Phebe John W. Brown G 69-70 1830 (daughter of Elisha Parker of Chesterfield District)
Parkins, Elizabeth J. Dr. William Riley Jones W 1-4 1852 (marriage settlement 19 May 1852) (daughter of Allen R. Parkins)
Parnell, Laura A. John J. Stuckey X 559 1854 (marriage settlement 14 September 1854)
Parr, Caroline Edward F. Braithwaite I 413 1836
Parrott, Mary John Heller H 145-146 1832 (marriage settlement 14 June 1832)
Parrott, Winny Charles W. Garner N 348-349 1844 (daughter of Benjamin Parrott of Darlington District)
Paterson, Katharine James Eadie D 109-114 1818 (daughter of James Paterson) (of Clackmanan, Scotland)
Patterson, Jane Archibald Bradly W 184-188 1852 (in Abbeville District)
Patterson, Lucretia A. W. Atkinson 2B 457-458 1861 (daughter of Angus Patterson) (in Barnwell District)
Patterson, Sarah William Stewart E 64-65 1822 (daughter of James Paterson) (of Feliciana Parish, Louisiana)
Patton, Jane M. Thomas Whitesides 2B 806-809 1864 (marriage agreement 12 April 1864) (widow)
Pawley, Hannah E. Archibald H. Waring Y 182-185 1855 (marriage settlement 18 April 1855) (she of Darlington District) (he of Colleton District)
Pawley, Mary A. _____ McClenaghan Y 182-185 1855 (widow)
Payne, Elizabeth _____ Grigsby H 85 1831 (widow) (she of Newberry District) [See also page 155]
Payne, Lucinda William B. Boyd 2A 348-349 1858 (marriage settlement 17 April 1858) (widow of John W. Payne) (both of Laurens District)
Peake, Mariah Dr. C. T. Murphy 2B 434-435 1861 Louisa (daughter of David D. Peake of Union District)

238

Implied South Carolina Marriages Volume IV 1787-1875

| WOMAN | MAN | VOL | PAGES | LIVED |
|---|---|---|---|---|
| Peake, Martha A. | Clough McCreight | 2A | 307-308 | 1858 |

(marriage contract 2 January 1858) (of Union District)

| | | | | |
|---|---|---|---|---|
| Pearce, Elizabeth S. | Andrew W. Lewis | 2C | 3-4 | 1864 |

(daughter of Samuel Pearce of Richland District, S.C.) (Lewis of Richmond County, Georgia)

| | | | | |
|---|---|---|---|---|
| Pearse, Elizabeth S. | ___ Lewis | 2B | 755-756 | 1863 |

(daughter of Samuel Pearse of Columbia)

| | | | | |
|---|---|---|---|---|
| Pearson, Anna | Thomas Hollis | S | 352-355 | 1848 |

(widow) (he was married before) (in Union District)

| | | | | |
|---|---|---|---|---|
| Pearson, Emeline S. | W. W. Herbert | W | 74-81 | 1852 |

(daughter of George B. Pearson Sr. of Fairfield District)

| | | | | |
|---|---|---|---|---|
| Pearson, Martha Ann | James Rush | F | 408-409 | 1829 |

(daughter of John Pearson of Fairfield District) (Rush of Columbia)

| | | | | |
|---|---|---|---|---|
| Pearson, Martha Ann | James Rush | H | 105 | 1831 |

(daughter of John Pearson of Fairfield District)

| | | | | |
|---|---|---|---|---|
| Pearson, Martha C. | William Taylor | I | 459 | 1836 |
| Pearson, Mary E. | ___ Boyce | W | 74-81 | 1845 |

(daughter of George B. Pearson Sr. of Fairfield District)

| | | | | |
|---|---|---|---|---|
| Peay, Martha K. | Joseph A. Black | L | 199-200 | 1841 |

(daughter of Austin F. Peay of Fairfield District)

| | | | | |
|---|---|---|---|---|
| Peay, Martha K. | Joseph A. Black | 2A | 35-38 | 1857 |

(daughter of Austin F. Peay of Fairfield District)

| | | | | |
|---|---|---|---|---|
| Peckham, Caroline E. | William C. Brown | Y | 411-412 | 1856 |

(daughter of James Peckham of Columbia, Richland District) (of Columbia, Richland District)

| | | | | |
|---|---|---|---|---|
| Pedrean, Lydia Ann | John Miller | F | 399-400 | 1829 |

(in Anderson District)

| | | | | |
|---|---|---|---|---|
| Pegues, Eliza Ann | James Jerry Dejarnett | K | 236-238 | 1838 |
| Pegues, Martha J. | Samuel D. Sanders | S | 90-93 | 1848 |

(marriage settlement 26 January 1848) (she of Marlborough District) (he of Chesterfield District)

| | | | | |
|---|---|---|---|---|
| Pegues, Mary Jane | Reuben Pickett | K | 236-238 | 1838 |
| Pegues, Sarah C. | James D. Jones | K | 236-238 | 1838 |
| Pemble, Washington Ann | Artemas E. Glover | X | 118-120 | 1853 |

(marriage settlement 12 November 1853) (of Orangeburg District)

| | | | | |
|---|---|---|---|---|
| Perkins, Temperance | William White | U | 193-195 | 1849 |

(daughter of Alfred Perkins) (in Chesterfield District)

| | | | | |
|---|---|---|---|---|
| Perrit, Martha J. | Robert Fullwood | 2A | 472-473 | 1858 |
| Perritt, Frances America | James Meroney (Maroney) | W | 625-629 | 1853 |

(widow of Perry Bryant Perritt) (in Edgefield District)

Implied South Carolina Marriages Volume IV 1787-1875

| WOMAN | MAN | VOL | PAGES | LIVED |
|---|---|---|---|---|
| Perry, Mary | ____ Dixon | N | 310 | 1844 |

(widow) (she of Lancaster District)

| Perry, Mary | ____ Montgomery | C | 45 | 1817 |
|---|---|---|---|---|

(daughter of Lamuel Perry)

| Perry, Sarah | ____ Nelson | C | 45 | 1817 |
|---|---|---|---|---|

(daughter of Lamuel Perry)

| Perry, Susan | Thomas D. Long | 2A | 475-477 | 1858 |
|---|---|---|---|---|

(of Greenville District) (to Pickens District)

| Pervis, Laura S. | James C. Craig | S | 76-78 | 1848 |
|---|---|---|---|---|

(daughter of John Pervis of Chesterfield District)

Pervis. See Purvis

| Peterson, Clara | R. Wright Adams | 2B | 762-764 | 1863 |
|---|---|---|---|---|

(daughter of Basil Peterson) (in Edgefield District)

| Peterson, Frances | ____ Roach | 2B | 762-764 | 1863 |
|---|---|---|---|---|

W. (daughter of Basil Peterson) (in Edgefield District)

| Peterson, Polly | William Langford | F | 478 | 1829 |
|---|---|---|---|---|

(separation agreement 15 July 1829) (widow of David Peterson) (in Newberry District)

| Pettigrew, Ann | Reverend Samuel Eccles | B | 498-505 | 1808 |
|---|---|---|---|---|

(marriage settlement 21 April 1808) (widow of Alexander Pettigrew) (of Darlington District)

| Pettigrew, Ann Eugenia | Joseph Edward Wingate | Z | 411-412 | 1856 |
|---|---|---|---|---|

(marriage settlement 22 November 1856) (in Darlington District)

| Pettigrew, Cornelia M. | Doctor James A. Tillman | Z | 270-275 | 1856 |
|---|---|---|---|---|

(marriage settlement 27 May 1856) (she of Darlington District, S.C.) (he of North Carolina)

| Phillips, Annes | Abraham Giles | B | 295-300 | 1804 |
|---|---|---|---|---|

(marriage settlement 16 February 1804) (both of Marion District)

| Phillips, Nancy A. | Thomas Brenan | G | 333 | 1831 |
|---|---|---|---|---|

(daughter of Zachariah Phillips)

| Pickens, Margaret | Archibald Bowman | B | 497 | 1807 |
|---|---|---|---|---|

(did not marry; had child only) (she in Pendleton District, S.C.) (he to Stokes County, North Carolina)

| Pickens, Mary | Robert Anderson | W | 100-102 | 1852 |
|---|---|---|---|---|

(daughter of Ezekiel Pickens) (in Abbeville District)

| Pickens, Mary Barksdale | Robert Anderson | H | 153-155 | 1832 |
|---|---|---|---|---|

(marriage settlement 10 July 1832) (daughter of Ezekiel Pickens)

Pierce. See Pearse

| Pitts, Amanda A. | Thomas J. Wilder | K | 28-29 | 1837 |
|---|---|---|---|---|

(marriage settlement 26 July 1837) (widow) (in Sumter District)

Implied South Carolina Marriages Volume IV 1787-1875

| WOMAN | MAN | VOL | PAGES | LIVED |
|---|---|---|---|---|

Pitts, Rebecca ____ Loring G 90-91 1830
   (daughter of Jeremiah Pitts of Sumter District)
Plowden, ____ ____ Hays 2B 682-684 1863
   (daughter of Miles H. Plowden of Clarendon District)
Plowden, Rachael George J. McCaulley T 67-69 1849
   (in Sumter District)
Plowden, Rachel George J. McCarrley M 270-272 1842
   (widow) (of Sumter District)
Pollard, Mary Thomas B. Lockhart L 222-223 1841
   (daughter of James Pollard of Abbeville District) (in Laurens District?)
Pollard. Rebecca Dr James Ward L 222-223 1841
   (widow of James Pollard of Abbeville District)
Polock, Rebecca Abraham L. Solomon U 214-217 1850
   (marriage settlement 18 December 1850) (daughter of Levi Polock) (in Richland District)
Poole, Margaret H. Alpheus W. Current 2B 205-207 1860
   (daughter of John Poole) (of Spartanburg District)
Pope, Mary Jane Henry C. King 2B 801-804 1864
   (marriage settlement 14 April 1864) (both of Edgefield)
Porcher, Catharine Franklin Gaillard W 500-506 1853
   Cordes (marriage settlement 28 March 1853) (she of Charleston) (he of Winnsborough, Fairfield District)
Postell, Jane Alexander Houston E 505 1826
   (marriage settlement 13 July 1826) (widow of Colonel James Postell) (of Abbeville District) [Must also see Volume F, pages 48-50]
Pou, Ann Thomas Tatum I 622-623 1837
   (marriage settlement 18 July 1837) (both of Orangeburgh District)
Powe, Caroline Thomas G. Ellerbe L 441-444 1841
   (daughter of Thomas Powe of Chesterfield District)
Powe, Mary C. ____ Ellerbie I 439 1836
   (daughter of Erasmus Powe) (in Chesterfield District)
Powe, Sarah Gideon W. Duvall O 156-158 1844
   (marriage settlement 29 May 1844) (daughter of Thomas Powe) (both of Chesterfield District)
Powell, Caroline T. James H. Rumbough Z 421 1856
   (daughter of Joseph Powell of Greenville, S.C.) (Rumbough of Greene County, Tennessee)
Pratt, Caroline B. William Kincaid U 451-453 1849
   (marriage agreement 31 January 1849) (daughter of Thomas Pratt) (of Fairfield District)
Pratt, Louisa Patrick C. Haynie T 57-61 1848
   (marriage settlement 18 December 1848) (widow of William Pratt) (she of Abbeville District) (Haynie of Anderson District)

Implied South Carolina Marriages Volume IV 1787-1875

| WOMAN | MAN | VOL | PAGES | LIVED |
|---|---|---|---|---|
| Pratt, Sarah L. | William Tolleson | 2A | 660-662 | 1859 |

(in Abbeville District)
Pratt, Virginia P.    Washington W. Calmes    U    449-451    1849
(marriage agreement 31 January 1849) (daughter of Thomas Pratt) (of Laurens District)
Prescott, Emily    William E. Middleton    Y    139-140    1855
(daughter of Daniel Prescott of Edgefield District)
Prescott, Emily    William E. Middleton    2B    193-197    1860
(daughter of Daniel Prescott of Edgefield District)
Prescott, Rachel B.    Dr. James A. Devore    2B    193-197    1860
(daughter of Daniel Prescott of Edgefield District)
Presley, Meheathlan    Abner Landrum    F    338    1828
(daughter of John Presley) (of Edgefield District)
Presley, Sarah E.    Bailey Corley, Jr.    2B    472-473    1862
(daughter of Edward Presley of Edgefield District) (of Edgefield District)
Pressey, Elizabeth    William L. Conally    F    274-275    1828
(marriage settlement 9 February 1828) (widow of Samuel Pressey) (of Barnwell District)
Pressley, _____ Brown    Y    188-191    1855
Antoinette (daughter of Samuel P. Pressley who died in Georgia)
Pressley, Comma M.    William C. Harris    Y    188-191    1855
(daughter of Samuel P. Pressley who died in Georgia)
Pricher, Rebecca    _____ Rizer    2C    177-179    1866
Ann (daughter of Thomas Pricher)
Priester, Barbara    _____ Ruff    D    365-367    1821
(widow)
Priester, Sarah    John Eigleburger    D    365-367    1821
(marriage agreement 13 September 1821) (both of Newberry District)
Prince, Charlotte    _____ Inglis    K    224-226    1838
Laura (daughter of Laurence Prince) (in Chesterfield District)
Prior, Elizabeth    _____ Watkins    W    217    1852
(daughter of Tobias Prior of Edgefield District, S.C.) (she in Richmond County, Georgia)
Puckett, Frances    Nicholas Long    G    404-405    1831
(marriage settlement 21 April 1831) (both of Abbevile District)
Pulliam, Anna    Agrippa Cooper    D    174-178    1819
(of Abbeville District)
Purvis, Jane    Dugald McKellar    H    170-171    1832
(marriage settlement 17 August 1832) (both of Abbeville District)
Purvis. See Pervis

Implied South Carolina Marriages Volume IV 1787-1875

| WOMAN | MAN | VOL | PAGES | LIVED |
|---|---|---|---|---|

(Q)

Quarles, Sarah    Pleasant Thurmond    D    97-100    1818
   (marriage settlement 15 December 1818) (of Edgfield District)
Quarles, Susan    ___ Bozeman    G    345-346    1831
Quattlebum,    Lewis Staley    R    224-226    1847
   Elizabeth M. (marriage settlement 14 January 1847) (in Orangeburgh District)
Quick, Honor    Edward C. Butler    H    200-202    1832
   (marriage settlement 25 August 1832) (both of Marlborough District)

(R)

Rabb, Elizabeth C.    William R. Robertson    O    318    1845
   (daughter of Thomas A. Rabb of Fairfield District) (of Fairfield District)
Rabb, Elizabeth E.    Thomas Crumpton    O    319-320    1845
   (daughter of John Rabb of Fairfield District) (in Fairfield District)
Ragin, Julia E.    John J. Ragin    V    580-582    1852
   (widow of Charles C. Ragin)
Ragsdale, Amelia    William Beckham    2A    388-389    1858
   (daughter of Burr Ragsdale of Chester District)
Raiford, Nancy    Oswell (Oswald) E. Burt    H    256-257    1832
Rainsford, Esther    James Rainsford    H    461-463    1833
   (marriage settlement 26 October 1833) (in Edgefield District)
Rainsford, Mary Ann    Lewis C. Cantelou    H    329-331    1833
   (marriage settlement 28 February 1833) (both of Edgefield District)
Randol, Elizabeth    John Surginer    C    171-177    1815
   (Randell) (marriage settlement 18 March 1815) (widow of John Bond Randol) (of Richland District) [See also page 353]
Raoul, Caroline R.    ___ Stark    O    326    1845
   (daughter of Dr. J. L. Raoul of Richland District) (in Richland District)
Raoul, Caroline R.    ___ Stark    Y    555-558    1855
   (daughter of John L. Raoul)

243

Implied South Carolina Marriages Volume IV 1787-1875

| WOMAN | MAN | VOL | PAGES | LIVED |
|---|---|---|---|---|
| Raoul, Celestine | ____ Goodwyn | R | 159-164 | 1847 |

(daughter of Dr. John Louis Raoul de Champmanoir) [See also pages 216-219, 258-260]

| Raoul, Harriet P. | ____ Taylor | O | 327 | 1845 |
|---|---|---|---|---|

(daughter of Dr. J. L. Raoul of Richland District)

| Rasor, Nancy A. | S. M. Pyles | 2B | 190-191 | 1860 |
|---|---|---|---|---|

(daughter of Ezekiel Rasor of Abbeville District, S.C.) (Pyles of Cobb County, Georgia)

Rasor. See Razor

| Ratchford, Sarah C. W. | W. Garvin | 2A | 234-237 | 1858 |
|---|---|---|---|---|

(both of Barnwell District) [See also pages 240-241]

| Rawls, J. S. | James Clendening | 2C | 223-224 | 1866 |
|---|---|---|---|---|

(antenuptial settlement 18 September 1866) (widow) (in Richland District)

| Ray, Emily M. | Belfield Stark | G | 414-415 | 1831 |
|---|---|---|---|---|
| Ray, Louisa R. | Thomas McMillan | G | 414-415 | 1831 |
| Ray, Martha C. | John P. Blair | G | 414-415 | 1831 |
| Razor, Elizabeth Jane | Isaac Richey | Z | 493-495 | 1857 |
| Razor, Mary Ann | John Donald | Z | 493-495 | 1857 |
| Razor, Nancy Ophelia | Redmond Wyett | Z | 493-495 | 1857 |
| Razor, Sarah (widow) | James W. Blain (of Abbeville District) | Z | 493-495 | 1857 |
| Razor, Sarah Lutcha | Ebenezer Sharp | Z | 493-495 | 1857 |

Razor. See Rasor

| Rearden, Frances America | Perry Bryant Perritt | W | 625-629 | 1853 |
|---|---|---|---|---|

(daughter of Joseph Rearden)

| Reddle, ____ | ____ Smith | 2A | 799-800 | 1860 |
|---|---|---|---|---|

(sister of Napoleon B. Reddle, late of Louisiana)

| Reddle, Mary M. | John M. Boland | 2A | 799-800 | 1860 |
|---|---|---|---|---|

(of Newberry District)

| Reddle, Mary M. | ____ Witt | 2A | 799-800 | 1860 |
|---|---|---|---|---|
| Redman, Martha | James M. Richardson | 2B | 491 | 1848 |

(did not marry; had child only) (in Edgefield District)

| Reed, Laura | Richard H. Williams | G | 84-85 | 1828 |
|---|---|---|---|---|

(daughter of John Reed of Camden, who died 22 April 1821)

| Reed, Mary Elizabeth | Henry Brown | G | 86 | 1830 |
|---|---|---|---|---|

(daughter of John Reed of Camden, who died 22 April 1821)

| Rees, Julia E. | Marcus Reynolds | X | 274-276 | 1853 |
|---|---|---|---|---|
| Rees, Julia V. | Marcus Reynolds | S | 282-286 | 1848 |

(marriage settlement 15 June 1848) (daughter of F. W. Rees) (both of Sumter District)

Implied South Carolina Marriages Volume IV 1787-1875

| WOMAN | MAN | VOL | PAGES | LIVED |
|---|---|---|---|---|
| Rees, Margaret M. | James S. Moore | W | 600-606 | 1853 |

(marriage settlement 7 June 1853) (granddaughter of William J. Rees) (both of Sumter District) [pages 601-603 missing]

| Rees, Maria P. | John Mayrant Jr. | C | 117-123 | 1814 |
|---|---|---|---|---|

(marriage settlement 11 May 1814) (daughter of William Rees) (both of Sumter District)

| Rees, Vermeille | John S. Bradford | K | 300-302 | 1839 |
|---|---|---|---|---|

(marriage settlement 8 January 1839) (widow of F. W. Rees) (of Sumter District) [See also Volume L, pages 360-363, 406-408]

| Rees, Vermeille | John S. Bradford | X | 376-381 | 1839 |
|---|---|---|---|---|

(marriage settlement 8 January 1839) (widow of F. W. Rees) (both of Sumter District)

| Reese, Jannett A. | Isaac D. Witherspoon Junr. | Z | 231-233 | 1856 |
|---|---|---|---|---|

(daughter of George Reese of Chambers County, Alabama) (Witherspoon of York District, S.C.)

| Reid, Elizabeth | James Caldwell | U | 176-178 | 1850 |
|---|---|---|---|---|
| Reid, Eliza S. | James H. Alexander | Z | 3-4 | 1856 |

(daughter of William Reid Senr.) (of Union District)

Reid. See Ried

| Reilly, Catherine | James N. Steen | R | 12-13 | 1846 |
|---|---|---|---|---|

Elizabeth (daughter of Bernard Reilly of Columbia, Richland District)

| Reilly, Cornelia | Hugh P. Lynch | 2A | 62 | 1857 |
|---|---|---|---|---|

Agnes (daughter of Bernard Reilly of Columbia, Richland District) (Lynch of Cheraw)

| Reilly, Cornelia | Hugh P. Lynch | 2B | 61-62 | 1857 |
|---|---|---|---|---|

Agnes (Rielly) (daughter of Bernard Reilly of Richland District) (Lynch of Cheraw) [See also pages 375-376]

| Reynolds, Elizabeth | William Creighton | I | 422 | 1832 |
|---|---|---|---|---|

(Renolds, Runnels) (marriage contract 13 February 1832)

| Rhoden, Emiline | Lerkin C. Prator | 2A | 337-338 | 1858 |
|---|---|---|---|---|

(daughter of Thomas Rhoden) (in Edgefield District)

| Rice, Eliza Ann | Nathaniel W. Foulkes | I | 466-468 | 1836 |
|---|---|---|---|---|

(marriage settlement 2 August 1836) (widow of David B. Rice) (both of York District)

| Rice, Medora | ___ Duncan | 2B | 777-778 | 1864 |
|---|---|---|---|---|

(daughter of B. H. Rice of Union District)

| Rich, Caroline | James L. Jones | H | 360-362 | 1833 |
|---|---|---|---|---|

(in Sumter District)

| Richardson, ___ | John J. Moore | 2B | 496-502 | 1855 |
|---|---|---|---|---|

(daughter of Governor James B. Richardson)

| Richardson, Ann | William Mayrant Senr | G | 340-342 | 1831 |
|---|---|---|---|---|

(she in Sumter District)

Implied South Carolina Marriages Volume IV 1787-1875

| WOMAN | MAN | VOL | PAGES | LIVED |
|---|---|---|---|---|
| Richardson, Ann | John Shackelford | Y | 570-573 | 1852 |

(reference to marriage settlement 14 October 1852) (both of Marion District)

Richardson, Bethia Frances  Moses Liddell  G  349-351  1830
(of Wilkinson County, Mississippi)

Richardson, Dorothy A.  William H. B. Richardson  G  43-46  1829
(marriage settlement 4 November 1829) (daughter of Charles Richardson of Sumter District) (in Sumter District) [See also pages 161-170]

Richardson, Emily  John Ioor  B  289-295  1804
(marriage settlement 21 March 1804) (she of Georgetown) (he of Sumter District)

Richardson, Emily  John Ioor  G  348-349  1829
(of Wilkinson County, Mississippi) [See also pages 340-342]

Richardson, Epsey  Manning D. Brunson  U  105-107  1850
(in Sumter District)

Richardson, Evelina A.  William Ballard  I  428-429  1836
(marriage settlement 30 April 1836) (both of Sumter District)

Richardson, Frances (Fanny)  Steward (Stewart) Harrison  U  394-396  1851
(marriage settlement __ March 1851) (in Edgefield District)

Richardson, Juliana Augusta  John T. Richardson  F  338-339  1827
(marriage settlement 16 October 1827) (in Sumter District) [See also pages 397-399]

Richardson, Lacy Ann  Roland Moss  2A  549-550  1859
(daughter of Thomas Richardson of Fairfield District) (of Fairfield District)

Richardson, Lydia B.  Dr. John S. Rich  T  415-416  1849
(marriage settlement 1 November 1849) (in Sumter District)

Richardson, Mary Catherine  Elisha A. Ferguson  2B  246-247  1859
(daughter of Noah T. Richardson of Anderson District) (Ferguson of Pickens District)

Richardson, Susan W. A.  _____ Logan  U  126-128  1850

Richardson, Susannah  Young Allen  E  497-498  1826
(in Edgefield District)

Richardson, Susannah  Young Allen  F  347  1828
(she of Edgefield District)

Richbourg, Agness L.  John W. Ridgway  N  61-62  1843
(marriage settlement 31 January 1843) (in Sumter District)

Implied South Carolina Marriages Volume IV 1787-1875

| WOMAN | MAN | VOL | PAGES | LIVED |
|---|---|---|---|---|
| Richbourg, Harriett | Robert Ridgway | W | 441-443 | 1853 |

(marriage settlement 12 January 1853) (daughter of Eli Richbourg)

Richbourg, Leonora   Daniel Johnson   W   440-441   1853
(marriage settlement 28 February 1853) (daughter of Eli Richbourg) (in Sumter District)

Richey, Jannet   Thomas Jones   M   76   1842
(Jennet) (marriage contract 29 January 1842) (both of Newberry District)

Richey, Nancy   Simeon Spruill   H   101-103   1832
(marriage settlement 31 January 1832) (both of Abbeville District)

Richey, Nancy   Daniel Jones Jordan   T   224-228   1849
Adeline (marriage settlement 3 May 1849) (she of Abbeville District, S.C.) (he of Rockingham County, North Carolina)

Ricks, Sarah   William W. Wilder   Y   458-459   1855
(marriage settlement 11 October 1855) (in Sumter District)

Ridgill, Rebecca   Edward H. Tallon   I   295-297   1834
(marriage agreement 23 December 1834) (both of Sumter District)

Ried, Eliza Smith   James H. Alexander   U   385-386   1851
(Reid) (daughter of William Ried Sr. of Spartanburgh District) [Must also see pages 447-448; Volume V, pages 198-199]

Rielly, Cecelia V.   Robert P. McCants   2B   374-375   1861
(daughter of Bernard Rielly of Richland District, S.C.) (McCants of Ocala, Florida)

Rinehart, Catharine ____ Kinard   H   222-225   1832
Elizabeth [Must also see Volume G, pages 451-455]

Rinehart, Catharine   John Wise   G   451-455   1831
Elizabeth (reference to marriage contract - no date given) (of Newberry District) [Must also see Volume H, pages 222-225]

Roach, ____   William Wheeler   L   325-326   1833

Roach, M. E.   B. H. Brady   2B   239-240   1861
(daughter of Dr. Thomas J. Roach of Richland District)

Roach, Mary   Alfred China   L   325-326   1833
(in Sumter District)

Robbins, Henrietta ____ McIver   2B   459-466   1862
K. Jr. (reference to marriage settlement - no date given)

Robbins, Henrietta   Francis M. McIver   2A   399-407   1858
K. the Younger (marriage settlement 5 August 1858) (daughter of William H. Robbins) (both of Chesterfield District)

247

Implied South Carolina Marriages Volume IV 1787-1875

| WOMAN | MAN | VOL | PAGES | LIVED |
|---|---|---|---|---|

Robbins, Josephine   James H. Powe   2B   459-466   1862
E. (marriage settlement 15 March 1862) (both of
Chesterfield District)
Robertson, Eliza   Hugh Marshall   S   356-358   1848
Wardlaw
(marriage settlement 8 August 1848) (both of Abbeville
District)
Robertson, Ellen   Geo. Brown   P   178-180   1845
(daughter of William Robertson of Fairfield District,
S.C.) (of Mississippi)
Robertson, Louisa   William Pratt   T   57-66   1848
(daughter of Andrew Robertson of Abbeville District)
Robertson, Sarah M.   John J. Robertson   2A   766   1859
(daughter of John W. Robertson of Troup County, Georgia)
(of Richland District, S.C.)
Robeson, Mary   _____ Ford   F   393   1828
(daughter of Peter L. Robeson of Chesterfield District)
Robeson, Mary H.   Samuel J. Wilson   L   381-382   1841
(Robison) (daughter of Peter L. Robeson of Chesterfield
District) (of Darlington District)
Robeson, Rebecca F.   Robert E. Evans   2C   285-287   1867
(daughter of Thomas W. Robeson of Chesterfield District)
Robeson, Sarah A.   Sherwood L. Cox   Y   206-209   1855
(marriage settlement 19 April 1855) (widow of Peter L.
Robeson) (she of Chesterfield District, S.C.) (Cox of
Anson County, North Carolina)
Robinson, Gatsey   Levi Pate   2C   356-358   1865
(married 10 January 1865) (reference to marriage
settlement 10 January 1865) (both of Kershaw District)
Robinson, Mariah   _____ Ferrel   L   352-354   1841
Robinson, Martha M.   _____ Wylie   M   383-386   1843
(daughter of James Robinson) (in Chester District)
Robinson, Mary F.   _____ Orr   M   383-386   1843
(daughter of James Robinson) (in Chester District)
Robinson, Rachel   John W. Cartin   F   314-315   1828
(marriage settlement 20 February 1828) (both of
Orangeburgh District)
Robinson, Rebecca   David Studdard   R   479-481   1847
(marriage settlement 22 June 1847) (in Laurens District)
Robinson, Sarah   Samuel J. Murray   K   338-340   1839
Lang (daughter of John Robinson of Charleston) (of
Sumter District)
Rochell, Charlotte   John A. Kennedy   E   161-162   1824
(marriage settlement 5 February 1824) (she of Fairfield
District) (he of Camden, Kershaw District)
Rodgers, Amelia   Copeland Stiles   S   411-412   1848
Rosamond   (of Sumter District)

Implied South Carolina Marriages Volume IV 1787-1875

| WOMAN | MAN | VOL | PAGES | LIVED |
|---|---|---|---|---|
| Rogers, Mary E. M. | B. Bruno Poellwitz | 2A | 487-490 | 1858 |

(marriage settlement 25 November 1858) (she of Darlington District, S.C.) (he of Marengo County, Alabama)

| | | | | |
|---|---|---|---|---|
| Rogers, Susannah | Michael Andrews | D | 344-345 | 1820 |
| Rook, Catherine | Benjamin Lyles | V | 554-557 | 1824 |

(daughter of William Rook of Laurens District)

| | | | | |
|---|---|---|---|---|
| Rooks, Lydia L. | A. W. Wood | 2A | 656-657 | 1859 |

(marriage agreement 30 April 1859) (in Barnwell District)

| | | | | |
|---|---|---|---|---|
| Roper, Burchet R. | Thomas H. Todd | M | 249-252 | 1842 |

(marriage settlement 30 August 1842) (both of Mississippi) (in Greenville District, S.C.?)

| | | | | |
|---|---|---|---|---|
| Rose, Elizabeth | Thomas M. Brumby | F | 59-61 | 1827 |

(marriage settlement 20 April 1827) (widow) (both of Sumter District)

| | | | | |
|---|---|---|---|---|
| Rose, Henrietta | Samuel L. Hinckley | K | 110-114 | 1838 |

Elizabeth (marriage settlement 15 March 1838) (daughter of Daniel Rose) (she of Sumter District, S.C.) (Hinckley of Northampton, Massachusetts)

| | | | | |
|---|---|---|---|---|
| Ross, Jane (widow) | _____ Buchannon | U | 186-190 | 1845 |

(in Spartanburgh District)

| | | | | |
|---|---|---|---|---|
| Ross, Lucinda | _____ Thornton | 2B | 647-648 | 1863 |
| Rotten, Nancy | Marmaduke Coate | H | 65-66 | 1831 |

(marriage settlement 29 December 1831) (of Edgefield District)

| | | | | |
|---|---|---|---|---|
| Rountree, Christiana | James E. Black | Y | 598-599 | 1855 |

(daughter of Dudley Rountree of Edgefield District)

| | | | | |
|---|---|---|---|---|
| Rountree, Christiann | James E. Black | P | 294-296 | 1845 |

(daughter of Dudley Rountree of Edgefield District)

| | | | | |
|---|---|---|---|---|
| Rountree, Mary H. | John Rogers | P | 294-296 | 1845 |

(daughter of Dudley Rountree of Edgefield District)

| | | | | |
|---|---|---|---|---|
| Rowe, Ann | Thomas Griffin | O | 431-432 | 1845 |

(marriage settlement 7 April 1845) (widow) (both of Fairfield District)

| | | | | |
|---|---|---|---|---|
| Rowe, Maria S. | Jacob V. D. Wolfe | M | 146-147 | 1842 |

(in Orangeburgh District)

| | | | | |
|---|---|---|---|---|
| Rowe, Sarah | John Elders | C | 306-307 | 1816 |

("formerly Sarah Autry") (of Richland District)

| | | | | |
|---|---|---|---|---|
| Royston, _____ | _____ Johnston | A | 321-322 | 1797 |

(daughter of Thomas Royston)

| | | | | |
|---|---|---|---|---|
| Ruff, Charlotte | Frederic Wise | S | 17-19 | 1847 |

(marriage settlement 9 December 1847) (widow) (both of Lexington District)

Implied South Carolina Marriages Volume IV 1787-1875

| WOMAN | MAN | VOL | PAGES | LIVED |
|---|---|---|---|---|
| Ruff, Lavinia C. | George Burder Boozer | 2C | 16-18 | 1864 |

(marriage settlement 26 October 1864) (widow) (both of Newberry District)

| | | | | |
|---|---|---|---|---|
| Ruff, Martha H. | Nathaniel W. Davidson | U | 123-124 | 1845 |

(in Newberry District)

| | | | | |
|---|---|---|---|---|
| Ruff, Mary | William T. Crooks | U | 122-123 | 1849 |

(of Union District)

| | | | | |
|---|---|---|---|---|
| Ruff, Rebecca | _____ Counts | U | 69-71 | 1850 |

(daughter of John Henry Ruff)

| | | | | |
|---|---|---|---|---|
| Ruff, Sarah | John Pester | C | 141-143 | 1814 |

(separation 24 June 1814) (bill for alimony) (daughter of George Ruff) (of Newberry District)

| | | | | |
|---|---|---|---|---|
| Ruff, Tersea | Frederick Nance | G | 371-372 | 1831 |

(marriage settlement 26 March 1831) (widow) (of Newberry District)

| | | | | |
|---|---|---|---|---|
| Russell, Eliza D. | Hartwell Macon | F | 252-253 | 1828 |

(marriage settlement __ February 1828)

| | | | | |
|---|---|---|---|---|
| Russell, Jane | Reuben Goodin | U | 18-19 | 1850 |

(marriage settlement 23 February 1850) (she of Abbeville District)

| | | | | |
|---|---|---|---|---|
| Russell, Martha M. | _____ Wiggins | R | 438-440 | 1847 |
| Russell, Mary Parr | John M. Howie | Y | 446-449 | 1855 |

(marriage settlement 7 November 1855) (daughter of Robert Russell)

| | | | | |
|---|---|---|---|---|
| Russell, Rachel | William Knox | 2B | 234-235 | 1860 |

(in Abbeville District)

| | | | | |
|---|---|---|---|---|
| Rutherford, Elspeth | Thomas Hutson | E | 73-77 | 1820 |

(in Shielshaugh, County of Selkirk, Scotland)

| | | | | |
|---|---|---|---|---|
| Rutherford, Jean | Robert Inglis | E | 73-77 | 1820 |

(in Philipaugh, County of Selkirk and Mountevine, County of Roxburgh, Scotland)

| | | | | |
|---|---|---|---|---|
| Rutland, _____ | _____ Holland | 2A | 772-773 | 1860 |

(daughter of Abraham Rutland of Edgefield District)

| | | | | |
|---|---|---|---|---|
| Rutland, Martha | James White | 2A | 772-773 | 1860 |

(daughter of Abraham Rutland of Edgefield District)

| | | | | |
|---|---|---|---|---|
| Rutland, Morina | Emsley Lott | 2A | 772-773 | 1860 |

(daughter of Abraham Rutland of Edgefield District)

| | | | | |
|---|---|---|---|---|
| Rutland, Rebecca | Jesse Smith | 2A | 772-773 | 1860 |

(daughter of Abraham Rutland of Edgefield District)

| | | | | |
|---|---|---|---|---|
| Rutland, Sophronia | Henry Satcher | 2A | 772-773 | 1860 |

(daughter of Abraham Rutland of Edgefield District)

Implied South Carolina Marriages Volume IV 1787-1875

| WOMAN | MAN | VOL | PAGES | LIVED |
|---|---|---|---|---|
| | (S) | | | |

Salton, Caroline   John H. Koon          2B   156-157   1860
  (daughter of Michael Salton of Lexington District)
Salton, Julia      Elijah Austin         2B   156-157   1860
  (daughter of Michael Salton of Lexington District)
Salton, Kezia      Draton Epting         2B   156-157   1860
  (daughter of Michael Salton of Lexington District)
Sams, Adelaide     Laurent D.            2C   42-44     1865
                   Hallonquist
  (marriage settlement 20 March 1865) (she of Newberry
  District, S.C.) (he of Montgomery County, Alabama)
Sanders, Anna      George A. Tucker      2C   194-196   1863
  (Annie) L.
Sanders, Elizabeth John Gabriel          B    173-175   1792
                   Guignard
Sanders, Margaret  Malachi Ford          B    173-175   1792
  Ann
Sanders, Martha    Nathaniel S.          2A   303-304   1857
                   Harrison
Sanders, Martha    Ephraim Kendrick      H    31-33     1832
  (daughter of Robert Sanders of Sumter District)
Sanders, Mary E.   William C. S.         2C   412-413   1868
                   Ellerbe
  (daughter of William Sanders of Sumter District)
Sanders, Sarah A.  Thomas Kendrick       H    31-33     1832
  (daughter of Robert Sanders of Sumter District)
Sanders, Tabitha   Horace W. Bronson     H    31-33     1832
  (daughter of Robert Sanders of Sumter District)
Sarter, Mary A. R. James L. S. Hill      R    309-310   1847
  (daughter of John P. Sarter of Union District)
Satcher, Nancy     Lee R. Stringfellow   2A   225-226   1858
  (marriage settlement 18 January 1858)
Satterwhite, Epsey John C. Kennedy       2A   335       1858
  Jane (marriage settlement 23 February 1858) (both of
  Edgefield District)
Saxon, Isabella    Arnold Milner         P    110-111   1848
  (marriage contract 17 November 1848) (widow) (she of
  Laurens District, S.C.) (he of Cass County, Georgia)
Scarborough, Susan Oliver Perry Wheeler Z    426-430   1856
  W. (marriage contract 25 October 1856) (widow of Richard
  J. Scarborough) (in Marion District)
Schumpert,         Baily Conwell         P    135       1845
  Catharine (daughter of Fred. Schumpert of Newberry
  District)

Implied South Carolina Marriages Volume IV 1787-1875

| WOMAN | MAN | VOL | PAGES | LIVED |
|---|---|---|---|---|
| Schumpert, M. Elliott | Clamage H. Kingsmore | 2A | 423-424 | 1858 |

(daughter of Jacob K. Schumpert of Newberry District) (of Newberry District)

| | | | | |
|---|---|---|---|---|
| Schumpert, Magdalina | Jacob Long | P | 136 | 1845 |

(daughter of Frederick Schumpert of Newberry District)

| | | | | |
|---|---|---|---|---|
| Schumpert, Sarah | James Curton | P | 138-139 | 1845 |

(daughter of Frederick Schumpert of Newberry District, S.C.) (Curton of Coweta County, Georgia)

| Scott, _____ | Wm. A. Brownlee | 2A | 745-746 | 1846 |
|---|---|---|---|---|
| Scott, _____ | Thomas Dickson | 2A | 745-746 | 1846 |
| Scott, _____ | Wm. T. Drenan | 2A | 745-746 | 1846 |
| Scott, _____ | Wm McCaslan | 2A | 745-746 | 1846 |
| Scott, Maria Melinda | Charles W. Rolinson | Z | 471-473 | 1857 |

(daughter of John Scott of Richland District)

| Scott, Martha | J. L. Clark | T | 395-398 | 1849 |
|---|---|---|---|---|
| Scott, Martha Matilda | Joseph Bates | Z | 470-471 | 1857 |

(daughter of John Scott of Richland District)

| Scott, Mary | _____ Perry | N | 310 | 1844 |
|---|---|---|---|---|
| Scott, Mary D. | William T. Drennon | 2A | 566 | 1859 |
| Scott, Mary Elizabeth | Darling (or David) J. George | X | 602-603 | 1854 |

(daughter of John Scott of Richland District) [See also pages 640-641]

| Scott, Sally | Dr. Allen J. Green | T | 395-398 | 1849 |
|---|---|---|---|---|

(marriage settlement 15 October 1849)

| Scott, Sarah Ann | Dr. Samuel J. Dwight | W | 140-141 | 1852 |
|---|---|---|---|---|

(daughter of John Scott of Richland District)

| Scott, Sarah E. | William McCaslan | 2A | 453-454 | 1858 |
|---|---|---|---|---|
| Scott, Unity Jane | Josiah T. Ramsey | 2A | 761-762 | 1860 |

(daughter of John Scott of Richland District)

| Scruggs, Polly (widow) | Allen Kates | P | 32-33 | 1844 |
|---|---|---|---|---|

(of Newberry District)

| Scurry, Susan A. | Frederick A. Nance | 2A | 54-56 | 1857 |
|---|---|---|---|---|

(marriage settlement 2 July 1857) (in Newberry District)

| Seay, Lucy | Gamer Self | I | 18 | 1834 |
|---|---|---|---|---|

(daughter of James Seay Sr of Spartanburg District)

| Seibels, Caroline L. | Barnet Statham | K | 347-349 | 1839 |
|---|---|---|---|---|

(of Greenville District)

| Seibles, Ellen | Jacob G. Wannamaker | 2C | 358-360 | 1867 |
|---|---|---|---|---|

(of Lexington District)

| Seibles, Harriet | Henry Arthur | 2C | 358-360 | 1867 |
|---|---|---|---|---|

(of Lexington District)

| Seibles, Louisa | William G. Ligon | 2C | 358-360 | 1867 |
|---|---|---|---|---|

(of Lexington District)

Implied South Carolina Marriages Volume IV 1787-1875

| WOMAN | MAN | VOL | PAGES | LIVED |
|---|---|---|---|---|
| Sellers, Jerusha | Joel Gulledge Sr. | Y | 615-617 | 1855 |

(marriage settlement 29 December 1855) (both of Chesterfield District)

| | | | | |
|---|---|---|---|---|
| Senn, Ann | John H. G. Culler | G | 61-63 | 1829 |

(marriage settlement 19 December 1829) (widow) (of Lexington District) [See also pages 212-214]

| | | | | |
|---|---|---|---|---|
| Seymore, Mary | Wiley Coleman | E | 182 | 1824 |

(Seamore) (marriage settlement 1 January 1824) (in Fairfield District)

| | | | | |
|---|---|---|---|---|
| Sharp, Charlotte | Alexander Brodie | E | 32-34 | 1822 |

(marriage settlement 21 March 1822) (she of Lexington District) (he of Columbia)

| | | | | |
|---|---|---|---|---|
| Shaver, Mary C. | Robert Greenfield | Y | 513-515 | 1855 |

(marriage settlement 27 October 1855) (both of Greenville District)

| | | | | |
|---|---|---|---|---|
| Shedd, Catharine | Osmond S. Jones | Z | 185-186 | 1856 |

(daughter of William Shedd of Fairfield District)

| | | | | |
|---|---|---|---|---|
| Shellito, Mary Jane | Robert Keown | W | 16-19 | 1852 |

(daughter of John Shellito)

| | | | | |
|---|---|---|---|---|
| Shelton, Judah T. | John K. B. Sims | F | 229-230 | 1827 |
| Shelton, Nancy | Charles S. Sims | F | 229-230 | 1827 |
| Shelton, Sarah | Lemuel Farnandis | F | 229-230 | 1827 |
| Sheppard, Jemima | Thomas Seay (Sea) | E | 421-422 | 1826 |

(daughter of Abraham Sheppard Jr. of Richland District and granddaughter of Presley Garner of Richland District)

| | | | | |
|---|---|---|---|---|
| Sherly, Margaret Jane | Tarlton F. Keith | M | 414-415 | 1842 |

(in Edgefield District)

| | | | | |
|---|---|---|---|---|
| Shermon, Mary | Jesse Garrett | 2B | 525-527 | 1862 |

(of Anderson District)

| | | | | |
|---|---|---|---|---|
| Sherriff, Susan F. | Benjamin J. Hodge | W | 259-265 | 1852 |

(marriage settlement 28 December 1852) (daughter of James W. Sherriff) (both of Sumter District)

| | | | | |
|---|---|---|---|---|
| Shibley, Martha | Washington C. Hall | S | 13-15 | 1847 |

(marriage contract 28 September 1847) (widow of Jacob Shibley) (both of Edgefield District)

| | | | | |
|---|---|---|---|---|
| Shields, Martha Ann | Daniel A. Britt | Z | 496-497 | 1856 |

(daughter of James Shields)

| | | | | |
|---|---|---|---|---|
| Shields, Mary Caroline Allen | _____ Hind | Z | 496-497 | 1856 |

(or Caroline Mary Allen Shields)

| | | | | |
|---|---|---|---|---|
| Shields, Nancy Britton | _____ Crosland | Z | 496-497 | 1856 |
| Shiells, Margaret | Henry Jaffray | C | 326-338 | 1798 |

(daughter of James Shiells) (of County of Stirling, Scotland) [See also pages 340-344]

Shillito. See Shellito
Shirley. See Sherly

Implied South Carolina Marriages Volume IV 1787-1875

| WOMAN | MAN | VOL | PAGES | LIVED |
|---|---|---|---|---|
| Shockley, Sarah | Isaac Bradley | Y | 256-258 | 1855 |
| Shuler, Catherine | George Shuler | 2C | 184-186 | 1863 |

(marriage settlement 27 January 1863) (both of Orangeburg District)

Sibley, Elizabeth   Green B. Montgomery   V   236-237   1852
　　　　　　　　　Senior
(marriage agreement 24 January 1852) (widow) (in Chester District)

Simkins,            Daniel Bird           F   104-106   1827
Beheathland (marriage agreement 17 August 1827) (widow of Jesse Simkins of Edgefield District) (of Edgefield District)

Simkins, Elizabeth  Alfred B. Turpin      H   1-2       1831
S. (marriage settlement 29 November 1831) (daughter of Jesse Simkins) (she of Edgefield District, S.C.) (Turpin of Augusta, Georgia)

Simmons, Ann        Cleland Eveleigh      A   335-338   1787
Simmons, Mary Y.    J. R. Arthur          S   40-41     1848
(in Abbeville District)

Simonton, Sarah     William Watson        M   4-6       1843
(marriage settlement 21 February 1843) (she of Fairfield District) (he of York District)

Simpson, Elizabeth  James Darby           2A  579-580   1858
(marriage settlement 11 November 1858) (both of Chester District)

Sims, Dorothy       Eli Weeks             M   318-320   1842
(marriage settlement 2 September 1842) (widow of James S. Sims) (in Sumter District)

Sims, Elizabeth     ____ Bailey           Z   396-398   1856
Sims, Gertrude L.   J. Edward Nettles     2B  342-345   1861
(marriage settlement 7 February 1861) (of Darlington District)

Sims, Nancy         William B. Cauthen    Z   396-398   1856
(widow of Forney Sims) (in Lancaster District)

Sims, Nancy M.      Edward Roney          S   22        1847
(marriage contract 16 September 1847) (in Abbeville District)

Sims, Rebecca       ____ Kirk             Z   396-398   1856
Sims, Sophronia     ____ Bennett          Z   396-398   1856
Singleton, ____     Robert Marion         2B  496-502   1855
　　　　　　　　　DeVeaux
(daughter of Richard Singleton and granddaughter of John Singleton)

Singleton,          Isaac Lenoir          S   422-423   1848
Elizabeth (marriage contract 1 November 1848) (both of Sumter District)

Implied South Carolina Marriages Volume IV 1787-1875

| WOMAN | MAN | VOL | PAGES | LIVED |
|---|---|---|---|---|
| Singleton, Mary Carter | Robert W. Barnwell Jr. | 2A | 359-360 | 1858 |

(marriage settlement 23 June 1858) (daughter of John C. Singleton and granddaughter of Richard Singleton) (both of Richland District)

| Singleton, Susannah | ____ Wells | D | 46 | 1818 |
|---|---|---|---|---|

(daughter of Thomas Singleton) (she of Charlestown)

| Singleton, Videau Marion | Augustus L. Converse | 2A | 665-668 | 1859 |
|---|---|---|---|---|

(daughter of Richard Singleton) (in Sumter District)

| Singleton, Videau Marion | ____ Deveaux | T | 252 | 1849 |
|---|---|---|---|---|

(daughter of Richard Singleton) (in Sumter District) [Must also see pages 156-160]

| Singley, Caroline | Adam Hortman | M | 415-416 | 1842 |
|---|---|---|---|---|

(daughter of Martin Singley of Newberry District)

| Skinner, Mary C. | Charles W. Davis | Y | 406-407 | 1855 |
|---|---|---|---|---|

(marriage settlement 14 August 1855) (daughter of Harvey Skinner) (both of Sumter District)

| Sligh, Sarah | John Prester | H | 79-80 | 1832 |
|---|---|---|---|---|

(in Newberry District)

| Smith, Amanda E. | Eli McMahon | R | 467 | 1847 |
|---|---|---|---|---|

(daughter of William Smith of Union District)

| Smith, Catharine B. | James C. Kennerly | F | 83-84 | 1827 |
|---|---|---|---|---|

(marriage settlement 15 May 1827) (daughter of Thomas Smith) (she of Charleston District) (Kennerly of Lexington District)

| Smith, Charity | Henry Clark Senr | A | 255-259 | 1794 |
|---|---|---|---|---|

(marriage settlement 6 December 1794) (widow of Edward Smith) (both of Claremont County)

| Smith, Elizabeth A. C. | J. Mitchell Hill | 2B | 99-101 | 1858 |
|---|---|---|---|---|

(marriage settlement __ November 1858) (in Abbeville District)

| Smith, Elizabeth B. | Nathaniel Heyward Junr. | 2B | 656-658 | 1838 |
|---|---|---|---|---|

(reference to marriage settlement 30 March 1838)

| Smith, Eliza C. | ____ Graham | S | 157 | 1848 |
|---|---|---|---|---|

(in Barnwell District)

| Smith, Francis | Samuel Wilson | P | 264-265 | 1828 |
|---|---|---|---|---|

(reference to marriage settlement 18 December 1828) (she of Darlington District)

| Smith, Francis | Samuel Wilson | R | 460-461 | 1828 |
|---|---|---|---|---|

(reference to marriage settlement 18 January 1828)

| Smith, Hannah Louisa | Isaac M. Bass | F | 405-407 | 1825 |
|---|---|---|---|---|

(daughter of Robert Smith of Orangeburgh District)

Implied South Carolina Marriages Volume IV 1787-1875

| WOMAN | MAN | VOL | PAGES | LIVED |
|---|---|---|---|---|

Smith, Hannah Isaac M. Bass H 344-346 1829
 Louisa (daughter of Robert Smith) (in Orangeburgh
 District)
Smith, Jane ____ Marshall 2C 23-25 1864
 (daughter of William Smith of Abbeville District)
Smith, Margaret Christian Arant F 330 1828
 (marriage settlement 26 August 1828) (widow of Robert
 Smith of Orangeburgh District) (of Orangeburgh District)
 [Must also see pages 405-407, 412-413]
Smith, Margaret Christian Arant H 344-346 1829
 (daughter of Robert Smith) (in Orangeburgh District)
Smith, Margaret Andrew J. Stokes 2A 689-690 1859
 Shand (married 8 September 1859 in Greenville)
Smith, Margaret W. J. H. R. Farr P 302-304 1846
 (to be married 5 February 1846) (marriage settlement 5
 February 1846) (both of Union District)
Smith, Martha Gabriel Moore 2A 637-638 1859
 (daughter of Enoch H. Smith of Spartanburg District)
Smith, Martha Jane John M. Kennedy H 100-101 1832
 (daughter of William Smith)
Smith, Mary Charles Smith W 155-157 1852
 (widow) (of Abbeville District)
Smith, Mary A. Jacob J. Duckworth 2A 195-197 1858
 (marriage settlement 13 January 1858) (widow) (she of
 Anderson District)
Smith, Mary J. John J. E. Gregory X 46-47 1853
 (daughter of John Smith of Chester District) (of Union
 District)
Smith, Nancy James Patterson F 120-121 1827
 (his first marriage) (daughter of Robert Smith)
 (Patterson of Abbeville District)
Smith, Polly Isaac Hughes C 129-130 1814
 (daughter of George Smith of Richland District) (of
 Richland District)
Smith, Rachael ____ Burke G 109-110 1830
 (widow) (she in Richland District)
Smith, Rebecca ____ McElvine H 100-101 1832
 (daughter of William Smith)
Smith, Regina Allbin Boulware 2B 201-202 1860
 (she of Fairfield District)
Smith, Reginia Allen Boulware O 400-401 1845
 (marriage contract 16 January 1845) (in Fairfield
 District)
Smith, Sarah Coonrod Zeagler G 77-78 1829
 (marriage settlement 23 November 1830) (widow of George
 P. Smith) (Zeagler was married before) (in Barnwell
 District)

Implied South Carolina Marriages Volume IV 1787-1875

| WOMAN | MAN | VOL | PAGES | LIVED |
|---|---|---|---|---|
| Smith, Sarah North | William Cuttino Smith | I | 300-302 | 1834 |

(daughter of Benjamin Smith of Anderson District) (of Abbeville) [See also pages 297-299]

| Smithson, Violet | John M. Bowman | Z | 659-660 | 1851 |

(marriage settlement 11 July 1851) (in Pickens District)

| Smyth, Caroline | Nicholas Herbemont | H | 482-485 | 1808 |

(marriage agreement 21 July 1808) (both of Columbia, Richland District)

| Snelgrove, Susanna | _____ Harmon | B | 622-623 | 1810 |

(she of Newberry District)

| Snelling, Emily | Richard H. Bradley | R | 310-313 | 1847 |

(marriage settlement 17 February 1847) (daughter of Henry Snelling) (both of Barnwell District)

| Sowden, Martha Ann | _____ Davis | V | 305-306 | 1852 |

[see also pages 310-311]

| Sowden, Martha Ann | Richard Davis | W | 214-216 | 1853 |
| Spann, Ellen | Franklin M. Ballard | H | 518-520 | 1833 |

(of Sumter District)

| Spann, McConico G. | James L. Haynsworth | S | 72-74 | 1848 |

(marriage settlement 6 January 1848) (both of Sumter District)

| Spann, Mary | John Murray | S | 428-431 | 1848 |

(marriage settlement 13 December 1848) (daughter of Col. James G. Spann) (both of Sumter District)

| Spann, Mary W. | _____ Carrigan | 2B | 51 | 1860 |

(widow) (in Sumter District)

| Sparks, Margaret Jane | Isaac D. Wilson | R | 517-520 | 1835 |

(married 27 May 1835) (daughter of Alexander Sparks of Darlington District)

| Sparks, Margaret Jane Samuel | William L. Robeson | S | 453-454 | 1849 |

(he was married before) (of Chesterfield District)

| Spearman, Drusilla S. | George Henry Werts | 2B | 784-785 | 1864 |

(daughter of Graves Spearman of Newberry District)

| Spearman, Elizabeth D. | Levi Slawson | 2A | 417 | 1858 |

(in Newberry District)

| Spearman, Mary C. H. | Jonathan Werts | 2A | 777 | 1860 |

(daughter of Graves Spearman of Newberry District)

| Spears, Emily E. | James Edwin Spears | 2A | 770-771 | 1860 |

(marriage settlement 9 February 1860) (daughter of Joshua A. Spears) (she of Sumter District) (James Edwin Spears of Marlborough District)

| Speed, Floride | John Holt | G | 94 | 1830 |

(marriage settlement 3 February 1830) (in Abbeville District)

Implied South Carolina Marriages Volume IV 1787-1875

WOMAN                MAN                     VOL   PAGES      LIVED

Speer, Margaret E.   Lawson Summit            R    432        1847
    (daughter of William Speer of Abbeville District)
Speer, Mary E.       _____ McCord            T    114-115    1849
    (daughter of William Speer of Abbeville District)
Speights, Mary C.    Stephen Hankinson        E    186-187    1824
    (marriage settlement 10 April 1824) (she of Edgefield
    District) (he of Barnwell District)
Speigner, Elizabeth  James Rowan              K    370-371    1831
    (Eliza) (married 16 February 1831) (widow of Samuel
    Speigner) (of Richland District)
Spencer, Sarah J.    John H. Walsh            2C   292-294    1867
    (daughter of Oliver H. Spencer of Chesterfield District)
Spigner, Ann B.      Peter Oliver Senr.       H    225-229    1832
    (marriage settlement 27 October 1832) (both of
    Orangeburgh District)
Spires, Mary         Robert R. Hunter         L    45-47      1839
    Elizabeth (marriage settlement 17 December 1839)
    (daughter of Henry Spires) (both of Edgefield
    District)
Spivey, Sarah Ann    Lewis Holloway           2B   301-303    1861
    (marriage settlement 1 January 1861) (she of Richmond
    County, Georgia) (he of Edgefield District, S.C.)
Stack, Caroline      Morgan Brandenburg       W    167-168    1852
    (marriage settlement 14 September 1852) (of St.
    Matthew's Parish, Orangeburg District)
Staggers, Mary       Laurence H. Belser       Z    97-101     1856
    Anastasia (daughter of William Staggers of Williamsburg
    District)
Stark, Caroline E.   Joseph J. Richardson     L    261-263    1840
    (marriage settlement 12 December 1840) (daughter of Eli
    Stark) (in Sumter District)
Stark, Harriet A.    _____ Anderson          O    22-24      1844
    (widow)
Stark, Martha E.     Thomas N. Broughton      O    22-24      1844
    (marriage settlement 27 February 1844) (in Sumter
    District)
Stark, Martha E.     Thomas N. Broughton      T    531        1844
    (reference to marriage settlement 27 February 1844)
Steed, Sarah         Daniel L. Britton        H    99-100     1832
    (widow of Griffin Steed)
Steel, Eliza A.      Wm G. Erwin              W    62-64      1852
    (marriage settlement 15 June 1852) (widow of J. J.
    Steel) (in York District)
Steen, Frances       John Taylor              Y    568-570    1855
    (daughter of Col. Gideon Steen) (in Union District)

Implied South Carolina Marriages Volume IV 1787-1875

| WOMAN | MAN | VOL | PAGES | LIVED |
|---|---|---|---|---|
| Stephens, Edna (Edney) | Henry Dickert | I | 469-470 | 1836 |

(marriage agreement 2 August 1836) (widow of John Stephens of Newberry District) (in Newberry District)

| Stephens, Julia F. | Samuel T. Agnew | 2A | 580-581 | 1856 |
|---|---|---|---|---|

(marriage settlement 7 April 1856) (in Newberry District)

| Stephenson, Mary | William C. Brunson | M | 263-265 | 1842 |
|---|---|---|---|---|

(marriage settlement 30 June 1842) (both of Darlington District)

| Stevens, Helen Fayssoux | Lionel C. Kennedy | N | 110-111 | 1843 |
|---|---|---|---|---|

(in Spartanburgh District)

| Stewart, Eliza L. | John P. Heath | 2B | 109-110 | 1860 |
|---|---|---|---|---|

(marriage settlement 1 March 1860) (in Lancaster District)

| Stewart, Sarah | Robert Russell | Y | 446-449 | 1855 |
|---|---|---|---|---|

(of Columbia, Richland District)

| Still, Harriet Elizabeth Ann | Thomas M. Dendy | N | 89-90 | 1843 |
|---|---|---|---|---|

(marriage settlement 9 March 1843) (both of Edgefield District)

| Still, Jane E. | Samuel Reed | 2C | 451-453 | 1868 |
|---|---|---|---|---|

(marriage settlement 17 February 1868) (both of Barnwell District)

| Stone, Elizabeth | Micajah Dinkins | D | 207-208 | 1820 |
|---|---|---|---|---|

(daughter of Enoch Stone of Lexington District)

| Stone, Francis G. | Abner Pyles | E | 14-15 | 1822 |
|---|---|---|---|---|

(marriage contract 10 May 1822) (widow) (both of Laurens District)

| Stroman, Elizabeth | Thomas R. Brown | E | 368-369 | 1811 |
|---|---|---|---|---|

(marriage settlement 4 June 1811)

| Stuart, Claudia S. the Younger | Charles R. Thomson | 2B | 85-86 | 1860 |
|---|---|---|---|---|

(marriage agreement 17 April 1860)

| Stubbs, Caroline A. | Charles M. Breaker | O | 68-69 | 1844 |
|---|---|---|---|---|

(marriage settlement 22 April 1844) (in Marlboro District)

| Stubbs, Elizabeth | Murphy C. McNair | S | 201-204 | 1848 |
|---|---|---|---|---|

(marriage settlement 21 March 1848) (both of Marlborough District)

| Stukes, Sarah E. | Jacob H. Whitehead | O | 17-18 | 1844 |
|---|---|---|---|---|

(marriage settlement 5 March 1844) (in Sumter District)

| Suber, Elizabeth J. | John S. Sitgreaves | Z | 220-223 | 1856 |
|---|---|---|---|---|

(marriage settlement 17 April 1856) (widow of Micajah Suber) (she of Newberry District) (Sitgreaves formerly of York District)

| Suber, Sarah (widow) | Lewis Boatner | I | 25-26 | 1834 |
|---|---|---|---|---|

Implied South Carolina Marriages Volume IV 1787-1875

| WOMAN | MAN | VOL | PAGES | LIVED |
|---|---|---|---|---|
| Suber, Tenah | Jacob Cromer | G | 445-446 | 1831 |

(marriage settlement 11 July 1831) (widow) (both of Newberry District)

| Sullivan, Catharine L. | Robert Anderson (of Edgefield District) | U | 272-274 | 1851 |
|---|---|---|---|---|
| Sullivan, Elizabeth | William G. Quarls | K | 508-510 | 1839 |

(marriage settlement 29 November 1839) (daughter of John Sullivan)

| Sullivan, Lucy | William G. Quarls | K | 508-510 | 1836 |
|---|---|---|---|---|

(daughter of John Sullivan)

| Sullivan, Mary | Samuel Getsam | K | 508-510 | 1836 |
|---|---|---|---|---|
| Summer, Magdalina | Jacob Sligh | D | 18 | 1819 |

(daughter of George A. Summer Senr. of Lexington District) [See also pages 116-117]

| Summer, Maria Eve | Henry Ruff | D | 118 | 1819 |
|---|---|---|---|---|

(daughter of George A. Summer Senr. of Lexington District) [See also pages 116-117]

| Summer, Susannah | John Hipp | D | 118 | 1819 |
|---|---|---|---|---|

Margaret (daughter of George A. Summer Senr. of Lexington District) [See also pages 116-117]

| Summers, Alse | Robert Worthington | G | 97-98 | 1830 |
|---|---|---|---|---|

(marriage settlement 4 January 1830) (both of Newberry District)

| Sutton, Martha E. | Thomas McDowell | M | 18-19 | 1841 |
|---|---|---|---|---|

(marriage settlement 3 November 1841) (widow) (both of Fairfield District)

| Swaford, _____ | _____ Alexander | X | 585-586 | 1854 |
|---|---|---|---|---|

(daughter of John Swaford of Pickens District)

| Swoford, _____ | _____ Alexander | Y | 280-281 | 1855 |
|---|---|---|---|---|

(daughter of John Swoford of Pickens District)

| Swoford, Mary | _____ Rogers | Y | 280-281 | 1855 |
|---|---|---|---|---|

(daughter of John Swoford of Pickens District)

(T)

| Tarrant, D. E. L. | C. H. Dillard | V | 385-389 | 1852 |
|---|---|---|---|---|

(marriage contract 3 January 1852) (widow) (both of Union District)

| Tart, Elizabeth | _____ Kirven | X | 646-649 | 1854 |
|---|---|---|---|---|
| Tatom, Caroline S. | George Graves | N | 297-301 | 1844 |

(marriage settlement 30 January 1844) (widow of Orville Tatom) (she of Abbeville District. S.C.) (Graves of Jefferson County, Florida)

Implied South Carolina Marriages Volume IV 1787-1875

| WOMAN | MAN | VOL | PAGES | LIVED |
|---|---|---|---|---|

Taylor, Eliza        John Elmore            Y    608-609    1855
  (marriage settlement 3 December 1855) (widow) (both of
  Newberry District) [See also pages 613-615]
Taylor, Elizabeth    Dr. A. P. Moore        K    546-552    1840
  M. (daugher of Henry P. Taylor and granddaughter of Col.
  Thomas Taylor)
Taylor, Harriet      Franklin H. Elmore     H    26-27      1831
  Chesnut (daughter of John Taylor of Columbia, Richland
  District)
Taylor, Jane         William Black Yates    I    306-309    1835
  (marriage contract 28 October 1835) (widow) (she of
  Columbia) (he of Charleston)
Taylor, Janet        John Macfarlan         W    259-265    1852
Taylor, Martha       Robert E. Russell      D    363-364    1821
  (marriage settlement 16 May 1821) (separation agreement
  27 May 1824) (of Columbia, Richland District) [Must also
  see Volume E, pages 191-193]
Taylor, Martha Ann   David S. Yates         K    546-552    1840
  (married 23 January 1840) (marriage settlement 22
  January 1840) (daughter of Henry P. Taylor and granddaughter of Col. Thomas Taylor) (she of Columbia) (Yates
  of Charleston)
Taylor, Mary Ann     _____ McGregor         R    86-87      1846
  (daughter of William Taylor of Kershaw District)
Taylor, Nannie W.    William St. J.         2A   201-203    1858
                     Mazyck
  (daughter of Benjamin F. Taylor) (of Charleston)
Taylor, Sally        Edward Edwards Evans   S    377-384    1848
  Chesnut (marriage settlement 15 November 1848) (daughter
  of John Chesnut Taylor) (in Richland District)
Taylor, Sarah        Albert Smith           I    236-237    1835
  Cantey (marriage contract 13 May 1835) (she of Columbia)
  (he of Beaufort)
Taylor, Virginia     Halcot P. Green        R    189-191    1847
  (daughter of Benjamin F. Taylor)
Teague, Charlotte    Dr Abner Teague        T    398-400    1849
Teague, Mary         H. W. Garlington       T    398-400    1849
Teague, Nancy        L. Miles               T    398-400    1849
  (marriage settlement 4 October 1849) (widow) (he was
  married before) (in Laurens District)
Telford, Rachel E.   George F. Thompson     N    278-279    1844
Telford, Sarah       B. W. Tradewell        N    278-279    1844
                     (of Richland District)
Tennent, Elizabeth   Alex R. Houston        2A   214-215    1857
  S. (daughter of William Tennent of Abbeville District)

Implied South Carolina Marriages Volume IV 1787-1875

| WOMAN | MAN | VOL | PAGES | LIVED |
|---|---|---|---|---|

Tennent, Elizabeth    Alexander Houston    Y    221-222    1855
    Smith (daughter of William Tennent of Abbeville
    District) (of Abbeville District)
Tennent, Martha C.    Dr. J. A. Gibert    2A    213-214    1857
    (daughter of Wiliam Tennent of Abbeville District) (of
    Abbeville District)
Terrill, Elizabeth    Jesse E. Dent    M    364    1842
    W. (common-law marriage?) (of Columbia, Richland
    District)
Thames, Anna E.    McCauley J. White    2A    788-789    1860
    (daughter of John C. Thames) (in Sumter District)
Thomas, Frances    Joel Easterling    2A    527-528    1859
    (Fannie) (marriage settlement 19 February 1859) (widow)
    (widower) (both of Marlborough District) [See also page
    748]
Thomas, Malinda    William Owings    W    454-455    1853
    (daughter of Reuben Thomas of Laurens District) (of
    Laurens District)
Thomas, Mary    John Bunch    B    51    1801
    (of Richland District)
Thomas, Sarah    John A. Fant    2A    206-208    1857
    (marriage contract 24 October 1857) (widow) (of Union
    District)
Thomas, Susannah    John W. Mondy    K    253    1838
    (Monday)
    (marriage settlement 15 September 1838) (widow of
    Charles Thomas) (both of Edgefield District)
Thompson, Charlotte    Joshua Player    I    150-173    1835
    Elizabeth (Thomson) (reference to marriage settlement -
    no date given) (in Fairfield District)
Thompson, Eliza J.    Thomas J. Spurrier    W    381-382    1852
    (marriage settlement 28 December 1852) (in Kershaw
    District)
Thompson, Eliza W.    _____ Jones    V    344-345    1850
    (daughter of Waddy Thompson)
Thompson, Frances    Josiah M. Wilder    2B    95-97    1860
    Ann (marriage settlement __ __ 1860 - proven 4 May
    1860) (daughter of Hilliard L. Thompson and grand-
    daughter of Robert Hudson) (in Sumter District)
Thompson, Frances    Robert C. Oliver    2C    372-374    1860
    Mary (reference to marriage settlement 4 January 1860)
    (in Clarendon District)
Thompson, Martha    _____ Barwick    Z    187-188    1856
    (daughter of John Thompson)
Thomson, Caroline    John B. Lewis    S    281-282    1848
    S. (daughter of William R. Thomson) (of Orangeburgh
    District)

Implied South Carolina Marriages Volume IV 1787-1875

| WOMAN | MAN | VOL | PAGES | LIVED |
|---|---|---|---|---|
| Thomson, Caroline Sophia | John B. Lewis (in Orangeburgh District) | K | 269 | 1839 |
| Thomson, Emma V. (Thompson) | Benjamin R. Stuart | 2B | 91-93 | 1860 |

(marriage settlement 1 May 1860) (she of St. Matthew's Parish) (he of Richland District) [Must also see pages 136-138] [See also pages 260-261]

Thomson, Margaret C.  Dr. Artemas T. Darby  I  45-49  1834
(marriage settlement 19 April 1834) (daughter of John L. Thomson and granddaughter of William R. Thomson) (of Richland District) [Must also see pages 449-450, 452]

Thorn, Delilah  Philip J. Hammond  M  342-343  1842
(daughter of Charles Thorn)

Thorn, Mary  Thomas Mason  M  342-343  1842
(daughter of Charles Thorn)

Thorn, Olive Lee  John Ross  M  342-343  1842
(daughter of Charles Thorn)

Thorn, Sarah  James McCrorey  M  342-343  1842
(daughter of Charles Thorn)

Thornton, Lucinda  S. J. Burnett  2B  647-648  1863
(marriage contract 1 June 1863) (widow) (she of Abbeville District) (he of Edgefield District)

Threewits, Catharine  Joseph Griffin  K  246-248  1838
(marriage settlement 17 September 1838) (widow) (both of Edgefield District)

Thurmond, Elizabeth  Solomon G. Ward  E  146  1821
(marriage agreement 25 September 1821) (she of Greenville District, S.C.) (he late of New York)

Tierse, Ainre (Amie) Rimi (Turse)  Frederick Seybt  Q  96-97  1822
(she was born about 1775 in Paris) (he was born about 1769 in Bayreuth, Franconia) (arrived 19 July 1818, Alexandria, District of Columbia, then to S.C.)

Tillman, Nancy T.  James Tate  L  178-181  1840
(marriage settlement 7 November 1840) (widow of Hiram Tillman) (she of Abbeville District, S.C.) (Tate of Mississippi)

Tillman, Tabitha  James F. Adams  X  208-211  1853
(marriage settlement 3 May 1853) (widow) (he was married before) (both of Edgefield District)

Timmerman, Sarah T.  H. W. Walter  E  260-263  1824
(marriage settlement 19 September 1824) (in Columbia, Richland District)

Timmons, Angerona J.  M. R. Sturges  2C  117-118  1866
(marriage contract 2 January 1866) (widow of Luther R. Timmons) (in Marion District)

Timmons, Elizabeth H.  Thomas L. James (in Marion District)  P  399-400  1846

Implied South Carolina Marriages Volume IV 1787-1875

| WOMAN | MAN | VOL | PAGES | LIVED |
|---|---|---|---|---|
| Tims, Winifred | James Hogan | U | 396-397 | 1851 |

(marriage contract 4 March 1851) (in Chester District)

| Tobin, Agnes Elizabeth | Beverly Cooper Hughes | 2A | 279-281 | 1858 |
|---|---|---|---|---|
| Tollison, Sarah | Berryman S. Holder | F | 16-17 | 1826 |

(marriage agreement 4 December 1826) (she of Franklin County, West Tennessee) (he of Spartanburgh District, S.C.)

| Tomkins, Elizabeth | Abiah (Biah) Morgan | I | 485-486 | 1836 |
|---|---|---|---|---|

(marriage agreement 1 July 1836) (widow of Stephen Tomkins) (both of Edgefield District)

| Tomkins, Elizabeth | John Rochelle | F | 65-67 | 1827 |
|---|---|---|---|---|

(Tompkins) (marriage settlement 13 April 1827) (widow of Samuel Tomkins of Edgefield District) (of Edgefield District)

| Tomkins, Elizabeth | Willard Smith | 2B | 598-599 | 1847 |
|---|---|---|---|---|

(Tompkins) (marriage agreement 16 June 1847) (widow) (in Abbeville District)

| Tomlinson, Ann Eliza | James F. Drake | 2A | 426-429 | 1858 |
|---|---|---|---|---|

(marriage settlement 11 September 1858) (daughter of Henry M. Tomlinson)

| Tomlinson, Ann Eliza | James F. Drake | 2B | 493-496 | 1858 |
|---|---|---|---|---|

(reference to antenuptial settlement 11 September 1858) (daughter of Henry M. Tomlinson) (in Chesterfield District)

| Toole, Kesiah | George M. Owens | 2B | 276-277 | 1861 |
|---|---|---|---|---|

(daughter of Stephen Toole of Barnwell District)

| Towels, _____ (Towles) | Ridley M. Scurry (of Edgefield District) | Y | 600-601 | 1855 |
|---|---|---|---|---|
| Towels, Mary Catharine | Pickens B. Wever | Y | 600-601 | 1855 |

(Towles) (of Emanuel County, Georgia)

| Towles, Mary C. | Pickens B. Wever (in Edgefield District) | X | 93-94 | 1853 |
|---|---|---|---|---|
| Towles, Susan Elvira | Ridley M. Scurry (in Edgefield District) | X | 93-94 | 1853 |
| Townes, Fanny | George Butler | 2B | 537-538 | 1862 |

(daughter of S. A. Townes) (in Greenville District)

| Tradewell, Mary E. | John H. Boatwright (in Richland District) | Z | 196-200 | 1855 |
|---|---|---|---|---|
| Trapp, Rachel | _____ Wooten | Z | 293-295 | 1856 |

(she of Fairfield District)

| Tredaway, Mary | Edward Bomar | I | 39-40 | 1834 |
|---|---|---|---|---|

(marriage settlement 17 April 1834) (he was married before) (of Spartanburgh District)

| Trowell, Ann Haseltine | William McBride | 2B | 690-695 | 1863 |
|---|---|---|---|---|

(daughter of James Trowell) (in Beaufort District)

Implied South Carolina Marriages Volume IV 1787-1875

| WOMAN | MAN | VOL | PAGES | LIVED |
|---|---|---|---|---|
| Tucker, Agness J. | _____ Moss (Moses) | W | 415-417 | 1853 |
| (daughter of Bartley Tucker of Abbeville District) | | | | |
| Tucker, Anna (Annie) L. | Dr. William F. Holmes | 2C | 194-196 | 1863 |
| (married 29 June 1863) (widow of George A. Tucker) (both of Union District) | | | | |
| Tucker, Annabella Martha | James D. Erwin | Z | 452-454 | 1856 |
| (daughter of Daniel R. Tucker of Baldwin County, Georgia) (Erwin of Barnwell District, S.C.) | | | | |
| Tucker, Mary Ann Elizabeth | Ulysses M. Erwin | Z | 450-452 | 1856 |
| (daughter of Daniel R. Tucker of Baldwin County, Georgia) (Erwin of Barnwell District, S.C.) | | | | |
| Tucker, Mary Ann | C. E. Sims | 2B | 570-571 | 1863 |
| (daughter of George B. Tucker) | | | | |
| Tucker, Sarah | _____ Betsel | R | 438-440 | 1824 |
| Tucker, Sarah | Charles Stone | C | 219-220 | 1803 |
| Turner, Polly | David Peterson | F | 478 | 1829 |
| Turner, Sarah | Douglass Nisbett | 2B | 585-586 | 1863 |
| (daughter of Franklin Turner of Chesterfield District) (Nisbett of Charleston) | | | | |
| Turner, Susan (Susannah) | Nathan O. Nelson | X | 108-110 | 1853 |
| (marriage settlement 20 October 1853) (widow) (both of Barnwell District) | | | | |
| Turner, Susannah | John Edmonson | F | 175 | 1826 |
| (marriage contract 29 January 1826) (both of Newberry District) | | | | |
| Turnipseed, Charlotte | Daniel Souter | U | 148-150 | 1850 |
| (daughter of Felix Turnipseed of Richland District) (of Richland District) | | | | |
| Turnipseed, Rebecca | James M. Beard | U | 148-150 | 1850 |
| (daughter of Felix Turnipseed of Richland District) | | | | |
| Turpin, Caroline | _____ Hardy | V | 385-389 | 1852 |
| Turpin, Catherine W. H. | _____ Clark | V | 385-389 | 1852 |
| Turpin, D. E. L. | _____ Tarrant | V | 385-389 | 1852 |
| (daughter of William Turpin of Greenville District) | | | | |
| Turpin, Laura A. H. | _____ Green | V | 385-389 | 1852 |
| Turpin, Mary R. L. B. | _____ Rouley | V | 385-389 | 1852 |
| Turquand, Hannah | Russell McCord | A | 166-167 | 1791 |
| (daughter of Paul Turquand of Orangeburgh District) (McCord of Camden District) | | | | |
| Turquand, Martha | Joseph McCord | A | 167 | 1791 |
| (daughter of Paul Turquand of Orangeburgh District) | | | | |
| Tyler, Ann R. | James W. Reed | 2C | 450-451 | 1851 |

Implied South Carolina Marriages Volume IV 1787-1875

| WOMAN | MAN | VOL | PAGES | LIVED |
|---|---|---|---|---|

(U)

Ussery, Gincy    Isham Spears    Z   15-18   1852
   (both of Barnwell District)

(V)

Vance, Mary F.    Elihu Alton    U   111-112   1850
   (in Laurens District, S.C.) (of Pontotoc County, Mississippi)
Vance, Susan C.    Richard Satterwhite    X   452-454   1854
   (marriage settlement 24 March 1854) (she of Laurens District) (he of Newberry District)
Vandeperr, Cecile    Simon Homot    Q   63   1805
   (divorced) (she was born about 1757 in Bruxelles, French Flanders) (to Georgia, then S.C.)
VanLew, Eleonor    Ledford Rogers    U   152-154   1850
   (Vanlew) (marriage contract 20 August 1850) (of Union District) [See also pages 150-152]
Vanlew, Mary S.    Benjamin Gregory    K   79-80   1838
   (marriage settlement 3 January 1838) (of Union District)
Vaughan, Alice D.    Benjamin Mitchell    O   101-103   1844
   (in Sumter District) [See also pages 176-178]
Vaughan, Elizabeth    John T. Brunson    2A   33-35   1857
   Alice (marriage settlement 20 June 1857) (granddaughter of William Vaughan) (in Sumter District)
Vaughan, Emily E.    John M. Dargan    O   176-179   1844
   (in Sumter District) [See also pages 101-103]
Vaughan, Frances M.    Hugh G. Cassels    V   323-325   1851
Vaughan, Francis M.    Hugh G. Cassels    O   179   1844
   [See also pages 101-103, 176-178]
Vaughan, Leonora C.    Samuel C. Mitchell    L   38-40   1840
   (marriage settlement 11 January 1840) (daughter of William Vaughan) (both of Sumter District)
Vaughan, Mary    Edward K. Mellichamp    P   196-202   1845
   Theodosia (marriage settlement 4 December 1845) (daughter of John H. Vaughan) (she of Sumter District) (Mellichamp of Charleston)
Vaughan, Victoria    Timothy L. Jones    P   196-198   1843
   A. (widow of John H. Vaughan)

Implied South Carolina Marriages Volume IV 1787-1875

| WOMAN | MAN | VOL | PAGES | LIVED |
|---|---|---|---|---|
| Vaughn, Barbara | Solomon Galespy (Galespe) | V | 11-13 | 1851 |

(separation agreement 13 May 1851) (daughter of John Vaughn) (in Laurens District)

| Vernon, Ann V. | _____ Hicks | G | 39-42 | 1829 |
|---|---|---|---|---|
| Vernon, Mary Elizabeth | Charles Gee | G | 175-176 | 1829 |

[See also pages 39-42]

| Villepontoux, Loveridge Lewis | _____ Godbee | A | 198-199 | 1791 |
|---|---|---|---|---|
| Voss, Barbara | John Rhoderwits (Rodewits) (of East Granby) | D | 339-341 | 1820 |

(marriage contract 27 April 1820) [Must also see Volume E, pages 53-54]

(W)

| Waddill, Martha Ann | _____ McCarter | S | 62-64 | 1847 |
|---|---|---|---|---|
| Waddill, Susan | Peter Shockley | S | 62-64 | 1847 |

(marriage settlement 21 December 1847) (widow) (both of Greenville District)

| Wade, Mary B. | _____ McCaine (in Barnwell District) | S | 343-344 | 1840 |
|---|---|---|---|---|
| Wade, Sarah B. | _____ Johnson (in Barnwell District) | S | 343-344 | 1840 |
| Wadlington, Dorothy Ann | Jefferson L. Edmonds | I | 107-108 | 1834 |
| Wadlington, Mary B. | M. W. Gracey | K | 535-542 | 1835 |
| Wadlington, Sarah T. S. F. | Robert H. Spencer | K | 535-542 | 1835 |
| Wadlington, Sarah T. Susannah F. | Robert H. Spencer | I | 74-76 | 1834 |

[Must also see pages 107-108] [See also pages 7-8]

| Waldrop, Anna | Levi Longshow (in Newberry District) | F | 364-365 | 1828 |
|---|---|---|---|---|
| Waldrop, Hetty | John Golding | F | 364-365 | 1828 |

(marriage settlement 23 September 1828) (in Newberry District)

| Waldrop, Martha G. | J. Quincy Wilber | 2C | 243-245 | 1866 |
|---|---|---|---|---|

(marriage settlement 8 October 1866) (in Laurens District)

| Waldrop, Matilda | Young Longshow | F | 364-365 | 1828 |
|---|---|---|---|---|

(in Newberry District)

| Waldrum, Elizabeth T. | Thomas B. Reese | 2C | 302-304 | 1866 |
|---|---|---|---|---|

(marriage settlement 10 December 1866) (widow of William Waldrum) (both of Edgefield District)

Implied South Carolina Marriages Volume IV 1787-1875

| WOMAN | MAN | VOL | PAGES | LIVED |
|---|---|---|---|---|
| Walker, Caroline | Joseph Randall | X | 493-494 | 1851 |
| Walker, Eleanor | Robert Henry Goldthwaite | E | 155-156 | 1823 |

(married 10 August 1823) (marriage settlement 25 September 1823) (both of Lexington District) [See also pages 193-194]

| Walker, Letty Jane | Leroy Stroud | 2A | 297-298 | 1858 |
|---|---|---|---|---|

(daughter of Drury Walker)

| Walker, Mary | _____ Allsbrook | P | 150-152 | 1845 |
|---|---|---|---|---|

(widow)

| Walker, Sarah A. | Thomas McCully | 2B | 562 | 1861 |
|---|---|---|---|---|

(daughter of Adam T. Walker of Chester District)

| Walker, Sarah C. | John Smith | Z | 714-716 | 1857 |
|---|---|---|---|---|

(marriage settlement 17 March 1857) (both of Chester District)

| Wall, Elizabeth | _____ Ragsdale | R | 370-371 | 1847 |
|---|---|---|---|---|

(daughter of Charles Wall of Chester District)

| Wallace, Agnes | Dr. Edward H. Barton | S | 375-376 | 1848 |
|---|---|---|---|---|

(daughter of Andrew Wallace of Richland District, S.C.) (of New Orleans, Louisiana)

| Wallace, Agnes | Dr. Edward H. Barton | T | 326-328 | 1849 |
|---|---|---|---|---|

(daughter of Andrew Wallace of Richland District, S.C.) (of New Orleans, Louisiana)

| Wallace, Alescina | Samuel W. Evans | S | 34-35 | 1848 |
|---|---|---|---|---|

(daughter of Andrew Wallace of Richland District) (Evans of Chesterfield District)

| Wallace, Elizabeth | Robert McCollough | F | 255-256 | 1827 |
|---|---|---|---|---|

(marriage settlement 23 January 1827) (in Union District)

| Wallace, Elizabeth | Robert McCollough | P | 369-371 | 1827 |
|---|---|---|---|---|

(reference to marriage settlement 23 January 1827) (in Edgefield District)

| Wallace, Ellen | John H. Pearson | U | 269-271 | 1851 |
|---|---|---|---|---|

(daughter of Andrew Wallace of Richland District) (of Richland District)

| Wallace, Emma | Dr. John S. Murdock | T | 130-131 | 1849 |
|---|---|---|---|---|

(daughter of Andrew Wallace of Richland District, S.C.) (to Jacksonville, Florida) [See also pages 355-357]

| Waller, Rosa H. | Elijah Webb | T | 47-49 | 1849 |
|---|---|---|---|---|

(marriage settlement 15 January 1849) (both of Anderson District)

| Walter, Mary | Thomas Ford | B | 391-398 | 1805 |
|---|---|---|---|---|

(marriage settlement 16 December 1805) (widow of Richard Charles Walter who died 17__) (she of Stateburg) (Ford of Black River)

Implied South Carolina Marriages Volume IV 1787-1875

| WOMAN | MAN | VOL | PAGES | LIVED |
|---|---|---|---|---|

Walter, Sarah C.    Benjamin G. Ioor    B    702-705    1811
   (marriage agreement 20 April 1811) (she of Clarendon
   County) (he of Claremont County)
Wannamaker, Selina   _____ Shire    G    192    1830
   (daughter of Henry Wannamaker)
Ward, Emeline    Harry R. Godman    X    457-458    1854
   (daughter of Richard Ward of Edgefield District)
Ward, Emiline    _____ Godman    2A    47-49    1857
Ward, Susannah    David Greer    F    80    1827
   (marriage agreement 7 June 1827) (in Laurens District)
Wardlaw, Elizabeth    Simion S. Bonham    F    379-380    1829
   Amanda (daughter of James Wardlaw of Abbeville District)
   (of Abbeville District)
Ware, Eliza    James Killingsworth    Z    128-130    1856
   (daughter of William Ware of Abbeville District) (of
   Abbeville District)
Ware, Lucy F. E.    John R. Jayroe    2C    115-117    1865
   (postnuptial settlement 22 December 1865) (in Sumter
   District)
Ware, Lucy S.    Nathaniel H. Whitlaw    H    516-517    1834
   (marriage settlement 1 January 1834) (she of Edgefield
   District, S.C.) (he of Augusta, Georgia)
Ware, Malinda    James M. Vandiver    Z    125-126    1856
   (daughter of William Ware of Abbeville District) (of
   Abbeville District)
Ware. Sarah.    See Sarah Mullen
Waring, Sarah E.    Thomas R. Center    2A    231-233    1858
   (marriage settlement 12 January 1858) (widow) [See also
   pages 627-629]
Waring, Selina    Samuel Green    E    317-318    1825
   (marriage contract 4 August 1825) (both of Columbia,
   Richland District)
Warren, Amanda F.    Morris J. Wheeler    G    485    1831
   (daughter of Peter Warren of Camden, Kershaw District)
   (of Camden, Kershaw District)
Warren, Mary W.    Hall T. McGee    G    486-487    1829
   (daughter of Peter Warren of Camden, Kershaw District)
   (of Camden, Kershaw District)
Waters, Louisa    Robert Melton    U    103-105    1850
   (marriage settlement 17 July 1850) (both of Chester
   District)
Waters, Ruth    Starling (Sterling)    D    133-136    1819
                            Baldaree (Baldree)
   (marriage settlement 6 February 1819) (widow of Philemon
   Waters Senr.) (of Newberry District)
Waties, Charlotte    James Bracey    F    366-367    1818
   Alston (marriage settlement 2 February 1818)

Implied South Carolina Marriages Volume IV 1787-1875

| WOMAN | MAN | VOL | PAGES | LIVED |
|---|---|---|---|---|
| Waties, Elizabeth | Doctor William Wallace Anderson | H | 470-471 | 1833 |

(marriage settlement 29 October 1833) (daughter of Hon. Thomas Waties) (both of Stateburg, Claremont)

| Waties, Mary B. | Sebastian Sumter | T | 215-220 | 1849 |
|---|---|---|---|---|

(marriage settlement 12 May 1849) (both of Stateburg, Sumter District)

| Waties, Mary B. | Sebastian D. Sumter | V | 489-491 | 1849 |
|---|---|---|---|---|

(reference to marriage settlement 12 May 1849)

| Watkins, Mary Ann | Winfield Havird | Y | 141-142 | 1855 |
|---|---|---|---|---|

(daughter of Zedekiah Watkins of Edgefield District) (of Edgefield District)

| Watson, Almira Haseltine | Alexander McNeill | 2B | 532-533 | 1862 |
|---|---|---|---|---|

(marriage settlement 2 October 1862) (in Abbeville District)

| Watson, Ann | _____ Myers | S | 279-280 | 1848 |
|---|---|---|---|---|

(in Edgefield District)

| Watson, Ann C. | _____ Myers | U | 66-67 | 1850 |
|---|---|---|---|---|

(in Edgefield District)

| Watson, Elisar | _____ McCance | I | 210 | 1835 |
| Watson, Eliza | Joseph Kennedy | P | 108-110 | 1845 |

(daughter of Hardiway Watson) (of Fairfield District)

| Watson, Eliza Ann | Joseph Kennedy | S | 461-462 | 1845 |
| Watson, Eliza Ann | Joseph Kennedy | T | 384-385 | 1845 |

(in Fairfield District) [Must also see pages 555-557]

| Watson, Ellen | Benjamin McIntosh | S | 138-139 | 1847 |

(daughter of Francis C. Watson of Chesterfield District)

| Watson, Martha | _____ Davis | I | 210 | 1835 |

(widow of Mathew Watson)

| Watson, Martha | Reverend Chesley Davis | G | 73 | 1830 |

(marriage settlement 14 January 1830) (in Abbeville District)

| Watson, Mildred | Thomas L. Smith | 2B | 170-171 | 1860 |

(daughter of Elijah Watson Senior of Edgefield District) (of Edgefield District)

| Watson, Myra | Dr. J. C. W. Kennerly | 2B | 169-170 | 1860 |

(daughter of Elijah Watson of Edgefield District) (of Edgefield District)

| Watson, Myra | Dr. John C. W. Kennerly | 2C | 48-50 | 1865 |

(daughter of Elijah Watson Sr. of Edgefield District)

| Watson, Sarah | John D. Raiford | I | 524 | 1837 |

(daughter of Elijah Watson Senr. of Edgefield District) (in Edgefield District)

| Watson, Sophia | _____ Boatwright | 2A | 198 | 1858 |

Implied South Carolina Marriages Volume IV 1787-1875

| WOMAN | MAN | VOL | PAGES | LIVED |
|---|---|---|---|---|
| Watson, Sophia | Burrell Boatwright | S | 279-280 | 1848 |

(in Edgefield District)

| Watson, Sophia | Burrell T. Boatwright | 2A | 564-565 | 1859 |

(in Edgefield District) [Must also see page 742]

| Watson, Susan | Hinchey Winn | I | 606-607 | 1837 |

(marriage settlement 6 June 1837) (widow of John Watson of Edgefield District) (in Edgefield District)

| Watt, Nancy K. | John Glazier Rabb | 2C | 299-300 | 1867 |

(in Fairfield District)

| Watts, Elizabeth | William J. Lee | U | 331 | 1851 |

(daughter of Hampton Watts of Sumter District)

| Watts, Elizabeth | William J. Lee | Z | 485-487 | 1856 |

(daughter of Hampton Watts of Sumter District) (of Sumter District)

| Watts, Elizabeth E. | ____ Brown | V | 377-378 | 1852 |

(daughter of Richard Watts of Laurens District)

| Watts, Elizabeth E. | Robert C. Brown | Y | 214-215 | 1855 |

(in Abbeville District)

| Watts, Margaret E. | Stewart A. Godman | S | 331-333 | 1848 |

(marriage settlement 24 August 1848) (in Laurens District)

| Watts, Mary F. | James A. Johnson | Z | 485-487 | 1856 |

(daughter of Hampton Watts of Sumter District)

| Watts, Sarah R. | Joseph T. Cummings | U | 331 | 1851 |

(daughter of Hampton Watts of Sumter District)

| Watts, Sarah R. | Joseph T. Cummings | Z | 485-487 | 1856 |

(daughter of Hampton Watts of Sumter District)

| Watts, Susan A. | Robert L. Jones | X | 375-376 | 1854 |

(daughter of Hampton Watts of Sumter District)

| Watts, Susan A. | Robert L. Jones | Z | 485-487 | 1856 |

(daughter of Hampton Watts of Sumter District)

| Weathersbe, Mary | James H. Reed | Y | 378-379 | 1855 |

(daughter of John Weathersbe of Barnwell District) (of Barnwell District)

| Weaver, Martha E. | R. Furman Whilden | 2C | 492-493 | 1864 |

(reference to marriage settlement 24 August 1864) (in Greenville District)

| Weaver, Martha E. | Richard Furman Whilden | 2C | 18-21 | 1864 |

(marriage settlement 24 August 1864) (in Greenville District) [See also pages 492-493]

| Webb, Frances E. | Isaac A. McKagen | 2B | 521-523 | 1862 |

(marriage settlement 9 September 1862) (daughter of William Webb) (in Sumter District)

Implied South Carolina Marriages Volume IV 1787-1875

| WOMAN | MAN | VOL | PAGES | LIVED |
|---|---|---|---|---|

Weeks, Dolly        Thomas H. Osteen     W    496-499     1853
    (marriage settlement 5 April 1853) (daughter of Chosel
    Weeks) (in Sumter District)
Welbourn, Maria     Robert Black         I    555         1837
    (marriage settlement 21 February 1837) (both of Union
    District)
Wells, Elizabeth E. _____ Law            U    107-109     1850
    (daughter of Irby S. Wells and granddaughter of Thomas
    Wells)
Wells, Elizabeth E. William Snider       2A   559-560     1859
    (daughter of Henry H. Wells of Sumter District) (Snider
    of Orangeburg District)
Wells, Laura E.     Samuel N. Lacoste    2A   750-752     1859
    (marriage settlement 1 November 1859) (granddaughter of
    Thomas Wells) (both of Sumter District)
Wells, Lydia A.     John Tindall         P    202-204     1845
    (marriage settlement 29 December 1845) (both of Sumter
    District)
Wells, Margaret Ann George Washington    T    413-415     1849
                    Stukes
    (marriage settlement 18 October 1849) (daughter of John
    W. Wells) (both of Sumter District)
Wells, Mary A.      _____ Teague         2A   678-680     1859
    (daughter of Chesley Wells of Edgefield District)
Wells, Mary Ann     David W. Cuttino     2A   782-783     1860
    (daughter of Henry H. Wells of Sumter District) (of
    Clarendon District)
Wells, Rachel       Lamuel Perry         D    187         1817
    (marriage contract 24 February 1817)
Wells, Sophia       Frederick A. Nance   N    275-276     1843
    (daughter of David Wells) [See also Volume O, pages 204-
    205]
Werts, Eve (Wertz)  Harmon Aull          H    140-143     1832
    (marriage settlement 8 May 1832) (widow of John Werts)
    (in Newberry District)
Wescott, Mary       _____ Elders         M    13-14       1842
    (widow) (she of Richland District)
Wescott, Nancy D.   Jesse Cooper         M    13-14       1842
    (daughter of Thomas Wescott)
West, Ellen         _____ Tisdale        K    318-320     1830
    (in Sumter District)
West, Nancy E.      _____ Dyson          K    318-320     1830
    (in Sumter District)
Weston, Sally F.    D. W. Ray            V    103-105     1850
    (marriage settlement 14 November 1850) (daughter of
    William Weston) (she of Richland District)

Implied South Carolina Marriages Volume IV 1787-1875

| WOMAN | MAN | VOL | PAGES | LIVED |
|---|---|---|---|---|
| Wetherby, Jane | John E. Williams (of Spartanburgh District) | K | 33-34 | 1837 |
| Wheeler, Mary | Thomas N. Moye | T | 221-223 | 1849 |

Catherine (marriage settlement 22 May 1849) (in Sumter District)

| Wheeler, Rose B. | John F. Quinn | 2A | 658-659 | 1859 |
|---|---|---|---|---|

(marriage contract 28 June 1859) (in Marion District)

| Wheler, Sarah Ann | Robert Sidney Mellett | T | 206-209 | 1849 |
|---|---|---|---|---|

(marriage settlement 15 May 1849) (in Sumter District)

| Whetstone, Leah | _____ Kennerly | C | 373 | 1817 |
|---|---|---|---|---|
| Whitaker, Eliza | Robert Man | S | 338-342 | 1848 |

Jane (daughter of William Whitaker)

| Whitaker, Margaret | Richard T. Powell | S | 338-342 | 1848 |
|---|---|---|---|---|

G. (postnuptial settlement 31 August 1848) (daughter of William Whitaker) (both of Cheraw)

| Whitaker, Mary | Burwell Boykin | A | 243-246 | 1793 |
|---|---|---|---|---|

(marriage settlement 21 October 1793) (both of Kershaw County)

| Whitaker, Sally W. | Rufus A. Nott | K | 527-530 | 1840 |
|---|---|---|---|---|

(marriage settlement 1 January 1840)

| White, Agnes P. | Julius L. Bartlett | 2C | 392-396 | 1867 |
|---|---|---|---|---|

(daughter of Leonard White) (of Sumter)

| White, Charlotte | John P. Bossard | H | 307-308 | 1832 |
|---|---|---|---|---|

(daughter of Joseph B. White of Sumter District)

| White, Elizabeth | Peter Mouzon | G | 419-420 | 1830 |
|---|---|---|---|---|

(of Sumter District) [See also pages 417-419]

| White, Hannah | Joshua E. Kirven | L | 156-159 | 1840 |
|---|---|---|---|---|

(marriage settlement 7 September 1840) (daughter of William White of Montgomery County, Alabama) (in Darlington District, S.C.)

| White, Mary Ann | William M. Delorme | G | 48-49 | 1829 |
|---|---|---|---|---|

(daughter of Joseph B. White of Sumter District) (of Sumter District)

| White, Sarah | Henry Haynsworth | T | 525-528 | 1850 |
|---|---|---|---|---|

(marriage settlement 13 February 1850) (daughter of William White) (both of Sumter District)

| White, Sarah | Henry Haynsworth | Y | 386-388 | 1855 |
|---|---|---|---|---|

(reference to marriage settlement 13 February 1850)

| Whiting, Servina | Col. William Toney | E | 431-432 | 1826 |
|---|---|---|---|---|

(marriage agreement 14 February 1826) (widow) (he was married before) (of Greenville District) [See also pages 475-477; Volume F, pages 148-149]

| Whitmire, Mary | Warren E. Davis | 2A | 229-230 | 1858 |
|---|---|---|---|---|

(marriage settlement 2 February 1858) (widow) (in Union District)

Implied South Carolina Marriages Volume IV 1787-1875

| WOMAN | MAN | VOL | PAGES | LIVED |
|---|---|---|---|---|
| Whittemore, Lydia G. | James S. Rhodes | 2B | 750-753 | 1863 |

(marriage settlement 24 December 1863) (daughter of Cephas Whittemore of Orangeburg) (Rhodes of Charleston)

| Wienchy, Sarah T. | Jesse H. Goodwyn | G | 322-323 | 1831 |
|---|---|---|---|---|
| Wigfall, Eliza | Erasmus J. Youngblood | G | 326-327 | 1831 |
| Wiggins, Emma | John S. Due | R | 212-213 | 1846 |

(of Fairfield District)

| Wilder, Leonora W. | John D. Jones | P | 188-189 | 1846 |
|---|---|---|---|---|

(daughter of Thomas J. Wilder Senior of Sumter District)

| Wilder, Sarah | Daniel Brunson | N | 104-105 | 1843 |
|---|---|---|---|---|

(of Sumter District)

| Wilds, _____ | Peter C. Coggeshall | 2B | 480-490 | 1861 |
|---|---|---|---|---|
| Wilds, Julia E. | Layton (Leighton) W. Lide | 2B | 480-490 | 1861 |

(marriage settlement 25 April 1861) (daughter of Peter A. Wilds) (in Darlington District)

| Wilds, Mary Ann | Peter C. Coggeshall | E | 41-43 | 1822 |
|---|---|---|---|---|

(marriage settlement 13 June 1822) (in Darlington District)

| Wilds, Nancy L. | Peter C. Coggeshall | X | 385-391 | 1854 |
|---|---|---|---|---|

(marriage settlement 12 April 1854) (daughter of Peter A. Wilds of Darlington District) (both of Darlington District)

| Wilkinson, Tabitha | William Donaldson | E | 22-24 | 1822 |
|---|---|---|---|---|

(marriage contract 27 June 1822) (both of York District)

| Wilks, Victoria T. | John C. Walker | W | 637-640 | 1853 |
|---|---|---|---|---|

(marriage settlement 23 July 1853) (of Columbia)

| Williams, _____ | T. Edwin Ware | V | 564-567 | 1842 |
|---|---|---|---|---|
| Williams, Caroline E. | Leonidas King | H | 422-423 | 1833 |

(marriage contract 8 July 1833) (in Darlington District)

| Williams, Elizabeth | Jeremiah Gardner | K | 66 | 1837 |
|---|---|---|---|---|

(of Abbeville District)

| Williams, Elvira G. | Jacob Shrum | 2A | 795-796 | 1859 |
|---|---|---|---|---|

(marriage settlement 19 October 1859) (in Pickens District)

| Williams, Frances E. | J. N. Whitner Vermillion | Z | 725-726 | 1857 |
|---|---|---|---|---|

(married 12 March 1857) (of Anderson District)

| Williams, Harrietta Sarah | Andrew A. Dexter | M | 300 | 1840 |
|---|---|---|---|---|

(daughter of Wm. W. Williams) (Dexter of Alabama)

| Williams, Jane | _____ Jones | V | 564-567 | 1842 |
|---|---|---|---|---|

(daughter of Samuel Williams of Greenville District)

Implied South Carolina Marriages Volume IV 1787-1875

| WOMAN | MAN | VOL | PAGES | LIVED |
|---|---|---|---|---|
| Williams, Mary Ann | Allen Gibson | G | 177-181 | 1830 |

(marriage settlement 17 April 1830) (daughter of Eli Williams) (she of Richland District) (Gibson of Columbia, Richland District)

| Williams, Mary F. | Noah White | 2C | 111-113 | 1866 |
|---|---|---|---|---|

(marriage settlement 8 March 1866) (both of Aiken, Barnwell District)

| Williams, Susan Caroline | _____ Lorick | 2A | 767-769 | 1860 |
|---|---|---|---|---|

(widow of Thomas B. Williams)

| Williamson, Mary | George A. Hillegas | F | 171-174 | 1827 |
|---|---|---|---|---|

(marriage settlement 25 October 1827) (widow)

| Williamson, Sarah K. | _____ Wells | 2B | 707-708 | 1863 |
|---|---|---|---|---|
| Willis, Angaline | _____ Rice | X | 22-27 | 1853 |

(in Barnwell District)

| Willis, Susan | John K. Johnston | X | 22-27 | 1853 |
|---|---|---|---|---|

(marriage settlement 11 July 1853) (widow of Robert Willis) (Johnton was married before) (she of Barnwell District) (Johnston of Edgefield District)

| Willis, Susan | John K. Johnston (Johnson) | Z | 738-741 | 1853 |
|---|---|---|---|---|

(reference to marriage settlement 11 July 1853) (widow of Robert M. Willis) (of Barnwell District)

| Wilmore, Eliza | Vincent Brown | H | 351-354 | 1833 |
|---|---|---|---|---|

(marriage settlement 11 April 1833) (widow) (she of Fairfield District) (he of Chester District)

| Wilson, Ann | Benjamin T. Nunnery | N | 7-8 | 1843 |
|---|---|---|---|---|

(marriage settlement 18 January 1843) (in Sumter District)

| Wilson, Elizabeth T. | William Lewis | W | 455-458 | 1853 |
|---|---|---|---|---|

(marriage settlement 21 February 1853) (widow) (she of Georgetown) (he of Sumterville)

| Wilson, Frances Adaline | _____ Crane | 2A | 3-4 | 1857 |
|---|---|---|---|---|

(daughter of Absalom Wilson of Sumter District)

| Wilson, Harriet E. | John B. Bowers | S | 221-222 | 1848 |
|---|---|---|---|---|

(of Barnwell District)

| Wilson, Henrietta | Thomas B. Chalmers | O | 138-140 | 1844 |
|---|---|---|---|---|

(granddaughter of James Wilson Senior)

| Wilson, Jane Almira (Elmira) | George Q. (or D.) McIntosh | H | 514 | 1833 |
|---|---|---|---|---|

(daughter of Hugh Wilson of Sumter District) [See also Volume I, pages 29-30]

| Wilson, Lucy | _____ Beecham | K | 29 | 1837 |
|---|---|---|---|---|

(widow) (she of Newberry District)

| Wilson, Mariah | _____ Cappleman | M | 71-72 | 1842 |
|---|---|---|---|---|

(daughter of James Wilson of Newberry District)

Implied South Carolina Marriages Volume IV 1787-1875

| WOMAN | MAN | VOL | PAGES | LIVED |
|---|---|---|---|---|
| Wilson, Sarah | Jacob Blizzard | L | 314-316 | 1840 |

(widow of James Wilson Senr.) (in Fairfield District)
[See also pages 309-314]

| Wilson, Sarah | Thomas B. Chalmers | T | 449-452 | 1844 |

(granddaughter of James Wilson)

| Wilson, Sarah J. | Sidney McFaddin | U | 471-473 | 1851 |

(marriage settlement 13 May 1851) (both of Sumter District)

| Wilson, Susan E. | James G. McCrackin | K | 356-357 | 1839 |

(marriage settlement 8 April 1839) (both of Newberry District)

| Winfield, Mariah B. | James Moffett | E | 449-452 | 1826 |

(marriage settlement __ __ 1826) (she of Marlborough District) (he of Cheraw)

| Wingate, Sophenisba | Richard Branham | F | 424-425 | 1829 |

E. M. [See also pages 430-431, 439]

| Withers, Rachel C. | Osgood A. Darby | 2A | 466-468 | 1858 |

(marriage settlement 22 November 1858) (widow of Benjamin F. Withers) (in York District)

| Witherspoon, Catharine D. | Davidson McDowell | U | 302-304 | 1827 |

(reference to marriage settlement 17 December 1827)

| Witherspoon, Louisa | Silvester E. Hart | U | 115-117 | 1850 |

(daughter of John S. Witherspoon) (in Darlington District)

| Witherspoon, M. M. | W. J. Barnes | U | 115-117 | 1850 |

(daughter of John S. Witherspoon) (in Darlington District)

| Witherspoon, Margaret J. E. | ____ Sadler | M | 192-193 | 1842 |

(in Lancaster District)

| Witherspoon, Rebecca Frances | ____ Pringle | Z | 35-38 | 1856 |

(widow)

| Witherspoon, Rebecca W. | John Wallace | T | 538-539 | 1850 |

(daughter of John D. Witherspoon of Darlington District)

| Witherspoon, Sarah Ann | John Johnson Knox | H | 467-470 | 1833 |

(marriage settlement 23 October 1833) (in Sumter District)

| Wolfe, Henrietta C. | Samuel J. Kennerly | O | 328-329 | 1845 |
| Wolfe, Henrietta C. | Samuel J. Kennerly | S | 328-329 | 1848 |

(daughter of Joseph A. Wolfe) (in Lexington District)

| Wood, Gracy | Charles Fooshe | D | 201-202 | 1820 |

(marriage settlement 13 June 1820) (in Abbeville District)

| Wood, Margaret E. | Joseph Eubanks | 2C | 438-440 | 1868 |

(daughter of Wiley Wood of Union District)

Implied South Carolina Marriages Volume IV 1787-1875

| WOMAN | MAN | VOL | PAGES | LIVED |
|---|---|---|---|---|
| Wood, Rebecca F. | John F. Peyton | I | 110-111 | 1834 |

(marriage settlement 29 October 1834) (of Barnwell District)

| Wood, Rebecca F. | John F. Peyton | K | 215-216 | 1838 |
|---|---|---|---|---|

(reference to marriage settlement 9 October 1834)

| Wood, Sarah | Sebastian Fritzmann | M | 253 | 1842 |
|---|---|---|---|---|

(marriage settlement 30 June 1842) (in Newberry District)

| Wood, Winny | Joseph Tims | K | 31-33 | 1837 |
|---|---|---|---|---|

(marriage settlement 2 December 1837) (he was married before) (both of Chester District)

| Woodberry, Desdemonea | David D. Salmon | I | 599-600 | 1837 |
|---|---|---|---|---|

(marriage settlement 17 May 1837) (she of Marion District, S.C.) (he of Fayetteville, North Carolina)

| Woodward, Alice | John M. Willie | F | 78-80 | 1827 |
|---|---|---|---|---|

(Ailsey) (Woodard) (Willey) (marriage agreement 22 March 1827) (widow of Major John Woodward) (in Fairfield District)

| Woodward, Caroline | William Weston | 2B | 645-646 | 1863 |
|---|---|---|---|---|

(daughter of Lewellen Woodward) (of Richland District)

| Woodward, Esther Caroline | Edward P. Woodward | X | 607-610 | 1851 |
|---|---|---|---|---|

(marriage settlement 14 December 1851) (daughter of William T. Woodward of Fairfield District)

| Woodward, Sallie S. | Jesse T. Owens | X | 631-632 | 1854 |
|---|---|---|---|---|

(daughter of Osmund Woodward of Fairfield District) (of Fairfield District)

| Woolf, Charlotte Augusta | Lipman T. Levin | V | 550-553 | 1844 |
|---|---|---|---|---|

(marriage settlement 10 January 1844) (post-nuptial settlement 23 March 1852) (of Columbia, Richland District)

| Woolf, Charlotte Augusta | Lipman T. Levin | X | 340-343 | 1854 |
|---|---|---|---|---|

(reference to marriage settlement 10 January 1854) (of Columbia, Richland District)

| Worthy, Rebecca | David Pendergrass | 2A | 385-386 | 1858 |
|---|---|---|---|---|

(marriage settlement 16 June 1858) (both of Chester District)

| Wright, Anna | Masten Williamson | S | 358-360 | 1848 |
|---|---|---|---|---|

(marriage settlement 8 August 1848) (widow) (both of Anderson District)

| Wright, Elizabeth | William C. Glenn | G | 258 | 1830 |
|---|---|---|---|---|

(daughter of Thomas Wright) (in Union District)

| Wright, Jane L. | William A. Kennedy | V | 577-580 | 1852 |
|---|---|---|---|---|

(daughter of James Wright) (of Chester District)

| Wright, Lucy C. | John A. Bedenbaugh | P | 83-84 | 1845 |
|---|---|---|---|---|

(daughter of Zacheus Wright of Newberry District) (of Newberry District)

Implied South Carolina Marriages Volume IV 1787-1875

| WOMAN | MAN | VOL | PAGES | LIVED |
|---|---|---|---|---|
| Wright, Sarah E. | Noah Crane | K | 442-444 | 1839 |

(marriage settlement 11 July 1839) (both of Sumter District)

(Y)

| Yarborough, Drusilla | Oliver Taggart (in Abbeville District) | L | 145-147 | 1840 |
|---|---|---|---|---|
| Yarbrough, Behethlen | ____ Calbreth | Z | 12-14 | 1856 |
| Yarbrough, Caroline | ____ Dozier | Z | 12-14 | 1856 |
| Yarbrough, Cornelia | Joseph Weatherall | M | 92-96 | 1842 |
| Yarbrough, Drucilla | Oliver Taggart | M | 92-96 | 1842 |
| Yarbrough, Elizabeth | William Davis | M | 92-96 | 1842 |

(marriage settlement 17 January 1842) (she of Abbeville District, S.C.) (he of Monroe County, Georgia)

| Yarbrough, Frances | James Murray | M | 92-96 | 1842 |
|---|---|---|---|---|
| Yarbrough, Haret | ____ Gibson | Z | 12 | 1856 |

[her first name illegible] (Gelder) [his last name illegible]

| Yarbrough, Mary | Nicholas Miller | M | 92-96 | 1842 |
|---|---|---|---|---|
| Yarbrough, Nancy | ____ Grant | Z | 12-14 | 1856 |
| Yarbrough, Sarah | ____ Nelson | M | 92-96 | 1842 |
| Yates, Anna Eleanor | William R. Bracey | L | 439-441 | 1841 |

(marriage settlement 6 November 1841) (both of Sumter District)

| Yongue, Sarah | William P. McFadden | 2B | 649-651 | 1863 |
|---|---|---|---|---|

(marriage settlement 9 July 1863) (widow)

| Young, Elizabeth | Elhanon Crocker | C | 229-230 | 1815 |
|---|---|---|---|---|

(marriage settlement 11 November 1815) (in Laurens District)

| Young, Lurana (Uraniah) | ____ Jeffers | A | 301-302 | 1801 |
|---|---|---|---|---|

(from North Carolina to Camden District, S.C.)

| Young, Mary | William Giles | H | 207-208 | 1827 |
|---|---|---|---|---|

(marriage settlement 27 April 1827) (in Abbeville District)

| Youngblood, Jane | William Wright | M | 459-461 | 1843 |
|---|---|---|---|---|

(of Yorkville, York District)

(Z)

| Zeigler, Catherine | William Dent | D | 168-169 | 1820 |
|---|---|---|---|---|

(daughter of Nicholas Zeigler) [See also pages 169-172]

Implied South Carolina Marriages Volume IV 1787-1875

| WOMAN | MAN | VOL | PAGES | LIVED |
|---|---|---|---|---|
| Zeigler, Margaret | Gunrod Hare | D | 237-239 | 1821 |

(daughter of Jacob Zeigler) (in Orangeburgh District)

| Zimmerman, A. E. | Robert Cates | R | 13-16 | 1846 |
|---|---|---|---|---|

(daughter of John C. Zimmerman)

| Zimmerman, Rebecca | George W. Burton | Z | 295-297 | 1856 |
|---|---|---|---|---|

(marriage settlement 10 June 1856) (both of Edgefield District)

| Zimmerman, Sarah A. | William K. Davis | R | 374-375 | 1847 |
|---|---|---|---|---|

(in Darlington District)

| Zinn, Agnes | _____ Edmunds | C | 210-207 | 1815 |
|---|---|---|---|---|

(daughter of Jacob Zinn Senior of Beach Island, Edgefield District)

| Zinn, Mary | _____ Gardner | C | 201-207 | 1815 |
|---|---|---|---|---|

(daughter of Jacob Zinn Senior of Beach Island, Edgefield District)

## SUBINDEX

THIS BOOK IS SELF-INDEXED.
THIS INDEX IS TO OTHER NAMED INDIVIDUALS IN THE ADDITIONAL
NOTATIONS CONTAINED IN SOME OF THE REFERENCES.

Ables, John J., 45,101,146
Adams, Ephram (Ephraim), 98, 146
Adams, George, 105,146
Adams, James F., 1,97,146
Adams, Jesse S., 143,146
Adams, Richard Wright, 128, 146
Addison, Joseph, 100,146
Adger, Robert, 134,147
Aiken, James, 25,40,91,147
Aldrich, Alfred P., 37,147
Allen, Bannister, 7,147
Allen, Charles, 98
Allen, Francis, 17,26,147
Allen, George, 2,147
Allen, John C., 10,42,147
Allen, Josiah G., 2,147
Allen, Thomas, 19,147
Alston, James, 100,148
Anderson, James, 46,148
Anderson, John, 22,148
Anderson, Richard L., 3,148
Anderson, Thomas, 127,148
Ardis, Abram, 89,116,148
Arledge, Isaac, 16,148
Arthur, J. R., 127,149
Ash, Samuel, 28,149
Ashley, Barnett, 3,149
Ashmore, William H., 54,149
Atkin, David, 12,149
Ayer, Hutwell, 87,149

Bacot, Samuel, 9,150
Bailey, Thomas, 135,141,150
Ballard, John, 118,150
Barber, James, 140,150
Barksdale, George, 102,151
Barksdale, Higgerson, 103,151
Barnard, Robert, 66,151
Barnett, Jorial, 14,151
Barr, William H., 22,151
Bartley, Thomas, 79,151
Bates, John, 8,9,51,65,116, 123,130,151,152
Bates, William, 93,152
Bauskett, John, 24,152
Beacham, Daniel S., 89,152
Beall, Duke, 116,152
Bean, James, 113,152
Beard, James, 75,152
Beard, Joshua, 87,142,152
Beaty, Jonathan, 107,152
Beatty, Jonathan, 41,152
Beckham, William M., 116,152
Bedgegood, Malachi N., 10,153
Bee, Robert R., 75,153
Bellinger, Edmund C., 48,153
Belton, John, 89,153
Bender, George, 5,153
Benson, E. B., 92,153
Benson, William P., 34,153
Benson, Willis, 95,153
Bently, Joel, 10,154
Berly, John, 109,154
Berry, James, 127,154
Bethea, Francis, 81,154
Bethea, W. S., 42,154
Bigger, A. B., 119,154
Bishop, Rev. P. E., 133,154
Black, James A., 103,154
Black, John, 25,154
Bledsoe, Lewis, 1,155
Blewer, John G., 26,155
Blocker, James, 1,155
Blount, Charles, 90,155
Boatwright, Drury, 51,155
Boatwright, James, 27,64,155, 203
Bobo, John E., 62,135,136,155
Bogan, William, 50,155
Bookter, Jacob, 8,155
Boone, Thomas, 102,156
Boozer, George, 41,156
Boulware, Thomas, 100,156
Bowman, John, 108,156
Bowman, John A., 20,156
Box, Thomas, 19,156
Boyd, John, 107,156

## SUBINDEX

Boykin, A. Hamilton, 21,157
Boykin, Alexander Hamilton, 21,157
Boyle, Cunningham, 67,119,157
Bracy, Philip, 111,157
Bracy, Solly, 88,157
Bradford, William W., 65,99, 139,157
Bradley, Isaac, 13,158
Bradley, John, 55,85,157,158
Brady, Robert, 97,158
Bratten, Dr. John S., 79,158
Breithaupt, Christian, 50,158
Brewer, John, 76,158
Britt, Daniel A., 135,158
Brock, William, 134,158
Brockington, William T., 121, 158
Brogdon, Isaac B., 62,158
Brooks, Col. Zachariah S., 10, 101,154,159
Brooks, Col. Zachariah Smith, 11,159
Brooks, Whitfield, 37,159
Brooks, Z. S., 29
Brough, Thomas, 63,159
Brown, James, 40,159
Brown, Joseph, 135,159
Brown, Lewis, 120,159
Brown, Peter, 78,159
Brown, Wm., 6,159
Brown, Wm C., 137,159
Brunson, Daniel, 59,160
Brunson, Daniel D., 67,160
Brunson, William L, 41,78,79, 160
Bryan, Allen, 66,160
Bryan, John, 7,160
Bryan, Joseph, 2,161
Burton, Aaron, 25,60,115,161
Burton, Peter, 12,161
Bush, George, 13,161
Bush, Thomas, 135,161
Bussey, Demcy, 39,111,161
Butler, Peter M., 16,35,161, 162
Butler, Seth, 3,161
Buzzard, Jacob, 68,162
Bynum, Nathaniel, 91,162

Byrd, Miller, 42,162
Byrd, Reddin, 91,162

Caldwell, James, 85,162
Caldwell, James E., 91,162
Caldwell, John, 110,162
Calhoun, John A., 112,163
Calhoun, Nathan, 105,137,163
Calhoun, William, 19,129,163
Calvert, Jesse, 37,163
Cameron, Joseph, 52,163
Cammer, James, 32,163
Campbell, Dr. Robert E., 95, 163
Cannon, David, 107,114,163,164
Cannon, David M., 74,164
Cannon, George S., 47,67,121, 163,164
Cannon, Richard S., 132,164
Cannon, Wm, 66,163
Cantelou, Lemuel, 19,164
Carey, W. H., 12,164
Carson, James, 141,164
Carter, Benjamin, 69,139,165
Carter, Larkin G., 46,165
Cartledge, Edmund, 53,66,87, 165
Cary, William H., 58,165
Cason, Cannon, 73,165
Cates, Aaron, 131,165
Chalmers, Thomas B., 143,165, 166
Chandler, Genl. Samuel R., 7, 166
Chandler, George, 49,166
Chandler, Samuel, 85,166
Chapman, Allen, 11,166
Charles, Edgar W., 56,166
Chatham, Thomas, 1,166
Cheatham, Guthredge, 38,166
Cheatham, Robert, 125,166
Chesnut, John, 52,166,167
Cheves, Langdon, 62,167
Clark, J. W., 40,167
Clark, William, 63,167
Clarke, Caleb, 24,167
Clarke, George, 60,167
Clarkson, Thomas B., 24,128,

## SUBINDEX

168
Clarkson, William, 124,168
Clayton, Edmond, 43,168
Cleckly, D. F., 9,168
Clemens, C. W., 119,168
Cleveland, Benjamin Milton, 69,168
Cloud, Austin N., 59,168
Cloud, William, 21,168
Cochran, L. B., 137,169
Coggeshall, Peter C., 31,40, 169
Cohen, John J., 93,169
Colclough, John A., 34,169
Colclough, William A., 82,169
Cole, William, 48,169
Converse, Augustus L., 43,170
Cook, Henry R., 113,170
Cook, John, 29,116,170
Cook, Nathaniel, 50,170
Corley, Josiah, 113,170
Courtney, Martin, 103,170
Cowan, Col. Isaac, 55,171
Coward, Solomon, 137,171
Cowie, Archibald, 100,171
Craig, John H., 139,171
Crankfield, Littleton, 59,74, 90,171
Crawford, Andrew, 58,171
Crawley, John, 72,171
Croft, Edward, 120,171
Crook, Dr. A. B., 76,172
Crooks, John A., 124,172
Crooks, Thomas C., 64,172
Crosby, David, 120,172
Crossle, George, 100,172
Crumpton, David, 55,172
Culler, Jacob, 22,172
Cunningham, Alexander, 128, 173
Cunningham, Arthur, 110,172
Cunningham, John S., 30,173
Cunningham, Joseph, 115
Cunningham, O. H. P., 77,173
Cureton, Jere, 37,173

Dain, Hyder A., 9,173
Daniel, Richard, 63,173

Darby, James, 53,173
Dargan, Geo. W., 102,173
Darlington, John, 74,174
Darrington, Robert, 14,174
Davenport, Isaac, 132,174
Davenport, William, 80,174
Davidson, Robert, 44,174
Davis, Bushrod Washington, 118,174
Davis, William W., 133,174
Dawkins, Col. Benjamin F., 103,174
Dean, Alfred, 62,174
Dean, John, 42,174
Deas, William, 101,174
Deason, John, 104,174
DeBruhl, Jesse, 41,87,174
Deen, William, 144,175
De Graffenreid, Allen, 71,175
DeVeaux, Robert Marion, 92,175
DeVeaux, S. G., 92,175
Deveaux, Stephen G., 17,103, 175
Dew, William, 56,175
Dewalt, Daniel, 1,63,134,136, 140,176
De Walt, Daniel, 136,176
Dillard, John A., 97,176
Dingle, Adam, 130,176
Dinkins, L. T., 76,177
Diseker, Jacob, 69,139,177
Dixon, Abel, 142,177
Dixon, Benjamin, 82,177
Dogan, Joseph H., 5,177
Douglas, James K., 3,177
Douglass, James K., 4,177
Douglass, Dr. John, 54,57,177
Dove, Daniel, 33,177
Drafts, Jesse, 37,216
Drake, Lemuel S., 54,178
Drake, Micajah, 110,178
Dreher, Godfrey, 89,178
DuBose, Isaac, 72,178
DuBose, Samuel, 13,178
DuBose, Theodore S., 15,103, 178
Dukes, James T., 106,178
Duncan, Willis J., 129,178
Dunlap, William, 10,178

## SUBINDEX

Dunn, William, 132,179
Duren, Thomas, 9,179

Earle, Elias Drayton, 56,179
Earle, James W., 12,179
Eckhard, Jacob, 69,179
Edgerton, Otis, 95,179
Edgeworth, Richard L., 63,180
Edwards, Philip Gadsden, 51, 180
Eigleberger, Col. John, 124, 180
Elkins, James, 62,112,180
Ellerbe, Thomas G., 37,180
Ellerbe, William, 39,180
Ellerbe, William C., 22,180
Ellerbe, William F., 104,180
Ellis, Benjamin, 117,181
Elmore, F. H., 126,181
Elmore, Mathias, 43,181
Elrod, Jeremiah, 80,181
Eppes, Daniel, 132,181
Eppes, William, 64,181
Epting, John, 125,181
Eubanks, James J., 88,181
Evans, Gideon, 60,181
Evans, John, 110,182
Evans, William, 136,181
Eveleigh, Thomas, 108,182
Evins, M. P., 86,182

Fair, James, 20,182
Falls, Alexander, 70,182
Fant, David J., 103,127,182
Farr, James, 117,183
Farr, John P., 49,114,123,182
Faster, Robert, 62,183
Faucett, Samuel, 100,183
Felder, John H., 18,183
Fellers, John, 117,183
Ferguson, Wade, 134,183
Ford, Elijah, 113,184
Ford, George, 133,184
Ford, William, 60,183
Foster, Jariahr, 6,99,121,184
Fountain, George, 6,184
Fountain, George H., 6,184

Fraser, John B., 91,184
Fraser, John Baxter, 17,185
Fraser, Ladson L., 17,18,91, 184,185
Frazer, Joseph, 114,185
Frean, Thomas, 132,185
Frost, _____, 8,155
Fuller, Messer, 73,185
Fullwood, Robert, 13,185
Fulmer, John H., 44,186
Furginson, William, 99,186

Gahagan, John, 62,186
Gaillard, David, 66,186
Gaillard, James, 107,186
Gallman, Harman, 6,186
Gantt, Richard, 128,186
Gardner, Jeremiah, 12,187
Garner, Presley, 114
Garner, Presly, 115,187
Garrett, Henry W., 67,187
Garrett, John C., 67,187
Garvin, David, 7,187
Garvin, James, 77,187
Gaskins, Daniel, 8,100,187
Gaskins, John, 84,187
Gassaway, Thos., 98,187
Gee, Edmund, 96,187
Geiger, Abram, 136,188
Geiger, Godfrey H., 45,188
Gibbs, Churchill, 50,188
Gibson, Absolom, 22,188
Gibson, Jacob, 115,188
Gibson, John C., 75,188
Gill, Lewis, 44,189
Gill, Robert, 77,189
Gilliam, Reuben, 46,189
Glover, Jethro, 94,189
Goode, George M., 20,189
Goodlett, Spartan, 63,189
Goodwyn, Jesse, 61,190
Gordon, Charles F., 23,190
Gordon, Mansfield, 79,190
Gossett, John T., 47,190
Gowen, John, 40,190
Graetz, _____ Wolff, 142,190
Graham, James, 13,190
Graham, John, 65,190

## SUBINDEX

Gray, John J., 5,74,111,191
Gray, M. M., 88,191
Gray, William W., 113,191
Green, Henry C., 57,191
Greer, Thomas S., 94,192
Gregory, Benjamin J., 50,192
Griffin, Ira, 11,192
Griffin, Reuben, 144,192
Griffith, Stephen, 3,193
Groves, Joseph, 5,44,193
Gruber, John, 118,193
Guignard, James S., 88,114, 193

Hadden, John T., 139,193
Hagood, Benjamin, 87,90,110, 193
Haigood, Buckner, 109,194
Haile, Benjamin, 71,88,194
Hails, Capt. Robert, 10,194
Hamer, Thomas C., 15,194
Hamilton, Alexander C., 13,194
Haney, Orashea, 106,194
Harden, Silas, 47,195
Hardy, William, 99,195
Hare, Gunrod, 100,195
Harkness, John, 44,195
Harmon, Stephen, 131,195
Harrell, James, 11,195
Harris, David, 94,141,196
Harris, John, 2,27,103,122, 139,144,195,196
Hartley, Henry, 104,196
Hartzog, George F., 106,196
Haskew, Zacheus, 35,196
Hatcher, John, 74,196
Havis, Jesse, 40,49,196,197
Hawthorn, Jasper N., 47,197
Hay, James, 99,197
Haynsworth, Doctor James, 90, 197
Haynsworth, Dr. James, 90,197
Haywood, James, 90,197
Hearst, John, 4,197
Heath, Thomas, 98,136,197
Henderson, Hugh L., 43,198
Henry, George, 143,198
Henry, James, 26,28,76,89,120, 198
Hewitt, Frances M., 4,198
Hickson, John, 57,199
Hickson, Levi, 52,66,199
Hickson, Thomas J., 117,199
Hill, John, 109,199
Hill, Littleton, 119,199
Hinton, William, 56,199
Hiron, John, 22,199
Hirons, John, 32,199
Hodges, Gabriel, 13,200
Hodges, Robert H. W., 69,200
Hoke, John, 76,172
Holder, Daniel, 77,200
Hollingsworth, John, 18,126, 132,139,185,200
Hollis, John, 119,200
Holstein, Wade, 71,144,200, 201
Holston, Moses, 113,201
Hope, John C., 59,201
Hopkins, James, 15,201
Hopkins, Newton, 117,201
Hornsby, Daniel, 33,119,201
Horton, Joseph, 84,201
Howard, Charles B., 54,138,201
Howell, Jesse M., 130,202
Howell, Joseph, 34,202
Howell, Matthew, 98,202
Hubbard, William, 23,202
Huckabee, G. W., 37,202
Hudson, Robert, 128,138,202, 262
Hughey, Daniel, 39,55,202
Huiet, John, 131,202
Humphries, Thomas, 97,202
Hunter, John, 139,202
Hunter, Joseph Y., 38,202
Hutchinson, A. S., 87,203
Hutchison, Robert, 104,203

Irby, Dr. Wm, 134,203

Jacks, Isaac Calmes, 86,203
Jaffray, Henry, 58,77,203,204
James, George C., 114,204
James, John, 15,204

## SUBINDEX

James, Joseph, 106,142,204
James, Matthew, 28,204
James, Walter, 6,34,35,204
Jennings, Joseph, 67,87,104, 130,204,205
Jennings, Larkin, 83,205
Jennings, Rev. John, 117,205
Jeter, James R., 73,205
Jeter, Thomas C., 53,205
Jeter, William, 86,205
Johnson, Alexander, 144,206
Johnson, David, 136,205
Johnson, Taley, 16,205
Johnston, John, 41,206
Johnston, John K., 54,105,206
Johnston, Samuel, 1,23,103, 206
Jones, Abraham, 75,78,85,206, 207
Jones, Benjamin T., 127,207
Jones, Elijah, 25,206
Jones, Lewis, 68,206
Jones, Ralph, 32,207
Jones, Samuel P., 29,207
Jordan, John, 118,207
Jumelle, Peter L., 99,101,207

Keeler, Samuel, 106,208
Kellogg, Daniel, 26,43,169, 208
Kelly, Frederick, 53,208
Kelly, John, 16,208
Kelly, William, 59,61,84,127, 208
Kennedy, John M., 15,208
Kennedy, Lionel H., 75,208
Kennedy, Richard E., 102,209
Kennedy, William, 71,209
Kenner, Samuel E., 93,209
Kennerly, Eli, 47,209
Kershaw, George, 47,209
Kibler, John Adam, 91,209
Kilcrease, Lewis, 115,209
Killen, James F., 95,209
Killingsworth, Mark, 78,210
Kimbrel, G. W., 83,210
King, Gillam, 85,210
King, John G., 106,210

King, Mitchell, 21,210
King, William, 79,210
Kirk, Alexander, 59,210
Kirkland, George, 2,210
Kirkland, John D., 11,210
Kirksey, William, 45,211
Knighton, Moses, 88,93,211
Koon, John, 125,211
Koppel, Jacob, 54,211

Lacoste, Stephen, 14,28,97,211
Lagrone, John, 87,212
Lake, Enoch, 115,212
Lamar, Mack, 30,44,186,212
Lamar, Thomas, 75,212
Lark, John, 105,212
LaRoche, J. J., 82,212
Latta, Robert, 67,212
Leaman, Hugh, 68,213
Leapheart, William, 36,213
Ledingham, John, 24,213
Lee, Horace, 74,213
Lee, Timothy, 137,213
Leever, Jacob, 36,213
Leister, Craven, 20,213
Leitner, Daniel W., 49,213
Lemon, James, 99,144,213
Lenhardt, Lawrence, 8,130,213
Lenoir, John, 88,213
Lesesne, Charles, 15,214
Lesly, William, 92,97,214
Lester, Archibald, 50,88,99, 110,191,214
Lewis, James, 141,214
Lewis, Joseph, 27,214
Lide, Hugh, 56,166
Lightfoot, Francis, 66,80,113, 214,215
Lindsey, Benjamin, 58,215
Littlejohn, Samuel, 118,215
Logan, Andrew, 28,215
Lomax, G., 35,70,215
Lomax, Jas, 108,215
Long, Jacob S., 52,216
Looper, Jeremiah, 69,216
Lorick, John, 36,37,115,140, 216
Lorick, Michael, 45,188

## SUBINDEX

Loveland, Roger, 122,216
Lucas, Benjamin, 22,216
Lunsford, Swanson, 93,216
Lyles, Reuben S., 64,216
Lyles, Thomas M., 103,217
Lyons, Isaac, 93,217
Lyons, Jacob C., 65,217

McAdams, Hiram A., 31,217
McBride, Samuel, 88,217
McBride, William, 51,110,143, 217
McCall, James S., 38,218
McCaslan, William, 103,218
McCaw, Dr. William, 142,218
McClanahan, Samuel G., 41,51, 218
McCoy, Joseph, 24,219
McCreary, John, 82,219
McCreless, John, 104,219
McDaniel, John C., 110,219
McDonald, Charles A., 82,219
McDonald, William, 75,219
McDowell, Davidson, 108,219
McDowell, William, 57,219
McFadden, Col. Thomas, 142, 220
McFadden, Isaac, 41,220
McFaddin, James D., 11,20,115, 121,220
McFall, Andrew N., 128,220
McHarg, William, 138,220
McKellar, John W., 12,220
McKenzie, John, 142,221
McKenzie, William, 58,221
McKie, Daniel, 5,35,221
McKittrick, Benjamin, 130,221
McLemore, Majr. John, 132,221
McLeod, James Henry, 18,221
McLure, Hugh, 31,114,222
McLure, Thomas, 104,222
McMakin, Thomas, 83,222
McMullin, Cullin, 45,222
McPherson, James, 9,222
McRae, Duncan, 86,222
McWillie, Adam, 86,222
McWillie, William, 113,115, 222,223

Macfarlan, John, 84,223
Maddon, Samuel L., 60,223
Maddox, Augustus (Augustin), 140,223
Marks, Alexander, 113,223
Marks, Mordecai, 113,223
Mars, John A., 3,4,224
Marsh, John, 64,224
Marshall, George, 82,224
Marshall, Martin (or A.), 128, 224
Martin, Robert, 98,224
Martindale, William, 126,224
Massey, James R., 9,225
Matheson, Christopher, 80,225
Mauldin, Samuel, 23,225
Maxwell, John, 38,69,76,117, 136,225
Maxwell, Robert A., 134,143, 225
Mayer, Major Adam, 122,225
Mayrant, William, 108,226
Mays, Sampson B., 61,226
Mays, Stephen W., 61,226
Mayson, Archy, 80,226
Mellett, Dr. James L., 83,226
Mellett, Peter, 102,226
Melton, Elisha, 29,80,226
Mercer, Thomas, 31,226
Merriman, John, 97,226
Meyer, David, 8,227
Michau, Manasseth, 91,227
Mickle, Joseph, 36,79,227
Middleton, John, 45,227
Miles, Jeremiah, 102,227
Miller, Andrew, 86,88,126,228
Miller, Benjamin, 119,227
Miller, James, 4,228
Miller, John, 27,228
Miller, John B., 96,228
Miller, Robert, 144,228
Milling, John, 89,91,229
Mills, Thomas, 57,229
Mitchell, Daniel A., 94,229
Mixson, William J., 30,229
Mobley, Dr. Isaiah, 37,229
Mobley, Edward P., 58,85,229
Mobley, John, 82,91,229
Mobley, John M., 37,229

## SUBINDEX

Moncrieff, Richard, 100,230
Montgomery, David, 36,230
Montgomery, John, 121,230
Montgomery, John W., 140,230
Montgomery, Samuel, 102,230
Montgomery, William, 26,230
Moon, Peter, 51,230
Moor, Moses, 127,230
Moore, Captain Matthew S., 63, 134,230
Moore, Col. Richard, 25,230
Moore, James, 20,230
Moore, Moses, 109,230
Morgan, Mark, 50,231
Morris, Thomas, 127,138,231
Morse, Whitfield, 135,231
Moseley, Henry, 20,231
Moseley, John M., 7,62,137,231
Moses, Franklin J., 7,90,121, 231,232
Mosley, John, 2,232
Motley, John, 142,232
Moye, George W., 94,232
Muffett, James, 138,232
Muldrow, Matthew D., 56,232
Muldrow, Matthew E., 43,55,88, 232
Muldrow, Robert B., 37,232
Murray, Samuel J., 96,233
Myers, Col. David, 2,233

Nail, Casper, 45,89,234
Nail, John, 87,234
Nance, Zachariah, 77,234
Neal, John, 135,234
Nettles, Amos A., 70,235
Nettles, James, 84,235
Nettles, Joseph B., 54,235
Nettles, Joseph M., 138,234
Nettles, Samuel M., 95,235
Nettles, Zachariah, 28,235
Neuffer, Charles, 71,235
Nickels, John, 3,60,235
Nixon, Washington F., 87,235
Noble, William, 25,235
Nobles, William, 68,236
Norton, Allen, 102,124,236
Norton, Jeptha, 10,236

O'Brien, William, 29,236
OCain, Daniel, 57,236
Oeland, John, 131,237
Oneal, Richard, 5,237
Orr, Joab, 44,237

Palmer, Champion D., 31,238
Palmer, Ellis, 54,84,122,237, 238
Parker, Elisha, 17,238
Parkins, Allen R., 68,238
Parrott, Benjamin, 45,238
Paterson, James, 38,123,238
Patterson, Angus, 5,238
Patterson, James, 123,238
Payne, John W., 13,238
Peake, David D., 94,238
Pearce, Samuel, 76,239
Pearse, Samuel, 76,239
Pearson, George B., 13,57,239
Pearson, John, 112,239
Peay, Austin F., 11,239
Peckham, James, 18,239
Perkins, Alfred, 137,239
Perritt, Perry Bryant, 89,239
Perry, Bennet, 36
Perry, Lamuel, 92,96,240
Pervis, John, 28,240
Peterson, Basil, 1,109,240
Peterson, David, 74,240
Pettigrew, Alexander, 38,240
Phillips, Zachariah, 15,240
Pickens, Ezekiel, 4,240
Pitts, Jeremiah, 78,241
Plowden, Miles H., 56,241
Pollard, James, 78,133,241
Polock, Levi, 120,241
Poole, John, 30,241
Postell, Colonel James, 61,241
Powe, Erasmus, 39,241
Powe, Thomas, 37,39,241
Powell, Joseph, 112,241
Pratt, Thomas, 21,72,241,242
Pratt, William, 55,241
Prescott, Daniel, 33,90,242
Presley, Edward, 27,242
Presley, John, 74,242
Pressey, Samuel, 26,242

## SUBINDEX

Pressley, Samuel P., 16,54, 242
Pricher, Thomas, 61,109,242
Prince, Laurence, 64,242
Prior, Tobias, 134,242

Rabb, John, 29,243
Rabb, Thomas A., 110,243
Ragin, Charles C., 106,243
Ragsdale, Burr, 9,243
Randol, John Bond, 125,243
Raoul, Dr. J. L., 122,126,243, 244
Raoul, Dr. John Louis, 49,244
Raoul, John L., 122,243
Rasor, Ezekiel, 105,244
Rearden, Joseph, 101,244
Reddle, Napoleon B., 118,244
Reed, John, 17,139,244
Rees, F. W., 14,107,244,245
Rees, William, 88,245
Rees, William J., 92,245
Reese, George, 142,245
Reid, William, 2,245
Reilly, Bernard, 79,122,245
Reynolds, William, 102
Rhoden, Thomas, 104,245
Rice, B. H., 37,245
Rice, David B., 42,245
Richardson, Charles, 108,246
Richardson, Governor James B., 92,245
Richardson, Judge John S., 144,215
Richardson, Noah T., 42,246
Richardson, Thomas, 93,246
Richbourg, Eli, 66,109,247
Ried, William, 2,247
Rielly, Bernard, 80,247
Roach, Dr. Thomas J., 14,247
Robbins, William H., 84,247
Robertson, Andrew, 104,248
Robertson, John W., 110,248
Robertson, William., 16,248
Robeson, Peter L., 28,42,140, 248
Robeson, Thomas W., 40,248
Robinson, James, 98,143,248

Robinson, John, 95,248
Rook, William, 79,249
Rose, Daniel, 58,249
Rountree, Dudley, 10,111,249
Royston, Thomas, 67,249
Ruff, George, 101,250
Ruff, John Henry, 27,250
Russell, Robert, 62,250
Rutland, Abraham, 60,79,114, 119,137,250

Salton, Michael, 5,39,73,251
Sanders, Robert, 16,70,251
Sanders, William, 39,251
Sarter, John P., 58,251
Scarborough, Richard J., 136, 251
Schumpert, Fred., 26,251
Schumpert, Frederick, 30,78, 252
Schumpert, Jacob K., 73,252
Scott, John, 8,38,46,106,111, 252
Seay, James, 114,252
Shedd, William, 68,253
Shellito, John, 72,253
Sheppard, Abraham, 114,253
Sherriff, James W., 59,253
Shibley, Jacob, 52,253
Shields, James, 15,253
Shiells, James, 65,253
Simkins, Jesse, 10,130,254
Sims, Forney, 23,254
Sims, James S., 135,254
Singleton, John, 33,254
Singleton, John C., 8,255
Singleton, Richard, 8,26,33, 254,255
Singleton, Thomas, 135,255
Singley, Martin, 61,255
Skinner, Harvey, 31,255
Smith, Benjamin, 120,257
Smith, Edward, 24,255
Smith, Enoch H., 92,256
Smith, George, 62,256
Smith, George P., 145,256
Smith, John, 50,256
Smith, Robert, 4,8,100,255,

## SUBINDEX

256
Smith, Thomas, 71,255
Smith, William, 71,83,85,87, 255,256
Snelling, Henry, 14,257
Spann, Col. James G., 94,257
Sparks, Alexander, 140,257
Spearman, Graves, 135,257
Spears, Joshua A., 121,257
Speer, William, 81,125,258
Speigner, Samuel, 112,258
Spencer, Oliver H., 133,258
Spires, Henry, 63,258
Staggers, William, 10,258
Stark, Eli, 108,258
Steed, Griffin, 15,258
Steel, J. J., 40,258
Steele, General _____, 121,222
Steen, Col. Gideon, 126,258
Stephens, John, 34,259
Stone, Enoch, 34,259
Suber, Micajah, 117,259
Sullivan, John, 105,260
Summer, George A., 58,112,117, 260
Swaford, John, 2,260
Swoford, John, 2,111,260

Talbot, Daniel, 140,194
Tatom, Orville, 49,260
Taylor, Benjamin F., 50,89,261
Taylor, Col. Thomas, 92,144, 261
Taylor, Henry P., 92,144,261
Taylor, John, 39,261
Taylor, John Chesnut, 40,261
Taylor, William, 83,261
Tennent, William, 46,61,261, 262
Terry, Benjamin, 63
Thames, John C., 137,262
Thomas, Charles, 92,262
Thomas, Reuben, 99,262
Thompson, Hilliard L., 138,262
Thompson, John, 8,262
Thompson, Waddy, 68,262
Thomson, John L., 30,263
Thomson, William R., 30,76,262

Thorn, Charles, 53,81,87,111, 263
Tillman, Hiram, 126,263
Timmons, Luther R., 124,263
Tomkins, Samuel, 110,264
Tomkins, Stephen, 93,264
Tomlinson, Henry M., 36,264
Toole, Stephen, 98,264
Townes, S. A., 20,264
Trowell, James, 80,264
Tucker, Bartley, 93,265
Tucker, Daniel R., 40,265
Tucker, George A., 60,117,265
Tucker, George B., 117,265
Turner, Franklin, 97,265
Turnipseed, Felix, 9,120,265
Turpin, William, 126,265
Turquand, Paul, 81,265

Vaughan, John H., 69,89,266
Vaughan, William, 18,91,266
Vaughn, John, 44,267

Waldrum, William, 107,267
Walker, Adam T., 82,268
Walker, Drury, 123,268
Wall, Charles, 106,268
Wallace, Andrew, 8,40,94,101, 268
Walter, Richard Charles, 42, 268
Waltherer, Andrew, 99,218
Wannamaker, Henry, 116,269
Ward, Richard, 48,269
Wardlaw, James, 12,269
Ware, William, 72,131,269
Warren, Peter, 83,136,269
Waters, Philemon, 7,269
Waties, Hon. Thomas, 3,270
Watkins, Zedekiah, 55,270
Watson, Elijah, 71,106,119,270
Watson, Francis C., 84,270
Watson, Hardiway, 71,270
Watson, John, 141,271
Watson, Mathew, 31,270
Watts, Hampton, 29,67,68,75, 271

## SUBINDEX

Watts, Richard, 16,271
Weathersbe, John, 106,271
Webb, William, 84,271
Weeks, Chosel, 98,272
Wells, Chesley, 126,272
Wells, David, 95,272
Wells, Henry H., 30,120,272
Wells, Irby S., 75,272
Wells, John W., 124,272
Wells, Thomas, 74,75,272
Werts, John, 5,272
Wescott, Thomas, 27,272
Weston, William, 106,272
Whitaker, William, 86,104,273
White, Joseph B., 12,33,43,273
White, Leonard, 8,137,176,273
White, William, 55,73,273
Whittemore, Cephas, 107,274
Wilder, Thomas J., 68,274
Wilds, Peter A., 25,77,274
Williams, Eli, 46,275
Williams, Samuel, 68,274
Williams, Thomas B., 78,275
Williams, Wm. W., 33,274
Willis, Robert, 67,275
Willis, Robert M., 67,275
Wilson, Absalom, 28,275
Wilson, Hugh, 84,275
Wilson, James, 11,22,23,275, 276
Withers, Benjamin F., 30,276
Witherspoon, John D., 132,276
Witherspoon, John S., 7,55,276
Wolfe, Joseph A., 71,276
Wood, Wiley, 40,276
Woodward, Lewellen, 136,277
Woodward, Major John, 140,277
Woodward, Osmund, 98,277
Woodward, William T., 143,277
Wright, James, 71,277
Wright, Thomas, 48,277
Wright, Zacheus, 9,277


Zeigler, Jacob, 53,279
Zeigler, Nicholas, 33,278
Zimmerman, John C., 22,279
Zinn, Jacob, 39,45,279